THE

TWO TRUTHS

IN

INDIAN BUDDHISM

THE TWO TRUTHS IN INDIAN BUDDHISM

Reality, Knowledge, and Freedom

SONAM THAKCHOE

Wisdom

Wisdom Publications
199 Elm Street
Somerville, MA 02144 USA
wisdomexperience.org

Library of Congress Cataloging-in-Publication Data
Names: Thakchoe, Sonam, author.
Title: The two truths in Indian Buddhism: reality, knowledge, and freedom / Sonam Thakchoe.
Description: First edition. | Somerville: Wisdom Publications, 2023. | Includes bibliographical references and index.
Identifiers: LCCN 2022037784 (print) | LCCN 2022037785 (ebook) | ISBN 9781614297468 (paperback) | ISBN 9781614297611 (ebook)
Subjects: LCSH: Truth—Religious aspects—Buddhism. | Buddhism—Doctrines. | Mādhyamika (Buddhism)
Classification: LCC BQ4255 .T475 2023 (print) | LCC BQ4255 (ebook) | DDC 294.3/92—dc23/eng/20220825
LC record available at https://lccn.loc.gov/2022037784
LC ebook record available at https://lccn.loc.gov/2022037785

ISBN 978-1-61429-746-8   ebook ISBN 978-1-61429-761-1

27 26 25 24 23
5 4 3 2 1

Cover design by Jess Morphew. Interior design by James D. Skatges.

Printed on acid-free paper that meets the guidelines for permanence and durability of the Production Guidelines for Book Longevity of the Council on Library Resources.

Printed in the United States of America.

MIX
Paper from responsible sources
FSC www.fsc.org FSC® C011935

Please visit fscus.org.

Contents

I dedicate this book to
Ama Jetsun Pema-la.

Acknowledgments

I am indebted to all my present and past teachers from Tibetan Children's Village School, Central University of Tibetan Studies, and the University of Tasmania. I would especially like to extend my sincere gratitude to my philosophy and academic mentor, colleague, and friend, Professor Jay L. Garfield, for his unwavering support and guidance over the years.

I am extremely grateful to my *kalyāṇamitra*, *ācārya* S. N. Goenka, my *vipassanā* teacher, for skillfully opening my Dharma eye, enabling me to see within myself the fragility of human conditions.

Many other friends and colleagues have directly or indirectly contributed toward this book. I owe a great debt to my colleagues and friends in Buddhist studies who have contributed much to my understanding of the subject. In particular I am incredibly indebted to the Yakherds Research Team—Jay L. Garfield, John Powers, Geshe Yeshe Thabkhas, Khenpo Tashi Tsering, José Cabezón, Thomas Doctor, Douglas Duckworth, Jed Forman, and Ryan Conlon—with whom I have had the real privilege and honor to work closely for nearly a decade (2014–2021) on two major successful research manuscripts: *Knowing Illusion: Bringing a Tibetan Debate into Contemporary Discourse: Vol. I Philosophical History of the Debate* (Oxford University Press, 2021) and *Knowing Illusion: Bringing a Tibetan Debate into Contemporary*

Discourse: Vol. II Translations (Oxford University Press, 2021). I benefitted enormously from the breadth and depth of the Yakherds' scholarship and insight, and from them I have learned how to prosecute Buddhist studies rigoriously with an open mind, collaboratively, and colleagially. I also had the great fortune to collaborative on two successful book projects—*Moonpaths: Ethics and Emptiness* (Oxford University Press, 2015) and *Moonshadows: Conventional Truth in Buddhist Philosophy* (Oxford University Press, 2016)—with the Cowherds Research Team: Jay L. Garfield, Jan Westerhoff, Tom J. F. Tillemans, Guy M. Newland, Georges Dreyfus, Graham Priest, Mark Siderits, Charles Goodman, Stephen Jenkins, Bronwyn Finnigan, Koji Tanaka, and Amber Carpenter. They are some of most influential Buddhist scholars and philosophers working cross-culturally, exploring the intersection between Buddhist studies and Western philosophy. I am especially indebted to the Cowherds for arousing and deepening my interest in Western philosophy—phenomenology, cross-cultural philosophy, logic, philosophy of mind, metaphysics, epistemology, and ethics.

I am very grateful to the University of Tasmania for awarding me with Study Leave programs (2012, 2019) and the Australian Research Council for awarding my team the four-year Discovery Project grant (2015–2019) to work on my research projects. I am also grateful to my friend and colleague, Joshua Quinn-Watson, for the time he invested in carefully editing previous drafts of the manuscript.

My sincere thanks go to Dr. Daniel Aitken, CEO of Wisdom Publications, for kindly publishing this book, and in particular to Brianna Quick for undertaking a careful copyediting of the manuscript.

Finally, I pay tribute to my dear wife, Tenzin Sangmo, whose companionship, love, and support made it possible to bring this book project to a successful completion.

INTRODUCTION

Mahāyāna and the Two Truths

According to the Tibetan schools of Mahāyāna Buddhism, the doctrine of the two truths begins in India, naturally, with the historical Buddha, Siddhārtha Gautama. It is claimed that Siddhārtha Gautama became a buddha, or "awakened one," precisely because he came to fully understand the two truths: conventional truth (*saṃvṛtisatya*) and ultimate truth (*paramārthasatya*). After attaining awakening the Buddha turned the Dharma wheel three times. The first turning of the Dharma wheel[1] represents his teachings on the four noble truths given at Sarnath, from which arose the philosophical foundationalism, essentialism, realism, and representationalism of the two truths as they are understood by the Vaibhāṣika and Sautrāntika schools. The second turning of the Dharma wheel represents his teachings on emptiness and signlessness given on Vulture Peak at Rājagṛha, found in the Perfection of Wisdom (*Prajñāparamitā*) sūtras,[2] and from which arose the philosophical nonfoundationalism, nonessentialism, and nonrealism of the Madhyamaka school's view of the two truths. From the third turning of the Dharma wheel, as outlined in the *Unraveling the Intent Sūtra* (*Saṃdhinirmocanasūtra*) and including sūtras such as the *Buddha Essence Sūtra* (*Tathāgatagarbhasūtra*) and the *Descent into Laṅka Sūtra (Laṅkāvatārasūtra)*, arose the phenomenology and idealism of the two truths asserted by the Yogācāra school. The Tibetan scholars claim that the two truths are the very heart of the Buddha's teachings, which they see reflected in the massive philosophical literature on the two truths by various Indian Buddhist philosophers belonging to all four major Buddhist schools. But that philosophical literature is not monolithic—it is diverse even among the Indians, a point that will be one of the key objectives of this book to demonstrate.

The Mahāyāna tradition—to which the Yogācāra and Madhyamaka schools belong—historically became influential only in the second century CE, first in northwestern India and later in other areas, and the Mahāyāna sūtras began to emerge and become popular in the first century BCE and were fully flourishing by the seventh and eighth centuries CE. Nevertheless, the Tibetan Buddhist tradition believes that the doctrine of the two truths is a direct teaching of the Buddha. The Tibetans identified themselves as belonging to the Mahāyāna (or Bodhisattvayāna) tradition that arose in India, which is a historical offshoot of the Mahāsaṅghika lineage.[3] Therefore Mahāyāna sūtras—such as the well-known Perfection of Wisdom sūtras that proclaim the two truths doctrine—are, for the Tibetan Mahāyānists, discourses spoken by the Buddha himself, and thus, the teachings of the two truths contained therein are directly attributable to the historical Buddha.[4] Indeed, the two truths occupy the central philosophical space in much of the Mahāyāna sūtras. Some sūtras in particular are entirely devoted to the exposition of the two truths, such as the *Sūtra on the Exposition of Conventional Truth and Ultimate Truth* (*Saṃvṛtiparamārthasatyanirdeśa*),[5] according to which both truths are means to understanding all phenomena (Skt. *dharmas*). In the *Discourse on the Meeting of the Father and the Son* (*Pitāpūtrasamāgamasūtra*), the Buddha claims that he became fully awakened precisely because he came to fully realize the meaning of the two truths.[6] In this sūtra the Buddha explains that because he came to know things as they are conventionally and ultimately, he rid himself of the ignorance under whose sway his life had been but a self-perpetuating cycle of dissatisfaction. Engaging things as they are not, he saw, is what drives that cycle, while engaging things as they are, in other words, in accordance with the two truths, brings that cycle to a close. Having penetrated these two truths, he taught them to others so that they too might retrace their journey from the ignorance that yields dissatisfaction to the wisdom that is free from it. The Buddha taught extensively and with such variety as to yield apparent contradictions, but all of his teachings shared a common purpose: to bring his students closer to a correct understanding of these two truths. "The Dharma," the Indian scholar Nāgārjuna says, is "precisely based on the two truths."[7]

In Tibet the topic of the two truths is still a richly contested issue among philosophers, as my previous book, *The Two Truths Debate: Tsongkhapa and Gorampa on the Middle Way*, showcases the debates between Tsongkhapa Lobsang Drakpa (Tsong kha pa Blo bzang grags pa, 1357–1419) and Gorampa Sönam Sengé (Go rams pa Bsod nams seng ge, 1429–89) on how to interpret Candrakīrti's Madhyamaka view. The sheer range of the Buddha's teachings, and the philosophical ambiguities contained therein, provides ample scope for debate. That debate began immediately with the Buddha's passing and has continued unabated since. Philosophical and doctrinal differences were behind a progression of schisms among the followers of the Buddha, which resulted in the development of myriad Buddhist schools, some eighteen in India alone. Eventually, a handful of schools rose to particular historical and philosophical prominence, among them the two Abhidharma schools—Vaibhāṣika and Saūtrāntika—and two Mahāyāna schools—Yogācāra and Madhyamaka—and it is the philosophies of these four schools that will be the focus of this work.

The two truths have been contested in India with philological and philosophical strategies of great variety, and the accounts of the two truths generated by debate are no less various. In some cases, the differences between these theories will be extremely subtle, in other cases quite staggering. Some draw from a limited conception of the Buddhist canon, while others draw from a considerably more inclusive interpretation of it. Some Indian Buddhist philosophers emphasize the Buddha's own statements, whereas others emphasize the exercise of reasoning in relation to them. Some are not far removed from our intuitive worldview, others jarringly counterintuitive. Some are philosophically straightforward, others the endpoint of an extremely complex process of reasoning. Some are partially foundationalist, others entirely nonfoundationalist. From the Tibetan doxographical standpoint, the Indian Buddhist schools may be unanimous that the two truths are the centerpiece of the Buddha's teachings, but they are anything but unanimous on the questions of what exactly those two truths are and how they relate to one another.

Vaibhāṣika, Saūtrāntika, Yogācāra, and Madhyamaka—these schools imperfectly divide a continuum of philosophical debate that is far more interrelated, and internally complex, than one may presume. This is to be expected, for it is the nature of debate to generate increasingly fine distinctions and also to establish what is common among the parties' assertions. Nevertheless, philosophers traditionally saw these schools for the convenienence they afford, as a method of efficiently grouping scores of Buddhist thinkers—imperfectly contained and often shared—and also of efficiently navigating the different theories of the two truths these thinkers have given rise to.

WHY THE PHILOSOPHICAL APPROACH?

The account of the two truths in Indian Buddhist philosophy detailed in this book is modeled on the work by Gashar Nyagri Sharchö Rinpoche Jetsun Lobsang Nyima, *An Outline of the Two Truths: The Pinnacle of All the Positions.* In his book, Jetsun Lobsang Nyima employs a *grub mtha'* (Skt. *siddhānta*) styled presentation of the two truths in Indian Buddhism, following the well-known works by Losang Chökyi Nyima, *The Crystal Mirror of Philosophical Systems: A Tibetan Study of Asian Religious Thought*, and Changkya Rölpai Dorjé, *Beautiful Adornment of Mount Meru: A Presentation of Classical Indian Philosophy.*

The English phrase that corresponds most closely with the Tibetan phrase *grub mtha'i rnam bzhag* (*siddhāntavyavasthāpana*) is "presentation of philosophical systems," although academics often use "tenets" or "doxography" (which in Greek refers to "an opinion" or "a point of view")—terms employed to describe the conclusions by various philosophical views.

Broadly speaking, the *siddhānta* approach to the topic of the two truths in Indian Buddhism provides justifications for the doctrine of the two truths, in which the philosophical views of the schools are not pitted against each other as fixed and static competing positions; rather, the detailed argumentations and analyses of each school's approach to the two truths are presented to weave together the unique contributions each brings to supporting and strengthening the practice. And this practice requires the networking of the system and the positions in order to form a unified path, like the rungs of the ladder upon which each practitioner can traverse. We may say the Tibetans took the *siddhānta* approach from the Buddha's teaching in the *Descent into Laṅkā Sūtra* (*Laṅkāvatārasūtra*):

> Mahāmati, this is the characteristic of the way of *siddhānta* and the teachings, which you and other great bodhisattvas should work hard to embark on. So it is said:
> I have two ways:
> schools and teachings.
> To the childish I give teachings,
> and schools for the practioners.[8]

The *siddhānta* method though is not specific to any particular school but is a trenchant philosophical practice in all schools of Indian and Tibetan Buddhism. This method, however, is not a new invention on the part of Tibetans. The *siddhānta* tendency in India can be traced back as early as the late fifth century to the Grammarian Bhartṛhari, who often used *siddhānta* language in his description of various philosophical thoughts, developing the term *darśana* ("view").[9] Through the *darśana* approach, doxography came to play a central role in the presentation styles of various schools of thought in India. The Tibetans adopted the *siddhānta* approach from their Indian counterparts, emulating the doxographical work of the great Indian master Bhāviveka (490–570 CE). His method exerted a strong influence on later

Buddhist scholars, including the great philosophical works of Candrakīrti, Śāntarakṣita, Kamalaśīla, Śāntideva, Ātiśa, and others who followed them. The Buddhist *siddhānta* approaches and arranges the Indian Buddhist schools of thought from a hierarchical standpoint. By the time Ātiśa was teaching in Tibet in the eleventh century, Tibetan Buddhist *siddhānta* had successfully absorbed the hierarchical structure of the Indian Buddhist schools, starting with Vaibhāṣika, Sautrāntika, Yogācāra, Svātantrika Madhyamaka, and finally Prāsaṅgika Madhyamaka.

Not surprisingly, I have adopted the same *siddhānta* presentation structure in this book. This approach is not without its drawbacks—approaching the two truths through representive schools is far from perfect in representing what is in reality a far more complex intellectual continuum. I nevertheless decided upon its use for several reasons.

First, the *siddhānta* approach is convenient for the purposes of this book, which is not to attempt a complete historical record of every position ever taken by an Indian Buddhist thinker on the two truths, but to provide an accurate and useful account of the overall introductory debate. The *siddhānta* approach, approximate as it is, is suited to separating the key lines of the argument from the side skirmishes.

Second, the *siddhānta* approach reminds us that we must examine the respective two truths theories not in a vacuum, but within the contexts of ontological, epistemological, soteriological, phenomenological, and ethical concerns of the schools that propose them. As we shall see as we progress, a school's position on the two truths is inseparable from the philosophical commitments that school makes: its view of what exists, and how that which exists may be reliably known. The schools have starkly different positions on these questions, starkly different ideas of what kind of psycho-physical world the two truths comprise and describe. Progressing through the schools sequentially keeps my discussion of the two truths in step with their philosophical context, averts the confusion that can arise by judging one school's theory in relation to another's ontology or epistemology, and leads to more precision in debate.

Third, the *siddhānta* approach is by its very structure a reminder of Buddhism's soteriological project: the gradual replacement of our current ignorance with the wisdom of enlightenment. All Buddhist schools agree that the root of our current ignorance is an excess of foundationalism: we invest things with more substance and solidity than they warrant. The route from that ignorance to wisdom is to divest ourselves of surplus foundationalism, to invest things only with the substance and solidity that they warrant. The schools in the *siddhānta* schema all advance positions that are less foundationalist than we intuitively advance ourselves, but not equally so. They are arranged, quite deliberately, in descending order of foundationalism. As we examine the schools in this sequence, we are studying positions that deny, in steady progression, slightly more substance. The substance we intuit, that of gross objects, is rejected for the substance of their tiny, momentary components; the substance of the physical is rejected for the substance of the mental; the substance of the mental is rejected for the substance of convention; the substance of convention is rejected for an utter lack of substance. While the schools disagree, quite understandably, about where on this scale of diminishing foundationalism reality itself sits, the fact of the scale itself is a useful reminder of the soteriological task all schools accept.

The adoption of the *siddhānta* approach, the sequence of the schools, and the placement of the Prāsaṅgika school at the end of that sequence does in this work, as it does in most Tibetan Buddhist traditions, indicate a doxographic hierarchy, or a clear soteriological progression. The *siddhānta* approach indicates that there is much more at stake in the two truths than just a spectrum of unrelated and fragmented philosophical views. The value of philosophical views lies in the strength of the arguments enabling a journey through the progressive soteriological path toward awakening, not in their allocated positions on this spectrum. Following the *siddhānta* tradition, the aim of this book is to lay out the rich and complex philosophical journey undertaken by our understanding of the two truths, progressively moving from the commitment to foundationalism (or ontological realism) of the Vaibhāṣika, to the representationalism of the Sautrāntika, to the idealism or phenomenology of the Yogācāra (making stops at the partial idealism/phenomenology of the Yogācāra-Svātantrika Madhyamaka and partial realism/representationism of the Sautrāntika Svātantrika), and finally arriving at the thoroughgoing nonfoundationalism, the relinquishing of all foundationalist commitments, of the Prāsaṅgika Madhyamaka.

Although I follow Jetsun Lobsang Nyima's *An Outline of the Two Truths* as the source of inspiration behind this book, this work draws primarily and extensively from canonical sources—from the texts attributed to the Indian masters themselves and their most influential Indian interpreters. My intention is to recount the philosophies of the two truths in Indian Buddhism from the perspective of my interpretive lens, sketching the contours of rich hermeneutic approaches to the two truths that remain very much alive and unsettled, at least in so far as the modern exegetes see it. The philosophical arguments and counter-arguments here are not presented to serve as an inert historical record, but as the basis for the reader to test and interrogate the competing positions, to locate their philosophical strengths and vulnerabilities, and to determine which, if any, have the superior claim.

That there exists in Indian Buddhism such radical differences on so fundamental a matter is of great interest and is, I believe, deserving of a dedicated work. Despite the centrality of the two truths to Buddhism generally, and especially its philosophical development in India, there is not yet such a work. While there are two works dedicated to the two truths in Tibetan Buddhism,[10] a form of Buddhism that absorbed much of the Indian philosophical tradition, there are very few academic resources dedicated to the two truths in the root Indian Buddhist tradition. The absence of such resources, and the absence of English translations of many of the critical texts that comprise the two truths debate across all four philosophical systems, significantly deprives students and scholars of the opportunity to engage this rich philosophical tradition by way of its central philosophy. This is a critical lacuna and one this work aims to address.

Moreover, the absence of such a work has allowed a view quite the opposite to that supported by the primary literature to gain unwarranted traction—that is, that there is a *single* theory of two truths accepted by all Indian Buddhist schools, in particular, the Madhyamaka, which distinguishes itself according to other philosophical commitments. By simply surveying, as this work does, the many competing theories of the two truths presented by Indian Buddhist thinkers, the falsity of this view quickly becomes self-evident. Indian Buddhism houses so many theories of the two truths, in fact, that even the considerable number discussed here can be no more than a representative sample.

This work is the result of a decade of methodical research and teaching experience. Since my goal is to set out the two truths debate in Indian Buddhism, I have taken as my primary sources the works of the Indian Buddhist philosophers most involved in that debate and deliberately avoided foregrounding secondary materials. That I deliberately avoid emphasizing this material is no reflection on its worth—there is, in fact, some extraordinary scholarship relating to the material we will cover. Where possible, these works are referenced in the notes in the hope that they will guide the interested reader's subsequent study.

While many of the primary sources remain extant in their original Indic languages, many do not, in which case we have used the Tibetan editions of these texts. In most cases, I have offered my own translations, appropriating available alternative translations only rarely. Throughout, I have attempted to render the original sources into English that is both readable and faithful to the original, using precise equivalents wherever it has been possible to do so without rendering the text unaccommodating. Throughout the book, in the interest of accessibility of the main discussion, I have deliberately avoided using foreign terms as much as possible. However, where necessary the key foreign terms in parentheses are Sanskrit, unless otherwise noted. Wherever possible I have supported my translations and my interpretations with relevant textual references, and have cited the original source text for my translated excerpts in the notes in all but the few instances where the excerpts were too long to allow it.

The majority of the materials in this work have arrived here after being trialed and refined by their use in undergraduate and graduate Buddhist philosophy courses at the University of Tasmania. The responses of my students, representing a spectrum of expertise ranging from the absolute beginner to the graduate researcher, have shaped the approach I have taken in selecting, arranging, and presenting the sources and arguments used. Throughout, my approach is to present this long and complex debate in a way that is accessible to a nonspecialist audience without compromising the complexity and sophistication of the ideas that make up that debate.

I have argued throughout the course of this work a philosophically fruitful debate on the status of the two truths. In each of the individual chapters, I have set out each school's contribution to that debate, its key thinkers and treatises, and its most innovative and influential philosophical moves. I have observed throughout that each school's position on the two truths reflects the extent of our commitment to something foundational—particularly to essence, or to intrinsic nature (*svabhāva*) and unique particulars (*svalakṣaṇa*).

The Tibetans took philosophical hierarchy among the Indian Buddhist philosophies very seriously. During the time of the "early dissemination" of Buddhism to Tibet (seventh to ninth centuries), Śāntarakṣita (eighth century) and his student Kamalaśīla were the first prominent Indian Mādhyamika luminaries to travel to Tibet, a voyage made at the request of King Trisong Detsen (Khri Srong lde'u btsan, r. 754–c. 799). The two philosophers promoted the Yogācāra Madhyamaka (or Yogācāra-Svātantrika Madhyamaka) school in Tibet, which enjoyed initial success. After the great Samyé debate[11] held at Samyé Monastery between Kamalaśīla and the Chan master Hwashang Mahayana (Ch. Heshang Moheyan), the Tibetan king Trisong Detsen declared Kamalaśīla victorious, and thereafter the king and the central Tibetan administration further decreed that the Madhyamaka of Nāgārjuna would be the normative philosophical system to be adopted throughout Tibet by all four of its major Buddhist schools.[12]

Śāntarakṣita and Kamalaśīla's philosophy was adopted by a number of Tibetan luminaries during the time of the "early dissemination" of Buddhism to Tibet. With government support for importation of Buddhist texts and translation of materials from India and China, as well as the development of exegetical traditions, the study of Madhyamaka became a Tibetan national project. During the period of the "early dissemination," important works attributed to Nāgārjuna, Candrakīrti, and other Indian philosophers were translated, and an indigenous tradition of commentary emerged. Tibetan scholars traveled to India, and many studied at the great monastic universities in the north of the subcontinent or with masters in Kashmir or Nepal. Although from an early period in Tibet Madhyamaka was widely influential, as Tibetans worked to understand the implications of the literature they inherited from India, fissures developed and schools of interpretation emerged. The most prominent disagreements concerned the interpretation of Nāgārjuna's works. By the end of the eleventh century, four main movements of Indian Madhyamaka thought had taken shape in Tibet: (1) the foundational Madhyamaka works attributed to Nāgārjuna and Āryadeva; (2) the Prāsaṅgika Mādhyamika works attributed to Buddhapālita and Candrakīrti, which later came to be appreciated by most Tibetan exegetes as the preeminent Buddhist philosophical system on the ground of its utter rejection of any form of foundationalism; (3) the Svātantrika Madhyamaka works by Bhāviveka; and (4) the Yogācāra-Svātantrika Madhyamaka works (most closely associated with Śāntarakṣita and Kamalaśila), which were generally ranked below the Prāsaṅgika but were still considered more sophisticated than the Vaibhāṣika, Sautrāntika, and Yogācāra systems because they were seen to embrace some form of foundationalism smuggled through the back door.[13]

From the eleventh century up until the present day, most of Tibet's leading intellectual figures have endorsed Buddhapālita and Candrakīrti's Madhyamaka to be the most authoritative interpretive works on Nāgārjuna's Madhyamaka and agree that the Prāsaṅgika system is superior to Svātantrika of Bhāviveka. But there are still significant disagreements about how precisely to capture this distinction. The debates between the Geluk and other schools of Tibetan Buddhism concerning what really counts as authentic Prāsaṅgika Madhyamaka and how it should be differentiated from the Svātantrika Madhyamaka can be deep and subtle.[14]

Nevertheless, the Tibetans unanimously and continuously identified themselves as the champions of the Prāsaṅgika Madhyamaka school who are committed to eschewing foundationalism of any stripe. Accordingly at one end of their philosophical spectrum is the battle against foundationalism of Brahmanism, in particular, the Ābhidharmikas—Vaibhāṣika and Sautrāntika—representing our ordinary intuitive attraction toward realism of the external things. At the other end of the spectrum is the difficult task of achieving the nonfoundationalism of the Prāsaṅgika, representing the *ārya*'s, or exalted being's, freedom from all views, or relinquishing any commitment to realism of both external and internal realities. And between these two ends of the spectrum lies the partial foundationalism of the Yogācāra, representing our attachment to an internal world of subjectivity, as well as the inner experiences and partial foundationalism of the Svātantrika, represented by the soft realism of internal dharmas (according to Svātantrika-Yogācāra Madhyamaka) and the soft realism of external dharmas (according to Svātantrika-Sautrāntika Madhyamaka).

I will consider the broader implications of the degree of foundationalism that each school admits into its theory of the two truths. Specifically, I will consider the schools' positions against a variety of related spectrums—ontology, soteriology, causality, and the roles of reasoned analysis and language.

ONTOLOGY

The Vaibhāṣika and Sautrāntika schools, representing the Abhidharma system, are unanimous in their critiques of the Nyāya-Vaiśeṣika substance metaphysics that claims reality constitutes substances possessed of qualities. Substances are substrates of qualities but are distinct from the qualities they possess. The most fundamental of the Vaiśeṣika ontological categories is undoubtedly substance (*dravya*). Substance denotes the objective reality of things, the subjective reality of consciousness in and of itself, and the self-subsistence of things. It argues that reality of experience dictates the existence of substances in which qualities inhere, parts inhere, and action inheres. Substances are either eternal or noneternal. Substance that depends on something else is noneternal, hence composite substances (*avayavidravya*) are dependent and impermanent. The eternal substances are simple, independent, and unique. The eternal substances consist of earth, water, fire, air, ether, time, space, self, and mind. These nine substances are all eternal and infinitesimal, and they form the basis for composite and destructible substances. Eternal substances are neither caused nor destroyed, whereas noneternal substances are caused and destroyed—not by themselves, but by the force of something other than them.[15] The noncorporeal world of consciousness includes cognitions, desires, aversions, volitions, and the feelings of pleasure and pain—all these are transitory, they all are viewed as qualities of the substance called the "soul."[16]

The Abhidharmika's rejection of the substance metaphysics of the Vaiśeṣika represents antifoundationalist tendencies however, its rejection of foundationalism is still only partial; intrinsic reality is simply confined to event metaphysics of fundamental spatial and temporal units, to atoms and instants. Though the Vaibhāṣika and Sautrāntika schools differ in their use of terminology, they broadly agree that these units—unique and irreducible—are the ultimate reality, while the composites that are conceptually constructed from them are merely conventional.

Yogācāra rejects the realism of these schools, the assumption that experience indicates an objectively real external world. But like those realist schools, their rejection of intrinsic reality is not categorical; it is simply confined to the mind. The only reality for the Yogācāra is mental impressions. Perceived ignorantly—as indicating something external and enduring—they are conventional reality; perceived as they are—as nondual, empty, and ineffable—they are ultimate reality.

Svātantrika Madhyamaka rejects the shared position of the realist schools that intrinsic reality can be ultimately located; analysis, its proponents argue, exposes its ultimate absence both materially and mentally. But their rejection of intrinsic nature, too, is not total; intrinsic nature is simply confined to the conventional. The Svātantrika Madhyamaka subschools, Sautrāntika-Svātantrika and Yogācāra-Svātantrika, are distinguished by their chosen model of the conventional. Each imports that ontology from its namesake school—the conventional reality of the former permits matter, that of the latter is entirely mental.

It is for the Prāsaṅgika that intrinsic reality is entirely rejected. To attempt to confine intrinsic reality is folly, they argue, indicative of an underlying foundationalism. To confine it to the conventional domain is not possible, because the conventional (dependent arising) and ultimate (emptiness) are ontologically equated. Only that which is empty of intrinsic nature may dependently arise, and the dependent arising of all things demonstrates their emptiness.

ANALYSIS

Ontology and analysis are deeply interlinked: where analysis ends is precisely where intrinsic reality begins. For the realist schools (Vaibhāṣika and Sautrāntika), analysis is employed devastatingly against conceptual composites—conventional truth—but is exhausted at the level of atoms and instants, their basic ontological units—ultimate reality. For the idealist Yogācāra, analysis is deployed to entirely dismantle the external world, including the atoms of the realists. That analysis exhausts itself though at the level of nondual consciousness, whose resistance to analysis confirms its ultimacy.

For the semi-realist Svātantrika, analysis is used to clear the ultimate domain of intrinsic reality entirely—reasoned analysis arrives at the ultimate truth of emptiness. But the conventional domain is spared analysis, lest it rob conventionality of the intrinsic reality that the Svātantrika believe is essential to causality.

For the Prāsaṅgika, analysis is deployed without exception, and there is nothing that can withstand it. Ultimately everything, seen analytically, is empty of intrinsic reality, including emptiness itself; conventionally, everything seen analytically exists only relationally, including relations themselves. Rather than robbing things of causality, the Prāsaṅgika argue that analysis, by showing that things exist insubstantially and relationally, confirms it. Only things that lack intrinsic nature can contribute to causal interdependence, and analysis confirms that lack.

CAUSALITY

For all the schools, except the Prāsaṅgika, causality is a function of something foundational; it is intrinsic reality that possesses causal power.

For the Vaibhāṣika and Sautrāntika, causal efficacy is attributed to ultimately real unique particulars. For the Yogācāra, it is attributed to mental representations; causality is entirely mental. While the Svātantrika Madhyamaka reject intrinsic reality ultimately, they retain the previous schools' equation of intrinsic reality and causal power in the conventional domain. Causal efficacy is attributed to what is conventionally intrinsically real—to conventional unique particulars.

The Prāsaṅgika Madhyamaka distinguishes itself by delinking intrinsic reality and causal power, arguing that the two mutually exclude each other. Anything intrinsically real would be causally inert; only things empty of intrinsic nature can causally, which is to say, dependently, arise. To permit intrinsic reality in the conventional domain, as the Svātantrika Madhyamaka do, would be to deny it its role as the domain of dependent arising. For the Prāsaṅgika, everything, both ultimately (a rebuke to Vaibhāṣika, Sautrāntika, and Yogācāra) and conventionally (a rebuke to the Svātantrika Madhyamaka), owes its existence *only* to its causes and conditions, and not to anything intrinsic to it.

LANGUAGE

A similar division appears when the role of language is considered. For all of the schools except the Prāsaṅgika, language and ultimate reality mutually exclude each other. For the Vaibhāṣika and Sautrāntika, we saw, language is exclusively the domain of the conventional. Language, gross and approximate, marks conventional concepts; it applies singular labels to composite, constructed things; it attributes identity to abstractions and causal efficacy to that which is causally inactive.

For the Yogācāra, the distinction between language and ultimate reality is equally sharply drawn. In terms of their theory of the three natures—dependent nature (*paratantra*), conceptual or imaginary nature (*parikalpita*), and ultimate or perfect nature (*parinispanna*)—only the first two, which account for conventional reality, are linguistic; the third, ultimate nature, is entirely nonlinguistic. Language has only a conventional role: a linguistic signifier (*śabda*) is one of the three forms of convention (the others are fabrication and consciousness) that gives rise to conventional truths.

The subschools of the Svātantrika Madhyamaka borrow their namesakes' treatment of language: the Sautrāntika-Svātantrika Madhyamaka's treatment accords with the Sautrāntika, the Yogācāra-Svātantrika Madhyamaka with the Yogācāra. In either case, language is exclusively conventional; ultimate reality is always extralinguistic.

In other words, the majority of Buddhist philosophers hold that ultimate reality and language are divorced from each other. But the Prāsaṅgika disagree. They argue that reality and language do not exclude each other, that in fact they intersect. For the Prāsaṅgika, everything exists dependently and is only a "thing" at all because it is designated a "thing" by the linguistic consciousness that names it. Everything is, in other words, nominally dependent. Everything, including ultimate truth, is unavoidably linguistic. As Nāgārjuna says in his *Seventy Verses on Emptiness* (*Śūnyatāsaptatikārikā*):

> The Buddha says that due to the power of linguistic conventions, not the power of reality, things are said to be "produced," "destroyed," to "exist," "to not exist," to be "inferior," "mediocre," "superior."[17]

In the utter absence of intrinsic reality, it is language and concepts that give the phenomenal world its shape, structure, and character. In his *Commentary on the Four Hundred Verses* (*Catuḥṣatakaṭīkā*), Candrakīrti argues that realities are:

> Like the snake that is conceptually imputed on the coiled ropes, the [realities] exist due to the existence of the concepts . . . [and are] not established through their intrinsic nature.[18]

In his commentary on Nāgārjuna's *Sixty Verses on Reasoning* (*Yuktiṣaṣṭikārikā*),[19] Candrakīrti expands this further. All categories, all phenomenological experiences, are dependent upon our conceptual constructs, which are themselves shaped by accepted linguistic conventions. All phenomena we know are linguistically influenced: we know them only within a linguistic framework.[20] Even nirvāṇa and ultimate truth are linguistic concepts that exist merely as names or concepts:

> It is just so! Since saṃsāra is also a concept, nirvāṇa too must be a concept, for they both exist as mundane linguistic conventions (*loka-vyvahāra*).[21]

That they are dependent upon language does not disqualify them as ultimate truths. For the Prāsaṅgika, we come to understand their ultimacy not by abandoning language, but by appreciating the linguistic dimension of their dependent existence.

SOTERIOLOGY

The ultimate purpose of each philosophical program is the same for all schools. It is soteriological release: to rid ourselves of the ignorance that yields constant dissatisfaction by bringing ourselves into accord with the reality of things. To know the two truths accurately is simply to be in accord with that reality.

For the Vaibhāṣika and Sautrāntika, the ultimate soteriological release available to us is nirvāṇa, which requires the direct perception of the ultimate truth of selflessness. In accordance with their theory of the two truths, that is the direct perception that reality is no more than atomic particles in a state of constant, momentary flux, bereft of any abiding or underlying reality.

In the case of the Mahāyāna schools, the ultimate soteriological release available to us is complete enlightenment—to not just break free of suffering but to attain the capacity of a buddha who may assist others in the same task. To attain enlightenment requires the direct realization of the ultimate truth of emptiness. In accordance with the Yogācāra theory of the two truths, that is to realize the emptiness of everything external to nondual consciousness, if not the emptiness of nondual consciousness itself. In accordance with the Svātantrika and Prāsaṅgika theories of the two truths, that is to realize the emptiness of both subject and object—the emptiness of both oneself and all phenomena.

There are many reasonable objections to the *siddhānta* approach, chief among them that by abbreviating and simplifying a philosophical continuum into a sequence of separate schools, a certain amount of distortion takes place. In the process of simplification, positions are attributed to philosophers and schools that they never explicitly advanced, and philosophers are identified with one school at the expense of others to which they have contributed. In order to avoid the first problem, misattribution, I have been careful not to attribute a philosophical position to a person or school on the basis of hearsay. Only when I have located in the primary literature an instance of that position being explicitly made will I attribute it to the person who has explicitly made it. My provision of the original text from which all citations and translated excerpts are taken in my notes is an additional safeguard against misattribution.

Avoiding the second problem, miscategorization, is simpler. Though I use the *siddhānta* structure, I do not intend to definitively house individual philosophers within any particular school. It is never my view that the position a philosopher takes at one time or in one text is final or representative of their entire career. It is always simply a specific contribution—even if sometimes an enormously influential one—to the debate. No philosopher arrives fully formed or remains intellectually stagnant. The example of Vasubandhu, who makes important philosophical contributions in several separate chapters, demonstrates the folly of attempting to categorize thinkers. In the *Treasury of Abhidharma* (*Abhidharmakośa*), Vasubandhu is the spokesperson for both the Vaibhāṣika and the Sautrāntika. In the Yogācāra literature, he represents that school's position vigorously. In Madhyamaka texts, like his *Commentary on the Diamond Sūtra* (*Vajracchedikaṭīka*), he speaks as a Mādhyamika. I am not concerned here with finding out Vasubandhu's final view, as interesting a subject as that may be. I am concerned more with the debate than the historical figures themselves.

STRUCTURE OF THE BOOK

As we progress through the schools, I will, where relevant, set out their definitions of the two truths, the relationship between them, their ontological status, the epistemic standards they must satisfy, their relation to the limits of language and thought, and the implications their realization has for the Buddhist soteriological project.

The first chapter takes up the Vaibhāṣika school's account of the two truths, which, while sharing much of the spirit of the Sautrāntika account, adheres to a more elaborate ontology. Relying on this school's canonical text, Vasubandhu's *Treasury of Abhidharma* and its commentary, I will outline the five categories of that ontology—matter, primary minds, secondary minds, nonassociated composite phenomena, and unconditioned phenomena—before turning to the two truths that apply to them. Ultimate truth consists of the basic spatial and temporal units—atoms and moments—of the five basic categories, and such ultimate truths exhibit three interrelated qualities: irreducibility, independence, and unconstructedness. Again, conventional truths are the inverse of ultimate truths. They are spatial or temporal aggregates—atomic groupings and temporal continua—and they exhibit the opposite three qualities. They are reducible, derivative, and constructed. A notable innovation of the Vaibhāṣika is their subclassification of ultimate truths according to whether they are subject to causality: as being either compounded (the five aggregates) or uncompounded (the "uncompounded trio" of space and the two varieties of cessation). While the Vaibhāṣika attempt, quite inventively, to preserve the ultimate status of the aggregates they concede are compounded, that concession will be prosecuted to quite different conclusions by subsequent schools.

In the second chapter, I turn to the Sautrāntika school, which itself comprises two related subschools, the "textualists" (Āgamānusāra

Sautrāntika) and the "logicians" (Nyāyānusāra Sautrāntika). The textualists account of the two truths is, like the Vaibhāṣika school, shaped largely by Vasubandhu's *Treasury of Abhidharma* and closely resembles the Vaibhāṣika account. The textualists largely accept the Vaibhāṣika positions, denying only the ultimacy of the "uncompounded trio," the aggregates, and shape.

The account of the logicians, on the other hand, is largely shaped by Dignāga and Dharmakīrti's treatises on epistemology, and accordingly, has a more epistemological and logical bent. Ultimate truths for the logicians are unique particulars, which are causally efficacious and thus capable of being correctly perceived. They exhibit four qualities (in contrast to the Vaibhāṣika's three): they are causally efficacious, uniquely defined, cognizable absent language and thought, and not denotable by words. The only things that satisfy those criteria, the logicians argue, are moments of matter, of consciousness, and of nonassociated composite phenomena. Conventional truths, naturally, are those things that fail those four criteria—which are, in other words, causally incapable, indistinct, apprehendable by language and thought, and denotable by words.

In the third chapter, I turn to the Yogācāra school's account of the two truths, which is bound up in its distinctive ontological position that the only reality is mental. Exploiting the Sautrāntika's concession that we engage external objects not directly but via the mental representations they cause, the Yogācāra argues on logical and epistemological grounds that positing an external world to explain these representations is both unnecessary and philosophically fraught. Mental representations, they argue, indicate no extra-mental reality, nothing beyond the activity of mind itself. Both truths, then, refer to twin perceptions of the same thing: that which mentally appears. Conventional truth is these appearances occurring to an ignorant cognition, which sees them as indicating a substantive external "other." Ultimate truth is these appearances seen by a cognition free from ignorance, which sees them for what they are—mere appearance, empty, nondual, and ineffable.

In the fourth chapter, we arrive at the Madhyamaka school, whose foundational philosophical works belong to Nāgārjuna and Āryadeva, and whose signature philosophical position is nonfoundationalism, the view that, at least ultimately, things lack an identity all of their own, an intrinsic nature. Yet the correct interpretation of these works is the source of a deep and philosophically productive division between their followers. I immediately address the nature of the split between the two Madhyamaka subschools, the Svātantrika and Prāsaṅgika. This is critical, since it is sometimes argued that the split between these two schools is a methodological rather than philosophical one; that both schools prosecute an identical understanding of Madhyamaka philosophy and account of the two truths, but with alternative philosophical tools. Were this the case, I would have no cause to address the accounts of these schools separately, which I do in the remaining chapters. But this is not the case. There are very real methodological differences—the Svātantrika's philosophical tool of choice is the syllogism or probative argument, the Prāsaṅgika's the *reductio* argument—but there are also very real, interrelated *philosophical* differences. The methodological differences reflect a deeper ontological and epistemological divide that yields very different accounts of the two truths. Whereas the Svātantrika Madhyamaka accepts the intrinsic nature of conventional things, the Prāsaṅgika Madhyamaka's entire philosophical project is the total rejection of intrinsic nature, both ultimately and conventionally. Their methodological choices reflect and also reinforce this philosophical divide.

I turn first to the Svātantrika Madhyamaka, which itself houses two subschools, the Sautrāntika-Svātantrika Madhyamaka and Yogācāra-Svātantrika Madhyamaka. They are, as the names suggest, differentiated according to their view on the ontological status of external objects. Where the former fuses Madhyamaka nonfoundationalism with the realism of the Sautrāntika, the latter fuses it with Yogācāra idealism.

In the fifth chapter, I examine the Sautrāntika-Svātantrika Madhyamaka school's account of the two truths, laid out in the works of Bhāviveka and Jñānagarbha. For the Sautrāntika-Svātantrika Madhyamaka, the ultimate truth is that *all* phenomena lack intrinsic reality, a fact exposed by the analytical cognition whose unsuccessful search for it exposes its absence. From the standpoint of conventional truth, though, the intrinsic reality of external things is accepted, since the nonanalytical cognitions of ordinary beings that perceive it are considered a reliable arbiter of the conventional.

In the sixth chapter, I examine the Yogācāra-Svātantrika Madhyamaka school's account of the two truths, laid out in the work of Śāntarakṣita and his student Kamalaśīla. This school shares with the previous one a Madhyamaka account of the ultimate truth, the view that, ultimately, analysis exposes all things as empty of intrinsic reality. The key difference between this and the previous school is their conception of the conventional. Whereas for the previous school the conventional truth—an external world perceived to exist intrinsically—was supplied by the Sautrāntika, here it is supplied by the Yogācāra. All that is intrinsically conventionally real is *mind*. Any extra-mental posits are fictions, false even conventionally.

In the seventh chapter, I turn to the Prāsaṅgika Madhyamaka account, laid out primarily in the works of Candrakīrti. Here we find the philosophical culmination of the trend toward nonfoundationalism observed in the schools discussed previously. In the previous schools, we saw what was considered foundational progressively shrink, intrinsic nature turns to smaller spatio-temporal units, to unique particulars, to the mind itself, and to the conventional domain. In the Prāsaṅgika Madhyamaka account of the two truths, intrinsic nature is eliminated entirely. Both conventional and ultimate truths are empty of it. Intrinsic nature does not exist, not anywhere, because it cannot. Things that exist intrinsically exist independently, and such things have no place in a world that is utterly interdependent, utterly causal. The conventional truth is the fact of things arising dependently, the ultimate truth is the absence of any intrinsic reality that would prevent it from so arising dependently. In the Prāsaṅgika account, the conventional and ultimate, dependent arising and emptiness, are closely linked—they are twin aspects of a single reality. This is especially important to countering the charge most frequently leveled against the Prāsaṅgika Madhyamaka, that they extend beyond nonfoundationalism into outright nihilism. It demonstrates that the Prāsaṅgika Madhyamaka accept the existence of things and challenge only the mode by which things exist. Things exist, they say, because they dependently arise, and they do so precisely because they are entirely empty of intrinsic nature.

Finally, in chapter eight, we briefly look at the implications of the truths in contemporary academic studies of Buddhism. Contemporary studies of the two truths debates among the Buddhist philosophers stem in large part from the way in which they each differently interpret and understand the traditional sources on the two truths and their philosophical implications, predominantly from epistemological and metaphysical standpoints. From these standpoints the two truths are presumably taken to be concerned with property that some statements, beliefs, propositions, ideas, and representations may have. Academic studies reveal that the theory of two truths in Indian Buddhist thought is not in any way directly equivalent to any of the Western philosophical conceptions of truth. Even when the two truths are approached semantically, the predominant practice in Western philosophy, the traditional Buddhist philosophers are not strict correspondence theorists and neither are they strictly coherentists. They are neither pragmatists nor realists, not even fictionalist or deflationary theorists in a strict Western philosophical sense. And yet the Buddhist notions of truth do share many aspects in common with Western philosophical treatments of truth. Hence Buddhist philosophers are putting forward some tentative proposals to articulate the relationship between Western philosophical theories of truth and Buddhist theories of truth.

Let us turn now to our discussions of the individual schools.

CHAPTER ONE

Vaibhāṣika: Vasubandhu

Between the first and second century CE, the Vaibhāṣika, a subschool of the panrealist Sarvāstivāda school, became the dominant non-Mahāyāna school in northern India. Its influence soon spread across central Asia and would eventually reach China. By the seventh century, the famous Chinese pilgrim Yijing (635–713) traveled to India to study at Nālanda University, and after a period of twenty-five years (671–695) recorded, in his *Record of the Buddhist Religion as Practiced in India and the Malay Archipelago,*[22] the widespread currency of this philosophy in the kingdoms of central Asia, on the islands of Sumatra and Java in Southeast Asia, as well as in southern, western, and eastern China.

The Vaibhāṣika, like the Sautrāntika, recognize the Abhidharma as the actual words of the Buddha and classify it as one of the three *piṭakas*, literally three "baskets" or "scriptural collections." The Vaibhāṣika school held its council in Pāṭaliputra around the turn of the second century, which produced a sweeping commentary called the *Great Commentary* (*Mahāvibhāṣāśāstra*, also known as *Vibhāṣā*), a monumental *Encyclopedia of Abhidharma* commentary on Kātyāyanīputra's *Engaging with the Higher Insight of the Abhidharma* (*Abhidharma-jñānaprasthāna*),[23] and six supplementary treatises (*Padaśāstras*).[24] According to the *Great Commentary*, the four great masters of the school were Ghoṣak, Buddhadeva, Bhadanta Vasumitra, and Bhadanta Dharmatrāta; they were contemporaries who produced original works supplementing the canonical texts.[25]

In the fourth century, Vasubandhu undertook a comprehensive survey of the Sarvāstivāda school's thought, the results of which were a landmark compendium, the *Treasury of Abhidharma*, and its accompanying commentary (*Abhidharmakośabhāṣya*). Vasubandhu based his works on the *Great Commentary*, a comprehensive commentary on Kātyāyanīputra's *Engaging with the Higher Insight of the Abhidharma*, which according to the tradition was initially drafted and compiled during the Emperor Kaniṣka's council through the collaborative works of the four great contemporary master philosophers of the Sarvāstivāda: Ghoṣak, Buddhadeva, Bhadanta Vasumitra,[26] and Bhadanta Dharmatrāta.[27] These scholars also produced their own original works supplementing the Sarvastivādin canonical texts. Paul Demiéville observes that the authors of the Vibhāṣā were from Kaśmīra themselves. The followers of *The Great Commentary* came to be known as Vaibhāṣika, a term especially appropriated for the Kāśmīri. Vasubandhu's works, drawn on the *Great Commentary* on which the Vaibhāṣika philosophical positions are based, offer a generally reliable and probing critique of the Vaibhāṣika views from the Sautrāntika standpoint, including the theory of the two truths.

The Vaibhāṣika ontology classifies all the objects of knowledge within five basic categories:

1) *Matter* (*rūpa*), which consists of eleven forms. These are the ten revealing forms (*vijñaptirūpa*)—the five senses (eyes, ears, nose, tongue, and body) and five sensory objects (forms, sounds, smell, taste, and tangible objects)—and the nonrevealing form (*avijñāptirūpa*) that is not perceptible to the five senses.[28]
2) *Primary minds* are cognitions (*citta*) that range from visual consciousness to mental consciousness.[29] These apprehend the generalities of objects.

3) *Secondary minds* (*caitta*). These apprehend the particularities of the objects.
4) *Nonassociated composite phenomena* (*cittacaittaviprayuktasaṃskāra*), which are neither material nor mental, because they are disjoined from the mind and yet resemble the mind. These include life force, attainment, nonattainment, absorption, production, aging, enduring, cessation, and the like, which are neither mental nor physical.[30]
5) *Noncontingent* or *unconditioned phenomena* (*asaṃskṛta*), which are not causally produced. These include space, analytical cessation (*pratisaṁkhyānirodha*), and nonanalytical cessation (*apratisaṁkhyānirodha*).[31]

This ontology is foundational to the Vaibhāṣika theory of the two truths. In regard to the ontology of the two truths, in the *Treasury of Abhidharma*, Vasubandhu defines the two truths as follows:

> An entity, the cognition of which does not arise when it is destroyed and mentally divided, conventionally exists (*saṃvṛtisat*), like a pot and water. Ultimate existence (*paramārthasad*) is otherwise.[32]

Vasubandhu's *Commentary on the Treasury of Abhidharma* (*Abhidharmakośabhāṣya*) explains the above definitions more fully:

> Something conventionally exists if the cognition of it does not arise upon its division into parts, like a pot. There is no cognition of a pot when it is broken into pieces. And something conventionally exists if the concept of it does not arise when its properties are mentally stripped away, like water. The cognition of water does not arise when properties such as shape and the like have been excluded from it by the mind. It is on the basis of these properties that the conventional designations are formed. Thus the statement "there is a pot,

> there is water" is true through the power of convention. It is not false; it is conventional truth.[33]

Vasubandhu undertakes making a distinction between two truths. Conventional truth, the common-sense reality that is often called "truth of designation" (*prajñāptisatya*), expresses *wholes* as real (persons, jars, etc.); *collections* as real (a nation, armies, a forest, etc.); and a *continuum*, *causation*, or *motion*, etc., as real (a series, chain, stream, and so forth). To be sure, these entities are far removed from any real entities (*dravya*); nevertheless, all of these entities are conventionally real and they satisfy the truth conditions of conventional truth, even though they are not ultimately real. Conventional truth, after all, consists of reducible spatial groupings or temporal continua. Conventional reality is composite, in contrast with the ultimate reality, which is discrete.

Ultimate truth has unique particulars (*svalakṣaṇa*) of real entities as its object, which consist of irreducible spatial units (e.g., atoms) and irreducible temporal units (e.g., moments of consciousnesses) of the five aggregates. In this sense, according to the Vaibhāṣika that follow Vasubandhu, ultimate reality and the "reality of real entities" (*dravyasatya*) are synonymous terms. Bhadanta Vasumitra, one of the Vaibhāṣika school's greatest known philosophers, held the view that ultimate reality consists of complex moments underlying each conventional designation, which are not expressible through discursive linguistic and conceptual expressions, characterizable by most general designations as being causally conditioned. Echoing this point, the *Great Commentary*, offering an alternative position, goes so far as to saying that there is only one theory regarding conditioned events that can be ultimately true, that "all things are empty of self."[34] I propose this is Vasubandhu's final philosophical position, which he advances in his works such as *An Extensive Commentary on the Diamond Sūtra* (*Prajñāpāramitāvajracchedikāsaptārthaṭīkā*). The Vaibhāṣika that followVasubandhu, however, adopt the Sarvāstivāda approach. Although the progressive nature of its philosophy importantly noted that the Sautrāntrika that follow Vasubandhu critique Vaibhāṣika metaphysics.

According to the Vaibhāṣika, ultimate truth consists of irreducible spatial units (e.g., atoms) and irreducible temporal units (e.g., an instant of consciousness) of the five basic categories of objects of knowledge. Conventional truth, on the other hand, consists of reducible spatial groupings and temporal continua. Put simply, the conventional is composite, the ultimate discrete.

CONVENTIONAL TRUTH

We turn now to examine conventional truth in greater detail first. For the Vaibhāṣika, *conventional truth*, *composite-existence*, and *lack of intrinsic nature* are all equivalents. A conventional truth therefore has three interrelated qualities; it is:

1) *Reducible.* Conventional truths are physically and logically reducible. They disintegrate when subjected to physical destruction and disappear from our minds when their parts are separated in logical analysis.
2) *Derivative.* Conventional truths borrow their identity from other things, including their parts and properties. They lack the intrinsic nature required for independent existence.
3) *Constructed.* Conventional truth is a product of mental constructions, which give composite things an appearance of singularity and give reducible things an appearance of irreducibility. Such mental constructions include conventionally real wholes (as opposed to parts), causation, and temporal continuum—which, intuition notwithstanding, are conventions, not ultimate truths.

The three qualities are interrelated, and it is from the first of the qualities—reducibility—that the other two necessarily follow. For the Vaibhāṣika, conventional truth consists of reducible spatial wholes or temporal continua. In the definition of conventional truth cited above in the *Treasury of Abhidharma*, Vasubandhu uses a two-step process. He first determines what it is to conventionally exist, and subsequently he equates conventional existence with conventional truth. They are, Vasubandhu says, mutually coextensive. Whatever is "conventionally existent" is also "conventionally true." To conventionally exist, Vasubandhu says, is to be subject to physical destruction (a pot when it is broken into pieces) and intellectual deconstruction (water stripped of its component qualities). Destruction and deconstruction put the lie to something's ultimate existence: the concept of "pot" cannot survive the dismemberment of its material components; the concept of "water" cannot survive the subtraction of its component qualities.

In his *Commentary on the Treasury of Abhidharma: Following the Defining Characteristics* (*Abhidharmakośaṭīkālakṣaṇānusāriṇī*), the philosopher Pūrṇavardhana (date unknown) argues that Vasubandhu's examples of conventional truths, pot and water, are particularly significant.[35] First, they explain the distinct ways in which conventional truth may be reduced. A pot, easily destroyed, demonstrates physical reduction, whereas water, not easily physically separated from its properties, demonstrates conceptual reduction. Second, this distinction signals a necessary division of conventional truth into two subcategories: (1) *shapes*, conventions whose existence depends upon other conventions, and (2) *composites*, conventions whose existence depends on other entities.The pot represents *shapes*: conventional truths that exist in dependence on other conventional truths, by which they may be readily physically divided. A shape is simply the convention applied to a collection of physical components, an amalgam of more basic shapes. A "pot" is simply the convention applied to the collection of "mud" and "water," themselves simply conventions applied to certain configurations of atomic particles.

Water represents *composites*: conventional truths that exist in dependence on abstract properties such as form and color.[36] Since they are not readily physically divided, composites are subject only to conceptual reduction: the separation of water from its form, taste, and smell may be physically confounding and deceptive but it is analytically simple—logically singular and irreducible.

A further important point, which Dignāga notes in his *Commentary on the Treasury of Abhidharma: The Lamp Illuminating the Central*

Issues (*Abhidharmakośavṛttimarmapradīpa*), is that although shapes demonstrate the process of physical reduction, such as a pot being easily broken into pieces, they too are subject to conceptual reduction. To treat the pot as a whole rather than its assorted subcomponents is a conceptual leap, and, of course, one of those subcomponents is water—Vasubandhu's archetypal composite, which may be effectively reduced only by analysis.[37]

Still, pots and water are not nonexistent. They are conventionally real things, which means they exist through the force of conventional designations and conceptual imputations. Here we see that the second and third qualities—to be *derivative* and *constructed*—flow from the first quality, the quality of *reducibility*. As composite and reducible as "pot" and "water" may be, we nevertheless think of and refer to them in solid, singular terms. We refer to a single "pot," not to each of its manifold atomic components. We refer simply to "water," not to each of its manifold abstract properties. The identities to which these names refer do not intrinsically exist. They are instead derived from their component parts and properties. This is the second quality of conventional truths, to be *derivative*. Their identity derives from myriad other things, rather than the single intrinsic nature (*svabhāva*) required for independent existence.

How is it that we affix qualities to things that are anything but singular conceptual labels? We do so, the Vaibhāṣika argue, with the powerful but imprecise adhesive of convention. This is the third quality of conventional truths, to be *constructed*. Conventional truths are not themselves irreducible or singular, but are the products of mental constructions, conventions that lend an appearance to phenomena. Solid concepts like "pot" and "water," applied to things so vulnerable to physical and analytical deconstruction, are the work of a mind that constructs a unified conceptual framework from disparate parts.

Thus we see the interrelationship between the three qualities: conventional truths are *reducible*, liable to be deconstructed, because they are *constructed* in the first place—constructed by the mind from manifold *derivative* components.

In our discussion of conventional truth so far we have focused on the examples of pots and water. Though these examples may effectively demonstrate the varying ways in which analysis exposes phenomena as merely conventional, soteriologically speaking, understanding the nature of pots and water is not the primary target. As was the case in the previous discussion, and will be the case in each subsequent one, the assumption that Buddhist philosophy is primarily concerned with rejecting is that which makes the greatest contribution to our ongoing dissatisfaction: the assumption of a solid and enduring "self," which is true for all stripes of Buddhism—Theravāda, Mahāyāna, and Vajrayāna.

As for the schools we will examine, the Vaibhāṣika also regards the "self" as a conventional truth—a convenient, but ultimately inaccurate, name applied to an assemblage of the aggregates. The only "self" the Vaibhāṣika refrain from negating is that which refers to, as Vasubandhu tells us, "the aggregates, conditioned by defilement and action, of perpetuating themselves by means of the series of intermediate existence, like a lamp."[38] And such a self is a mere convention. His own commentary expands on this:

> We do not deny a self (*ātman*) that exists through designation, a self that is only a name given to the aggregates (*skandhas*). But far from us is the thought that the aggregates pass into another world! They are momentary and incapable of transmigrating.[39]

Having approached the definition of conventional truth positively—that is, what conventional truth *is*—it is equally instructive to approach it negatively—that is, to determine what conventional truth *is not*. We turn now to ultimate truth.

ULTIMATE TRUTH

We have seen that what is conventionally true exists under the power of linguistic and conceptual conventions. By implication, what is ultimately true is something whose existence does not depend at all on the power of convention. For the Vaibhāṣika, such a thing is "foundationally existent" (*dravyasat*).[40] We have also seen that to apply singular concepts to "compositely existent" things (*avayavidravya*) requires the intervening glue of convention. For foundationally existent things, though, that glue is totally unnecessary, since such things are as simple and irreducible as the concepts that refer to them. In the case of something foundationally existent, there always remains something irreducible to which the concept of the thing applies. Foundationally existent things are ultimately true since they are true irrespective of convention. I will address this point at greater length later.

The Vaibhāṣika treat as conventional those things that possess the three intertwined qualities of reducibility, derivation, and construction. Ultimate truths are therefore their opposite—that is, they are:

1) *Irreducible.* Ultimate truths are immune to physical destruction and resist the logical analysis that would otherwise undermine their identity by separating them from their parts.
2) *Independent.* Ultimate truths do not borrow their nature from elsewhere, including from their parts. They exist simply by virtue of their intrinsic nature (*svabhāva*).
3) *Unconstructed.* Ultimate truths are not the product of mental constructions. Their intrinsic nature exists independently of all things, including the conceptual mind.

For the Vaibhāṣika, ultimate truths fall into two categories: the uncompounded ultimate (*asaṃskṛta*) and the compounded ultimate (*saṃskṛta*).

The uncompounded ultimate

The uncompounded ultimate consists of space (*akāśa*) and *nirvāṇa*, the latter of which is a complete freedom from afflictive states of existence and further subdivided into analytical cessation or freedom (*pratisaṃkhyānirodha*) and nonanalytical cessation or freedom (*apratisaṃkhyānirodha*). Together, these three are referred to as the "uncompounded trio," a grouping that will be further discussed in regard to other schools in subsequent chapters.

The uncompounded ulitmate is called "uncompounded" on the grounds that such phenomena are immune to reduction. They resist physical reduction because they are nonspatial concepts devoid of the slightest physical referent. Space is a mere absence of entity. Analytical and nonanalytical cessations are the two forms of nirvāṇa, which is itself the mere absence of (or freedom from) suffering.[41]

These concepts are not physical and so may not be physically dismantled. The Vaibhāṣika treat them as immune to logical reduction too, because in their ontological estimation, they are not subjected to causal conditioning. Since anything composite or compounded is vulnerable to physical deconstruction (such as pots) or analytical deconstruction (such as water), anything that resists such deconstruction does so because it is primary and uncompounded. Thus, the Vaibhāṣika treats the uncompounded trio (space and the two forms of cessation) as ultimately real, as foundational entities.

The compounded ultimate

For the Vaibhāṣika, the compounded ultimate consists of the five aggregates: the material aggregate (*rūpa*), feeling aggregate (*vedanā*), perception aggregate (*saṁjñā*), dispositional aggregate (*saṃskāra*), and consciousness aggregate (*vijñāna*). Vasubandhu writes:

> Ultimate truth constitutes ultimate existence, e.g., material form, the concept of which survives its destruction and the mental exclusion of other properties. Even when form [aggregate] is divided up into atoms, and even when the mind takes away from it properties such as taste and the like, there is still the concept of the intrinsic nature (*svabhāva*) of the form. Feeling [and the other aggregates] must be seen in the same way. Because this exists ultimately, it is known as ultimate truth.[42]

These aggregates are treated as compounded phenomena because although they are causally produced, they can only be conceived individually. Were it possible to conceive of the aggregates as mere collections and psychophysical continua, they could not be ultimately real. But, the Vaibhāṣika argue, such a conception is beyond the realm of cognitive possibility. The aggregates are objective and indissoluble domains of cognition and so can only be conceived of as such. One's *ideas* of the aggregates are natural, singular, and indestructible, and so the aggregates can be nothing other than ultimately real. Ideas—which are nonphysical by nature—may not be physically dismantled, and ideas this primary to our perception of self and phenomena may not be dismantled by analysis. Pūrṇavardhana, in glossing the previous passage by Vasubandhu, explains:

> Collectively, feeling, dispositions, consciousness, etc. should be treated as conventionally real. Nevertheless, considered in isolation, they should be treated only as foundational existents (*dravyas*). But why so? Feeling and the other aggregates are realities on the ground for which, despite attempts to mentally exclude them, the idea of feeling and the other aggregates arises intrinsically.[43]

In other words, though the aggregates are not exempt from reduction, the *idea* of each aggregate is: the idea of perception, the idea of disposition, the idea that consciousness persists. None of these, the Vaibhāṣika argue, may be excluded logically or physically and so are ultimately real.

CONCLUSION

In this chapter we have seen that the Vaibhāṣika, or Sarvāstivāda, school excludes the second and third turnings of the wheel and includes the Abhidharma Piṭaka, which is the basis for much of its original commentary and philosophical interpretation.

We have seen that for the Vaibhāṣika, a conventional truth is that which exists under the power of conceptual construction. It is constructed from more basic physical, temporal, and conceptual entities, and it can be physically or analytically deconstructed, or reduced, back into the same. A conventional truth, in other words, is that which possesses three qualities: it is reducible, derivative, and constructed. Physical deconstruction is the domain of shapes and analytical deconstruction the domain of composites, and these two forms of deconstruction overlap—that which is vulnerable to physical deconstruction may also be further analytically deconstructed. The most insidious conventional truth, which most urgently requires deconstruction, is, as it will be discussed in the subsequent chapters on other schools of philosophy, the "self."

The Vaibhāṣika concept of the ultimate truth is, we saw, essentially the inverse of its position on conventional truth. Where conventional truths are reducible, derivative, and constructed, ultimate truths are irreducible, independent, and unconstructed. Vaibhāṣika subclassifies ultimate truths according to whether they are subject to causality, as either *uncompounded* (not subject to causality) or *compounded* (subject to causality). In the former category fall the "uncompounded trio" (space, analytical cessation, and nonanalytical cessation), and in the latter the five aggregates, which, although they are causal continua (and so temporally reducible), can only be conceived of independently and irreducibly—they are objective and indissoluble domains of cognition. It is the mind that is tasked with exposing phenomena as reducible, derivative, and constructed, and so far as the aggregates are concerned, it is constitutionally incapable of it. It is in the final regard—the classification of ultimate truths according to their susceptibility to causality, and maintaining the ultimacy of the aggregates by appealing to epistemology, to the limits of cognitive possibility—that the Vaibhāṣika most distinguish themselves from the Sautrāntika with whose position on the two truths they are otherwise in substantial agreement.

The Vaibhāṣika, as represented in Vasubandhu's *Treasury of Abhidharma*, may be described as robustly panrealist. Vasubandhu argues that ultimate reality consists of spatial *svabhāvas*—intrinsically real, irreducible spatial particles (i.e., atoms)—and temporal *svabhāvas*—irreducible temporal units (i.e., instants of consciousness). Vaibhāṣika's approach to ultimate truth can be described as a form of correspondence theory of truth, meaning that ultimate truth consists in a relation to, or correspondence with, *svabhāvas* as the ultimate reality. That is to say, ultimate truth is a relational property involving a characteristic correspondence or congruence relation to ultimately real *svabhāvas*, in which *svabhāvas* play the role of genuine truthmakers and ultimately true statements play the role of genuine truthbearers.[44] As the contemporary scholar Fraser MacBride has remarked, "The notion truthmaker, like that of a clapping hand, cannot ultimately be understood in isolation from the notion of what it makes true, the other hand with which it claps, a truthbearer."[45] Thus the statement "entities with intrinsic nature (*svabhāva*) are ultimately real" is an ultimately true statement if it accurately represents the way that ultimately real entities may then be said to be ultimately true.[46] "It's painful" is an ultimately true statement since it denotes the intrinsic nature of pain is the intrinsic characteristic of any pain; whatever the pain results from, *svabhāva* makes it be the sort of pain it is. Thus, pain's *svabhāva* can be an ultimately real truthmaker.

Conventional reality, on the other hand, lacks *svabhāva* and consists of reducible spatial wholes (such as a person, self, table, etc.) or temporal continua (such as a stream of consciousness, etc.). Put simply, conventional reality is composite, consisting of wholes and continua, whereas ultimate reality is a discrete moment. It is clear the Vaibhāṣika do not assert a robust realist form of correspondence theory insofar as the treatment of conventional truth goes. Since conventionally true statements denote collections, wholes, and continua such as a person, self, car, and table, etc.—all of which are conventionally real, but only conceptually constructed fictions—they are ultimately unreal and possess only *parabhāvas*—meaning extrinsic natures or contingent characteristics, which are borrowed property from elsewhere (as opposed to being an intrinsic nature of conventionally real entities).

Representing the Vaibhāṣika school, Vasubandhu argues that linguistic truth expresses and applies strictly to conventional reality. He maintains that conventional truth, composite existence (*avayavidravya*), and the lack of intrinsic nature (*niḥsvabhāva*) are more or less equivalents. The Vaibhāṣika maintain that linguistic truth applies to types of things that are *reducible*, *derived*, and *constructed*. Concepts that disintegrate when subjected to physical destruction and disappear from our minds when their parts are separated in logical analysis are thus *reducible* physically and logically. Concepts that borrow their identity from other things, including their parts and properties that lack the intrinsic nature required for independent existence, are *derived* properties. Concepts that are products of mental constructions are aggregations of appearance of inherence—such as wholes, causation, and temporal continuums—and are thus *constructed*. As such, these conventionally real entities cannot play the role of genuine truthmakers. In this sense, conventional truth, though useful pragmatically, only represents conceptual fictions, entities whose nature is purely extrinsic, and therefore cannot play the role of genuine truthbearer in the sense of a robust realist correspondence theory of truth.[47] Yet there is a sense that the Vaibhāṣika employ a weaker notion of correspondence theory for conventional truth. After all there is no denying that conventional truth genuinely leads to success in pragmatic purposes, so in this sense, conventional truth for the Ābhidharmika appears to follow the pragmatic theory of truth.

As we turn to the subschools of the Sautrāntika, we can immediately notice their philosophical positions are formed in relation to the Vaibhāṣika. It is to the Sautrāntika we now turn.

CHAPTER TWO

Sautrāntika: Vasubandhu and Dharmakīrti

The Sautrāntika school is home to some of the most significant Indian logicians and epistemologists. It was originally founded by Dignāga (480–540), who wrote the *Compendium of Epistemology* (*Pramāṇasamuccaya*). In the seventh century Dharmakīrti (600–660), one of the best-known Buddhist phenomenologists, championed Sautrāntika metaphysics, logic, and epistemology through some of his influential works. Dharmakīrti developed much of the philosophical machinery concerning the two truths that we will consider, especially through his works such as *Verses on Epistemology* (*Pramāṇavārttikakārikā*), *Ascertaining Epistemology* (*Pramāṇaviniścaya*), *Dose of Logical Reasoning* (*Nyāyabindu*), *Doses of Reasoning* (*Hetubindu*), *The Logic of Debate (Vādanyāya)*, *Establishing the Other Continuum* (*Saṃtānāntarasiddhi*), and *Commentary on Analysis of Relations (Sambandhaparīkṣāvṛtti*). After Dharmakīrti, philosophical works of his disciple Devendrabuddhi (630–690),[48] followed by his student Śākyabuddhi (660–720),[49] and others such as Vinitadeva (630–700),[50] Dharmottara (750–810),[51] and Mokṣakaragupta (ca. 1100–1200), just to name few, further refined the Sautrāntika school and defended it from rival Brahmanical schools, most notably the Nyāya.

The Sautrāntika system has two subschools: the scripturalists and the logicians, who, in their positions on the two truths, differ markedly. The philosophical approach of the scripturalists is largely shaped by Vasubandhu's *Treasury of Abhidharma* (*Abhidharmakośa*) and *Commentary on the Treasury of Abhidharma* (*Abhidharmakośabhāṣyam*), as well as other commentaries on Vasubandhu's work. The philosophical approach of the logicians is largely shaped by Dignāga and Dharmakīrti's treatises on epistemology, among other works.

SCRIPTURALISTS

The position the Sautrāntika-scripturalists take on the theory of the two truths is largely compatible with the position held by the Vaibhāṣika, as discussed in the previous chapter. There are however important issues over which the two schools part company.

First, the Sautrāntika and the Vaibhāṣika disagree on where to place the division between foundational entities (*dravyasat*) and conceptual entities (*prajñaptisat*), namely the status of the "uncompounded trio," the five aggregates, and shape. The Vaibhāṣika regard each as foundational and ultimate; the Sautrāntika regard each as conceptual and conventional.

1. The uncompounded trio

As we saw earlier, the Vaibhāṣika treat the uncompounded trio—space and the two forms of cessation—as ultimately real on the ground that they are foundational entities.[52] They are, the Vaibhāṣika say, irreducible, independent, and unconstructed. They are immune to physical and analytical deconstruction because, being nonphysical and not subject to causation, they are not physically or conceptually constructed from their derivatives. The Sautrāntika, on the other hand, treat the trio as only conventionally real because they are conceptual entities, mere negative phenomena.[53] They are conceptually constructed from—or in other words, derived and dependent upon—the absence of other things. Space, they argue, is conceptually constructed from the absence of any obstructive property or point of contact. Analytical cessation is conceptually constructed from the absence of the afflictions and their dispositions—a cessation brought about by the wisdom of the analytical mind. Finally, nonanalytical cessation is conceptually constructed from the absence of the afflictions, not because of their elimination by the analytical mind, but simply because they lack the conditions necessary for them to arise.

2. The five aggregates

The Vaibhāṣika treats the five aggregates as ultimately real because they are foundational entities. The Vaibhāṣika's argument for this claim is that each individual aggregate is foundationally existent, as each atom of the aggregate is fundamental—both logically and physically irreducible. A peculiar feature of the Vaibhāṣika approach is that the same atoms regarded as immune to mereological reductionism into parts and wholes are acknowledged as being composite. As Vasubandhu puts it: "each atomic particle is a composite in itself."[54] Each atom is, the Vaibhāṣika argue, both ultimately real *and* constituted by the bare octad: the four elements of cohesion (earth), moisture (water), maturation (fire), motion (air), and their four derivatives (*bhautika*), which are the domains (*āyatana*) of visual form or shape, smell, taste, and tactile sensation.[55] For an atom to be both composite and irreducible is not seen to be contradictory. On the contrary, form and form aggregate are seen as mutually coextensive. Whatever is form is necessarily a form aggregate and necessarily a composite. So too feeling and feeling aggregate, perception and perception aggregate, disposition and disposition aggregate, consciousness and consciousness aggregate. This allows Vaibhāṣika to argue that atoms, the fundaments of the five aggregates, are themselves aggregates, but the aggregates of atoms do *withstand* conceptual analysis and hence are logically irreducible.

The Sautrāntika reject this possibility. Instead, they argue that anything composite *must* be subject to decomposition, and anything so reducible can be no more than conventionally real—a figment of conceptual thought that constructs a whole from the parts. For something to be both indivisible and composite is, they argue, a logical impossibility. The two properties mutually contradict: an indivisible atom cannot be an aggregate, and an aggregate cannot be an indivisible atom.[56] Therefore, the Sautrāntika that follow Vasubandhu argue that the Vaibhāṣika's attempted marriage of aggregates and ultimate is unsound and based on a perversion of the term "aggregate."

3. *Shape*

The Vaibhāṣika argue that a shape is ultimately real on the ground that it is an independent, foundational entity whose cognition is not dependent on environmental causes, sensory contact, or component phenomena like color. For example, evidence of shape's independence is the fact that the properties of a shape—its length, for instance—might be apprehended without the visual cognition required to apprehend its colors. According to the Sarvāstivādin, it is possible to apprehend shape based on the tactile sense, because shape and tactility copresent. In other words, a direct tactile knowledge yields inferential knowledge of the shape in the same way one can infer a fire's heat from seeing it's color, and one can infer a flower's color from its fragrance.[57] This argument is bound up with the Sarvāstivāda theory of the relation of shape and color, according to which a phenomenon can have (1) color but no shape, e.g., white, blue, black; (2) shape but no color, e.g., long, short, tall, small; (3) both shape and color, e.g., an oblong blue box, a circular black table; or (5) neither shape nor color, e.g., a sweet taste.

The Sautrāntika object to this claim. Shape, they argue, is plainly not independent of environmental causes. The various shapes of the fire's flames are causal functions (*arthakriya*) of, say, the configuration of fuel, the fire's present temperature, available oxygen, and prevailing wind. Nor can shape be independent of its subcomponents and colors, since shape is simply a conventional designation given to the various atomic structures or formations that constitute both it and the color it presents to our visual consciousness. Just as cognition of the height or the length of a shape is comprised of multiple and diverse atomic compositions, the Sautrāntika argue, so too, is cognition of color.[58] And, were it the case that shape was independent of sense contact, then shape would be experienced constantly and extrasensorily. This, they argue, is plainly not the case; we do apprehend shape, just not independent of its causes, color, and apprehending sense.

LOGICIANS

The second Sautrāntika subschool, home to some of the most significant Indian logicians and epistemologists, diverges further from the Vaibhāṣika position of the two truths. A standard Sautrāntika-logician statement regarding the division is found in Dharmakīrti's *Verses on Epistemology*:

> That which is ultimately causally efficacious is an ultimate existent; that which is not is a conventionally existent. These are the definitions of the unique particular and the universal respectively.[59]

Let us now turn to the two truths, beginning once again with the ultimate truth.

ULTIMATE TRUTH

Ultimate truths are, Dharmakīrti says in his above definition, "ultimately existent," which is to say, "ultimately causally efficacious" or a "unique particular" (*svalakṣaṇa*). Dharmakīrti equates these three phrases; to be ultimately real is to ultimately *exist*, which is to be ultimately *causally efficacious*, which is to be a unique particular.[60]

The very nature of existence dictates that this is the case, Dharmakīrti argues. "All things that exist or are produced are," says Dharmakīrti in his *Logic of Debate* (*Vādanyāya*), "impermanent,"[61] meaning they are part of a thoroughly interconnected and unsubstantial causal web whose very nature is change. Thus, to "ultimately exist" in an ontology whose very nature is change means either to be a causal actor—to be "causally efficacious"—or not to exist at all. To exist is to be causally produced and to, in turn, causally produce—to be an active, momentary participant, in an utterly causal system. It is, Dharmakīrti says, only momentary, individual objects that so participate. The real things populating a causal reality are particular things—discrete in space and time, and established by their unique causal characteristics, or their signature makeup and capacities. Such things are called "unique particulars." In short, to be ultimately true is to exist; to exist in a momentary, causal reality is to be a momentary, causal actor; and actions of such causal actors are the preserve of individual objects, or unique particulars.

Dharmakīrti thus substitutes a four-criteria schema for the Vaibhāṣika's three criteria for ultimate truth—which are to be irreducible, independent, and unconstructed. Unique particulars, he says, are (1) causally efficacious, (2) unique and distinctly defined individuals, (3) not denotable by language, and (4) cognizable without reliance on other factors such as language and thought. We will now address each of these criteria in turn.

1. Causally efficacious[62]

We have seen that to exist in a causal reality is to participate in it, to be causally produced, and to causally produce in turn. It is unique particulars, Dharmakīrti argues, that so participate. They are momentary points in material or cognitive activity, the results of the conditions that precede them and the causes of the effects that succeed them. We have seen also that to exist in a momentary reality is to be momentary. Unique particulars are, Dharmakīrti argues, causal processes devoid of substrata, arising and perishing simultaneously in a single moment.[63] Inherently self-destructive,[64] unique particulars perish instantly, inevitably, and without the intervention of any extrinsic factors.[65] Utterly momentary, they do not move or endure, though they may appear to do so. That appearance is an illusion, contributed by a conceptual mind synthesizing similar, successive instants. The conceptual mind, as we shall see, has no contribution to make in the identification and perception of unique particulars.

In his *Commentary on the Doses of Reasoning* (*Nyāyabinduṭīkā*), Dharmottara discusses two aspects of causal efficacy that bear individual mention: *practical efficiency* and *cognitive efficiency*. Practical efficiency is the ability to affect beings, to serve the purposes of life. After all, it is the unique particulars of a fire that warm us, not the abstract property of "fire-ness." Cognitive efficiency refers to the unique particular's ability to affect the cognitive image that corresponds to it by its relative proximity to the perceiver. Our cognitive image of a close unique particular is large and vivid, the image of its remote counterpart is commensurately small and indistinct.[66] This is not the case with universals.

2. *Distinct and uniquely defined individuals*

Unique particulars are, by nature, distinct and uniquely defined, requiring no conceptual involvement in their definition. As Dharmakīrti says:

> Because things intrinsically exist individually and as distinct entities, there is differentiation between similar and dissimilar things."[67]

Unique particulars are distinct and differentiable, Dharmakīrti explains in his *Commentary on the Verses of Epistemology*, on account of three properties.[68]

First, if they are material, unique particulars are *spatially determinate*. In other words, if they occupy space at all, they occupy a precise and dedicated location, which they share with nothing else. We can identify a unique particular in part because it can be spatially located and isolated—it is near or far, in a particular direction, or at a particular height or depth. By contrast, univerals cannot be spatially located and isolated; the universal "fire-ness," for example, is spatially indeterminate, a property not just of a specific fire but of all conceivable fires.

Second, whether material or cognitive, unique particulars are *temporarily determinate*. They are momentary instants that spontaneously go out of existence the moment they come into it. They are the momentary components of an utterly causal system. By contrast, universals, being abstract and constructed, stand outside of causality; they are enduring concepts fashioned from the conceptual synthesis of momentary individuals. Dharmakīrti thus describes universals as atemporal and static.[69]

Third, unique particulars are *ontologically determinate*. Unique particulars are causally conditioned—produced by the interplay of the conditions that have conspired to produce them—and also produce their own effects. They are thus ontologically determined by their unique causal makeup and capacities. They are established by, and can be distinguished from their fellow unique particulars by, their causal characteristics.

In short, the "determinate intrinsic natures of the unique particulars," Dharmakīrti argues, "are not accidental or fortuitous since . . . [they are] spatially, temporally, and ontologically determinate."[70] Ultimate real things are determinate in time and space, and individuated precisely and constantly by their causal conditions.

3. Not denotable by language

Unique particulars, as we have just observed, are established and distinguished by their own spatio-temporal location and causal characteristics. As a result, they need no further establishment or distinction by language and concepts. As Dharmakīrti puts it, language does not denote the real particulars, since "all particulars exist by virtue of their own identities."[71] Language and concepts, so essential to the construction of universals, are irrelevant to the identities of unique particulars. Language and thought can *refer* to unique particulars (after all, we have been doing just that in this chapter), but they do so only approximately. Unique particulars, beyond the full grasp of any conceptual mind, are likewise beyond the grasp of language, which gives names to concepts.

4. Cognizable without reliance on other factors

If unique particulars are not apprehended by language and concepts, how is it that they are apprehended? Unique particulars, Dharmakīrti says in *Verses on Epistemology*, are apprehended by perception. "The objects of [perception] are the unique particulars," he says, "the objects whose nearness or remoteness correspondingly alters our cognitive image. That alone is ultimately real because it is causally efficacious, the defining characteristic of things."[72] We may initially be inclined to believe this refers to our ordinary perception, which, after all, is not consciously linguistic or conceptual. This, according to Dignāga's *Investigation of the Percept* (*Ālambanaparīkṣā*), would be a mistake. Though we typically assume that our ordinary perception is a satisfactory epistemic yardstick, capable of perceiving unique particulars and the reality of things as they are, we assume wrongly. Though not consciously conceptual, it is conceptual nonetheless. Dignāga, describes our regular perceptual cognition as but a quasi-perception, epistemically distorted by the conception that inevitably accompanies it. Ordinary perception, he says, cannot perceive without also compulsively reifing the unique particulars it perceives.[73]

If, as Dharmakīrti says, unique particulars are "objects of perception," then they must be objects of a type of perception different and superior to ordinary perception. Such a perception is one that is free from cognitive defects and independent of language and thought. It is a perception that perceives unique particulars as they are without rushing to reify or to interpret, conceptualize, or name them. It is such a perception that unmistakenly perceives things, as it avoids the distortive effect of applying concepts to nonconceptual objects. Such a perception is correct and warrants epistemic authority about its objects; likewise, to be apprehended by such a perception qualifies that object as a unique particular.

So, what then are the objects that meet these four criteria and thus qualify as unique particulars? In the Sautrāntika ontology, the range of unique particulars falls under the following three categories:

1) *Momentary instants of matter* (*rūpa*). These can be subdivided into (a) matter that correlates to the mental continuum consisting of the five senses (of the eyes, ears, nose, tongue, and body) and (b) matter unrelated to the mental continuum

consisting of the five sensory objects (form, sound, taste, smell, tactility).

2) *Momentary instants of consciousness* (*vijñāna*). This can be subdivided into (a) sensory consciousness (eye-consciousness, ear-consciousness, nose-consciousness, tongue-consciousness, and bodily consciousness) whose unique dominant condition (*adhipatirūpa*)[74] is its corresponding sense faculty, and (b) mental consciousness whose dominant condition is the mental sense faculty. This is true in the case of both the primary minds (*citta*) that apprehend the abstract characteristics of objects and the secondary minds (*caitta*)[75] that apprehend the individual characteristics of objects.
3) *Momentary instants of nonassociated composite phenomena.* These phenomena are neither material nor mental. This grouping includes persons dependently designated upon their aggregates and the phenomena such as arising, cessation, causality, and so on, which are designations made on the basis of fabricated temporal divisions.

Finally, it is important to note that there is a soteriological and an ontological dimension to unique particulars' ultimate status. According to Dharmakīrti's *Logic of Debate*, a necessary condition of the attainment of nirvāṇa—the attainment of ultimate freedom from the afflictions of life through apprehending the final nature of things—is an immediate perception of the unique particulars.[76] We turn now to conventional truth.

CONVENTIONAL TRUTH

According to the Sautrāntika-logicians, as we have seen, to be ultimately true is to ultimately exist, which is to be causally efficacious, and in turn be a unique particular.[77] Accordingly, they define conventional truth in inverse terms: to be conventionally true is to conventionally exist, which is to be causally inefficacious, and in turn be a *universal*.[78] By "universal," the Sautrāntika-logicians mean a conceptual entity apprehended not by virtue of its own being, but a general property that is conceptually constructed and appears to be common to objects of a certain class.

We also saw that qualifying as an ultimate truth, as a unique particular, required meeting four criteria: to be causally efficacious,[79] distinct and uniquely defined, denotable by language, and cognizable without reliance on other factors. Conventional truths, as *universals*, are therefore their opposite—that is, they are (1) causally inefficacious, (2) indistinct, (3) denotable by language, and (4) apprehendable by language and thought. Let us briefly address each in turn.

1. *Causally inefficacious*

Unique particulars are *causally* efficacious: they are both causally produced and causally productive. Universals, on the other hand, are mental fabrications that exist outside of the network of causation composed of momentary unique particulars. Universals are abstract mental phenomena—both immune to change and unable to effect it. And, just as unique particulars are both practically and cognitively efficient, universals are practically and cognitively inefficient: Dharmottara's *Commentary on Doses of Reasoning* (*Nyāyabinduṭīkā*) notes that abstract properties do not contribute to the welfare of beings, nor do they present anything but a uniform cognitive image that bears no relation to its proximity to the perceiver.[80]

2. *Indistinct*

Whereas unique particulars are distinct in space, time, and their causal characteristics, universals, on the other hand, are entirely conceptual and therefore *not* situated in space, time, or a causal network. Not only are they themselves indistinct, but they are *obscuring*: universals obscure the individualities of the unique particulars from being directly apprehended. This is to say, because universals are conceptually constructed, according to Dharmakīrti's *Verses on Epistemology*[81] and its autocommentary,[82] they are the result of crudely synthesizing the distinct individualities of unique particulars. The critical point is the conceptual mind is ignorant of its constructive role and treats its creation as uncreated and unchanging—as the perception of a natural property rather than the superposition of conceptual thought. As a result, the conceptual mind prevents us from seeing directly the individual characteristics of particulars to which the concept has been applied.

Take a conceptual mind apprehending a tree, for instance. Grasping at the "tree" as universal prevents us from seeing the unique particulars of the tree—its distinctive characteristics or individuality. The property "treeness," or "not non-tree," appears to be held in common by all individual trees regardless of how distinct each may be. The "treeness" of a sapling palm, for instance, appears to the conceptual mind as indistinguishable to the "treeness" of a centuries-old oak. In this way, the universal distracts the cognition from apprehending the ultimate reality—the unique particulars of each individual tree. We cannot, the Sautrāntikas might say, see the trees for the "treeness."

3. Denotable by language

While unique particulars, distinguished by their own characteristics, do not require the involvement of language and can only be denoted approximately by it, universals, on the other hand, are very much denotable by language—they are, in fact, linguistic conventions. In contrast to the Naiyāyika-Vaiśeṣika position that language describes *real* universals, the Sautrāntika-logicians propose a nominalist theory of the universal, *apoha theory*, in which language describes universals that have no extra-mental reality, and does so negatively, by eliminating the other (*anyāpoha*). Unique particulars can only be denoted approximately by language; universals simply are that approximate denotion.

According to this theory, the function of language, specifically the act of naming, is to eliminate the object it names from the classes of objects to which it does not belong. "One might say," as Bimal Krishna Matilal puts it, "that the function of a name is to locate the object outside of the class of those to which it cannot be applied."[83] To use a commonplace example, the phrase "white cow" linguistically approximates the unique particulars it refers to *negatively* by sequentially excluding the universals "non-cow" and "non-white cow." In this way, language can, via the negative application of universals, approximate its referent unique particulars, though it remains at best a blunt approximation. It is a convention by which the component unique particulars—themselves beyond the domain of language—are identified by the conceptual, linguistic amalgam: "white cow."

4. *Apprehendable by language and thought*

While unique particulars are beyond the grasp of thought and language, it is only by thought and language that universals are grasped.[84] They are in fact the very product of thought and language, a result of their intrusion into the process of perception. Universals are conceptual amalgams, superimposed by thought and language upon unique particulars, which are quite independent from them. Universals render in our minds what is by nature ineffably complex as simple, what is discrete as unified and singular, what is a part as a whole.

They are amalgams that answer to intuition rather than critical analysis. Because they are constructed conceptually and linguistically, they ought also to be deconstructed in kind. Our failure to subjecting them to critical analysis, the Sautrāntika argues, disguises their constructed nature and confines our belief in them as they are to the realm of intuition.

CONCLUSION

In this chapter, we have seen that the Sautrāntika school contains two subschools, one asserting the primacy of scripture, the other of reason; one whose textual focus is Vasubandhu's *Treasury of Abhidharma*, the other Dignāga's and Dharmakīrti's treatises on epistemology. The first of these subschools, the scripturalists, largely adopts the Vaibhāṣika theory of the two truths, accepting its criteria for dividing truths (whether or not they are reducible, derivative, and constructed) but disputing them on which side of the division the uncompounded trio, the aggregates, and shape fall. For the Vaibhāṣika these are ultimate truths, but for the Sautrāntika-scripturalists they are mere conventions.

The second subschool, the logicians, propose a related, but distinct, division between the two truths. For the Sautrāntika-logicians, the division between ultimate and conventional truth is the division between unique particulars and universals, and they propose a fourfold criteria by which the two are divided. Ultimate truths are causally efficacious, unique and distinctly defined, not denotable by language, and apprehended without reliance on language and thought; conventional truths are their inverse. To be causally efficacious, we saw, is to be a momentary participant in an utterly causal reality, to be both produced and productive. To be unique and distinctly defined is to be determinate in space, time, and causal characteristics. To be unique and distinctly defined also obviates the intervention of language, and instead, ultimate truths are perceived by a direct and correct perception, unaccompanied by conceptualization. In short, ultimate truths are unique particulars: causally constructed, distinct, momentary, productive, and the objective domain of direct perception. Conventional truths, by contrast, are universal: conceptually constructed amalgams, static, causally unproductive, and the domain of inference.

CHAPTER THREE

Yogācāra: Vasubandhu

The Madhyamaka and Yogācāra schools belong to the Mahāyāna tradition, a historical offshoot of the Mahāsaṅghika lineage. The Mahāyāna tradition distinguishes itself on a variety of doctrinal issues. In contrast with the *arhatship* of Śrāvakayāna, Mahāyāna followers aspired to the soteriological trajectory of the *bodhisattva*, in which the spiritual journey culminates in the achievement of ultimate buddhahood for the benefit of all sentient beings; this aim is so central to Mahāyāna that it is sometimes called the Bodhisattvayāna tradition. In contrast with the nonself ontology of the Śrāvakayāna, the Mahāyāna ontology centers on emptiness (*śūnyatā*) as the ultimate mode of being of all phenomena. In contrast with the Śrāvakayāna epistemology directed to the knowledge of the nonself of the five aggregates, the Mahāyāna epistemology demands knowledge of the emptiness of *all* phenomena. In addition, in contrast with the stringent ethical codes of the Śrāvakayāna Vinaya, the Mahāyāna emphasis on the concept of "skillful means" (*upāyakauśalya*) allowed Mahāyānists the ethical flexibility to contravene moral codes where necessary to promote the welfare of beings.

The Mahāyāna claims that its sūtras, written in Hybrid Sanskrit, are as much authentic teachings given by the historical Buddha (the word of the Buddha, or *Buddhavacana*) as the Pāḷi suttas; they are simply teachings given to his bodhisattva disciples rather than śrāvaka disciples. It claims that those sūtras record the second and third "turnings of the Dharma wheel"—turnings that, we have seen, are not recognized as an authentic record of the words of the Buddha by the Śrāvakayāna schools. For the Mahāyāna, however, they are not just part of that record, but an especially important part, containing teachings of a scope and profundity beyond that found in the Pāḷi Canon or the Abhidharma literature. The sūtras were held to be either directly spoken or orally transmitted by the historical Buddha through the meditative visions and lucid dreams of adepts of remarkable capacity, or as records concealed by the Buddha to be recovered later by those capable of comprehending and interpreting their profundity.

There are two main surviving schools that belong to the Mahāyāna tradition, namely, Madhyamaka and Yogācāra. Though these two schools share the soteriological goal of buddhahood, they have marked philosophical differences. Madhyamaka (which began to flourish around the first century BCE) precedes Yogācāra (from the third and fourth century CE) chronologically,[85] but in the Madhyamaka philosophical doxography in which the schools are ranked in ascending order of philosophical sophistication, the sequence is reversed: Madhyamaka, the earlier school, is considered preeminent. At least so far as the theory of two truths is concerned, this sequence is convenient. I will accordingly consider the Yogācāra theory of the two truths first.

Inspired by the various sūtras of an apparently idealistic or phenomenological character, many Indian philosophers in the third or fourth century CE developed and systematized a coherent Idealist school. In the beginning of his *Twenty Verses* (*Viṃśatikā*), Vasubandhu treats consciousness (*citta*), mind (*manas*), cognition (*vijñāna*), and impressions (*vijñāpti*) as synonymous and uses these terms as the basis for three of the four names of the Idealist school: Mind Only (Cittamātra), Consciousness Only (Vijñānamātra), and Impressions Only (Vijñāptimātra). The names give the Idealist doctrine in its most condensed form—all existing things are only mind, consciousness, or impressions. The fourth name is Yogācāra, derived from its proponents' dedication to the practice (*ācāra*) of meditation or mental discipline (*yoga*).

The Yogācāra system was founded by Maitreya, often known as "Maitreyanātha," (ca. 270–350 CE) and Asaṅga (ca. 315–390), and later propagated by Vasubandhu (ca. 320–380), Dignāga (ca. 480–540), Sthiramati (475–555), Dharmapāla (530–561),[86] Xuanzang (602–664), Dharmakīrti (ca. 600–660), Śāntarakṣita (ca. 725–788), and Kamalaśīla (ca. 740–795). Vasubandhu, Dignāga, and Dharmakīrti are familiar to us for their involvement in the schools previously considered. Śāntarakṣita and Kamalaśīla, it should be noted, also have mixed affiliations; they are identified as Yogācāra Mādhyamikas.

Like other Buddhist schools, the theory of the two truths is central to Yogācāra doctrine. Maitreya asserts in his *Verses on the Distinction Between Phenomena and Reality* (*Dharmadharmatāvibhaṅgakārikā*): "All this is understood to be condensed in two categories, phenomena (*dharma*) and reality (*dharmatā*), because they encompass all."[87] By *dharma*, Maitreya means conventional truth, and by *dharmatā*, he means ultimate truth. In other words, the categories of the two truths are exhaustive and include all possible objects of knowledge.

As it is for the previous schools, in the Yogācāra school, the ontology of the two truths is thoroughly interlinked with its epistemology. Defined epistemologically, the ultimate and conventional truths present the objects of correct transcendent cognition and correct mundane cognition, respectively. As Vasubandhu's *The Principles of Exegesis* (*Vyākhyāyukti*) points out:

> The Buddha taught the two truths: conventional truth, which is the object of correct mundane cognitions, and ultimate truth, which is the object of world-transcending cognition.[88]

Here, Vasubandhu means that mundane cognition apprehends uncritically and superficially, unthinkingly *reifying* every object with which it comes in contact. It is perception from behind a veil of cognitive confusion, which superimposes substance on sense data that offer it no basis for such presupposition. Therefore, the object of a mundane cognition can be no more than a conventional truth. A transcendent cognition, however, apprehends critically and objectively, perceiving the true characteristics of its object without any reification. Therefore the object of a transcendent cognition is always ultimate truth.

Defined soteriologically, as we have done for the previous schools, the ultimate and conventional truths extinguish and fuel the causes of suffering, respectively. More specifically, Yogācāra discriminates between the two truths on the basis of their relationship with the mental afflictions that produce suffering and prevent buddhahood. Conventional truths are objects of knowledge whose cognition may give rise to the afflictive mental states of confusion, desire, and aversion. Ultimate truths, by contrast, are objects of knowledge whose cognition may not give rise to these afflictive states. Instead, since it is the final or the ultimate object of knowledge, cognition of ultimate truth is the method by which those afflictions are extinguished. Let us now turn to the two truths separately and in greater detail.

CONVENTIONAL TRUTH

For the Yogācāra school, the term "conventional truth" refers to objects of knowledge that are false, unreal, and deceptive, and whose mode of existence and mode of appearance conflict. To the extent they are truths, they are truths as a function of three forms of convention: (1) fabrication (*asatkalpita*), (2) consciousness (*vijñāna*), and (3) a linguistic signifier (*śabda*). Respectively, a conventional truth is (1) *fabricated* by the conceptual mind, (2) apprehended in error by the dualistic *consciousness*, or (3) invested with meaning by its *signifier*. The Yogācāra school treats the products of the three conventions as separate categories of conventional truths: the truths of fabrication, consciousness, and language. Truths of fabrication and language are labeled "imaginary phenomena" (*parikalpita*), while truths of consciousness are labeled "dependent phenomena" (*paratantra*). Before we explore these categories in depth, however, we must first be clear about one central point in Yogācāra philosophy: its idealistic thesis.

The central thesis in Yogācāra philosophy is the assertion that conventional reality is but the ideas, images, and creations of the mind, outside of which no corresponding objects exist. The universe is a mental universe. All physical objects are fictions, unreal even conventionally, and similar to a dream or mirage in which all we seem to outwardly perceive has actually been inwardly produced.

The central claim that only mind is conventionally real is the focus of the Yogācāra treatises,[89] including Vasubandhu's fundamental treatise, the *Twenty Verses*. In it, he states:

> All this is indeed only consciousness because of the appearance in it of nonexisting objects, just like the vision of the nonexistent net of hairs, moons, etc., by someone afflicted with an optical illusion.[90]

In the way we imbue our mental representations with objective reality, Vasubandhu argues, we are just like a person seeing double who treats the two moons he sees as an astronomic fact, or the person who perceives the hair-like "floaters" in his eyes' vitreous humor as a meteorological occurrence. In fact, Vasubandhu argues, that which we perceive *does not* exist apart from the creative workings of the mind. The reality of the phenomenal world is reducible to our mental representations, which we create independent of any corresponding objective counterpart. What we take as basic ontological and epistemological facts are *ideas*, and ideas need not and do not have any ultimately real referent. Vasubandhu traces this claim back to *The Sūtra of Ten Grounds* (*Daśabhūmikasūtra*), which says that the three worlds systems—the desire realm, form realm, and formless realm—are only mind (*citta*).[91]

As radical as the Yogācāra position is, in many ways it is a natural evolution from the epistemological positions of the Vaibhāṣika and Sautrāntika schools. The Vaibhāṣika take a *direct realist* position, in which perception directly knows its external object. The Sautrāntika, on the other hand, advance a *representationalist* position, in which one knows not the external object but the mental representation of it. The Sautrāntika thus reject the Vaibhāṣika's claim that perception offers direct access to the external object, but agree that there *are* external objects, simply ones accessed via their representations. The Yogācāra agree with the Sautrāntika's claim that mental representations are primary—the *intentional object*—but reject the Sautrāntika's claim that this means there must be physical objects, since representations must be externally caused by contact between the senses and the objects represented. The Yogācāra school rejects the link between external causes and mental representation, arguing that the "subliminal impressions" (*vāsanās*) from the foundational consciousness (*ālayavijñāna*) alone cause mental representations. The physical world and the physical senses that apprehend it are redundant, rejected even conventionally. Yogācāra denies the conventional reality of all physical objects and argues that the only conventional realities are mental representations, creations, and cognitions.

The Yogācāra school's claim that external objects are entirely unreal and that only mental objects may be conventionally real finds expression in their theory of the three natures (*trisvabhāva*). In his *Identifying the Three Natures* (*Trisvabhāvanirdeśa*), Vasubandhu explains the Yogācāra ontology and phenomenology as consisting of the unity of three natures (*svabhāva*): (1) dependent nature (*paratantra*), (2) imaginary nature (*parikalpita*), and (3) perfect nature (*pariniṣpanna*).[92] The first two account for conventional truth and the latter ultimate truth. We shall consider the three in turn.

Dependent nature

Asaṅga, in his *Compendium of the Mahāyāna* (*Mahāyānasaṃgraha*), defines *dependent nature* as "cognition that, having its roots in the storehouse consciousness, constitutes erroneous conceptions."[93] Vasubandhu defines it as that which exists due to being causally conditioned (*pratyayādhīnavṛttitvāt*) and as the basis of both "what appears" (*yat khyāti*) incorrectly as conventionally real and the "unreal conceptual fabrication" (*asatkalpa*) from which the appearance of reified subjects and objects arises.[94]

The dependent nature is causally conditioned because it exists entirely due to the force of the subliminal impressions (*vāsanās*). By "subliminal impressions," the Yogācāra proponents mean latent representations contained in the storehouse consciousness (*ālayavijñāna*),[95] which are reactivated in our consciousness under certain conditions and serve as the intentional objects of cognitions. So conditioned, they arise as "what appears."

That the phrase "what appears" describes dependent nature is significant in two ways. First, it emphasizes that, epistemically or cognitively, all we have access to is appearance. Our cognitive access is limited to intentional objects, and these intentional objects are no more than mental representations—representations that are just manifest forms of subliminal impressions. Although the representations are purely mental creations, the Yogācāra philosophers argue, we engage with them dualistically, as though they exist as external realities. Second, the phrase "what appears" emphasizes that every aspect of the entire world of appearance, whose phenomenological presentation varies so wildly, is but the figment of the central storehouse consciousness. Apart from those representations—consciousnesses masquerading as external objects—there is nothing conventionally real. Our conventional reality is simply our projections being perceived by, and perceived as apart from, the very mind that projected them.

Imaginary nature

If dependent nature is "what appears" (*yat khyāti*), imaginary nature is "as it appears" (*sau yathā khyāti*). If dependent nature is appearance itself, imaginary nature (*parikalpita*) is the *mode* in which it appears. That mode is "imaginary" because appearance is only an unreal conceptual fabrication (*asatkalpa*).[96]

It is imaginary, the Yogācāra argue, for two reasons. First, it is from these representations that we fabricate a sense of *ourself* as a subject apart from others—in other words, as an ultimately real self. In reality, there is no subject-object duality corresponding to the imaginary nature. There is simply a series of momentary representations—the dependent nature—that calcify into the sense of a self who knows. Second, it is from these representations that we fabricate a sense of objects as existing externally and objectively when there is no such reality.

The objective mode, which encompasses known beings and objects, is but the representational output of the storehouse impressions presented as perceptual input and falsely believed to be existing dually and externally.

On both counts, it is clear for the Yogācāra that the imaginary nature is an unreal mental fabrication since there is no reality that corresponds to the separation of an objectively real subject from objectively real objects that are imagined. It is also clear that the representations—dependent nature—provide the basis for the imaginary nature since it is these mental representations that are the basis for our ontological self-deception.

Perfect nature

Given that dependent nature is actually free from duality, the imaginary nature that appears as dualistic is a mere superimposition on it. Accordingly, nonduality, the perfect nature (*pariniṣpanna*), is the dependent nature's ultimate reality. We are now in the domain of ultimate truth.

ULTIMATE TRUTH

The *Unraveling the Intent Sūtra* (*Saṃdhinirmocanasūtra*) defines perfect nature as "reality as it is—the intentional object of a pure consciousness; it is with respect to it that the Buddha described all phenomena as ultimately natureless."[97] Vasubandhu's *Identifying the Three Natures* defines perfect nature as "the eternal, unalterable, absence of 'as it appears' from 'what appears.'"[98] "What appears" is the dependent nature, composed of a series of mental representations. "As it appears" is the imaginary nature, fabricating subjects and objects from that dependent nature. The representations—i.e., the dependent nature—appear to the cognition as though possessed of a subject-object duality of which they are wholly devoid. The perfect nature is thus the negation of the imaginary nature—the duality—superimposed upon the "natureless" dependent nature. Subtracting the imaginary nature from dependent nature yields the perfect nature, the ultimate truth.

Since the imaginary nature is dual, the perfect nature in which it is absent is nondual. Vasubandhu says, "The nonduality of the dependent nature is the reality (*dharmatā*)."[99] That is, the perfect nature of nonduality is an *inalienable* characteristic of consciousness. This is the sense in which Vasubandhu's above definition of perfect nature describes the absence of imagined duality from appearance as "eternal, unalterable." The perfect nature's nonduality is a basic ontological fact: the perfect nature has always been, is now, and must always be free from subject-object duality. As Maitreya's *Separating the Middle from the Extremes* (*Madhyāntavibhaṅgakārika*) says, it is reality as it is (*tathatā*), for whether or not we are buddhas—and so capable of perceiving it—the reality of things remains constant.[100]

In his autocommentary on the *Twenty Verses* (*Viṃśakārikāvṛtti*), Vasubandhu describes the perfect nature as "indescribable by nature" (*abhilāpyenātmanā*) and an "object of [knowledge] of buddhas" (*buddhānāṃ viṣya*)—meaning an object of transcendent cognition free from the deluded mental constructions of ordinary cognition.[101] Since it is mental fabrications (*vikalpajñāna*) that underwrite the imagined subject-object duality, transcendent nonconceptual awareness (*lokottara nirvikalpajñāna*) is the knowledge in which those fabrications are transcended, whereby one directly sees the falsity of that duality.[102]

The indescribable perfect nature is, in the same text, identified with emptiness (*śūnyatā*)—the nonself of all phenomena (*dharmanairātmya*) and of persons (*pudgalanairātmya*). Through the identity of perfect nature and the emptiness, Vasubandhu says, "we realize the nonself of the person. And yet in another way we develop the understanding of the nonself of the dharmas."[103]

Vasubandhu's rationale for the identification of the indescribable nonduality of reality and the insubstantiality of all things is that a substantial conception of self (*ātman*) and phenomena must presuppose a subject-object duality, in which the self is the subject and phenomena are its objects. It is impossible to sustain a conception of self and things as existing substantially without also believing the two to be substantially different. Having a correct knowledge of the nonself of all phenomena and persons thus negates the interlinked conceptions that self and object are substantial *and* dual. An understanding of the emptiness of phenomenal selfhood and personal selfhood is therefore *itself* a realization of nonduality. Such a realization, according to Vasubandhu, is like awakening from a deep slumber of ignorance.

In the *Thirty Verses* (*Triṃśikākārikā*), Vasubandhu also identifies perfect nature with mere consciousness:

> This is the ultimate truth (*paramārtha*) of the dharmas, and so it is the reality (*tathatā*) too. Because its reality is like this all the time, it is mere consciousness.[104]

Here Vasubandhu says the ultimate truth qua reality is none other than mere consciousness—mental impressions. According to Sthiramati's *Commentary on the Thirty Verses* (*Triṃśikābhāṣya*), "ultimate" in Vasubandhu's above verse refers to

> the world-transcending knowledge (*lokottara nirvikalpa-jñāna*), in that there is nothing that surpasses it. Since it is the object of the transcendent knowledge, it is the ultimate. It is like space in that it has the same taste everywhere. It is the perfect nature, which is stainless and unchangable. Therefore it is known as the ultimate.[105]

In other words, the ultimate reality in Yogācāra philosophy is the *perfect* nature—emptiness—the object of cognition of the transcendent mind, and consciousness in its nondual and nonconceptual natural state. As Maitreya says in *Separating the Middle from the Extremes*, ultimate truth takes three primary forms: as emptiness it is the ultimate object, as nirvāṇa it is the ultimate attainment, and as nonconceptual knowledge it is the ultimate realization.[106]

We have seen that the dependent and the imaginary natures together provide the foundation for the Yogācāra position on conventional reality, while the perfect nature provides the foundation for its position on ultimate reality. An important qualification, though, is that though imaginary nature is constitutive of conventional truth, it remains *imaginary*—that mode of appearance is false even by empirical and practical standards. Dependent nature alone is conventionally real, and perfect nature alone is ultimately real.

THE THEORY OF THE THREE NATURELESSNESSES

An understanding of the corresponding theory of the three naturelessnesses is critical for a proper understanding of the Yogācāra theory of the two truths. This theory is shaped in response to the following objection: if there are three natures, why did the Buddha teach that all dharmas are natureless? To resolve this objection, in his *Thirty Verses*, Vasubandhu introduces the doctrine of the three naturelessnesses. According to this theory, he says, "The naturelessness of all dharmas has been explained with the understanding that the three natures constitute the three naturelessnesses."[107] In other words, the three natures are themselves devoid of any real nature. Still, the three natures serve as the ontological foundation upon which the three naturelessnesses stand. These three are, as described in the *Thirty Verses*: (1) naturelessness with respect to the lack of *identity*, (2) naturelessness with respect to the lack of *self-production*, and (3) naturelessness with respect to the lack of being *ultimately real*.[108]

The first, naturelessness with respect to the lack of identity, corresponds to imaginary nature. This is the case since, as we have seen, any solid ontological identity, even conventionally, is imagined—meaning it is superimposed by cognitive confusion. Sthiramati explains this further in his *Commentary on the Thirty Verses*: its identity is wholly fabricated since it lacks intrinsic nature. It is like the fabricated identities of an objectively real attractive form or an objectively real pleasant feeling. They are natureless as they do not have objectively real intrinsic nature, similar to a sky-flower.[109]

The second, naturelessness with respect to the lack of self-production, corresponds to dependent nature. That which exists in dependence on other phenomena plainly does not self-produce—there is no such ability for a cognition to generate itself independently of other supporting conditions. Hence dependent nature is natureless by origin because it is devoid of the external causal production that appears to dualistic cognition. Sthiramati's commentary explains:

> The dependent nature, similar to an illusion, is a product of its conditions; therefore it lacks its own nature [in that sense it is natureless]. It is natureless with respect to its production because the way it appears does not cohere with the way it is produced.[110]

Dependent nature appears as if it is externally existent but is, of course, merely a product of our own mental representation.

The third, naturelessness with respect to the lack of being ultimately real, corresponds to perfect nature. "The perfect nature is ultimately natureless," says Sthiramati, because "it is the ultimate reality of all the dharmas whose nature is dependent. Thus it is the reality (*dharmatā*) of the dependent nature. This follows since the perfect nature is the nature of the [dual] things that do not exist."[111] Vasubandhu summarizes in his *Identifying the Three Natures*: "The three natures are also nondual and ungraspable because [imaginary nature] is simply nonexistent; [the dependent nature] does not exist as (it appears), and the perfect nature is the nonexistence of that [duality]."[112]

In short, the Yogācāra conception of ultimate reality consists of the perfect nature—the nondual mind, empty of subject-object duality. As we have read in Maitreya's *Separating the Middle from the Extremes*, perfect nature is reality as it is (*tathatā*). Whether or not we are buddhas, and thus aware of this reality, it remains constant. The perfect nature is, he continues, also:

> the ultimate limit (*bhūtakoṭi*), since it represents the climax of moral perfection. It is naturelessness (*niḥsvabhāva*) as it is free from all conceptual fabrications. It is the ultimate object

> (*paramārtha*) as it is the final object of engagement by the transcendent wisdom of the awakened beings. And it is the root of righteousness (*dharmadhātu*) as it nourishes all virtues of the noble beings.[113]

We have observed so far that, for the Yogācāra, there are no external objects that are even conventionally real—all conventional truths are entirely mental. This is a radical claim that runs counter to our commonplace beliefs and deserves a robust philosophical defense. The Yogācāra philosophers provide just such a defense, and it is to that we now turn.

ARGUMENTS REJECTING THE REALITY OF EXTERNAL OBJECTS

The obvious objection to a "mind only" ontology is that if there is only mind, then how do representations arise in it, and from where do they come? Vasubandhu acknowledges this objection at the beginning of his *Thirty Verses*, where he asks:

> If there is only consciousness or series of representations, why do people and the Buddhist texts speak about the existence of self (*ātman*) and phenomena (*dharmas*)?

Vasubandhu initially responds to this hypothetical question by expounding Yogācāra's theory of mind, according to which mind has eight activities, which are of three kinds: the maturation (*vipāka*) of the storehouse consciousness (*ālayavijñāna*), the afflicted (or ego) consciousness (*kliṣṭamanas*), and the six sensory cognitive functions.[114]

The storehouse consciousness contains subliminal impressions, dispositions, and tendencies accumulated across the previous moments of one's existence.[115] With the intervention of the afflictive consciousness and karma, the Yogācāra argues those impressions mature from the subliminal state and then pass on to the conscious state, where they present as representations to the six sensory consciousnesses. It is these representations that appear as though they are external objects.

We fail to realize that the externality we impose on these impressions is baseless, the Yogācāra philosophers say, because we are intoxicated by our ignorance. The person who is sleeping is not aware of the nonexistence of the objects of his vision in a dream; just so, when people are submerged in the impressions (*vāsanās*) of ignorance with false mental creations, they do not understand the unreality of the objects of their cognition. But when they are awake from the impressions of ignorance, by means of correct knowledge, they become aware of the unreality and therefore the nonexistence of the external objects.[116]

The Yogācāra are able to explain knowledge without external objects by positing the concept of the storehouse consciousness, which functions in three key modes:

1) As the *active storehouse*, it transforms and matures the seeds (*bījas*) of sense impressions and karma into actual representations—the intentional objects of our cognition, which are stored by the passive storehouse.
2) As the *passive storehouse*, it collects, receives, and retains the impressions created by the afflictive consciousness, volitional actions (*karmas*), and other defiling factors (*sāṃkleśika*).
3) As the *substrate consciousness* of all that there is, it is the source of all external appearances of objects or subjects.

By positing the storehouse consciousness in his *Twenty Verses*, Vasubandhu demonstrates that external objects are not the only method of explaining perception—the machinery of the mind offers a tenable alternative. The second and more substantial of Vasubandhu's arguments against the realism of external objects is that the realists' argument, which presupposes the reality of external objects, is a considerably less tenable explanation for our perception of reality than the mind alone.

Vasubandhu fully develops this idealistic theory elsewhere in his *Twenty Verses*, as does Dignāga in his *Commentary on Investigation of the Percept* (*Ālambanaparīkṣāvṛtti*), which systematically examines the nature of intentional object or cognitive support (*ālambana*).

In both these texts, the argument is made in opposition to the realist schools that propose the reality of eternal things, such as the Vaibhāṣika and Sautrāntika, as well as competing Hindu philosophical schools, including the Sāṃkhya-Yoga, Nyāya-Vaiśeṣika, and Pūrva Mīmāṃsā.[117] These schools, which we will group under the label "realists," raise three objections to the Yogācāra thesis: that the absence of external objects would render logically impossible (1) the determinacy (*niyama*) in regard to place (*deśa*) and time (*kāla*), (2) the inexclusivity (*aniyama*) in regard to the series of consciousness, and (3) the performance of the specific function (*kṛtyakriya*).[118]

Vasubandhu's *Commentary on the Twenty Verses*[119] lays out the three objections in greater detail. The first objection concerns *spatio-temporal determinacy*. The realists argue that but for the fact that representations *represent* external objects fixed in space and time, there is no reason why those representations should be likewise fixed. Representations plainly arise at specific times and in specific forms, for example, as colors and shapes. The words of this chapter, for instance, are amalgams of shapes and colors of component letters, and make sense only because they appear to us in the sequence in which we read them, rather than all at once and constantly. The realists say that such behavior would be impossible absent the contribution of an external world governed by space and time with which our senses make contact. And since that behavior is not just possible but *actually* the case, that external world must exist.

The second objection concerns *intersubjective agreement*. Were representations the invention of a single mind, the realists argue, there would be no way to explain the fact that representations appearing in separate minds often agree. It is a fact that observers in similar locations at similar times observe similar things—two people seated next to each other in a cinema typically see the same movie, for instance. The only possible explanation for the fact of two separate mental streams sharing a similar sensory experience, the realists argue, is that that experience is being governed by sensory stimuli that are external to and shared by both. Absent external sensory stimuli, we would expect any experience to be radically subjective. Our sensory experience would be as individual and idiosyncratic as, for example, the visual experience of someone suffering from cataracts.

The third objection concerns *causal efficacy*. If an impression in the consciousness is devoid of an external object, the realists argue, it would fail to perform the causal function expected of that object. For instance, food and drink in a dream, no matter how vast their quantity, simply do not serve the nutritional function of food consumed in waking life. Therefore, since our representations are causally effective, they mustn't be entirely imagined—they must correspond to the external.

Vasubandhu replies to these realist objections in the *Twenty Verses*, offering a Yogācāra-based account of all three objections. The first problem is resolved by noting that dreams also exhibit spatio-temporal determination. In dreams, even with external objects absent, one still has the cognition of a dream-person in a specific time and place, rather than everywhere and at any or all moments. Therefore external objects are not necessary conditions of spatio-temporal specificity.

The second problem is answered with an appeal to Buddhist cosmology, in which inter-subjective agreement is observed among beings of specific karmic classes. For instance, hungry ghosts, observing what we humans would see as water, are said to see rivers of pus, urine, and excrement, while hell-beings collectively hallucinate demons as hell guardians. Although pus, urine, excrement, and hell guardians are nonexistent externally, these beings experience a series of cognitions leading them to see these things on account of their collective karma. Without this karma, other beings do not encounter these cognitions.[120] Since, according to Buddhist doctrine, similar karma can account for similar sensory experiences, positing shared external objects for the purpose of explaining shared experiences is unnecessary.

The third problem is resolved by noting the causal efficacy of imagined impressions, such as wet dreams, which cause the emission of semen absent physical contact. Since illusions may be causally effective, positing the existence of external objects to explain causal function is unnecessary.

In sum, the coherence of the experienced world is not evidence of its externality because karma is entirely capable of giving coherence to a universe of appearance. To the extent that beings' karmic histories resemble each other, the worlds of their perception will accord. It is for this reason and no other, the Yogācāra philosophers argue, that the world of our impressions is orderly rather than chaotic and arbitrary. We simply mistake that order for objectivity.

However strong the Yogācāra's defensive arguments are, they are inconclusive without a successful offense against the core realist thesis—the reality of external objects composed of atoms. In fact, the Yogācāra *do* mount a sustained attack on that thesis, to which we now turn. The mind only and realist theses agree on what the observables are: mental entities, including mental images and emotions. The realist theory, though, must posit the reality of additional physical objects that are in principle unobservable, given our cognitive access extends no further than our impressions. On this point, Dignāga's *Investigation of the Percept* reads:

> Those who postulate the existence of real external objects as the intentional object of cognitions claim that either the atoms are [the intentional objects of the cognition] because they are its causes, or that an [atomic] composite is [the intentional object] because there arises a cognition which appears under the form of that [composite object].[121]

The realist thesis is that external things composed of atoms exist substantively and act as the intentional objects of cognition. Perception (*pratyakṣa*), it argues, is only possible if it is anchored in something external and substantive. The fact of perception is therefore proof of the substantive, external things that we seem to perceive. For that thesis to hold, the Yogācāra contend, the "anchors" must be viable objects of cognition. And for that to be the case, one of the following must be true:

1) Objects are *wholes*, things that are constituted by atoms and parts but are different from those parts and have a real existence apart from them.

2) Objects are a collection of *multiple* atoms and parts, which coexist without forming a composite whole or mutually cohering.
3) Objects are atoms and parts *grouped together*, unified in a cohesive mass.

None of the three possibilities, the Yogācāra argue, provide an admissible object of cognition.

The first is inadmissible because it is impossible for an external object to be grasped as a whole removed from its parts. Were there to be such an apprehension of the whole, it would be no more than a symptom of a defective cognition: the whole is no more real, argues Dignāga, than the "second moon" perceived by someone seeing double. And, something that does not exist at all, he concludes, can hardly be the cause of cognition.[122]

The second option is inadmissible because we simply cannot perceive atoms individually; because of their size, they are well below the threshold of visibility. So vision of the "thing" can hardly be attributed to vision of its component atoms. And, since we require something substantive to anchor the realist perceptual chain, vision of the collection is also excluded because something that is the sum of its parts can never be substantive.

The third option is inadmissible since the only possible method of bringing atoms above that threshold—combining them—is excluded by the realists' definition of atoms as partless and indivisible (recall our discussion of the ultimate truth in the chapters on Vaibhāṣika and Sautrāntika). The conjunction of partless atoms is not logical since if atoms were to form a composite, they would no longer be partless.[123] To allow them the power of combination is also to admit they have the power of division, because it is a tacit acknowledgment they have parts by which and points at which they might combine. Something possessed of both parts and the power of division cannot also be *partless and indivisible*; in other words, were atoms capable of combination, they would not be atoms at all.

To aggregate, Vasubandhu argues, requires that atoms both occupy and defend a distinct space, otherwise aggregation would simply be convergence: the "entire aggregate"—regardless of the quantity of composite atoms—would never exceed the size of a single atom. This, aside from being nonsensical, also defies the point of aggregation: leaving the aggregates below the threshold of perception. The occupants of the locus would mutually exclude each other, precluding the possibility of visible mass.[124] The achievement of visible mass requires that the atoms that cohere occupy separate locations, according to which the amalgam could then be divided.

The achievement of visible mass also requires that the component atoms have some size. The combination of sizeless things will not bring us any closer to a size capable of crossing the threshold of perception. But to have size, Vasubandhu continues in his *Commentary on The Twenty Verses*, is to have directional dimensions, and to have such dimensions is to be divisible by them. In other words, a space-occupying atom must possess aspects, or axes, and it is along these axes that it may be divided into distinct spatial parts (in Vasubandhu's terms, "in front," "on bottom," "east," "north," and so on). Here, Vasubandhu is not arguing that the atom may be physically divided, but rather conceptually so. Anything possessed of space is possessed of infinitely divisible space, and its nature must depend on its constituent spatial parts. A conceptual aggregate, it thus cannot be "individually existent." Thus, aggregation of atoms is logically impossible; for atoms to meaningfully aggregate, they would be divisible individually (on account of their size) and collectively (on account of their aggregation in multiple loci).

All three possibilities are thus excluded. Vasubandhu summarizes the Yogācāra objections against the reality of the external sense objects (*āyatanas*):

> An external sense object is unreal because it cannot be the intentional object of cognition either as a single thing, as a multiple in [isolated] atoms, or as an aggregate because the atom is not proven to [substantively] exist.[125]

So far we have seen that for the Yogācāra, an atomic external world is logically problematic. The Yogācāra augment this argument with another: that even if atoms are logically tolerable, they could not function as the intentional objects of perception. Atoms, the Yogācāra argue, do not satisfy the criteria of intentional objects. Were atoms the intentional object of the perceptual cognition, they must, according to Dignāga, satisfy two criteria of an intentional object (*ālambana*): they must be (1) directly present to the cognition that cognizes them and (2) responsible for the content of the cognition.[126] The atoms, though, fail both these criteria. Atoms do not directly present themselves to cognition, and so cognition cannot vouch for their existence. And since atoms do not present directly to cognition, they can't claim responsibility for its contents, the mental representations.

The disconnect between hypothetical atoms and perception is underscored in the "time-lag argument" used in Vasubandhu's *Commentary on the Twenty Verses* (see verses 16–17). According to this argument, perception takes *time*, and there is therefore a time gap between perception's stimulus and its conclusion. Were we to perceive an atomic thing, the image that appears to our mind at the end of the perceptual process could only be an image of the object as it existed at the start of that process—in other words, at some time in the past. This is significant because that object, like all things, is momentary, and if the process of perception lasts a moment or more, that object has passed into oblivion before it is perceived. Thus, the atoms of an external object cannot be the intentional object of perceptual cognition. They no longer exist at the point they are cognized. Accordingly, they cannot be responsible for the cognition having the content it has; instead, they are like the unseen events occurring on the far side of an impenetrable wall.

CONCLUSION

In this chapter, we have seen that the Yogācāra school represents a radical departure from the realist ontology of the previous schools, for whom the external world exists and is composed of the atoms, or "partless particles," which are its fundamental building blocks. For the Vaibhāṣika, the external world is engaged directly by cognition; for the Sautrāntika, it is engaged via the intermediary of a mental representation. The Yogācāra accept the fact of mental representations, but reject the assumption that they indicate any extra-mental reality. For the Yogācāra, not only does perception *not* require an external atomic anchor, but any such anchor would be logically and epistemologically tangled. We cannot perceive an external whole since they do not exist independently of their parts; we cannot perceive the whole's "indivisible" atomic parts because they are below the threshold of perception; and we cannot usefully combine those atomic parts to resolve that problem without conceding that they have spatial content that makes them eminently divisible.

The more tenable model of perception, the Yogācāra argue, is their own, in which perceptual cognition is understood simply as the subliminal impressions (*vāsanās*) moving from latency in the subconscious storehouse (*ālayavijñāna*) to patency in our conscious awareness. All that exists is simply mind, and in the Yogācāra theory of the two truths, both truths refer to the same object—appearance. Conventional truth is simply these appearances seen by a consciousness shrouded in ignorance that uses them to compulsively fabricate a substantive external. Ultimate truth is these appearances seen by the transcendent cognition that recognizes them for precisely what they are. In terms of their signature theory of the "three natures," conventional truth is dependent nature seen in the mode of imaginary nature, which is to say through the lens of the "unreal conceptual fabrication" by which we fabricate the false dualities of self and other, internal and external. Ultimate truth, on the other hand, is perfect nature—dependent nature apprehended just as it is, which is to say, empty, nondual, and ineffable, the object of a transcendent cognition and the basis of enlightenment.

CHAPTER FOUR

Madhyamaka: Nāgārjuna

The primary source for the Madhyamaka's theory of the two truths is the genre of literature called the Perfection of Wisdom (*Prajñāpāramitā*) sūtras.[127] According to the Madhyamaka tradition, all these sūtras were words spoken by the Buddha, and together represent the philosophical acme of Buddha's teachings. Known as the second turning of the wheel of Dharma, as outlined in the *Teaching of Akṣayamati* (*Akṣayamatinirdeśasūtra*), they surpass in profundity and sophistication, the Madhyamaka say, the turnings that preceded and succeeded them: the first turning—found in the *Sūtra of the Wheel of Dharma*, which taught the four noble truths that provided the philosophical basis of the Abhidharma realism of the Vaibhāṣika and Sautrāntika—and the third turning—as outlined in the *Unraveling the Intent Sūtra* (*Saṃdhinirmocanasūtra*), which provided the philosophical basis for Yogācāra idealism. Madhyamaka philosophers have argued that the first turning presupposes the ontological realism of everything—both subjects and objects—whereas the third turning presupposes that the subjects—mind and experience—have some privileged ontological status. Both these metaphysical assumptions, the Mādhyamika argue, are unacceptable, and as we shall see in this and the following chapters, these metaphysical claims are at the receiving end of sustained Madhyamaka critiques.

NĀGĀRJUNA'S THEORY OF THE TWO TRUTHS

The philosopher most responsible for fashioning the literature of the second turning into the Madhyamaka theory of the two truths was the South Indian monk Nāgārjuna (ca. 150–250 CE). He delineated the theory of two truths in a series of seminal philosophical works that include the the following: *Fundamental Verses on the Middle Way* (*Mūlamadhyamakakārikā*),[128] *Akutobhaya: Commentary on Fundamental Verses of the Middle Way* (*Mūlamadhyamakavṛttyakutobhaya*), *Rebutting Disputes* (*Vigrahavyāvartanīkārikā*), *Commentary on Rebutting Disputes* (*Vigrahavyāvartanīvṛtti*),[129] *Seventy Verses on Emptiness* (*Śūnyatāsaptatikārikā*) and its autocommentary (*Śūnyatāsaptativṛtti*), *Essence of Dependent Origination* (*Pratītyasamutapādahṛdayakārikā*) and its autocommentary (*Pratītyasamutapādahṛdayavyākhyāna*), *Sixty Verses on Reasoning* (*Yuktiṣaṣṭikā*), *Stages of Meditation* (*Bhāvanākrama*), and *Crushing the Categories* (*Vaidalyaprakaraṇa*), among other works.[130] Nāgārjuna's foremost student was Āryadeva (third century), whose work *Four Hundred Verses* (*Catuḥśatakaṣāstrakārikā*) is also considered one of the foundational texts setting out the Madhyamaka theory of the two truths.

According to Nāgārjuna, the very essence of the Buddha's teachings is the theory of the two truths: the truth of mundane conventions and the truth of the ultimate.[131] He accordingly believed that a failure to understand the distinction between these two truths would be fatal to the understanding and actualization of the Buddha's teaching.[132] This is the case, Nāgārjuna argues, because without relying on conventional truth the meaning of the ultimate cannot be explained, and without understanding the meaning of the ultimate nirvāṇa cannot be achieved.[133] One cannot understand the ultimate absent the conventional, because in isolation we tend to reify the former and disparage the latter. This is a philosophically fatal mistake since it is in mundane conventions, such as language and conceptual knowledge, that the ultimate truth is initially explained. We can only realize that which we understand, and we come to understand things by explanation rather than by accident. By cordoning the ultimate off from the conventional, we cordon ourselves off from an understanding of the ultimate. It is the case that we cannot attain nirvāṇa without realizing the ultimate truth because nirvāṇa is the absence of suffering, and the presence of suffering is a product of the mental afflictions whose cause is an ontological confusion that takes root in the absence of understanding of the ultimate truth. So, without realizing the ultimate truth, freedom from suffering is impossible; realizing it, it is inevitable.

As we saw, for the realism of the Vaibhāṣika and representationalism of the Sautrāntika, ultimate truth is logically irreducible. For the idealism of the Yogācāra, the nondual mind is the only ultimate reality and the appearances of that mind, which are perceived as "other," are mere conventions. Nāgārjuna's critiques of the positions of the Vaibhāṣika, Sautrāntika, and Yogācāra[134] predominantly target the ontological foundationalism that underpins their theories of the ultimate truth[135]—in the case of the former two schools, foundationalism relating to the external world, in the case of the latter, foundationalism relating to the mind.

The positions of the Vaibhāṣika and Sautrāntika are rejected on the basis that their ultimates—partless particles and unique particulars—cannot survive the scrutiny of analysis. Under the glare of analysis, the Vaibhāṣika's partless particles are found not just ultimately unreal but oxymoronic: any spatio-temporal unit can be infinitely further subdivided along spatial or temporal lines. Likewise, the Sautrāntika's unique particulars are found to be ultimately unreal, since they too dissolve under the glare of analytical cognition, which, rather than resting on unique particulars as the basic unit of reality, establishes everything as empty of ultimate reality, empty of unique particularity.

The Yogācāra position—that the nondual mind rather than external objects are the only ultimate reality—is rejected because the nondual mind is just as vulnerable to analytical cognition as the external objects it perceives. Analysis, Nāgārjuna argues, establishes the ultimate unreality of everything, including atoms, affirming the emptiness of both subject and object; on the other hand, nonanalytical cognition affirms the conventional reality, the dependent existence, of subject and object.

Thus, Nāgārjuna proposes that there is no ultimate reality but emptiness; all other truths are conventions at best.

For Nāgārjuna's Madhyamaka, all things, including ultimate truth, are ultimately unreal, empty of any intrinsic nature. No exception is made. All things are groundless; even emptiness is empty. It is for this reason that the Mādhyamika is also referred to as an advocate of emptiness (*śūnyavādin*) and of intrinsic naturelessness (*niḥsvabhāvavādin*).

Critically, to assert that all things are empty of anything intrinsic is not to say they are simply *nothing*—totally nonexistent. On the contrary, Nāgārjuna argues, to assert that the things are empty of any intrinsic nature is to explain the way things *actually exist*—that is, as causally conditioned phenomena. For Nāgārjuna, the conventional truth about phenomena is that they dependently arise, and the ultimate truth is that they are empty of intrinsic nature. These two truths coexist and dovetail each other: that which does not independently exist (i.e., lacks intrinsic nature) must exist dependently; that which arises dependently cannot also exist independently.

Nāgārjuna emphasizes this relationship repeatedly. In a famous passage in chapter 24 of the *Fundamental Verses on the Middle Way*, he says:

> To whoever emptiness as the ultimate truth makes sense, all conventional truths—including the truth of suffering, truth of origin, truth of cessation, and truth of the path leading to the cessation of suffering—make sense, whereas to whoever emptiness as the ultimate makes no sense, no conventional truths make sense.[136]

Later in the chapter, he puts it in stronger terms still: "Whatever is dependently arisen is itself explained to be empty. That being dependently designated is itself the middle path."[137] He goes on to say, "There is no thing that is not dependently arisen; therefore, there is no such thing that is not empty."[138] In his *Seventy Verses on Emptiness*, he argues that the Buddha's claim of dependent existence is valid "since all things are empty of essence."[139] Likewise, in *Rebutting the Disputes*, he says that wherever emptiness—the ultimate truth—applies, there is causal efficacy—the conventional truth—and wherever there is not emptiness, there is not causal efficacy.[140] In the salutation to the Buddha at the end of that text, Nāgārjuna pays homage to the Buddha, describing him as "peerless" because he "perfectly explained that the middle path constitutes the identity of emptiness and dependent arising."[141]

Finally, we see the same line of argument employed in the *Sixty Verses on Reasoning* to draw saṃsāra—here substituting for conventional truth—and nirvāṇa—ultimate truth—closer phenomenologically: "Saṃsāra and nirvāṇa do not exist as two individually. The exhaustive knowledge of saṃsāra is itself defined as nirvāṇa."[142]

Thus, it is clear that Nāgārjuna completely rejects the Vaibhāṣika, Sautrāntika, and Yogācāra characterizations of the two truths, according to which the two are ontologically and epistemically incompatible, hierarchical, and must not entail each other. According to Nāgārjuna the two truths are ontologically and epistemically completely compatible and nonhierarchical.

THE SVĀTANTRIKA/PRĀSAṄGIKA SPLINTER

The Madhyamaka philosophy brought forth by Nāgārjuna is not monolithic, and neither is its theory of the two truths. The most significant division within Madhyamaka is between two broad subschools: the Svātantrika and Prāsaṅgika. The beginnings of that division were sown in the fifth century CE in Buddhapālita's *Commentary on [Nāgārjuna's] Fundamental Verses of the Middle Way* (*Buddhapālitamūlamadhyamakavṛtti*). For Buddhapālita, Madhyamaka's rejection of foundationalism of all forms both demarcates a philosophical view and dictates a philosophical method. To negate the intrinsic existence proposed by the Brahmanical and Abhidharma philosophers requires a philosophical method that is equally negative. That method is the use of *prasaṅga* (*reductio ad absurdum*) arguments at the expense of the *svatantra* probative, or syllogistic, arguments. If the Madhyamaka are to prove that all things are empty of substantive identity, Buddhapālita argues, best that they do so without advancing probative arguments that make substantive claims. For this reason, Buddhapālita is frequently described as the founder of the Prāsaṅgika Madhyamaka school.

The seeds of division ripened three decades later in Bhāviveka's[143] challenge of Buddhapālita's philosophical and methodological position. Bhāviveka wrote some of the major Madhyamaka treatises, including *Jewel Lamp of the Middle Way* (*Madhyamakaratnapradīpa*), *Wisdom Lamp: Commentary on the Fundamental Verses of the Middle Way* (*Prajñāpradīpamūlamadhyamakavṛtti*), *Blaze of Reasoning: Commentary on the Essence of the Middle Way* (*Madhyamakahṛdayavṛttitarkajvālā*, alternatively *Tarkajvālā*) and *Essence of the Middle Way* (*Madhyamakahṛdaya*). Bhāviveka argues that the *reductio* arguments are incompatible with the Madhyamaka theory of the two truths, which is not entirely negative. It has a positive aspect, and it requires the use of formal *svatantra* arguments to posit it. Bhāviveka is therefore frequently identified as the founder of the Svātantrika subschool.

The most noted aspect of the split between Prāsaṅgika and Svātantrika is the aspect embedded in their very names: the methodological aspect. Indeed, there is a prominent and significant methodological divide, but we must ensure that its prominence doesn't obscure equally significant *philosophical* differences, which are critical to their respective understandings of the two truths. It has been a regrettable feature of many later commentaries that these philosophical differences have been so obscured, and it is frequently argued that the Prāsaṅgika/Svātantrika splinter is simply a pedagogical or methodological one. According to this view, the Prāsaṅgika and the Svātantrika prosecute an identical understanding of Nāgārjuna and Āryadeva's Madhyamaka philosophy with alternative methods. As we shall see, this is not the case.

But, in redressing the inattention to the philosophical differences, we must not ourselves make the corresponding mistake of ignoring the very real methodological differences. We will therefore address the two in turn.

The methodological split is best understood by example, of which there is none better than Buddhapālita and Bhāviveka's respective commentaries on Nāgārjuna's verse negating the four alternative causal theories:

> Neither from itself, nor from another,
> nor from both,
> nor without a cause,
> does anything anywhere ever arise.[144]

For the sake of brevity, we shall only consider the methodological difference between the Prāsaṅgika and the Svātantrika negation of the first of the four positions mentioned above: the rejection of the Sāṃkhya school's theory of self-causation ("from itself"). Buddhapālita's *Commentary on the Fundamental Verses of the Middle Way* negates the position as follows:

> Things do not arise from themselves, because such spontaneous arising would be pointless and because the arising would be endless (*anavastha*). There is no purpose in the repeated arising of things that [already] exist by their own selves. That is, if they do arise again even though they exist [already], they would never stop arising. But this you [Sāṃkhya] do not accept. Therefore, things do not arise from themselves.[145]

Here, Buddhapālita only employs *reductio* arguments. The *reductio* arguments demonstrate that the Sāṃkhya's causal claim entails either of two absurdities: either *futility*, since an effect that preexisted its cause would hardly need to be "effected," or *infinite regress*, since something that insisted on coming into existence despite already being in existence would create a feedback loop of self-production. It would, as Buddhapālita says, "never stop arising."

Bhāviveka, in his *Wisdom Lamp: Commentary on the Fundamental Verses of the Middle Way*, criticizes Buddhapālita's method as logically flawed:

> That is irrational because no reason and example are given and because the charges laid by the opponent are not answered. And because it is a *prāsaṇga* argument, the original meaning of the property to be proved (*sādhya-dharma*) and the proving property (*sādhanadharma*) could be reversed to represent the opposite meaning. [Specifically the opponent could rebut by stating that] entities arise from another, because arising has a result and because arising has an end. Thus [Buddhapālita's own] doctrine would be contradicted.[146]

In other words, Bhāviveka argues *reductio* arguments (absent "reason and example") lack probative power; a purely negative approach cannot be decisive since it disregards the terms of debate (the charges "are not answered"); and finally, Buddhapālita's own intentions are defeated, since *reductio* arguments aren't so immutably negative after all—by a simple process of inversion they can be phrased positively.

So unsatisfied with Buddhapālita's method, Bhāviveka attacks the same section of verse with formal probative argument (*prayogavākya*):

> [Thesis:] It is certain that ultimately the inner domains (*ādhyātmikāyatanas*) do not arise from themselves (*ātmanaḥ*),
> [Reason:] because they exist [already],
> [Example:] like consciousness (*caitanya*).[147]

Bhāviveka's critique consists of a probative argument and the application of the qualification. We will address these two in turn.

Bhāviveka's probative argument has three key components: the thesis (*pratijñā*), reason (*hetu*), and example (*udāhaṇa* or *dṛṣṭānta*). Of these, the thesis comprises both the subject (*pakṣa* or *dharmin*), which in this case is the "inner domains," as well as the property to be proved (*anumeya* or *sādya*), which in this case is the property of not ultimately self-producing.

The second component of the probative argument, the reason, provides the proving property, which in this case is "exist already." The final component is the example, which in this case is "consciousness." The example is decisive, Bhāviveka argues, for two reasons: it possesses the proving property (already existing) and the property to be proved (lack of ultimate self-production), *and* the fact it so exists is, like the subject and the reason, acknowledged by both parties of the debate (*vādin* and *prativādin*).[148]

The construction of the probative argument answers two of the three criticisms Bhāviveka leveled at the *reductio*. Unlike the *reductio*, the probative argument *is* possessed of "reason" and "example"; and unlike the *reductio*, the probative argument establishes some common ground upon which the debate can occur and, they argue, be decisively won. That common ground consists of the probative argument's subject, property, and example, which must be established (*siddha*) for both parties. Were it not for this requirement, Bhāviveka argues, the Madhyamaka proponent and his opponent would simply be ships passing in the philosophical night—two parties possessed of different philosophical positions, unable to engage. With this requirement, those different positions become sides in a live debate in which a philosophical result is unavoidable—the terms of the contest are agreed, and reason acts as arbiter.

We will shortly see that for the Prāsaṅgika, finding common ground is seen as simply sacrificing the philosophically higher ground. There is nothing to be gained and everything to lose, they argue, from lowering the nonfoundational insight of the Madhyamaka position into a false equivalence with other foundationalist philosophies for the sake of contest. The Svātantrika, while acknowledging that risk, argue that the form of the probative argument offers suitable protection. Though the philosophical opponent might not be expected to have the Madhyamaka's nonfoundational insight into the ultimate, the eighth-century philosopher Jñānagarbha argues, in his *Commentary on Distinguishing the Two Truths* (*Satyadvayavibhaṅgavṛtti*), that it will not be problematic so long as the agreed terms are entirely conventional. It is acceptable, he says, to agree on subject, property, and example, which commonly appear to the minds of both parties. Having done so, it becomes plausible to use reason to ask whether the subject in question is ultimately real or not.[149]

For Bhāviveka, the negation of Sāṃkhya's theory of self-causation cannot be accomplished without the use of a qualification—the second component—which in this case is the word "ultimately." In the probative argument we just examined, he says that "*ultimately* the inner domains do not arise from themselves, because they exist already, like consciousness."[150] In *Wisdom Lamp: Commentary on the Fundamental Verses of the Middle Way*, Bhāviveka qualifies similarly:

> In this context there is no *ultimately* (*paramārtha*) *intrinsic* (*svabhāvatā*) production of the earth [element] and so forth because, like consciousness, they are conditioned and caused.[151]

Bhāviveka's purpose of using the qualifying term "ultimately" is to negate only from the standpoint of ultimate truth—in this case to negate the ultimate intrinsic production of the earth element. This implies, a fact *Blaze of Reasoning* makes clear, that Bhāviveka accepts the intrinsic production of the earth element from the standpoint of the conventional truth.

Having seen the Svātantrika position, and its reliance on probative argument and qualification, I turn to the Prāsaṅgika response, which rejects both probative argument and qualification. The Prāsaṅgika response falls largely to Buddhapālita's follower, Candrakīrti, who fends off Bhāviveka's criticisms of Buddhapālita in his *Clear Words Commentary on the Fundamental Verses of the Middle Way* (*Mūlamadhyamakavṛttiprasannapadā*, alternatively *Prasannapadā*).

First, argues Candrakīrti, the *reductio* argument Buddhapālita employs is quite capable of negating the Sāṁkhya's theory of self-arising. The logical weakness Bhāviveka perceived in Buddhapālita's arguments are, Candrakīrti says, "baseless accusations."[152] And Bhāviveka's demands for arguments that do more than expose the absurdities of Madhyamaka's opponents would be, Candrakīrti argues, itself absurd for a Mādhyamika:

> [A Mādhyamika] cannot accept his opponent's premises. It is also unreasonable for a Mādhyamika to propound a probative inferential argument from his point of view.[153]

Moreover, Candrakīrti argues that abstention from probative argument has a compelling pedigree: it is the method employed by Nāgārjuna in his *Rebutting the Disputes*, a text in which probative arguments are absent and the Nyāya thesis is demolished by confronting it with its internal logical faults.[154]

Having thus attacked the argument in principle, Candrakīrti turns to its use in the present case:

> Being a logician, [Bhāviveka] shows off his expertise in logic texts. In spite of the fact that he claims to follow Madhyamaka philosophy, he advances probative arguments. He thus mounts up error after error. How is that? He advances the following syllogism: [Thesis:] "It is certain that ultimately the inner domains do not arise from themselves, [reason:] because they exist [already], [example:] like consciousness."[155] So he asserts.[156]

Second, Bhāviveka's qualification of the negation is unacceptable. Candrakīrti argues that the only two possible grounds on which this qualifier might be justified are themselves entirely unjustifiable. The first possibility is that it is to protect conventional self-arising from negation. This, however, would be a grave philosophical error:

> But what is the purpose of introducing the qualification "ultimately"? [Perhaps it is] because he thinks arising as it

> is accepted in mundane convention cannot be denied, for if it were denied, it would undermine the thesis. This is nonsensical, since the arising from self is not accepted even conventionally.[157]

The arbiter of mundane convention is the ordinary cognitive processes, but the theory of self-arising is a posit of high philosophy, not everyday intuition. Candrakīrti continues:

> The ordinary person, without analyzing whether arising is from self or from another, simply understands an effect to be produced from a cause [and not from itself]; Ācārya [Nāgārjuna] himself settles the matter in this way. It is clear therefore that this qualification is in every sense pointless.[158]

The second possibility is that the qualifier is present to give a fair account of the opponent's position. This, Candrakīrti argues, would be a grave methodological error:

> If he [Bhāviveka] says the qualification ["ultimately"] is introduced to articulate the opponent's position, that too is nonsensical, since the [Mādhyamika] does not accept the opponent's system even conventionally. The non-Buddhists (*tīrthika*) lack unerring insight into the nature of the two truths, so the exclusion of its position [on the two truths] is a virtue [rather than an error]. Therefore, it is nonsensical to introduce this qualification even when referring to the opponent's position.[159]

In this example, we have seen the essence of the methodological divide between Prāsaṅgika and Svātantrika. The Svātantrika employs a probative argument, the Prāsaṅgika a *reductio* argument. The Svātantrika qualifies its negations with "ultimate," an approach the Prāsaṅgika rejects.

Though we are still on methodological ground, the Svātantrika's use of the qualifying term here is philosophically significant. The term is used for the precise reason that in the Svātantrika's reckoning, Madhyamaka philosophy rejects intrinsic reality only in the *ultimate* domain: intrinsic reality exists, but is simply quarantined in the *conventional*. As Kamalaśīla writes in *Illuminating the Middle Way* (*Madhyamakāloka*):

> The nature of all entities is that they are not ultimately intrinsic, yet it is not the case that the [things] lack conventionally [intrinsic] nature. If they lack conventionally [intrinsic] nature then there would be no framework for positing afflictive dharmas and liberating dharmas.[160]

It is clear from Kamalaśīla's argument that if things were to exist conventionally, they must exist intrinsically. In other words, conventionally things are *intrinsically real*. This thesis is the lynchpin of the Svātantrika's probative argument, which argues that *the appearance of intrinsically real things* provides the subject, the very basis of the debate between the proponent and the opponent. The Svātantrika argue that the appearance of intrinsically real things presents itself to the nonanalytical cognition of both parties. Its conventional reality is not in dispute, though it provides the basis for a dispute about its ultimate status. Appearance, Jñānagarbha argues, becomes the commonly agreed subject, as well as the basis for the the other components of the probative argument: property, example, reason of an inference, and the property to be inferred. When these items appear to the cognitive processes of both the parties involved, there is an inference, and if they do not appear, there is no inference.[161]

Jñānagarbha argues that this must be the case. The subject, property, and example have to be established *nonanalytically*—that is, on the basis of the way they appear, intrinsically, to intuition—because establishing them analytically is an impossibility. The parties of a debate are analytically divided; they hold opposing philosophical positions. If the precondition to a debate was the mutual analytical establishment of subject, property, and example, no debate could ever occur.

If, however, intrinsically real conventional truth is accepted as providing a subject, property, and example that mutually appear to the intuitions of both parties, a debate can occur. Only once the appearance is established as conventionally existing for both parties is it reasonable to debate. According to Jñānagarbha it is plausible to use certain kinds of reason to adjudicate the ultimate status of a conventionally appearing subject, such as self-arising.[162] This is only possible, he insists, as a result of accepting self-arising as an *intrinsic* conventional reality.

Accordingly, the Svātantrika reject only the ultimate reality of the four causal theses—arising from self, other, both, or neither—while according them the status of conventional reality. The Prāsaṅgika, in contrast, categorically reject the four causal theses. For the Prāsaṅgika, the four causal theses are reified philosophical positions in which intrinsic nature is implicitly endorsed and so must be rejected conventionally *and* ultimately. Candrakīrti writes in his *Introduction to the Middle Way (Madhyamakāvatāra)*:

> The argument that shows arising from self or other is unreasonable from the point of view of reality also shows that it is unreasonable conventionally. So how can you have any arising at all? Things such as reflections, which are empty and depend on a synthesis of causes, are not unacceptable just as from empty things, such as reflections, arise cognitions with the representations of those [things]. Thus, while all things are empty, they arise from empty [things]. There is no intrinsic nature from the point of view of either truth, so things are neither permanent nor destroyed.[163]

The Svātantrika challenge this line of argument. Although neither Jñānagarbha nor the subcommentator states Candrakīrti by name, Jñānagarbha criticizes Candrakīrti's position when he says, "Some who are notorious for their bad arguments argue that because things do not arise in a real sense (*tattvataḥ*), they do not arise in a conventional sense either, like the son of a barren woman and so on."[164] Candrakīrti's position is implausible, Jñānagarbha argues in the commentary, since it is refuted by common sense (*loka*) and direct perception, which verify the conventional existence of arising.[165]

Jñānagarbha's response is effective against the argument he attacks—unfortunately, that argument is not Candrakīrti's. The autocommentary and the subcommentary make clear that Jñānagarbha sees the Prāsaṅgika's categorical rejection of the four metaphysical causal theses as representing a wholesale rejection of natural causality.[166] This is not the case.

To understand why it is not, we need to understand more completely the Prāsaṅgika's position on qualifiers and probative arguments. We have seen the Prāsaṅgika's disdain for the qualification "ultimate" in the case of the first causal thesis, but this disdain does not extend to all qualifications. The Prāsaṅgika does not refuse to predicate *all* negations. They do so only when the *opponent's position* demands it.

When the opponent's position is a reified philosophical position, the kind that the Prāsaṅgika do not accept even conventionally, the negation is categorical. No qualification is needed. For the Prāsaṅgika, philosophically reified positions of any kind advanced by philosophers of any stripe—Buddhist or non-Buddhist—are unacceptable both ultimately and conventionally. They are so because, for the Prāsaṅgika, the arbiter of conventional truth is ordinary nonanalytical cognition, whereas highly analytical cognition is the arbiter of the ultimate.

These two cognitive processes are related to the twin ontological questions: do things exist, and if so, in what manner? For Candrakīrti, the answer to the first ontological question must come from the nonanalytic process—the type of cognition that accesses superficial appearance. That which exists as conventional truth appears to one's cognition, and that which doesn't does not.

The analytical process has no access to appearances as they arise and so cannot begin to answer the first question. Instead, subsequent to the affirmation of existence by nonanalytical cognition, it can approach with analysis the *manner* in which the things that appear actually exist. The important thing is that we cannot begin to answer the second question without having answered the first. Only when we are sure of the existence of conventional truths can we begin to analyze their ultimate nature.

What makes philosophically reified positions conventionally and ultimately intolerable to the Prāsaṅgika is that they are abstractions of the *analytical* mind. The philosophical opponents are attempting to answer the second ontological question without asking the first. Lofty metaphysical positions do not occur to the ordinary person engaging the world without analysis, they appear *only* to the analytical minds of the philosophers—in the case of the self-production thesis, these are the Sāṃkhya philosophers—who construct them. Such philosophical positions are thus entirely false—too philosophically flawed to be ultimately true, and too philosophical at all to be conventionally so.

Earlier we saw that Jñānagarbha defended the Svātantra's probative argument on the grounds that its agreed terms were simply conventional truths that would routinely appear to both parties of the debate. The basis for the Prāsaṅgika rejection of this defense should now be clear. There is no commonly agreed subject, property, or example, they say, because those terms would only appear to the analytical minds of the opponents. They would not routinely appear to the mundane cognition of the Mādhyamika for the reason that they are not conventional truths. The terms here may be analytically established for the Sāṃkhya, but are neither analytically nor nonanalytically established for the Mādhyamika. There is therefore no genuine possibility of common ground. In such contexts, therefore, the Prāsaṅgika rejects the use of probative argument and endorses categorical negation without qualification.

An interesting implication of this position is that it may be possible to form a probative argument of which the Prāsaṅgika approve by taking as the common ground something that *is*, for the Prāsaṅgika, conventionally true. If it is possible to take as subject, property, and example the unanalyzed appearance that presents to the nonanalytic minds of both parties—as opposed to the reified theories arrived at through reasoned analysis of the Sāṃkhya and the like—then it is possible to formulate a probative argument of which the Prāsaṅgika approve, in which a reason tests that subject's ultimacy. The key is not so much the method but the sequence—that is, that the two ontological questions are answered in the correct order. Based on the unanalyzed mode of appearance, the Prāsaṅgika could formulate a probative argument: for instance, a sprout arises dependently (the thesis) because it is produced from the collocation of its causes and conditions (the reason)—such as the seed, moisture, temperature, air, soil, etc. Just like a reflected image (the example), which dependently arises from the collocation of its causes and conditions—such as a face, a clean mirror, proper lighting, appropriate distance between the face and the mirror, etc.

Having seen the context in which Prāsaṅgika rejects qualification, let us now note that there are contexts in which the Prāsaṅgika insist on the use of qualifying terms to predicate the negations at issue. The reason is interlinked with our previous discussion—that is, having appointed nonanalytical mundane cognition as the arbiter of conventional truth, the Prāsaṅgika can hardly categorically negate its conclusions. In discussing the things that appear to nonanalytical mundane cognitions, the Prāsaṅgika qualify their remarks very carefully. The following passage from Candrakīrti's *Commentary on* [Āryadeva's] *Four Hundred Verses* (*Catuḥṣatakaṭīkā*) is typical:

> [Question:] Have we negated the nature of these appropriated effects? It seemed so, for the eyes, etc., are negated. [Reply:] Our analysis only seeks to find out the intrinsic nature. Here we negate things being intrinsically real (*svabhāvasiddhi*, Tib. *rang gi ngo bo grub pa*). We do not negate the karmic effects, such as the eyes, which are conditioned and dependently arisen. They thus exist, and they are asserted as the effects. Thus the eyes, etc., exist."[167]

For Candrakīrti, the negation of the five aggregates must be qualified by the terms "intrinsic nature" or "intrinsic reality" to avoid any suggestion that the negation extends to the aggregates, as they are produced conditionally and dependently.

There is another argument as to why the Prāsaṅgika insist on the uses of qualifying terms when negating conventionally real things.

That is, anything but a carefully qualified negation would undercut the doctrine of dependent arising, which for the Prāsaṅgika is a bedrock position. Again, in the *Commentary on* [Āryadeva's] *Four Hundred Verses*, Candrakīrti states:

> When one sees dependent arising correctly, it is conditioned like an illusion but not [nonexistent] like the son of a barren woman. If one maintained that according to this analysis, conditioned phenomena are nonarisen, then dependent arising would not be illusion-like. Rather, it would be like something perceived by the son of a barren woman and the like. Concerned by the absurd consequence that there would be no dependent arising, one should not conciliate with those [who hold such positions]. One should not contradict this [i.e., dependent arising].[168]

He goes on to state:

> Therefore, when analyzed, things are not established as intrinsically real; the illusion-like nature of each individual phenomenon must nevertheless remain.[169]

The negation of conventional truth must be qualified by the terms "intrinsic" or "ultimate" because the point of negation in this context, unlike the previous one, is to negate only the superimposition of "intrinsically real" and "ultimately real" upon things that do exist, but only conventionally, dependently so—things that are "illusion-like." Were they not so qualified, conventional truths would no longer be truths at all—they would be as totally false as the "son of a barren woman." Such an outcome would be fatal to the doctrine of dependent arising, since things that cannot arise, like the the child of an infertile woman, can hardly be also said to arise dependently. But it would also be fatal to the doctrine of two truths, since it would effectively reduce their number to one, and given that two truths mutually entail each other, when one is absent, the other will be too—resulting in utter nihilism.

CONCLUSION

In dealing with the methodological divide, we have already seen that it has been impossible to separate methodology from philosophical differences. The two are inextricably linked. Both are concerned with decisively rejecting the foundationalism of their opponents, but diverge in their methods of doing so. For the Svātantrika, a decisive victory must occur on common ground, and they advocate the use of probative reasoning in which the subject is mutually established, at least conventionally, and *reason* acts as arbiter. It is the Svātantrika's acceptance of intrinsic reality conventionally that allows the mutual establishment of the subject, from which their probative arguments proceed. For the Prāsaṅgika, finding common philosophical ground with realists can only come at the expense of the higher philosophical ground they already occupy, and a decisive victory is possible only by dismissing, rather than philosophically engaging, their opponents' errors. Freed from the requirements of mutually establishing a probative subject, the Prāsaṅgika reject intrinsic reality entirely. Having noted its methodological provenance, it is to the philosophical content of this debate—between Prāsaṅgika and Svātantrika, Buddhapālita and Bhāviveka, Bhāviveka and Candrakīrti—that I now turn. I shall take up the Svātantrika's account first.

CHAPTER FIVE

Sautrāntika-Svātantrika Madhyamaka: Bhāviveka and Jñānagarbha

The Svātantrika Madhyamaka was founded by Bhāviveka and has two subschools: the Sautrāntika-Svātantrika Madhyamaka and the Yogācāra-Svātantrika Madhyamaka. As far as the presentation of the ultimate truth is concerned, both subschools are in agreement. Emptiness alone is the ultimate truth, and all phenomena—the entire range of *dharmas*—are empty of intrinsic reality. The two schools differ slightly on conventional truth, especially the conventional status of external, physical objects. As we have seen, the distinctive feature of the Svātantrika Madhyamaka schools is that they accept the intrinsic reality of conventional things.

For the Sautrāntika-Svātantrika Madhyamaka school, whose primary proponents include Bhāviveka and his student Jñānagarbha, both the outer domains (form, sound, smell, taste, tactility, and the contents of thought) and inner domains (the faculties of the eye, ear, nose, tongue, body, and mind, as well as their respective consciousnesses) are conventionally intrinsically real.

For the Yogācāra-Svātantrika Madhyamaka, whose proponents include Śāntarakṣita and his student Kamalaśīla, conventional truth and intrinsic existence are confined to the inner domains and denied the outer domains, which are considered conceptual fictions.

We have previously seen the arguments by which the Yogācāra deny the reality of external objects. To understand the basis of the split between these two subschools requires briefly examining the Sautrāntika-Svātantrika response to those arguments. We have also previously seen that the Svātantrika takes the probative reasoning as the basis for philosophical engagement. In this case, we can probatively reconstruct the Yogācarā's rejection of the reality of external objects as follows:

> [Thesis]: Cognition of a material object has no external reality
> [Reason]: because it arises from a mental image or inner representation
> [Example]: like the cognition of material form in a dream.

Recall that for the Yogācāra, all we have cognitive access to are our intentional objects, which are no more than mental representations. Absent any compelling evidence that those mental representations referentially designate something outside the mind, they argue we ought not construct a hypothetical material universe just to explain them. The more reasonable conclusion, they argue, is that everything is mind only—external objects do not exist.

The first plank of Bhāviveka's response is to attack the significance of cognitive access being limited to representation. In the *Verses on the Essence of the Middle Way*, he says that if the Yogācāra proponent "thinks that a cognition of material form is incorrect because it has the representation or the image of an object, the reason is mistaken (*vyabhicārin*), and the thesis fails."[170] According to his *Blaze of Reasoning* commentary, "mistaken" here means "contradicted" (*viruddha*). Bhāviveka argues that for the Yogācāra to regard the fact that form is cognized via immaterial representations as evidence of its material implausibility is entirely opposite to the correct conclusion—it is precisely this that makes cognition of the external plausible. It is the very *nature* of material form to present itself mentally. Thus, the Yogācāra position that "having the representation of an object" (*grāhyābhāsatā*) excludes *correctness* of the cognition is contradicted, because it contradicts the very nature of the subject.

Bhāviveka enlists perception (*pratyakṣa*), tradition (*āgama*), and common sense realism (*lokaprasiddha*) to support his claim for the subject's nature. All of these, he says, agree that it is the nature of material form to be accessed via its immaterial representations.[171] The Yogacara probative argument's reason, therefore, undercuts the same probative argument's subject.

The Yogācāra respond with a scriptural appeal, quoting perhaps one of the most cited and famed sūtras, the *Sūtra of Ten Grounds* (*Daśabhūmikasūtra*), which says:

> These twelve components of becoming, the division into which was taught by the Tathāgata, are also all based in a single mind. Why is that? Consciousness is the arising of a mind joined by desire to an object. The object is a formation. Delusion concerning that formation is ignorance.[172]

And continues on to say:

> They overcome the three realms as being 'mind only.' These twelve components of becoming are in a single mind. They are born from desire; they are the manifestation of the mind. Thus, creation and destruction also are aspects of the mind.[173]

This sūtra leaves little doubt that the three-world system—the desire realm, form-realm, and formless realm—are mind only (*cittamātra*) and external objects (*bāhyārtha*) are only made by the mind. For Bhāviveka, a literal gloss of this citation falls foul of both the scriptural mainstream and common sense:

> It is not true that [in cognition] we apprehend mind only and do not apprehend material form and so forth. This thesis is contradicted by what has been accepted and also by common sense realism.[174]

A literal reading of the *Sūtra of Ten Grounds* would, for instance, negate the foundational scriptural claim that, depending on the form and visual faculty, visual consciousness arises. And it contradicts the bedrock common sense notion that cognition apprehending visible forms is impossible without visible forms to apprehend.

Yogācāra objects that both of the above fall foul of the empirical fact that consciousness of material form *does* arise in isolation from material forms (*artha*) itself, in dream states.[175] The Yogācāra argue that their example, the dream state, models cognition more accurately than common intuition can.

For Bhāviveka, the Yogācāra argument overstates the isolation of "dream consciousness" from real form. In fact, he says dream consciousness does have real *dharmas* as their intentional objects (*ālambana*)—their remembered impressions. Dream objects are simply the recycled impressions of real objects, previously seen and now remembered.[176] Accordingly, the Yogācāra probative reasoning example is void for not being accepted by both parties to the debate, and the probative argument as a whole, Bhāviveka says, "lacks an example and inappropriately denies object (*viṣaya*)."[177]

Having sketched the grounds for the division of the subschools, I will now discuss the individual schools in detail. First I take up the theory of the two truths of Sautrāntika-Svātantrika Madhdyamaka. The key figures for the Sautrāntika-Svātantrika Madhyamaka theory of two truths are Bhāviveka and his disciple Jñānagarbha. The two philosophers, though, stressed different aspects of the theory of the two truths and will be discussed separately.

BHĀVIVEKA

The cornerstones of the Sautrāntika-Svātantrika Madhyamaka theory of two truths are the following claims:

1) That *conventionally*, all phenomena are intrinsically real. They are established as such by the nonanalytical cognitions of ordinary beings. Allied to this thesis is Bhāviveka's claim

that the Madhyamaka must accept the intrinsic reality of things conventionally, since intrinsic reality itself constitutes conventional reality.

2) That *ultimately* all phenomena are intrinsically unreal with the exception of emptiness, which is ultimately real. They are established as empty of intrinsic reality from the perspective of *ārya*—exalted beings who have attained a direct realization of nonself and emptiness, and have consequently been freed from desire, anger, and confusion. Allied to this thesis is Bhāviveka's claim that the Madhyamaka must reject the intrinsic reality of things ultimately, since what is intrinsically unreal (i.e., empty) itself constitutes ultimate reality.

Conventional truth

We begin with Bhāviveka's definition of the conventional truth. In the *Blaze of Reasoning*,[178] he defines it as an "incontrovertible linguistic convention applied to every category of phenomena. It is a truth for it is the basis of everything that is epistemically warranted."[179] For Bhāviveka, such conventional truths take two forms: unique particulars and universals. He explains in the *Blaze of Reasoning*:

> Phenomena have [one of] two characteristics: they are universals or unique particulars. Unique particulars are a thing's intrinsic nature. They constitute the domain apprehended by nonconceptual cognition. Universals constitute the domain apprehended by inferential, conceptual cognition.[180]

The features of conventional truths that Bhāviveka lists here provide a useful comparison with the other philosophical schools. Three points are significant.

First, Bhāviveka accepts unique particulars as an integral part of the ontological structure of the conventional. In contrast, the Sautrāntika and Sārvastivāda proponents assert them as the ultimate truths, while the Prāsaṅgika treat them as false, both ultimately and conventionally.

Second, Bhāviveka attributes to the unique particular "intrinsic nature" or "inherent reality." For Bhāviveka, these natures are the fundaments of conventional reality. For the Sautrāntika and Sārvastivāda, intrinsically real unique particulars are the ultimate truths. For the Prāsaṅgika, as we shall see, intrinsic nature and inherent reality are not found in either the ultimate or conventional domain.

Third, Bhāviveka endorses the Sautrāntika's epistemology in which perception is by nature *nonconceptual* and therefore authoritative: it apprehends and verifies the conventional existence of the intrinsically real particulars. On the other hand, inference is *conceptual* and serves to apprehend unreal, but conceptually constructed universals. This epistemology is rejected by the Prāsaṅgika, who argue that, buddhas notwithstanding, perception *is* conceptual in character. The Prāsaṅgika also reject the assumption that perception need to be nonperceptual to be authoritative and argue that conceptually loaded perception can safely meets the epistemic demands of conventional truths.

I turn now to Bhāviveka's explanation of these three elements. First, Bhāviveka identifies "unique particular" with the five aggregates,[181] apprehended qualities (such as being blue, yellow, long, short), and sensory information (such as form and sound).[182] Unique particulars are irreducible, independent, and unconstructed with spatially, temporally, and ontologically specific locations. This category is intended to incorporate all phenomena except the universals (*sāmānyalakṣaṇa*), which, he says, include "impermanence, suffering, emptiness, nonself, and the like."[183] These are universals in the sense that produced phenomena universally share these ultimate characteristics. But this is not an exhaustive list of universals; Bhāviveka also uses the label "universal" in a manner similar to the Sautrāntika-logicians, in which the universals constitute the domain of conceptual or inferential cognition.

Second, conventionally speaking, things are intrinsically real even though they are not ultimately so. This claim is made explicitly and repeatedly in Bhāviveka's works.[184] For instance, I have already noted that this position can be deduced by his resolute use of the qualifier "ultimate" when negating claims of intrinsic reality. Bhāviveka concludes his critique of the Sāṃkhya's theory of self-causation by stating:

> The statements "that is self-existent" and "that is a thing" are conventionalities. That which arises from them [i.e., is conventionally self-produced] ultimately lacks intrinsic reality, for such a thing is [ultimately] neither produced from self, nor from another, nor from both, nor [produced] causelessly.[185]

In other instances, Bhāviveka makes the claim more directly. When asked if it is "not the case that the reality of things is just as it appears," he replies:

> That is the mode of the conventional truth. Its reality is its dependence upon intrinsic nature. But the other [ultimately real intrinsic nature] is excluded.[186]

Similarly, in *Verses on the Essence of the Middle Way*, Bhāviveka answers the claim that a denial of ultimately intrinsic production would be a denial of the posits of direct perception and common sense, saying:

> Because productions such as a vase appear to accord with the mind of ordinary beings, they are not negated. Hence the fallacies [of denying the objects of direct experience and the common sense conventions] are avoided.[187]

Bhāviveka expands on this in his *Blaze of Reasoning*.[188] The intrinsic arising of things such as a vase cannot be ultimately real since they cannot withstand critical analysis. Thus, from the perspective of the exalted cognition of noble beings, a perspective that accords with such analysis, "ultimately things neither arise from self nor from another, nor from both, nor do they arise causelessly. . . . Therefore [ultimately] there is no thing whatsoever."[189]

Still, from the conventional perspective—the nonanalytical cognition of ordinary beings—there certainly *are* things, and those things arise and exist intrinsically. Conventional truth applies where there is agreement between the things' mode of appearance, and the mode is perceived by such cognition. In other words, if a thing presents as intrinsically real, and it is ordinarily perceived as such, then it is a conventional truth that *it is* intrinsically real. That thing is also the legitimate domain of direct experience and common sense convention.

Another place where we find this claim being defended is in Bhāviveka's theory of causation, in particular in his refutation of the theory of causation from another. Bhāviveka says that denial of that theory doesn't contradict the Madhyamaka position that things arise from their objective condition (*ālambanapratyaya*, Tib. *dmigs rkyen*), dominant condition (*adhipatipratyaya*, Tib. *bdag rkyen*), immediate condition (*samanantarapratyaya*, Tib. *de ma thag rkyen*), and causal condition (*hetupratyaya*, Tib. *rgyu rkyen*).[190] "This is because," according to Bhāviveka, "the arising from other conditions and so forth is a merely conventional discourse. Thus it does not undermine the thesis. Such arising is not ultimate."[191] The Mādhyamika is not a nihilist on Bhāviveka's account precisely because he accepts the conventional reality of all phenomenal processes as they appear—that is, intrinsically.[192]

Their extremely robust defense of the conventional does not detract from or conflict with the Svātantrika's position on the ultimate, Bhāviveka says, for two reasons. First, the claim that conventionally things are intrinsically real does not clash with the claim that ultimately things are not intrinsically real, because each claim is domain-specific. Since the two claims refer to separate cognitive domains, they are incapable of negating each other.

Second, the ultimate reality of emptiness is not undercut by conventional reality's accordance with direct perception, inference, and mundane convention. A direct perception does not undermine the ultimate status of emptiness because the objects it perceives are ultimately "unreal." They are so because the instruments of perception—the sensory organs—are blunt instruments, notoriously prone to error. Bhāviveka reminds us of such errors, for instance, the miniscule "floaters" suspended in the eye's vitreous humor that are perceived as substantial objects descending from the sky. More importantly though, even when they are operating at peak accuracy, they are still incapable of accessing the ultimate single-handedly. It is the nature of sense organs to engage with their respective objects "naively" and nonanalytically, and it is the nature of the ultimate truth to only reveal itself under refined critical analysis.

An inferential cognition does not undermine the ultimate status of emptiness, for the inferred emptiness is only a conceptual reflection of emptiness, not a direct understanding of emptiness. In the same way, mundane convention does not undermine the ultimate status of emptiness because it too is sequestered in the conventional and disqualified from commenting on it. The world is blinded by the cataract of confusion, and common sense may be useful in navigating *within* that confusion, but it has no role in extinguishing it. It is rather extinguished by the critical analysis that leads to the ultimate truth. In this task mundane convention is unqualified and to be disregarded, in the same way that the blind are unqualified to visually appraise a precious stone.[193] Hence, for Bhāviveka, the simultaneous commitment to conventional theses and eschewal of an ultimate thesis is entirely consistent.[194]

Nevertheless, domain-specific as they are, the two truths nevertheless relate. The knowledge of conventional truth is a proper mundane cognition, which is a precondition to knowledge of the ultimate truth.[195] For Bhāviveka, the relationship between the two is immutable: knowledge of the ultimate truth, as different as it is, nevertheless depends on the conventional. In *Verses on the Essence of the Middle Way*, he writes:

> Were it not for the ladder of real conventionalities, it would be impossible for [even] the competent to arrive at the grand mansion of the ultimate reality. . . . This being so, [the categories of conventional truth] are explained this way.[196]

Having examined Bhāviveka's justification of the first two claims—that unique particulars are the fundamentals of conventional reality, and that conventional reality is intrinsically real—we turn to the third. The final aspect of Bhāviveka's theory of the conventional is his embrace of the Sautrāntika's *pramāṇa*—or epistemology. This position argues that raw perception is always nonconceptual and its objects always unique particulars, as summarized by Bhāviveka in the *Blaze of Reasoning*: "Since perception is defined as nonconceptual, it is not involved with conception and memory."[197] Bhāviveka sees no problem whatsoever in synthesizing the emptiness ontology of the Madhyamaka with the foundationalist epistemology of the Sautrāntika, in claiming that perception is invariably nonconceptual and that its object must necessarily be unique particulars.

In short, we have seen that Bhāviveka's position on conventional truth is a three-way equation between conventional truth, intrinsic nature, and unique particulars. For him the arbiter of conventional truth is an accord between a thing's manner of appearance and the manner it is perceived by ordinary nonanalytical cognition. It is due to the fact that things are intrinsically real that they appear to ordinary perception, and they become a reality—a *conventional* reality—for that perceiver. It is therefore the unique particular's quality of "intrinsic nature" that, for Bhāviveka, makes conventional reality a reality at all. What is excluded, though, is *ultimate intrinsic reality*.[198] For while intrinsic reality is verified by ordinary perception—the arbiter of the conventional—it is unfindable under analysis—the arbiter of the ultimate.

In his definition of the conventional truth, one of Bhāviveka's overwhelming philosophical motives is to avoid the charge of nihilism, to which he feels the Madhyamaka would otherwise be vulnerable. To deny the intrinsic reality of conventional things is tantamount, he says, to a wholesale denial of conventionality. After all, to deny intrinsic reality would deprive conventional reality of the very bases of its existence—unique particulars possessed of intrinsic nature. He says:

> The Lord has taught the two truths. Based on this, conventionally things are posited in terms of their intrinsic natures and [unique] particulars. It is only ultimately that [things are] posited as having no intrinsic nature.[199]

By preserving intrinsic nature in the conventional domain, Bhāviveka argues, the conventional domain is itself preserved—as are the direct perception and worldly convention that perceive and govern it. The preservation of intrinsic nature in one domain—the conventional—and its simultaneous prohibition in another—the ultimate—is Bhāviveka's solution to a problem that has vexed many Madhyamaka philosophers, which is how to and how far to prosecute the deconstructive dialectic without descending into outright nihilism. This compromise position is the distinctive stance of the Svāntantrika subschool that Bhāviveka is credited to have founded.

Ultimate truth

I turn now to Bhāviveka's position on ultimate truth, which is that all phenomena are intrinsically unreal. Bhāviveka's *Blaze of Reasoning* identifies the ultimate truth with the compound word *paramārtha*, with which we are already acquainted, and which literally means "highest or ultimate object." *Paramārtha* can be understood in either of three ways, Bhāviveka says. It is either

1) an object that is to be known, which means to be analyzed and understood; or
2) the object of the ultimate, because it is the object of ultimate nonconceptual cognition; or
3) the cognition that accords with knowledge of the ultimate. The ultimate domain presents itself as the object of such cognition.[200]

Thus Bhāviveka offers three ways to read *paramārtha*: the first focuses on the ultimate object, the third its cognition, and the second both. According to the first, both the terms "ultimate" (*param*) and "domain" (*artha*) refer to emptiness (*śūnyatā*), which is not just *an* object of knowledge, but the ultimate object of knowledge. According to the second, the components have separate referents: *artha* refers to emptiness while *param* refers to the exalted nonconceptual cognition attained in meditative equipoise. According to the third, both terms refer to a concordant ultimate, a cognition that has the ultimate as its object and is in accord with the ultimate truth.

Each sense emphasizes the ultimacy of emptiness. Bhāviveka's *Wisdom Lamp* commentary on chapter 24, verse 8 of Nāgārjuna's *Fundamental Verses on the Middle Way* explains that emptiness is the ultimate for multiple reasons.

First, emptiness is beyond the reach of language; it is independent of concepts and the words that mark them. Bhāviveka argues that language and concepts are constructions, and so their use is only valid in the domain of the constructed—the conventional domain. Ultimate reality, since it is not constructed, remains beyond the limit of words and concepts, which necessarily are constructed.

Second, emptiness itself remains *constantly* as it is, even though empty phenomena are momentary instants. Being the final status of things, it must be *apart* from the dynamic of flux that regulates the conventional world because it is itself apart from the conventional. In our discussions of previous schools, we have seen that time and causality are not absolutes, but conventions usefully applied to relations between chains of moments and similar momentary events. We cannot expect the ultimate reality of things to heed such conventions, and Bhāviveka argues it does not. It is free from these concepts and the related concepts of arising, enduring, and ceasing. Though conventionally everything remains in flux, emptiness, which is the ultimate nature of everything that fluctuates, remains the same. All are empty, and that emptiness neither arises nor ceases.

Third, emptiness is the domain of the ultimate nonconceptual cognition by way of *not* being an object, in that it is perceived only in the negative. It must not be a positive object for the cognition that apprehends it, since emptiness is simply the absence of the conventions by which objects are ordinarily formed. To apprehend emptiness is precisely to understand that these conventions—whether they be temporal, dimensional, visual, auditory, tactile, or of any other variety—are just conventions, and the object they construct together does not exist aside from that construction. It is in this way that the emptiness acts as the basis for its cognition by *not* being an object. Since emptiness is the very absence of concepts, it is naturally the object of cognition in which concepts are similarly absent. Bhāviveka refers to such a cognition as the "exalted nonconceptual cognition." Such a cognition is entirely reliable, Bhāviveka says, and can itself be equated with the ultimate.[201]

But the ultimate is not the exclusive preserve of nonconceptual thought. Recall Bhāviveka's third description of the ultimate, as "the cognition that accords with knowledge of the ultimate. The ultimate domain presents itself as the object of such cognition."[202] Exalted nonconceptual cognition is such a cognition, but it is not the only such cognition. Bhāviveka includes conceptual cognition that accords with the ultimate: a "concordant ultimate." Conceptual thought, even though it may not directly engage the ultimate truth, may still *accord* with it. So, a concordant ultimate truth, for Bhāviveka, is a *conceptual* cognition that directly follows from nonconceptual meditative equipoise—technically, a "cognition of subsequent attainment" (*pṛṣṭhalabdhajñāna*, Tib. *rjes thob ye shes*). Bhāviveka argues that a conceptual knowledge of emptiness derived from hearing, reflection, and meditation still accords with nonconceptual knowledge of the ultimate reality even though, with the exception of the last, none of those three activities may be anything but conceptual. He argues that such a cognition nevertheless has the ultimate truth of emptiness as its intentional object, and argues that nonconceptual awareness of emptiness has conceptual awareness of emptiness as its causal condition.[203]

From this discussion we may conclude that for Bhāviveka the ultimate is of two kinds. The first kind is transcendent, undefiled, and free from elaboration. Accordingly, it is engaged without a deliberative effort. This corresponds to the exalted "nonconceptual cognition." The second kind, he explains in the *Blaze of Reasoning* is elaborative and may be engaged with the deliberative effort of a correct mundane cognition sustained by the collective force of moral virtues and insights.[204] This corresponds to the "concordant ultimate," the conceptual cognition that has emptiness as its intentional object and whose understanding accords with the ultimate truth of emptiness.

Let us now turn to the major argument with which Bhāviveka advances his position on the ultimate truth—that all things are empty of intrinsic reality. This we can call the "conditionality argument." According to it, if intrinsic reality is to be found, it must be found in the four elements of which all things are composed. But it cannot be—each element is empty of intrinsic reality since it is conditioned by the causal factors necessary for their coming into existence. As Bhāviveka says in the *Verses on the Essence of the Middle Way*:

> [Ultimately the] earth [element] is not inherently solid because it is an element like air. Cohesiveness does not indicate solidity because earth is conditioned like liquid [and all other elements].[205]

Each single element, Bhāviveka further argues in the *Blaze of Reasoning*, is conditioned by *all* elements. The earth element, for instance, is an amalgam of atomic particles of each of the other elements, and the functions of solidity, moisture, heat or maturation, and mobility are contributed by the elements of which they are characteristic (earth, water, fire, and air, respectively). We have previously observed that this conception of atomic construction dates back to the Sarvāstivāda school, though it was the schools that followed that fully prosecuted the implications of such a construction—that is, that anything so constructed could not be *ultimate*. As Bhāviveka notes, so totally intertwined with each other, the identity of the individual elements collapses under analysis and cannot be established ultimately.[206] He explains that the earth element can be no more analytically separated from its subcomponents than a forest from its trees:

> Apart from the collective parts such as its moisture, the so-called "earth" element is not apprehended, and that which cannot be apprehended without apprehending its collective parts cannot be a foundational substance. This is like a forest. The so-called "forest" cannot be apprehended without apprehending specific trees. . . . The name "forest" is only appropriate to a collection [of trees].[207]

We would be ill-advised to search within those subcomponents for the intrinsic reality they deny the whole. The process repeats. The atomic particles of which the elements are composed are themselves revealed as composites. In Bhāviveka's reckoning,

> each [atom] is composed of the eight substances—earth, water, fire, air, form, smell, taste, and tactility, none of which have characteristics or functions that show their individuality to be intrinsically real and [specifically] functional.[208]

The same things we saw Bhāviveka accept as intrinsically real *conventionally* he shows to be without a shard of intrinsic reality *ultimately*. Produced and composite, from the ultimate analytical perspective the elements and their atoms are disqualified as self-contained unique particulars.[209] Thus, from the ultimate perspective, all things are nonintrinsic, nonsubstantial, and nonfoundational.

It is just as well that they are so, Bhāviveka argues, because were the elements and atoms possessed of intrinsic reality, they would be condemned to stasis:

> Because intrinsic nature is not causally conditioned and because it is fixed, nothing could ever alter its status to something else.[210]

And, since the elements are the basis of all existence, the entire field of existence would also be static. This would be an indefensible claim, since it is empirically not the case. The universe is observably dynamic. The fact is that all the things composed by the elements are productive and are subject to change. That that is the case, Bhāviveka says, is a function of their ultimate lack of intrinsic reality.

This argument is a very intentional rejection of the foundationalist ontology favored by some Hindu and Buddhist schools, in which atoms possessed of intrinsic reality are the foundational entities upon which all other ontological structures stand. Within Buddhism, this is a rejection of the Ābhidharmika ontology, in which the atoms of the five elements are considered logically and physically irreducible, and so ultimately real. They may indeed be reduced, Bhāviveka says, and so may not be considered ultimately real.

Bhāviveka's next concern is to press the epistemological implications of this position. Foundationalist ontology, we have seen, is typically used to underwrite a foundationalist epistemology. The Nyāya and the Sautrāntika proponents are both epistemologists (*pramāṇavādins*) who, for instance, posit an epistemic model in which certain faculties are *foundational*—objective, self-warranting, and the foundation for all other epistemic activity.

For Bhāviveka, because the objects—elements such as earth—are nonfoundational entities, the subjects—the cognition that apprehends them—must also be nonfoundational. The apprehension of objects, Bhāviveka reasons, can hardly possess the unified reality the objects lack. Therefore, ultimately, no object can be regarded as a domain of cognition.

Bhāviveka presses this argument in a variety of forms. First, he presses from the side of the object that is cognized. Objects, he says, fail to be an ultimate domain of cognition because they are composite and produced:

> Visible form is not ultimately apprehended by the visual faculty because it is a composite, like sound. [Likewise] sound is not ultimately apprehended by the hearing faculty because it is a composite, like form.[211]

The *Blaze of Reasoning* unpacks these arguments as follows:

> Thesis: A visual form that is the object of the visual faculty is not *ultimately apprehended* by the visual faculty
>
> Reasons: because it is (1) a composite, as a visible form is composed of the eight substances, and it is (2) a product of the elements,
>
> Example: like a sound.

If this argument is valid, so is the following:

> Thesis: A sound that is the object of auditory faculty is not ultimately apprehended by the auditory faculty
> Reason: (1) because it is a composite and (2) because it is a product of the elements,
> Example: like a visual object.

If it is true that these arguments are valid on account of their subjects being composites and products, then no foundationalist thesis can apply to composite or produced things. Such things cannot be an ultimate domain of cognition. Therefore the two arguments above are not valid grounds to prove the foundationalist thesis that a visible form is ultimately apprehended by the visual faculty. The two arguments would equally fail to warrant the validity of the foundationalist thesis that a sound is ultimately apprehended by the hearing faculty.[212]

Next, Bhāviveka presses his argument from the side of the apprehending cognitions. Cognitions, like the objects they cognize, fall short of ultimacy because they are *causal processes*. The argument proceeds as follows:

> Thesis: The subjects—cognitions apprehending the elements such as the earth—are not the ultimate
> Reasons: because (1) they are causal phenomena and (2) they are subject to cessation,
> Example: like the elements, such as the earth, which are not ultimate entities.[213]

Here, two reasons are provided. In the first case, cognitions lack ultimacy for arising only from their causal conditions, just as the cognition of the forest arises only with the apprehension of the constituent trees. In the second, cognitions lack ultimacy for ceasing to exist in the absence of their causal conditions, just as the cognition of the forest ceases after its constituent trees have been felled.

Next, Bhāviveka attacks the faculties of apprehension. These, he argues, fall demonstrably short of the independent function required of something ultimate. He explains:

> The visual faculty does not ultimately see the visible form. For it is different from the mind and mental factors, like the faculty [apprehending] a mountain.[214]

In the *Blaze of Reasoning*, he explains the verse as follows:

> Thesis: The visual faculty does not ultimately see the visible form
>
> Reason: because it is different from the mind and mental factors,
>
> Example: like the faculty apprehending a mountain.[215]

Here he argues that the visual faculty cannot *ultimately* be the agent of seeing. Were it ultimately, which is to say independently, capable of seeing the visible, it would do so at all times—during sleep, madness, death—and regardless of whether objects are obscured by darkness or distance. But it is not the case that the visual faculty functions persistently and consistently and does so uniformly. Absent certain conditions, it cannot see. Under certain conditions, it can. Since its function is regulated by conditions, it cannot be the foundation of perception; as Bhāviveka states, the "visual faculty does not ultimately see the visible form."

One might respond by proposing consciousness is that which sees. But were it so, Bhāviveka replies, one would be forced to conclude that the blind would see on account of their consciousness.

Were one to instead respond that mental consciousness is that which sees when accompanied by functional sense organs, then one has already conceded the point that the response is intended to defend—that is, that the perceptive faculty is, independently and ultimately, the agent of perception.

The visual faculty alone is not, in fact, such an agent, for the act of seeing is collaborative: it is conditioned by the appropriation of the visible form, light, space, mental engagement with the object, and so on. A response that acknowledges this, such as "the visual faculty associated with the consciousness sees"—which by definition concedes ultimacy—is accepted as the conventional truth, Bhāviveka says.[216]

What is it, then, that perceives the ultimate? Something, it turns out, quite distinct from the ordinary components of perception. Bhāviveka's *Verses on the Essence of the Middle Way* states:

> What brings about a complete cessation of the web of conceptions is stillness, direct perception, and freedom from conception and linguistic expression. The knowledge that discerns the ultimate domain engages with it without engaging—neither identifying with it nor differentiating from it. Like space, it is stainless.[217]

In the *Blaze of Reasoning*, Bhāviveka explains that ultimate reality entails a complete cessation of the web of conceptions. The ultimate reality of things is reality absent conceptual binaries such as permanence and impermanence, existence and nonexistence, static and dynamic, annihilation and eternity, and so on. "Stillness" thus represents the transcendent silence of the ultimate reality beyond the discursive maze of conceptual elaborations. It is in this stillness that we come face-to-face with ultimate reality as a domain of direct perception.

Ultimate reality is free from "conceptions and linguistic expressions" since it cannot be contained within conceptual thought and utterances. These are contrived for practical purposes—to divide and demarcate the field of experience—but the ultimate reality is uncontrived and indivisible. Like stainless space, reality is expressible neither in terms of identity, nor in terms of difference, nor both, nor neither.[218]

Given the nature of ultimate reality, the cognition that discerns the ultimate domain, Bhāviveka says, "engages with its domain without engaging it," since there is no appearance of the intentional object with which it is engaged. In fact, "not seeing itself constitutes the seeing," he says.[219]

I began my discussion of Bhāviveka's position on the two truths by noting his school's methodological differences with the Prāsaṅgika.

As I conclude our discussion of Bhāviveka's thought, we can see how the Svātantrika methodological position neatly signals its wider philosophical project. We read in *Verses on the Essence of the Middle Way*:

> In this context there is ultimately no intrinsic production of the earth [element] and so forth because, like consciousness, they are conditioned and causal.[220]

Here, Bhāviveka's qualifying terms, "ultimate" and "intrinsic," represent the two Svātantrika theses: that intrinsic nature is the conventional reality and its absence the ultimate reality. His simultaneous use of these two qualifying terms is a product of the Svātantrika school's simultaneous affirmation of intrinsic reality in the conventional domain and its negation of it in the ultimate. This is the Svātantrika's signature position, and upon it the entire Svātantrika ontology and epistemology stand.

JÑĀNAGARBHA

In the late seventh and early eighth century Bhāviveka's conception of the two truths flourished in the work of three important figures often known as the "eastern trio": Jñānagarbha (ca. 700–760), Śāntarakṣita (725–788), and Kamalaśīla (ca. 740–795).

Jñānagarbha followed Bhāviveka's Sautrāntika-Svātantrika Madhyamaka line with only minor variations, whereas Śāntarakṣita and Kamalaśīla's deviations from that position gave rise to the second Svātantrika subschool, the Yogācāra-Svātantrika Madhyamaka, which will be the subject of the following chapter. As we shall note, where the Sautrāntika-Svātantrika fuse the epistemological realism of the Sautrāntika with Madhyamaka's nonfoundational ontology, the Yogācāra-Svātantrika fuse the epistemological idealism of the Yogācāra with Madhymaka ontology.

Jñānagarbha composed *Distinguishing the Two Truths* (*Satyadvayavibhaṅgakārikā*) and the *Commentary on Distinguishing the Two*

Truths (*Satyadvayavibhaṅgavṛtti*). In these works, he argues that the two truths satisfy three criteria. The first, according to Jñānagarbha's *Distinguishing the Two Truths*, is that conventional truth is that which appears to be real, while ultimate truth is the unreality of that which appears:

> The Sage taught the two truths: conventional and ultimate. That which corresponds to appearances is conventional [truth] whereas the other [i.e., ultimate truth] is its opposite.[221]

Glossing this verse in his autocommentary, Jñānagarbha argues that anything that appears, regardless of whether it appears to an ordinary or noble being, is conventionally real. Conventional reality is "conceived in accordance with the way in which things appear."[222] But that surface reality, according to Śāntarakṣita's *Commentary on the Difficult Points of Distinguishing the Two Truths* (*Satyadvayavibhaṅgapañjikā*), has no basis in reason, and critical analysis quickly ascertains its ultimate unreality.[223] Ultimate truth is simply the apprehension of that unreality. It is in this sense ultimate truth is the reverse, or the opposite, of conventional reality. Ultimate truth, the truth that can withstand critical analysis, is simply not the truth that cannot withstand critical analysis—namely, conventional appearance.

The second criteria is that conventional truth is deceptive and contradictory, while ultimate truth is neither deceptive nor contradictory. Conventional truth is deceptive and contradictory, Jñānagarbha says, because:

> [ultimately] the way in which things appear does not correspond to the way they exist since they do not appear at all . . . to [all-knowing] cognition.[224]

Jñānagarbha argues that were the appearance of a thing to correspond to its ultimate reality, then it would also have to correspond to the cognition that apprehends that reality—the cognition of an enlightened being. In fact, appearance is never the object of cognition of such a being. That it is not, therefore, indicates its ultimate unreality. Since an enlightened cognition "directly knows what exists and what does not exist," he says, "if it does not see a thing, the nature of that thing should be carefully scrutinized."[225] It is for this reason, Jñānagarbha says, that the sūtras state that "to not see anything is seeing reality itself."[226] The fact that appearance fails to arise as an object of enlightened cognition betrays its lack of ultimate reality.

Ultimate truth, by contrast, is neither deceptive nor contradictory, Jñānagarbha says, because it accords with reason:

> It is nondeceptive. Reason is an ultimate [truth], not a conventional [truth], because [conventional truth] deceives, it is real just as it appears.[227]

Reasoning is not a conventional truth because reasoning cannot be deceived. Deception, we have repeatedly observed, is a function of unthinking, intuitive perception[228]—precisely because such perception is divorced from reason. Perception in accord with reason, on the other hand, ascertains the ultimate reality that the same perception divorced from reason obscures. Reason that ascertains reality as it is, for Jñānagarbha, is the very definition of ultimate truth:

> That which is ultimately real is the ultimate truth, for it is the truth verified by a rational cognition. Ultimate truth is the nondeceptive reason, for the reality ascertained through the power of reasoning cognition never deceives. Therefore a cognition produced by the means of the triple criterion of reasoning is the ultimate truth as it is [both] "ultimate" as well as the "domain." The domain that reason ascertains is also an ultimate truth, just as a perception [can be either a cognition or an object].[229]

Jñānagarbha, like all other Buddhist epistemologists after Dharmakīrti, has held that reason is valid when it satisfies three criteria:

1) the *pakṣa dharmatā* (Tib. *phyogs chos*), the fact that the reason qualifies the subject or thesis;
2) the *anvayavyāpti* (Tib. *rjes khyab*), or the reason's occurrence in only "similar instances" (*sapakṣa*, Tib. *mthun phyogs*); and
3) the *vyatirekavyāpti* (Tib. *ldog khyab*), the reason's complete absence from "dissimilar instances" (*vipakṣa*, Tib. *mthun phyogs*).

Similar instances are those examples that are similar to the subject in possessing the property to be proved. Similar instances, however, cannot be identical with the subject. That means sound is not a similar instance for proving sound's ultimate truth, but a reason is, according to Jñānagarbha. Similar instances are all those items that have the property to be proven, with the exception of the subject.

Dissimilar instances are all those examples that do not possess a property to be proven. Similar instances and dissimilar instances are also known as, respectively, "homologous example" (*sādhyadharmyaḍṛṣṭānta*, Tib. *sgrub bya'i chos dang mthun phyogs kyi dpe*) and "heterologous example" (*vaidharmyaḍṛṣṭānta*, Tib. *sgrub bya'i chos dang mi mthun pa'i dpe*). On the basis of these, the reason's occurrence in only "similar instances" and the reason's complete absence from "dissimilar instances" are established. We can characterize similar instances and dissimilar instances as follows: For all *x*, *x* is a *similar instance* for proving sound's ultimate truth if and only if *x* is an ultimate truth. For all *x*, *x* is a dissimilar instance for proving sound's ultimate truth if and only if *x* is not an ultimate truth.

Let us turn now to Jñānagarbha's third criterion, which is that conventional truth cannot be analyzed since it does not withstand deductive reasoning, while ultimate truth can be analyzed since it does withstand such reasoning. To understand why Jñānagarbha holds the conventional to be unanalyzable requires that we understand Jñānagarbha's distinction between the two types of conventional truths—*real* and *unreal* conventional truths. Jñānagarbha's *Distinguishing the Two Truths* explains:

> Though alike in the way in which it appears, conventional [truth] is subdivided into *real* and *unreal* conventionalities on the basis of their causal efficacy or inefficiency.[230]

The autocommentary explains that conventional truths are alike in their actuality—that is, their lack of ultimately intrinsic reality—and the manner in which they appear to mundane cognitions. Nonetheless, they may be distinguished according to their causal efficacy. *Real* conventional truths are nondeceptive because their causal function corresponds to their appearance. They fulfill the functions their appearances advertise. *Unreal* conventional truths, on the other hand, are deceptive because their causal function and appearance contradict. They fail to fulfill the functions of their advertized appearance. Whether they are real or unreal with regard to causally efficiency is a matter of common sense agreement.

Let us illustrate the division between real and unreal conventional truths. Water is a real conventional truth. It appears to be water and efficiently functions as water. It is wet, transparent, liquid, and satiates thirst. A mirage, on the other hand, is an unreal conventional truth. It is conventionally deceptive, for though it appears to be water, it lacks all of water's relevant causal functions.[231]

To qualify as a real conventional truth, or a "mere thing," Jñānagarbha argues, requires satisfying four criteria—two prescriptive, two proscriptive: (1) to not be conceptually imagined, (2) to be dependently arisen,[232] (3) to be causally effective, and (4) to not be analyzable.[233] I will address each in turn.

To not be conceptually imagined

A real conventional truth cannot be an imaginary phenomenon. "Imaginary phenomena" (*kalpitārtha*, Tib. *brtags pa'i don*) is an umbrella term for conceptually constructed entities that violate the basic fundaments of Madhyamaka philosophy. They include ultimately real elements; the ultimately real arising, real cessation, and real continuation proclaimed by the Hindus and Ābhidharmikas; the ultimately real consciousness proclaimed by the Yogācāra; and the primal matter (*pradhāna*) proclaimed by the Sāṃkhya. For Jñānagarbha, all these imaginary objects fail to attain even conventional reality, much less ultimate reality. For something to be a real conventional truth (i.e., a "mere thing") thus requires that it not be such an imaginary object.[234]

Imaginary phenomena are described as "conceptually imagined"[235] because, for Jñānagarbha, anything believed to possess ultimate reality *can* only be a figment of the philosophical imagination. Ultimately real entities *do not appear* to us, and so they must be imagined. The very fact that there is disagreement between philosophical schools, Jñānagarbha says, is evidence of this fact. If such objects were directly perceived, there would be no disagreement between different philosophical schools, for neither the proponent nor the opponent could dispute that direct perception.[236]

Thus, such phenomena imagined to exist ultimately fail both the ultimate standard of critical analysis, since critical analysis finds only the absence of ultimate reality,[237] *and* the mundane standard of appearance, since they are philosophical posits that can be debated but never observed. In this way, they are unreal conventions.[238]

To be dependently arisen

A real conventional truth is a dependently arisen phenomenon, which comes into existence on account of a constellation of causes and conditions.[239] Ultimately real substances of time, space, ether, the self, and mind, as proclaimed by Nyāya-Vaiśeṣika; pure consciouness (*puruṣa*) and the primal matter (*pradhāna*), as proclaimed by the Sāṁkhya; the Brahman and ātman of the Vedānta; the indivisible atomic particles and consciousness moments of the Vaibhāṣika and Sautrāntika; and the foundational consciousness of the Yogacāra are all imaginary objects and do not exist even conventionally because none of them dependently arise. They are claimed to exist.

To be causally efficacious

A real conventional truth, or "mere thing," is causally efficacious, according to Jñānagarbha. It is able to effectively fulfill its advertised function, which is to say its behavior is consistent with its appearance in the mundane cognitions of all ordinary beings.[240] Ultimately real substances of time, space, ether, the self, and mind, as proclaimed by Nyāya-Vaiśeṣika; the pure consciousness (*puruṣa*) and primal matter (*pradhāna*) proclaimed by the Sāṁkhya; the Brahman and ātman of the Vedānta; the indivisible atomic particles and consciousness moments of the Vaibhāṣika and Sautrāntika; and the foundational consciousness of the Yogacāra: all are metaphysical entities, and none of these are causally efficacious since they are eternal and unchanging substances. This conclusion follows because whatever is causally efficacious must necessarily be subjected to change, according to the changing nature of causes and conditions, and yet these metaphysical entities are held to be noncausal entities.

To be unanalyzable

Finally, Jñānagarbha says a conventional truth "cannot be subjected to critical analysis, for its identity is derived from its appearance but, when analyzed, it contradicts itself by turning out to be something else."[241]

For the Madhyamaka, we have seen, conventional reality is simply a function of surface appearance. It is therefore inappropriate for us to subject conventional truth to the critical analysis that searches for substance below that surface. According to Śāntarakṣita's *Commentary on the Difficult Points of Distinguishing the Two Truths*, the specific "critical analysis"[242] at issue here is that discussed in verse 14 of *Distinguishing the Two Truths*.[243] Such critical analysis asks questions of the following order: Is the cognition of conventional reality an effect produced by many causes or one cause? Is conventional reality apprehended by cognition that has the representation of its object? The answers to such questions are plainly irrelevant to conventional discourses, hence real conventional truth must remain unanalyzed.[244]

If a conventional truth is nevertheless subjected to analysis, its truth status is quickly destabilized. Though it appears to be real, analysis exposes its ultimate unreality. Conventional truth corresponds to appearances, but not to reason. In the domain of appearances, conventional truth *is* true, but reason exposes the fraud of appearance, the ultimate untruth of all conventionalities. It is for this reason, according to Jñānagarbha, that the Mādhyamika does not analyze conventional truth.[245]

I will conclude with two final points on Jñānagarbha's theory of the two truths: the conventionality of the conventional and the conventionality of the ultimate.

The conventionality of the conventional

According to this argument there is no real basis for any conventional truth. All conventional truths are mere designations, Jñānagarbha says:

> The [real] basis of the designations does not appear anywhere to anyone. Even trees and so forth do not depend on a real basis.[246]

The example of a tree demonstrates how the search for a basis to designation is interminable. The layman designates "tree" on the basis of its major components—the trunk, branches, leaves, roots, and so forth. For the botanist, those components are crude markers designated on the strength of *their* components. A leaf, for instance, is designated on the basis of its epidermis, veins, and mesophyll, each of which can be further technically divided. For the chemist, the botanists' designations are themselves crude, and even the most precise botanical designation can be reduced to its component atomic and subatomic particles. The physicist would be inclined to similarly reduce the chemists' designations, and so on.

Jñānagarbha takes the analysis to the level of the atomic particles (*paramāṇu*, Tib. *rdul phran*) and determines that, for reasons identical to those advanced by Bhāviveka, atomic particles are themselves baseless. Madhyamaka, Jñānagarbha says, holds conventional truth only to be consistent with appearances and not to depend on any real basis or cause.[247] That conventional designations are thus without a real basis is precisely their point. Were they to have a real basis, they wouldn't be conventional at all—they would be ultimately real.

Since there is no real basis for conventionality, it must be a superimposition, and superimposed by shared ignorance. Jñānagarbha argues that, etymologically, *saṃvṛti* ("conventionality") means "either that by which or that *in* which reality is concealed."[248] In his commentary, Jñāngarbha explains that conventional truth is a type of cognitive error that conceals reality—the emptiness of intrinsic nature—in plain sight.[249] In support, he cites the *Descent into Laṅkā Sūtra*,[250] which says that things that arise conventionally are ultimately empty of intrinsic nature, and so their source is a cognition that fails to grasp the emptiness of intrinsic nature and reifies emptiness or that which is empty as existing intrinsically.[251] Since there is no basis otherwise, were it not for erroneous cognition, ordinary beings would not conceive of real entities at all. It is mistaken cognition that gives rise to the real entities about which we agree. In other words, consensus that comes from common sense agreement is evidence not of a common correctness, but of a common cognitive defect.

The conventionality of the ultimate

Jñāngarbha goes so far as to argue that even the so-called "ultimate" is also only a conventionality. He deploys two arguments in support of this claim. The first is that "ultimate statements" are self-defeating because they only make sense conventionally. For instance:

> The meaning of the statement "ultimately [things] do not arise" also does not arise from the ultimate stand-

> point of reason, and the same principle applies to all other statements.[252]

Statements about the ultimate truth are empty of ultimate truth. They can be deconstructed just as easily and totally as everything else, such as the things about which they make claims (arising, nonarising, and so on). Thus, "ultimate statements" are empty from the ultimate perspective of reason, and the same principle applies to the ultimate perspective. *Everything* is empty, including the reason itself.[253]

Jñānagarbha's second argument stresses the identity of the conventional and the ultimate:

> Whatever is the reality of the conventional is itself considered [by the Buddha] as the meaning of the ultimate, for they are not distinct. Reason corresponds to the way of its appearance.[254]

It is for this reason, Jñānagarbha says, that the Buddha stated:

> O Subhūti, the mundane convention is not one thing and the ultimate another. The reality of mundane convention is identical in nature to the reality of the ultimate.[255]

In other words, for Jñānagarbha, reason—the ultimate truth—corresponds to the way of its appearance—the conventional truth. Just as appearances "appear" strictly as conventional phenomena, so does reason *appear* and *function* strictly as a conventional phenomenon. It cannot appear and function any other way.

This follows because, according to Jñānagarbha, reason is probative, and the components of the argument—the subject, property, example, reason of an inference, and the property to be inferred—are things that *appear* to the minds of the parties to an argument.[256] Reason cannot function in a vacuum; it is *applied* to things that appear. It is appearance, Jñānagarbha says, that establishes the components of the probative argument for both parties and makes subsequent inquiries into their ultimacy possible.[257] Here again, we see the ontological implications of the Svātantrika's methodological position.

CONCLUSION

Bhāviveka's position on ultimate truth, which rejects all forms of foundationalism at the ultimate level, is that all phenomena are ultimately intrinsically unreal (*niḥsvabhāvataḥ*) and that emptiness is the ultimate truth on the ground of four reasons cited in the *Wisdom Lamp* (24.8): (1) emptiness is beyond the reach of language; (2) emptiness itself remains *constantly* as it is, even though empty phenomena are momentary instants; (3) emptiness is the domain of the nonconceptual exalted cognition by way of *not* being any object in particular and perceived only in the negative; and (4) a conceptual knowledge of emptiness still accords with nonconceptual knowledge of the ultimate reality even though, with the exception of the last, none of those three activities may be anything but conceptual.

The major argument with which Bhāviveka advances his nonfoundationalism on the level of ultimate truth—that all things are ultimately empty of intrinsic reality—is the *conditionality argument*. According to this argument, if intrinsic reality is to be found ultimately, it must be found in the four elements of which all things are composed. But it cannot be—each element is empty of intrinsic reality since it is conditioned by the causal factors necessary for them to come into existence.

This argument intentionally rejects the foundationalist ontology ultimately favored by some Indian and Buddhist realist schools, in which atoms possessed of intrinsic nature, which are the foundational entities, are claimed to be the ultimate realities upon which all other ontological structures stand. Foundationalist ontology, we have seen, is typically used to underwrite a foundationalist epistemology. The Nyāya and Sautrāntika, for instance, posit an epistemic model in which certain faculties are *foundational*—objective, self-warranting, and the foundation for all other epistemic activity.

For Bhāviveka, because the objects—elements such as the earth—are ultimately nonfoundational entities, the subjects—cognitions that apprehend them—must also be ultimately nonfoundational. The apprehension of objects, he reasons, can hardly possess the unified reality the objects lack. Therefore ultimately no object can be regarded as a domain of cognition.

Jñānagarbha follows Bhāviveka's Sautrāntika-Svātantrika Madhyamaka line without much variation, although his style, language, and emphasis are quite different. He argues that the two truths satisfy three criteria: (1) conventional truth is that which appears to be real, while ultimate truth is the unreality of that which appears; (2) conventional truth is deceptive and contradictory, while ultimate truth is neither deceptive nor contradictory; and (3) conventional truth cannot be analyzed since it does not withstand deductive reasoning, while ultimate truth can be analyzed since it does withstand such reasoning.

Jñānagarbha's partial foundationalism is implicated in his conventional truth theory. Though alike in the way in which it appears, conventional truth is subdivided (from the Madhyamaka's own perspective, not from the mundane perspective like the Prāsaṅgika) into *real* and *unreal* conventionalities, based on the former being causally efficacious and the latter being causally inefficacious.[258] Real conventional truth, Jñānagarbha argues, satisfies four criteria, two prescriptive, two proscriptive: (1) to not be conceptually imagined, (2) to be dependently arisen,[259] (3) to be causally effective, and (4) not to be analyzable.[260]

His nonfoundationalist thesis can partly be observed from the way in which he proposes the conventionality of the conventional and the conventionality of the ultimate. The former is the case because there is no real basis for any conventional truth; all conventional truths are mere designations. The latter is so because Jñāngarbha goes so far as to argue that even the so-called "ultimate" is also only a conventionality. He gives two reasons for this. The first is that "ultimate statements" are self-defeating because they only make sense conventionally. His second argument stresses the identity of the conventional and the ultimate;

whatever is the reality of the conventional is itself considered by the Buddha as the meaning of the ultimate, for they are not distinct.

Bhāviveka and Jñānagarbha's philosophy fuses the epistemological realism of the Sautrāntika with the nonfoundational ontology of the Madhyamaka, hence it is known as Sautrāntika-Svātantrika Madhyamaka. Their understanding of conventional truth endorses partial foundationalism and has three key features: (1) it accepts unique particulars as an integral part of the ontological structure of the conventional truth; (2) it maintains unique particulars as "intrinsically" or "inherently" real conventionally, but not ultimately; and (3) it embraces the Sautrāntika's epistemology, in which the nature of perception is always nonconceptual and invariably reliable, and its object is always unique particulars.

CHAPTER SIX

Yogācāra-Svātantrika Madhyamaka: Śāntarakṣita and Kamalaśīla

Bhāviveka and Jñānagarbha's theory of the two truths informed the eighth-century works of Śāntarakṣita and Kamalaśīla. Jñānagarbha's student Śāntarakṣita wrote several influential texts, including *Verses on the Ornament of the Middle Way* (*Madhyamakālaṃkārakārikā*), *Commentary on the Verses on the Ornament of the Middle Way* (*Madhyamakālaṃkāravṛtti*), the *Compendium of Verses on Reality* (*Tattvasaṃgraha*), and *Commentary on the Difficult Points of Distinghuishing the Two Truths* (*Satyadvayavibhaṅgapañjika*).[261] His philosophical works proposed a synthesis of Madhyamaka and Yogācāra theories of the two truths, a synthesis that was systemized by the Yogacārā-Svātantrika Madhyamaka subschool. Kamalaśīla, Śāntarakṣita's student, endorsed his teacher's formulation of the two truths in his many works, which include *Commentary on the Difficult Points of the Verses on the Ornament of the Middle Way* (*Madhyamakālaṃkārapañjika*), *Demonstrating All Phenomena Lack Intrinsic Nature* (*Sarvadharmāsvabhāvasiddhi*), *Illuminating the Middle Way* (*Madhyamakāloka*), and *Discussion on Illuminating Reality As It Is* (*Tattvāloka*).

We have seen that Jñānagarbha and Bhāviveka's Sautrāntika-Svātantrika Madhyamaka marries the Madhyamaka's nonfoundationalist ontology with the Sautrāntika's epistemological realism. The Madhyamaka supplies the ultimate truth, the Sautrāntika the conventional. By contrast, Śāntarakṣita and Kamalaśīla's Yogācāra-Svātantrika Madhyamaka marries the Madhyamaka's nonfoundationalist ontology with the epistemological idealism of Yogācāra. The Madhyamaka supplies the ultimate truth, the Yogācāra the conventional. Thus, the two fundaments of this syncretistic view are:

1) The Yogācāra account of the conventional truth: that all that is conventionally real is *mind.* All objects external to it are conventionally unreal.
2) The Madhyamaka account of the ultimate truth: that analysis exposes the mind as empty of any intrinsic nature under ultimate analysis. Thus, all that conventionally exists lacks ultimate existence.

In short, all that exists is mind, and even mind doesn't exist ultimately. These two systems are in accordance and are the two fundamental elements in the soteriological path. Śāntarakṣita says:

> By relying on the Mind Only [school] one understands that external phenomena do not exist. And by relying on this [i.e., Madhyamaka] one understands that even [the mind] is thoroughly nonself[262] . . . Therefore, one attains a Mahāyāna [path] when one is able to ride the chariots of the two systems by holding to the reigns of logic.[263]

Śāntaraṣita and Kamalaśīla explain at great length the way in which these two chariots may be logically yoked. It is to their explanations I now turn.

ULTIMATE TRUTH

For Śāntarașita and Kamalaśīla, the meaning of ultimate truth is that everything, including the mind, is ultimately unreal and empty. Ultimate truth is the universal emptiness of intrinsic reality, from which emptiness itself is not exempt. This truth, explains Kamalaśīla, is "nonfabricated (*asamāropa*, Tib. *sgro ma brtags pa*) and established by means of right cognition (*saṃyakpramāṇa*, Tib. *yang dag pa'i tshad ma*)."[264] Kamalaśīla proposes three senses in which the ultimate truth can be understood:[265]

1) As the *ultimate reality* of the nonself of persons and phenomena. That reality, *paramartha*, or ultimate object, is the object of knowledge that finally eliminates the obstructions to liberation and total awakening since these obstructions arise from the ignorance of the ultimate reality.
2) As the *transcendent knowledge* that apprehends ultimate reality truly and directly. Elsewhere, the ultimate truth is defined as "a nature of any entity established by means of a reliable cognition."[266]
3) As the *mundane knowledge* that complements and accords with transcendent knowledge. Mundane knowledge includes hearing, reflection, and meditation, which can all lead to transcendent knowledge.

For Kamalaśīla, the ultimate truth is thus the truth itself, the transcendent knowledge that directly apprehends ultimate reality, and the mundane knowledge that, though insufficient in itself, leads to and complements that transcendent knowledge.

Let us now turn to the Yogācāra-Svātantrika Madhyamaka's arguments in support of their position on the ultimate. There are several, and I will consider two of them in turn: the "diamond-slivers" argument and the "neither-one-nor-many" argument.

1. The diamond-slivers argument

Kamalaśīla's primary argument is the "diamond-sliver" argument (*vajrakaṅādiyukti*, Tib. *rdo rje gzegs ma'i gtan tshigs*), which reveals ultimate reality by refuting four broad ontological theses that obscure it. These four theses, the four edges of the philosophical "diamond," bracket the arguments of the Mādhyamika's Buddhist and non-Buddhist opponents. These four theses state that things *ultimately*[267] arise in one of the following ways:

1) From self
2) From another
3) From both self and other
4) Causelessly (i.e., from neither self nor other)

Kamalaśīla goes on to refute all four possibilities, and so conclude that ultimate arising is impossible and all things must be empty of the ultimate existence that requires it. What is "asserted as really existing by us [other Buddhists schools] and others [non-Buddhists]," Kamalaśīla says, is no more real than the mythical "sky-lotus and so forth."[268]

1.1. Arising from self

Kamalaśīla identifies the first causal thesis, that things arise from themselves (*satkāryavāda*),[269] with the Sāṃkhya and others.[270] The term *sat* means "real"[271] or "existent," *kārya* means "effect,"[272] and *vāda* the "theory" or the "thesis." *Satkāryavāda* is thus the theory that the effect is real or existent. The implication, though, is that the effect is *always* existent and preexists in its cause, from which it arises.[273] Kamalaśīla levels a number of objections against this theory.

First, if entities were to arise from themselves, then the entities that arise from themselves must be either nonexistent or existent. Both positions, Kamalaśīla argues, are untenable. Nonexistent entities do not arise from themselves. Things that do not exist cannot self-produce, because there is no self from which to produce. The son of an infertile woman, whose very existence is logically impossible, doesn't have the causal efficacy to produce itself.[274] Something that doesn't and cannot exist cannot simply will itself into existence.

Neither can existent entities arise from themselves, since, by virtue of their existence, they are already arisen. They need not self-produce because they are already produced. An essential component of the Sāṃkhya's self-production thesis is that cause and effect are *identical*—causally and spatio-temporally so. But this definitional feature leads to a functional absurdity: if a feature of self-production is the identity of cause and effect, there is nothing to be produced. If the effect preexists, production is redundant.

Kalamaśīla argues that the Sāṃkhya cannot avoid the fault of causal redundancy without sacrificing their claim of causal identity, and if they retain the claim of causal identity, then the fault of redundancy is compounded by further absurdities. Causality is surely a way of explaining change, which is to say differences in space and time, but an insistence on the identity of cause and effect permits no such difference. Under this theory causes and effects are spatio-temporally the same, all observable evidence to the contrary. This, Kalamaśīla says, is entirely absurd: for the Sāṃkhya everything would be causally identical to anything else anywhere, and presumably at all times.[275]

A genuine principle of causality, Kalamaśīla argues, is dynamic, and it describes the change produced by causes in their effects, not their identity. Causality, he says, describes an effect whose causes contribute to its arising, such that the function of its causes is to condition the arising of the effect—effect being the contribution and cause the contributor.[276] This relational principle is impossible in the Sāṃkhya's theory of self-production.

1.2. Arising from another

Second, Kamalaśīla refutes the thesis that ultimately things arise from another (*parata utpāda*, Tib. *gzhan skyes*).[277] The term "another" or "other" (*parata*) has the specific implication that it is an intrinsically real effect that arises from a separate and equally real cause. Kamalaśīla structures his objection in the same manner as his objection to the previous thesis. If entities were to ultimately arise from a separate cause, then the cause from which they arise must be either eternal or noneternal. Both positions, Kamalaśīla argues, are untenable.

Kamalaśīla identifies the first, the claim of an eternal cause,[278] with the Sāṃkhya's claim that *prakṛti* (primal matter) functions as the eternal cause of all things. The Hindu theistic schools—such as the Vaiṣṇava, the Śaiva, the Śākta, the Advaitam of Śāṁkāra (788-820),[279] the Viśiṣṭādvaita of Rāmānuja[280]—claim that Īśvara, or God, under various monikers, serves an identical purpose.

Kamalaśīla argues that it is logically incoherent for the entities to arise, even conventionally, from an eternal cause, for an eternal cause lacks the causal efficacy to produce either (1) successively, (2) nonsuccessively, or (3) simultaneously.

Eternal cause lacks the causal efficacy to produce *successively* because an eternal cause would be, by definition, constantly and uninterruptedly causally effective. An eternal cause's causal efficacy is totally unshackled—it is not contingent upon other conditions—and so in principle should produce its effect *perpetually* rather than successively. Successive effects are produced only by noneternal causes because the timing of their succession is governed by other conditions, without which the production of their effects is impossible.[281]

If proponents of eternal-cause theory were to reply to this objection by saying that an eternal cause does depend upon such conditions, that would, Kamalaśīla argues, deliver them into other inconsistencies. Because the cause is eternal, the conditions upon which it depends would also be eternal, and the problem would repeat. The inability to explain succession would just be shifted one link down the causal chain. On the other hand, accepting an eternal cause's dependence on impermanent conditions would be an admission of its impermanence—nothing conditioned can endure longer than the conditions that give rise to it, let alone eternally. In either case, it makes no sense for an eternal cause to depend upon supporting conditions. Either they too are eternal, and we are no closer to an explanation of succession, or they are temporary, and the eternality of *prakṛti* or God is undermined. As

Kamalaśīla puts it, entities produced by an eternal cause, on account of their nonexistence, could not depend upon other conditions.[282]

Likewise, it makes no sense for the proponent to claim that an eternal cause could produce its effect nonsuccessively, that is, without the need of successive causal change. Nonsuccessive effects are a theoretically valid solution to the logical problems posed by an eternal cause, but they are not found anywhere outside the domain of theory. Effects are observed occurring intermittently, in succession. In the case of actual causation, the arising of an effect inevitably proceeds from its cause. With the cessation of its cause the effect ceases too, a fact that entails successive causal change. For causation to continue beyond a single cause and effect, something must succeed it. Successive causal change is thus the very basis of causation itself. Causation simply is the succession of causes and effects, and succession requires cessation. But the cessation of an eternal cause, as we have repeatedly seen, is unreasonable, for the eternal is by definition unceasing. And if it were to cease, the cause would have to give up its claims to eternity; it must necessarily be accepted as impermanent. Thus, Kamalaśīla concludes that an eternal cause is no more able to produce effects nonsuccessively than it is successively.[283]

Finally, eternal causes lack the causal efficacy for simultaneous production, for an effect simultaneous to its cause would never stop being produced. It is the nature of a cause *to cause things*, and a cause that continues to exist past the moment of its effect's production would *persist* in its causation. A productive eternal cause, then, would create an absurd feedback loop of endless production. Again, the proponents of eternal causes cannot deny this function without denying the cause's eternality. A cause that ceased causing after it had caused its effect would have renounced its claims to eternity.

Kamalaśīla therefore concludes that eternal causes are an impossibility since they are logically incoherent. They are precluded from producing their effect successively, nonsuccessively, and simultaneously. Since production can only take these three forms, the failure of the eternal cause thesis to demonstrate competence in a single one of these forms disqualifies eternal causes from productive power entirely.[284]

If the first sliver of the diamond—arising from another—is plausible and going to survive critique, then the "other" from which things arise must be impermanent rather than eternal. Kamalaśīla's second objection is directed toward that possibility. Kamalaśīla identifies the Vaibhāṣika with this variant of the thesis, according to which things arise from four intrinsically real, but impermanent, conditions: (1) the primary condition (*hetupratyaya*, Tib. *rgyu rkyen*), (2) the objectively supporting condition (*ālambanapratyaya*, Tib. *dmigs rkyen*), (3) the immediately contiguous condition (*samanantarapratyaya*, Tib. *de ma thag rkyen*), and (4) the dominant condition (*adhipratyaya*, Tib. *bdag rkyen*).

Kamalaśīla's primary objection is that effects cannot arise from that which is impermanent, because effects arise in the future, a time that impermanent causes are incapable of reaching. Impermanent causes are necessarily momentary instants and hence are confined to the present. For the Vaibhāṣika, as we saw earlier, genuine impermanence is momentariness: the instant something impermanent comes into existence is the same instant it extinguishes. Nothing impermanent endures, even for two moments.

But, Kamalaśīla argues, causation implies a connection between cause and effect, and endurance beyond the present moment is *necessary* to connect the present cause with the future effect. But if, as the Vaibhāṣika's own doctrine of impermanence requires, they are distinct temporal units—separate moments in time—then the one can hardly be considered the cause of the other. They simply inhabit adjoining moments, neighbors in time.

On the other hand, if the Vaibhāṣika were to attempt to deny temporal distinctness, they could only do so by making some claim of temporal endurance. Not only does this undercut their doctrine of momentary impermanence; it would also require them to explain why something that endures beyond a moment ever stops enduring. If it is reasonable for something to endure for two moments in the past, Kamalaśīla contends, it is not unreasonable for it to endure for eons into the future.[285]

Kamalaśīla's secondary argument demonstrates the impossibility of a thing arising from a momentary cause in any of the three times—

past, present, or future. Effects cannot be produced by past moments because the past no longer exists, and thus to assert that effects arise from the past is tantamount to asserting that effects arise causelessly. This follows, says Kamalaśīla, for the past is the intrinsic identity of that which has ceased to exist, and thus it is causally inefficacious and lacks any productive power.[286] So too does the future, which is nonexistent, the intrinsic identity of that which is not yet real. Though effects plainly arise *in* the future, they cannot arise from it, because it has yet to exist. The future, Kamalaśīla says, is no more real or productive than the mythical sky-lotus.[287]

The only remaining option is that the effect is produced *in* the present, *by* the present. In other words, the effect is produced *concurrently*. But this too is problematic. If cause and effect were concurrent, they would exist simultaneously, which would violate the requirement, accepted by the Vaibhāṣika, that the cause's nonexistence precedes its effect. And it would render the separate designations "cause" and "effect" entirely nonsensical. If such concepts are applied where inapplicable, such as between an intrinsically real first moment of a visual consciousness (as a cause) and an intrinsically real second moment of a visual consciousness (as an effect), as they would be without distinct temporal phases, it would muddle up the concepts of cause and effect, says Kamalaśīla.[288]

Kamalaśīla concludes that the theory of causation from another is inadmissible. If they arise from another, then things would have to arise from either an eternal or an impermanent cause. Once these possibilities are subjected to ultimate analysis, Kamalaśīla says, it becomes clear that they are not possible at all.

1.3. Arising from both self and other

The third causal thesis Kamalaśīla rejects is proposing the combined causation of both self and other. Although Kamalaśīla does not explicitly identify his opponent in this debate, it is primarily the Jaina proponents.[289] The Jaina's causal thesis, *anekāntavāada*, is a synthesis of the two we have previously covered, under which things arise from both self and another. Consider a wooden table. Jaina argue that it arises from a combination of these two sorts of causes: the wood from which the table is made is identical with the table itself, and the other causal components—say the trained hands of the carpenter, the nuts and bolts—are other than the table itself. The former causes amount to "arising from the self," the latter to "arising from another." The Jaina advance a causal theory that seeks to avoid the problems that beset the previous two theories by synthesizing them. Kamalaśīla, though, rejects this project as flawed and the resultant causal theory as untenable. Rather than avoiding the problems of the previous two theories, any combination of them must also combine their logical flaws. Kamalaśīla treats this fact as so self-evident and damning that he does not discuss or criticize the Jaina theory further.[290]

1.4. Arising causelessly

The fourth causal thesis rejected by Kamalaśīla is that arising is causeless, and so all causal explanations are redundant. Though his opponent is again unnamed, the thesis is plainly that associated with the Indian materialists, the Cārvāka (or Lokāyata).[291] The theory is vividly evoked by the Cārvāka, who see no causal power behind the particularities of existence. Peacock feathers may be rich and colorful, they say, and one bush may be pointed while another is blunt. But no one or no thing in particular is responsible for these particularities—things are the way they are simply because that is the way they happen to be.[292]

Kamalaśīla advances several objections. First, he argues that the thesis has no ultimate basis, for it does not have an example to support it. There is no example that the Cārvāka could produce to prove the theory that *ultimately* things arise causelessly without undercutting their position that *ultimately* all phenomena are not produced.[293]

Second, the thesis has no conventional basis because it is refuted by the direct perception of conventional appearance. The Cārvāka's acausal world would be one of chance and chaos, but the world is in fact observably not chaotic, and in it simple causal relationships are routinely observed. As Kamalaśīla puts it:

> [There is no example the Cārvāka could produce] to prove that *even* conventionally things arise causelessly, for thorns, etc., are ascertained by means of direct perception to arise from their own seeds, etc. Thus none arise causelessly.[294]

And to so disregard the observable evidence, Kamalaśīla continues, would undercut the Cārvāka's signature epistemological position, that direct perception is the primary, and only, source of knowledge. He argues:

> A direct perception undermines this causal thesis because it is only by the means of direct perception that the world establishes seed and sprout, etc., to bear the cause-effect [relationship]. If the [Cārvāka], however, alternatively assert arising [but denies this direct perceived truth] then . . . they would contradict their own words [i.e., the claim that direct perception is the only source of knowledge and the reasoning is not].[295]

Therefore, Kamalaśīla concludes, "all scholars need to abandon . . . the theory of causeless causation, since it is undermined by direct perception and so forth.[296]

Third, the thesis fails to account for differentiation. The fact is that all entities arise at different times and in different forms. And differentiation, Kamalaśīla says, indicates dependency because, after all, what but a cause can determine when and how something arises? Without causes to account for differentiation, the identity of all phenomena would conflate, Kamalaśīla says:

> That entity to which it depends [for its arising] is considered its cause. The cause is, therefore, known to be that by means of which [the effect] is sustained. . . . If the Cārvāka were right that entities are causeless, nothing could bring upon them any differentiation whatsoever, even thorns, etc., are not certain to be sharp, etc. For all things would bear the identities of everything else.[297]

If entities did have any intrinsic nature, it would be revealed by its ability to withstand logical analysis and would be produced in one of the ways assigned to each of the diamond-slivers, either from itself, or from another, or both, or causelessly. Thus, by prosecuting the diamond-sliver argument to completion, Kamalaśīla can conclude that all entities must lack intrinsic nature, for no such nature is analytically found to arise.

2. The "neither-one-nor-many" argument

For the second of the Yogacārā-Svātantrika Madhyamaka's arguments, I turn to Śāntarakṣita, Kamalaśīla's teacher. This argument, the "neither-one-nor-many" argument (*ekānekaviyogahetu*, Tib. *gcid du bral gyi gtan tshigs*),[298] is his signature position. He makes the argument as follows:

> The entities that are proclaimed by our own [Buddhist] schools and the other [non-Buddhist] schools lack intrinsic identity, because in reality their identity is neither singular nor plural—like a reflection.[299]

I have discussed the probative form in my treatment of the Svātantrika/Prāsaṅgika division. Let us break this argument into its probative components.

- The subject is all entities—entities that are proclaimed by our own Buddhist schools and the non-Buddhist schools.
- The property to be proved is entities' lack of intrinsic identity.
- The thesis is that all entities lack intrinsic identity.
- The reason or means of proof is that in reality their identity is neither singular nor plural. (There is a suppressed premise here upon which the reason depends, that is that any intrinsic identity must be either singular or plural.) The analogous example is a reflection.

It is important that we observe the argument's formal structure here because Śāntarakṣita says the validity of the neither-one-nor-many argument depends on it. The argument must satisfy the triple criteria of probative reasoning if it is to succeed. The first criterion (Skt. *pakṣadharmatā*, Tib. *phyogs chos*) is that the reason qualifies the subject. In this case, that means that all entities must be shown to be neither single nor plural. Śāntarakṣita separates the two—singularity and plurality— and rejects them in turn. I turn first to the rejection of singularity.

2.1. Rejection of singularity

In the *Verses on the Ornament of the Middle Way* and *Commentary on the Verses on the Ornament of the Middle Way*, Śāntarakṣita takes two different approaches to his rejection of singularity, separately rejecting singularity in pervasive and discrete things. We will follow this division, which, as by now we ought to have come to expect, is also further subdivided. We turn first to pervasive things.

2.1.2. Pervasive singularity

The rejection of singularity in pervasive phenomena initially targets the Nyāya-Vaiśeṣika concepts of space and time. The Nyāya-Vaiśeṣika treat both space and time as pervading and eternal substances: the universe's unmoving spatio-temporal substrate.[300] Space and time, for the Nyāya-Vaiśeṣika, are infinite, ubiquitous, and do not have an atomic structure. Partless, they are indivisible. Together, they are the instrumental causes of all produced things. Space is the unchanging substrate undergirding all spatial divisions, dimensions, and relations. Time is the unchanging substrate that undergirds all production, destruction, and persistence, all change and movement.[301] It is space that makes possible cognitions of direction, of distance, and of depth and altitude. It is time that makes possible cognition of past, present, and future, of priority and posteriority, of simultaneity and sequence. Both space and time are indivisible, but they nonetheless make metaphysically possible the conventional divisions of space and time by which we measure and regulate our existence within them.

Śāntarakṣita rejects entirely the Nyāya-Vaiśeṣika characterization of space and time. If space and time are to be useful concepts rather than passive abstractions, they must help us explain the world and the things in it with which they relate. This would be so if the world were as singular and pervasive as its substrate: if, with time unchanging, things in time were unchanging too; if, with space being unitary, things in space were also unitary rather than multidirectional. But things in space and time plainly are multidirectional and changing, Śāntarakṣita argues. The Nyāya-Vaiśeṣika accept as much. And so there is a philosophically fatal disconnect between the Nyāya-Vaiśeṣika's concept of space and time and the things existing within them with which they are intended to relate. And, as soon as we accept that they do relate, things become problematic. If space and time are, as the Nyāya-Vaiśeṣika say, unitary and unchanging, how can they meaningfully relate with things in the world that are many and changing? "Pervasive [entities such as space and time] are associated with a variety of directions," Śāntarakṣita says, "so how can they be unitary?"[302]

In his *Commentary on the Verses on the Ornament of the Middle Way*, Śāntarakṣita argues against the possibility of "singular," "pervasive" entities such as time and space relating to entities that exist in different directions and at different times. Like must relate to like. Were time unchanging, things in time would have to be unchanging too; were space unitary, things in space would have to be unitary rather than multidirectional. This follows since time and space, as singular substances, cannot accommodate any relation with entities having various natures at different times, for doing so would require changing their unitary substantive identities. But things in space and time plainly are directional and moving, Śāntarakṣita continues. And as we have seen, the Nyāya-Vaiśeṣika accept as much. For example, entities such as trees, having various changing natures, cannot accommodate time and space as unitary substances since they do not have a singular nature.[303]

Gyaltsab Jé (Rgyal tshab Rje), the famous fourteenth-century student of Tsongkhapa, in his *Note of Reminder on the Ornament of the Middle Way* (*Dbu ma rgyan gyi brjed byang*), puts Śāntarakṣita's argument as follows:

> The subject, [pervasive] time and space, etc., would not be really unitary because it is simultaneously related to the dispersal or collection of trees and so forth, which belong to different directions like east.[304]

So, if the relation between space and time and the objects in them are to be maintained, Śāntarakṣita concludes, the Nyāya-Vaiśeṣika must abandon either their characterization of time and space as singular and permanent or their characterization of the things in it as diverse and momentary. Since things are observably so, a fact acknowledged by the Nyāya-Vaiśeṣika, it is their characterization of time and space that must be abandoned.

2.1.3. Nonpervasive singularity

Śāntarakṣita is particularly concerned with five phenomena that are considered nonpervasive and singular: (1) the Sāṃkhya's *prakṛti*, (2) the Vaibhāṣika's uncompounded trio, (3) the Vātsīputrīya's theory of persons, (4) the Vaibhāṣika and Sautrāntika's theory of macro objects, and (5) the atoms that compose them. Śāntarakṣita's attack on the singularity of nonpervasive or discrete things is organized according to what degree his opponents classify them as permanent. Among these five, the first two are held to be permanent, the third neither permanent nor impermanent, and the final two are considered impermanent.

2.1.3.1. The Sāṃkhya's prakṛti

Śāntarakṣita's first focus is the refutation of permanent causal entities postulated in Hindu systems, especially the primeval principal (*pradhāna* or *prakṛti*, Tib. *gtso bo*) posited by the Sāṃkhya school.

Such entities must be empty of a singular identity, he says, because they are held to contribute to the production of manifold successive effects:

> If each successive effect is temporally and spatially distinct from latter successive effects, and latter ones must arise from the cessation of the previous successive effects, it follows, then, that such entities lack a singular permanent identity.[305]

So we see something singular and permanent could never produce the successive effects attributed to them by the Hindu schools. The Sāṃkhya, for instance, claim the primeval principal to be the primary cause of the entire universe, although it is causeless, singular, and permanent. Productive power, Śāntarakṣita argues, requires a dynamic producer; creating change is something that permanent entities are constitutionally incapable of doing. He explains:

> The effects would arise simultaneously since the effects would only be delayed if the cause were incomplete. When the causal efficacy [i.e., of the *prakṛti* for instance] is present unobstructed, how would a delay in the arising of those [effects] be possible?[306]

Nevertheless, let us suppose that a singular primeval principal was causally effective. If it were, Śāntarakṣita argues, then surely all effects would occur in a single burst of productive power—an absurd result. Unimpeded production would mean that the universe's primary causal force would be spent in an instant.

2.1.3.2. The uncompounded trio

Śāntarakṣita's second focus is the Vaibhāṣika's[307] "uncompounded trio": analytical cessation, nonanalytical cessation, and space. The Vaibhāṣika, we saw earlier, treat these three as permanent unitary entities.

For the Vaibhāṣika, these three are ultimately real foundational entities because they are (1) independent though composite in nature, (2) uncompounded on account of not being causally produced, (3) intrinsically real, (4) the objective domains of meditative cognitions, (5) eternal and enduring, and (6) indissoluble entities, the cognitions of which persist even after their components parts are mentally stripped away.[308]

Śāntarakṣita argues that the six qualities ascribed above conflict with each other. Something uncompounded and uncaused (the second quality) cannot also function as a meditational cognition (the fourth quality), because such a cognition is relational and constantly changing. He explains:

> Those uncompounded entities, which, according to the [Vaibhāṣika] system, are the objects of knowledge of meditative cognition, cannot [also] be unitary because they are associated with successive moments of consciousness.[309]

The problem that Śāntarakṣita identifies is that for something to function as an object of knowledge, it has to exist in *relation* with knowing. There must be a subject-object relation between the cognition and its object. But something uncompounded and uncaused—which would exist outside of ordinary systems of causal relation—cannot serve that function. Something that by nature isn't relational cannot also be half of a cognitive relation. If the Vaibhāṣika are to maintain the subject-object relation between knowledge and knower, Śāntarakṣita says, then they will have to give up their claim that the trio are uncompounded.

They must also give up their claim that they are eternal and enduring (the fourth quality), because that which they are required to relate to, consciousness, they hold to be the opposite—in momentary flux. But a consciousness that is aware of a permanent unchanging object would itself be permanent and unchanging—successive moments of consciousness would be indistinguishable. Śāntarakṣita explains:

> If the nature of the object known by a previous moment of consciousness continues to exist [in the same form] subsequently, then the previous moment of consciousness would become the latter [because it is conscious of precisely the same thing]; likewise, the latter would become the former.[310]

The simultaneous assertion of a constantly changing consciousness and an unchanging object breeds absurd consequences. If consciousness were constantly changing but its object was not, then the nature of the uncompounded object, known by a previous moment of consciousness, would still exist at a later stage, despite the fact that the previous consciousness would not still exist at that time. Similarly, Śāntarakṣita continues, "the object known by the later consciousness would exist at the earlier stage despite the fact that the later consciousness does not exist [at the earlier stage]. Thus [the Vaibhāṣika's position] is undermined."[311]

The only way to avoid such absurdity is to give up the permanency thesis and accept the impermanence of the uncompounded trio. As Śāntarakṣita states:

> Uncompounded phenomena, like consciousness, must be objects known to arise momentarily since the nature of the later object does not arise in the earlier stage, and the earlier object does not arise at the later stage.[312]

If we accept that uncompounded phenomena are not permanent, then the other qualities soon collapse, too. Something momentary cannot arise independently (the first quality), otherwise it would either arise *ad infinitum* since it is independent of that which would make it cease—the expiry of its cause—or it would not arise at all, since it is independent of the cause that would make it arise.[313] Something that is not independent cannot also be uncompounded (the second quality); something that is compounded cannot be indissoluble (the sixth); and so on. Once the contradictions between the six qualities are prosecuted, the entire list collapses.

2.1.3.3. The Vātsīputrīya theory of persons

Although Śāntarakṣita does not name his opponent here,[314] it is plainly a proponent of the Vātsīputrīya school. Their position is that persons (*pudgala*, Tib. *gang zag*) are singular and intrinsically real but transcend questions of permanence: they hold them to be neither permanent nor impermanent. Śāntarakṣita rejects this position:

> It is clear that the [type of] person [asserted by the Vātsīputrīya] is to be understood as being neither singular nor manifold since it cannot be explained as momentary or nonmomentary.[315]

Here Śāntarakṣita is arguing that personal identity cannot transcend questions of permanence or plurality because the very possibility of identity is bound up in its answer. Personal identity is only possible if the person is impermanent (i.e., momentary) or permanent (i.e., nonmomentary). Impermanence makes possible manifold identities, permanence makes possible the singular identity the Vātsīputrīya assert. But the Vātsīputrīya exclude both and so exclude all possible identity by proxy. He explains in *Commentary on the Verses on the Ornament of the Middle Way*:

> If [the persons] were momentary then they would have a manifold identity, because in each successive moment would arise other identities. If they were not momentary then they would have a singular identity, because their single identity would be eternally fixed. Since neither of the possibilities were asserted, there is no difficulty in proving the emptiness of a singular and plural identity.[316]

Gyaltsab Jé neatly formulates Śāntarakṣita's argument in his *Note of Reminder on the Ornament of the Middle Way*:

> The subject, the person, would not really be singular because they are not expressed as permanent. [And] they would not really be manifold because they are not expressed as impermanent. There is an entailment in the reasoning because if an entity does not have a manifold identity, it must be singular [and] if entities are of many identities, they must be manifold. In brief, they must not be really singular because they are not expressed as impermanent or permanent.[317]

Gyaltsab Jé's argument is that the Vātsīputrīya could not claim that a person is singular because they refused to express it as permanent, but singularity must necessarily be permanent. Nor could the Vātsīputrīya claim that a person is plural or manifold because they refuse to express it as impermanent, whereas the manifold must necessarily be impermanent.

2.1.3.4. Macro objects

Next, Śāntarakṣita refutes the unitary nature of macro objects. Although Śāntarakṣita does not identify his opponents here, Kamalaśīla confirms they are the Vaibhāṣika and Sautrāntika. Śāntarakṣita argues, "macro entities are not unitary since they can be [partly] visible and [partly] invisible."[318] Gyaltsab Jé expands Śāntarakṣita's argument. He explains that a macro material object is not unitary because if it were, three contradictions would result. First, it is substantively contradictory for a unitary object to have some of its parts visible and the other parts invisible. It should be either entirely visible or entirely invisible; a unitary object cannot be both obscured and exposed at once. Second, it is functionally contradictory for a unitary object to have some of its parts in motion and other parts standing still. If a tree, for instance, is a unitary object, it would be contradictory for its branches to be moving while the trunk stands still. And third, it is qualitatively contradictory for a unitary object to possess various qualities such as different colors in different parts at different times.[319]

2.1.3.5. Atoms

Finally, having rejected the singularity of macro obects, Śāntarakṣita turns to rejecting the singularity of the atomic components from which the Vaibhāṣika and Sautrāntika argue macro objects are composed. We have seen that under Vaibhāṣika and Sautrāntika atomic theory, atomic particles are held to be unitary, irreducible, and independent. Śāntarakṣita responds by deploying the Yogācāra refutation of Vaibhāṣika and Sautrāntika atomic theory, which I discussed in the Yogācāra chapter. That is, that for invisible atoms to form visible objects they must combine across locations, rather than converge on the same location. They can combine, Śāntarakṣita asserts, in one of three ways: (1) directly adjoining each other, (2) surrounding each other but separated by space, or (3) surrounding each other with no separation.[320] Unless we accept one of these three methods, Śāntarakṣita says, then one cannot account for the development of the perceivable world of land, water, etc., since atomic particles would not spatially expand.[321]

But accepting *any* of the three methods of combination is, Śāntarakṣita says, to accept that the atoms involved in such combinations have dimensions and directional faces by which they combine. The prevailing view at the time was that atomic particles connect with ten other particles. For such connection to be spatially expansive, the atoms must combine in *separate* places, and this requires that atoms have separate directional faces by which they combine. Thus, he explains in the *Verses on the Ornament of the Middle Way*, the central atomic particle, held by the atomists to be partless, would require at least ten faces corresponding to the number of the particles in all directions. And if something has at least ten dimensional components, how can it also be unitary? Anything dimensional can be easily conceptually divided. And anything that can be so divided can hardly also be unified. "How," Śāntarakṣita asks, "could [even] the most minute particles be singular and partless?"[322] Gyaltsab Jé summarizes this point:

> If it is still possible for the indivisible atoms to form macro objects, then the particle in the center of the ten directions

> must not be singular and without parts as it is claimed by the theorist, for the subject would have ten different faces facing the surrounding particles in the ten directions.[323]

This completes Śāntarakṣita's arguments against the possibility of singularity in all phenomena, whether pervasive or discrete, permanent or momentary.

2.2. *Plurality*

We turn now to Śāntarakṣita's argument against plurality, which is comparatively brief since the impossibility of singularity is his key premise. Put simply, without single things, there is no possibility of plurality.

> When we analyze any entity, none is [found] to be a singular. For that for which nothing is singular, there must also be nothing that is plural.[324]

The concepts of singular and plural are essentially interdependent—if there are no singular entities, one must accept that there are no plural entities either since the latter is only the accumulation of the former. In the *Commentary on the Verses of the Ornament of the Middle Way*, Śāntarakṣita elaborates this argument: When the Buddhist and non-Buddhist concepts (such as permanence and impermanence, universals and particulars, indivisible particles and macro objects, and consciousness) are subjected to rational analysis to examine if they are singular, there is no entity whatsoever that can defy the heavy burden of such critical examination. No singular or unitary phenomenon can be located in nature. Accordingly, accepting a plural nature would also be unreasonable because if there is nothing singular, there can be nothing plural—there can be no plurality of singular things.[325]

Recall that the purpose of this discussion has been to determine whether the first of the "triple criteria" of valid reasoning is satisfied in Śāntarakṣita's probative argument, that the reason (nothing is ultimately singular nor plural) qualifies the subject (phenomena). Śāntarakṣita's arguments certainly make clear that all instances of the subject, namely the intrinsic identities of those entities asserted by Buddhist and non-Buddhist opponents, are instances of entities that are neither singular nor plural. Therefore the first criterion is satisfied.

Once the first criterion of a valid reasoning—that the subject is the property of the reason—is established, Śāntarakṣita proceeds to show the entailment of the argument, the domain of the remaining two criteria. The second criterion is the proof of the forward pervasion—that is, the proof that the reason occurs in only similar instances where all instances of the reason are the instances of the predicates. In the case of the neither-one-nor-many argument, the second criterion is satisfied if the reason—all phenomena are neither singular nor plural—are instances of the predicate—phenomena that lack identity.

The third criterion is the proof of counter pervasion, or the proof that the reason is completely absent from dissimilar instances of the predicate. This holds if there are no instances of the predicate that are not instances of the reason. In the case of the neither-one-nor-many argument, this requires there are no instances of phenomena lacking intrinsic identity that are not also instances of phenomena that are neither a singular nor a plural. In *Verses on the Ornament of the Middle Way*, Śāntarakṣita makes this point on the third criterion:

> The existence of an entity belonging to a class other than that which is singular or plural is not possible because the two are exhaustive of all possible alternatives.[326]

The categories of singular or plural, according to Śāntarakṣita's *Commentary on the Verses on the Ornament of the Middle Way*, exhaust all possibilities for the existence of an intrinsic identity. There is no alternative mode of its being, nor could the two modes be combined since being singular and being manifold are mutually exclusive (Tib. *phan tshun spang te gnas pa'i mtshan nyid*). The *Commentary* therefore concludes:

> Since a singular and a plural are characterized as being mutually exclusive, any other alternative is excluded. Therefore the counter pervasion holds since there are no entities that could be posited as existing in other possible alternatives.[327]

Once the pervasion of the argument is shown, having satisfied the triple criteria, the argument is considered logically watertight.[328]

CONVENTIONAL TRUTH

We have seen from the neither-one-nor-many argument that the Yogācāra-Svātantrika Madhyamaka hold entities to be empty of ultimate reality beause such reality is only possible for singular or plural things, and such things are not possible. Let us now turn to the Yogācāra-Svātantrika Madhyamaka theory of conventional truth: their explanation of the way things *do* exist.

The Yogācāra-Svātantrika Madhyamaka school adopts the Yogācāra position on conventional truth—that conventionally only mind is real, that all experiences are mental impressions with no extra-mental reality—a position they defend textually and logically. Textually, Śāntarakṣita and Kamalaśīla's arguments rely heavily on the sūtras—especially the *Unraveling the Intent Sūtra* and *Descent into Laṅkā Sūtra*, which traditionally support Yogācāra idealism. Their works produce abundant citations from these texts, stressing the significance of the passages that make the conclusion that there are no physical objects other than mental projections. Śāntarakṣita claims that the philosophical position of Madhyamaka and the idealistic doctrines taught in these scriptures are all consistent.[329]

Logically, we find Śāntarakṣita deploying several arguments to defend this position. First, he argues in the *Commentary on the Verses on the Ornament of the Middle Way*, "that which is cause and effect is mere consciousness only. And whatever is causally established abides in consciousness."[330] Everything has the characteristic, as he continues on to explain in the *Commentary*, of the material form that appears in dreams or as part of an illusion. They appear to be real external objects, yet analysis reveals that they do not causally arise in such a manner: they do not arise concurrently with or independently from the cognitions, such as the visual consciousness, that apprehend them. Therefore phenomena that appear to be real external objects are not distinct from phenomenological experience, just as material forms experienced in the dreams are not distinct from the experience of dreaming.[331]

The realists might object, Śāntarakṣita anticipates, that external objects are real, their reality inferred by the fact their representations appear to consciousness as intentional objects. In his reply Śāntarakṣita agrees that there is an inference, but mere inference does not warrant the conclusion that external objects are real. After all, the validity of inference depends on whether or not it is grounded in direct perception. We are, however, not able to directly experience the reality of the external objects independently from the representations. The only access we have are the representations. Furthermore, Śāntarakṣita argues that the representations in the consciousness are causally produced by immediately preceding mental events, events whose impressions shape the intentional objects of one's present cognition. The nonexistence of the external object is further evidenced from the Yogācāra's successful refutation of the reality of atomic particles.[332]

Things exist, Śāntarakṣita says, only conventionally (Tib. *kun rdzob kho na'i mtshan nyid 'dzin*):

> Therefore these entities are only conventionally defined. If [someone] accepts them as ultimate, what can I do?[333]

But what does Śāntarakṣita mean by conventional existence? One of his formulations is a three-fold definition. Conventionality:

- appeals to face value, not reasoned analysis;
- is causally efficacious; and
- is subjected to arising and disintegration.[334]

First, conventional reality is intuitive, rather than analytical in character. Like illusory objects it is posited by appealing only to face value rather than subjecting it to a reasoned analysis—such as the neither-one-nor-many argument—it could not withstand.[335] Kamalaśīla's *Illuminating the Middle Way* reinforces this point:

> Entities do not exist ultimately. Yet entities such as material forms are established by way of *not* analyzing them. Those entities whose production, etc., are fabricated are explained to be conventional truths.[336]

Second, conventional reality is causally efficacious. Śāntarakṣita, drawing on the ideas of Dignāga, Dharmakīrti, and Jñānagarbha, asks what the purpose is of examining objects that lack causal efficacy. Such an inquiry would be as pointless, he says, as a "lustful person probing whether a eunuch is attractive."[337] Here, Śāntarakṣita is distinguishing between what is conventionally real and conventionally unreal. As the commentary on this verse explains, entities that are causally efficacious are conventionally real, while entities that are causally inefficacious are conventionally unreal. Causally efficacious entites are those that are "well known,"[338] meaning they present themelves directly to perception. In contrast, causally inefficacious entities are conceptually constructed fictions such as Īśvara, the Sāṃkhya's primordial principle, pure consciousness, and so on. These the Madhyamaka rejects categorically.[339] Rather than being "well known," Kamalaśīla says, such entities are "metaphysically conceptualized beyond what is well known."[340]

Importantly the Madhyamaka doctrines of nonself of persons and phenomena, established through the school's own arguments, can only apply to those entities that are causally efficacious, for they alone are accepted by the Mādhyamika as conventionally real. "The subject of the discussion here," Śāntarakṣita says, "is confined to all those that are causally effective."[341] Excluded are entities that are causally ineffective. Being entirely unreal, they warrant no discussion.

Third, conventional reality is impermanent, subjected to arising and disintegration. This definition is a point about succession—the link between that which precedes and that which succeeds—a point Śāntarakṣita makes explicitly:

> Therefore that which is a causally efficacious must be momentary. Otherwise, it is not feasible for it to perform subsequent and other functions.[342]

If Śāntarakṣita emphasizes the ontological dimension of conventionality, Kamalaśīla emphasizes the epistemological dimension. Śāntarakṣita sets out the characteristics of the *things* that exist conventionally, while Kamalaśīla sets out the characteristics of the *cognitions* that apprehend them.

For Kamalaśīla, ultimate and conventional are distinguished by the veracity of the apprehending cognition. Nonerroneous cognition apprehends the ultimate; the conventional is apprehended by erroneous cognition:

> The nature of any entity fabricated by virtue of falsely representing cognition is designated as conventional truth. It is akin to the nature of things posited by a person who has erroneous cognitions of illusory persons and so forth.[343]

This is not to claim that conventional things are entirely illusory, like the horn of a rabbit, to use one of the stock examples of Kamalaśīla's philosophical milieu. Rather, it is simply that absent analysis, we labor under the illusion that they exist ultimately. Once analysis is deployed, the illusion falls away:

> For when [conventionality] is not subjected to analysis, its appearance does appeal [to us].[344]

Under cognitive error we reify appearances that aren't worthy of reification. They exist, but are devoid of real nature. By superimposing ultimate existence, conventionality therefore conceals or obstructs ultimate reality.[345] Here, Kamalaśīla follows the *Descent into Laṅkā Sūtra*, which reads:

> Things arise conventionally. [They are] not intrinsically natured in any ultimate sense. We accept the conventionally real as that which erroneously apprehends entities that lack intrinsic nature as having intrinsic nature.[346]

In his gloss of the text, Kamalaśīla identifies as the source of this error the maturation of the subliminal impressions of the beginningless cognitive error. All convention is cognitive error, and all cognitive errors are mental impressions.

THE RELATIONSHIP OF THE TWO TRUTHS

In *Illuminating the Middle Way*, Kamalaśīla provides an account of the relationship between the two truths, structured as a response to the objection that the two truths cannot fit any of the following four relationships. He presents his opponent's objections as follows:

- If conventional truth and ultimate truth are identical, then they would be indistinguishable; there would be no two entities to relate.
- If they are distinct, they would be entirely unrelated.
- To be both identical and distinct is not an available option since the two options mutually exclude each other.
- To be neither identical nor distinct is not an available option since the two options are exhaustive.[347]

In his reply, Kamalaśīla objects to the presumption of the fourth relationship, that the two options are exhaustive, for it undergirds the entire structure. The binary of identity/nonidentity may be useful when applied to entities, he argues, but is not at all valid applied to the *characteristics* of entities. Conventional and ultimate truths are characteristics and do not need to, nor do they, choose between identity and distinction in order to relate. The fourth relationship, of neither identity nor distinction, here applies. Kamalaśīla says:

> Ultimate truth is the characteristic of reality, whereas conventional truth is the characteristic of compounded phenomena. The two are accepted neither as identical nor as distinct.[348]

Not content simply to reject the presumption of exhaustion that opens up the fourth relationship, Kamalaśīla, following the *Unraveling the Intent Sūtra*,[349] renders absurd the possibilities that precede it. First, if one asserts the two truths are identical, the following absurdities arise:

- All ordinary beings would directly perceive ultimate reality just as they do conventional truth.
- All ordinary beings would be liberated or fully awakened.
- Just as compounded phenomena are characterized as afflictive, so would ultimate truth be afflictive.
- Just as all compounded phenomena are ultimately not differentiated from each other (as all are ultimately empty of intrinsic nature), all the conventional characteristics of compounded phenomena would not be differentiated. (This makes no sense since all compounded phenomena are conventionally differentiated with different characteristics.)
- It would make no sense for the yogis to pursue the realization of ultimate truth by means of meditative practices.[350]

Second, if one asserts that the two truths are distinct, the following absurdities arise:

- Those who realize the ultimate truth would not also have prevailed over the dispositional characteristic of compounded phenomena, thus they would not be freed from the dispositional bondage—tendencies of craving, aversion, and delusion—that prevents beings from attaining freedom.

- If yogis were freed from dispositional bondage, they would also not overcome the bondage of the conditioned existential state of affairs.
- Those who were not freed from the bondage of the conditioned existential state of affairs would not realize liberation and ultimate awakening.
- The universal characteristic of compounded phenomena would not be the characteristic of the ultimate truth; in other words, the characteristic of the ultimate truth would not be compounded phenomena's lack of self or intrinsic nature.
- Afflictive phenomena and liberative phenomena would coexist simultaneously.

The third relationship, that ultimate and conventional truth are both identical *and* distinct, aside from being logically impossible, would combine the logical flaws of the two relationships that preceded it.

Therefore, ultimate truth, like the white color of a conch shell, is neither defined as distinct from compounded phenomena nor identical to them.[351] Kamalaśīla's defense of the thesis that the two truths are neither identical nor distinct is based on Madhyamaka's nonfoundationalist metaphysics. For a foundationalist metaphysician who advocates the two truths as substantial entities, he says, it may be plausible to accept the two as either identical or distinct. If foundationalist metaphysics applied, after all, each truth would be a substantial entity, independent from the other. However, for a Mādhyamika, who asserts the nonsubstantiality of both truths, it is nonsensical to assert that the two truths are either identical or distinct, and there is logical reason to assert they are neither.[352] Thus:

> The ultimate truth of an exalted cognition is no different from illusion and the like, hence it is also characterized as a real conventionality. Even so, it coheres with the realization

> of reality as it is, and is thus characterized as the ultimate truth. Therefore, differentiated by standpoint, one [ultimate truth] can have the characteristics of both [truths].[353]

CONCLUSION

I have considered two key arguments of the Yogācāra-Svātantrika Madhyamaka. First among these is Kamalaśīla's primary argument, called the "diamond-sliver" argument, which reveals that emptiness is ultimate reality by eliminating four broad ontological theses: that ultimately, things arise (1) from self, (2) from another, (3) from both self and other, and (4) causelessly (i.e., neither from self nor from another). Kamalaśīla goes on to refute all four possibilities and so concludes that ultimate arising is impossible, and all things must be empty of ultimate existence. If entities did have any ultimately real intrinsic nature, it would be revealed by its ability to withstand four modes of logical analysis and would be produced in one of the ways assigned to each of the diamond slivers—either from itself, or from another, or both, or causelessly. Following the diamond-sliver argument through to completion, Kamalaśīla concludes that all entities must lack intrinsic nature ultimately, for no such nature is analytically found to arise.

For the second argument, we turn to Śāntarakśita's "neither-one-nor-many" argument, which is his signature position. Śāntarakṣita says the validity of the neither-one-nor-many argument must satisfy the triple criteria of probative reasoning if it is to succeed. The first criterion is that the reason—that all entities must be shown to be neither singular nor plural (nothing is ultimately singular or plural)—qualifies the subject, phenomena. The second criterion is the proof of the forward pervasion—that is, the proof that the reason occurs in only "similar instances" where all instances of the reason are the instances of the predicates. In the case of the neither-one-nor-many argument, the second criterion would be satisfied if the reason—all phenomena are neither singular nor plural—is an instance of the predicate—phenomena that lack identity. The third criterion is the proof of the counter pervasion, or the proof that the reason is completely absent from the dissimilar instances of the predicate. This holds if there are no instances of the predicate that are not instances of the reason. In the case of the neither-one-nor-many argument, this would hold if there were no instances of phenomena that lacked intrinsic identity that were not also instances of phenomena that were neither singular nor plural.

The categories of singular and plural, according to Śāntarakṣita's *Commentary on the Verses on the Ornament of the Middle Way*, exhaust all possibilities for the existence of an intrinsic identity. There cannot be a third alternative mode of its being, nor could the two modes be combined, since being singular and being manifold mutually exclude each other. Once the pervasion of the argument is shown, having satisfied the triple criteria, the argument is considered logically valid.

Kamalaśīla's diamond-sliver argument and Śāntarakṣita's neither-one-nor-many argument show that ultimately everything is empty of intrinsic reality. The former reveals the emptiness as ultimate reality by eliminating the four broad ontological theses that obscure it, and the latter argument reveals emptiness as the ultimate reality by showing that it is impossible for things to be singular or plural ultimately.

Thus things exist, Śāntarakṣita says, only conventionally; or in his words, "Therefore these entities are only conventionally defined."[354] He offers a three-fold definition of conventional truth: conventionality (1) appeals to face value, not reasoned analysis; (2) is causally efficacious; and (3) is subjected to arising and disintegration.[355]

If Śāntarakṣita's formulation emphasizes the characteristics of things that exist conventionally, Kamalaśīla emphasizes the characteristics of the cognition that apprehends them. For Kamalaśīla, ultimate and conventional are distinguished by the veracity of the apprehending cognition. Nonerroneous cognition apprehends the ultimate; the conventional is that which is apprehended by erroneous cognition. This is not to claim that conventional things are entirely illusory, simply that absent analysis, we labor under the illusion that they exist ultimately. Once analysis is deployed, the illusion falls away.

Śāntarakṣita and Kamalaśīla's Yogācāra-Svātantrika Madhyamaka therefore marries the Madhyamaka's nonfoundationalist ontology with the epistemological idealism of Yogācāra. The Madhyamaka supplies the ultimate truth, the Yogācāra the conventional. Thus, the two fundamental theses that underlie this syncretistic view are: (1) The Yogācāra account of the conventional truth—that is, that all that is conventionally real is mind and all objects external to it are conventionally unreal, and (2) the Madhyamaka account of the ultimate truth—that is, that analysis exposes the mind as empty of any intrinsic nature under ultimate analysis. Thus, all that conventionally exists lacks ultimate existence.

CHAPTER SEVEN

Prāsaṅgika Madhyamaka: Candrakīrti

The Svātantrika Madhyamaka theories of the two truths, which derive from Bhāviveka, soon came under attack from Candrakīrti (ca. 600–650),[356] who developed that attack across a body of work that includes several texts: *Clear Words* (*Prasannapadā*), *Introduction to the Middle Way* (*Madhyamakāvatāra*), *Commentary on the Introduction to the Middle Way* (*Madhyamakāvatārabhāśya*), *Commentary on the Four Hundred Verses* (*Catuḥśatakaṭīkā*), *Commentary on the Seventy Verses on Emptiness* (*Śūnayatāsaptativṛtti*), *Commentary on the Sixty Verses on Reasoning* (*Yuktiṣaṣṭikāvṛtti*), and *Discussion on the Five Aggregates* (*Pañcaskandhaprakaraṇa*). In these works, Candrakīrti responds to many of the theories of the two truths that precede him. He rejects those of the Brahmanical schools and all the Buddhist schools we have so far examined: Vaibhāṣika, Sautrāntika, Yogācāra, and Svātantrika Madhyamaka. His philosophical attacks express a profound mistrust of metaphysical and epistemological foundationalism of any sort, to which he believes all these theories subscribe in varying degrees. For instance, Candrakīrti rejects Bhāviveka's reading of Nāgārjuna on the grounds that Bhāviveka's adoption of an independent formal probative reasoning entails a foundationalist metaphysics that is intolerable to Nāgārjuna's antifoundationalist project. Candrakīrti launches a withering critique against Bhāviveka and a staunch defense of Buddhapālita's Prāsaṅgika approach, which Bhāviveka rejects, quite mistakenly in Candrakīrti's view.

Instead of following any of the theories of the preceding schools, Candrakīrti advances a radical, nonfoundationalist theory of the two truths. This school later came to be known as Prāsaṅgika Madhyamaka, an umbrella classification under which fall other seminal works including the ninth chapter of Śāntideva's *Engaging an Awakened Life* (*Bodhicaryāvatāra*) and Ātiśa's *Introduction to the Two Truths* (*Satyadvayāvatāra*). Fundamentally, the Prāsaṅgika Madhyamaka theory of the two truths states the following:

- Conventional truth is dependent arising. Dependent arising is causally efficacious and lacks conventional intrinsic nature.
- Ultimate truth is emptiness. Emptiness is causally efficacious and lacks ultimate intrinsic nature. Ultimate truth is ultimately unreal.

These two theses are advanced separately but are coextensive. That is, there is a compatible relationship between conventional truth and ultimate truth, between dependent arising (*pratītyasamutpāda*, Tib. *rten 'brel)* and emptiness (*śūnyatā*, Tib. *stong pa nyid*). There is no logical tension between the two. I turn now to the Prāsaṅgika Madhyamaka arguments in defense of these two positions.

CONVENTIONAL TRUTH

Earlier we saw the Vaibhāṣika and Sautrāntika attribute causal efficacy to *ultimate* intrinsic reality. The Svātantrika Madhyamaka rejected this position, instead attributing causal efficacy to *conventional* intrinsic reality or unique particularity. They argued that the Vaibhāṣika and Sautrāntika failed to prosecute their philosophical positions through to their conclusion, and that the Svātantrika Madhyamaka position represents that conclusion. To deny an ultimate intrinsic reality might be necessary, but to go any further, to deny things a conventional intrinsic reality or unique particularity on the conventional level, would be, they argue, to deny them the very possibility of a productive existence. That, though, is precisely what the Prāsaṅgika Madhyamaka deny. The Prāsaṅgika Madhyamaka reject the positions of the Vaibhāṣika, Sautrāntika, and Svātantrika, arguing that only what lacks all intrinsic reality—conventional *and* ultimate—can dependently arise, and conventional truth is the field of dependent arising itself. Conventional truth, thus, is *always* intrinsically unreal; it lacks intrinsic reality not just *ultimately* (as the Svātantrika argue) but also *conventionally*. Hence that which is conventionally (or dependently) coarisen strictly does not arise ultimately.

Candrakīrti's theory of conventional truth, unique in its ontological and epistemological stance, is a marked break from the Svātantrika, especially the theories posited by Bhāviveka, Śāntarakṣita, and Kamalaśīla. That the Svātantrika school explained causal efficacy in terms of conventional intrinsic reality can be partially explained in terms of its intellectual pedigree. Svātantrika thinkers owed a massive and clear debt to the logicians, Dignāga and Dharmakīrti in particular, and were self-confessed adherents of the Buddhist logic school.[357] Dignāga and Dharmakīrti's epistemology and metaphysics, we have seen, are foundationalist, and the Svātantrika attempt to preserve them in a philosophical union with Nāgārjuna's nonfoundationalist metaphysics. The Prāsaṅgika, as we shall see, feel no such debt to foundationalism and attempt no such union.

Candrakīrti's presentation of his nonfoundationalist theory of conventional truth is extensive and varied. Here, the following five aspects of the theory will suffice as representative: (1) the two-nature theory, (2) the theory of mundane epistemic convention, (3) the theory on mundane ontological convention, (4) the theory of the epistemic and ontological convention of the noble beings, and (5) the two-tiered illusion theory. I will address them in turn.

Two-nature theory

Two-nature theory is derived from Candrakīrti's definition of the two truths. In *Introduction to the Middle Way*, Candrakīrti explains:

> It is said that all things have two natures—that found by a perception of reality and [that found by a perception] of unreality (Tib. *brdzun pa*). The objects of a perception of reality are things as they are; the objects of a perception of unreality are conventional truths.[358]

The *first nature*, Candrakīrti explains in his commentary, is the ultimate object that lacks intrinsic objective reality (*svarūpatā*, Tib. *bdag gi ngo bo nyid*) and is found by an exalted cognitive process (Tib. *ye shes*) that perceives such lack.[359] The *second nature*, on the other hand, is the same object found by an ordinary cognitive process, a process filtered through the blurry cataract of confusion, and one that fails to perceive the lack of intrinsic objective reality.

All phenomena are possessed of these two natures: conventional and ultimate. In his commentary, Candrakīrti says:

> The buddhas who flawlessly mastered the defining characteristics of each of the two truths have shown that all phenomena—interior and exterior—such as conditioned phenomena and a sprout, have two natures, and they are conventional and ultimate.[360]

Conventional nature corresponds to conventional truth, and ultimate nature corresponds to ultimate truth. The two natures therefore provide a complete ontological explanation of all objects.

This theory has epistemic implications. Since each phenomenon possesses two natures, a complete knowledge of all phenomena requires epistemic collaboration between the two cognitive processes, mundane and exalted cognition. Each cognitive process is confined to the same entity, but is domain specific—engaging only with its respective nature. Total knowledge of that entity requires that both cognitive pathways be engaged.

Mundane epistemic convention

We have seen that under Candrakīrti's definition of the two truths, exalted cognitions associate with ultimate truth, mundane cognitions with conventional truth. For the time being, I will focus only on mundane cognitions and their role—a critical one—in defining conventional truth. After all, conventional truth simply *is* what is true to mundane cognition (a point I will deal with in greater detail in the next section). But, Candrakīrti warns, this critical role means we must be especially careful to define what types of cognition qualify as mundane, what type of cognition are reliable enough to identify conventional truth. In *Introduction to the Middle Way*, Candrakīrti says:

> [We] accept that there are two kinds of perception of the unreal: that of acute sensory faculties and that of defective sensory faculties. The cognitive processes of those who have defective sensory faculties are incorrect in comparison to those persons with acute sensory faculties.[361]

In other words, conventional cognition can be either conventionally correct or incorrect, and only the former sort is a reliable warrant of what is conventionally true. In *Clear Words*, Candrakīrti describes this distinction between correct and incorrect cognition as one between mundane convention (*lokasaṃvṛti*, Tib. *'jig rten gyi kun rdzob*) and nonmundane convention (*alokasaṃvṛti*, Tib. *'jig rten ma yin pa'i kun rdzob*). The correct cognitive process is associated with an acute sense faculty, unimpaired by various causes of misperception. Such cognition perceives clearly and (conventionally, if not ultimately) truly: "[Worldly convention] posits things as they are [conventionally], and it does not engage in analysis."[362]

The incorrect cognitive process perceives neither clearly nor truly. It is associated with defective sense faculties and impairment by various causes of misperception, among which Candrakīrti's *Commentary on the Introduction to the Middle Way* lists *internal* causes such as cataracts, jaundice, and ingested hallucinogens, and *external* causes, such as magical illusions and natural phenomena known to cause optical and sonic illusions—for example, motion, reflective water and mirrors, echo chambers, and the rays of the sun.[363] Mentioned too are mental obstacles to correct cognition, which include wrong philosophical beliefs, faulty inferences, and sleep.[364] Any conventional framework so afflicted cannot qualify as a mundane convention.[365]

Mundane ontological convention

This is the ontological corollary of the previous point, which was epistemologically focused: *mundane* convention is epistemically reliable, and what is true to a mundane convention simply *is* conventional truth. The pig observed by someone of sound mind and with sound sense faculties is conventionally true, warrants further inquiry into its ultimate status, and maintains its conventional status even if later revealed to lack ultimate reality. *Nonmundane* convention, on the other hand, is epistemically deceptive, and such conventions are conventionally false. The flying pig seen by an observer on psychotropic drugs, or the yellow pig seen by a jaundiced observer, are conventionally false and warrant no further inquiry into their ultimate status. Candrakīrti says:

> Objects grasped by all six mundane sense faculties not impaired by the above, mentioned defects are [conventionally] real, real from the perspective of ordinary beings but not noble beings. But objects, such as reflections, that appear objectively real only when the sense faculties are impaired by the causes of defects are [conventionally] unreal, false from the perspective of ordinary beings.[366]

In *Clear Words*, Candrakīrti substitutes the terms "conventional truth" and "unconventional truth" for the terms "conventionally real" and "conventionally unreal" used in the previous passage. What is conventionally real is "conventional truth" (*lokasaṃvṛtisatya*, Tib. *'jig rten kun rdzob bden pa*), meaning true for and posited by the mundane conventions and by healthy and undeceived sense faculties. What is conventionally unreal is described as "unconventional truth" (*alokasaṃvṛtisatya*, Tib. *'jig rten ma yin pa'i kun rdzob bden pa*), truths fabricated by nonmundane conventions and by defective and deceived sense faculties.

The terminology here is significant because it signals an important aspect of Candrakīrti's thought, that is, that the existence of what is conventionally unreal is not entirely denied. Even fabricated truths are still truths, simply unconventional ones. Because they appear, they exist; they are causally efficacious and Candrakīrti regards them as conventionally real. What he rejects, though, is their reification. The mirage appearing to the parched traveler is an illusion, but the fact of its appearance means it exists somehow. The parched traveler's mistake is not to believe its existence, but to fail to see that its existence is merely appearance. The sense percepts exist, but the concept that the traveler constructs from them—an oasis!—does not.

For Candrakīrti, acknowledging the partial reality of illusions is important because *all things* are analogous to illusions. All concepts are reifications, and the most insidious of these is the concept of the self.

> The reified self is imagined by non-Buddhists and by those overcome by confusion and reified concepts, which arise like magical illusions, mirages, and so on, and which are nonexistent even from the perspective of mundane cognitive processes.[367]

His commentary on the verse includes in the same category the Sāṁkhya's three principles attributed to primal matter.

The epistemic and ontological conventions of noble beings

While illusion and the self may be analogous from the perspective of ordinary beings, Candrakīrti argues that from the perspective of noble beings, the two are *equivalent*. Noble beings—hearers (*śrāvaka*, Tib. *nyan thos*), solitary buddhas (*pratyekabuddha*, Tib. *rang sang rgyas*), and awakening beings (*bodhisattva*, Tib. *byang chub sems dpa'*)—have freed themselves from the deeply entrenched ontological confusion in which ordinary beings are mired, and they are able to directly apprehend all phenomena as the illusions they ultimately are. From the analytical perspective of the noble beings, all things are seen as they are: empty of intrinsic reality and dependently coarisen. From the intuitive perspective of ordinary beings, the same things are seen as intrinsic realities, unique particulars, and ultimates.

This argument is reinforced in his etymological analysis of the term *convention* (*saṃvṛti*, Tib. *kun rdzob*).[368] In *Clear Words* Candrakīrti attributes three senses to the term "convention." Convention is:

1) *confusion*, for it obstructs the mundane cognitive processes of the ordinary beings from seeing the reality as it is by concealing its nature;
2) *codependence* (*paraparasaṃbhavana*, Tib. *phan tshun brtan pa*), for being *interdependent* phenomena; and
3) a *signifier* (*saṃket*, Tib. *rda*) or *worldly convention* (*lokavyavahven*, Tib. *'jig rten tha snyad*), since conventions are dependently designated by means of expression and expressed, consciousness and its object of consciousness, etc.[369]

Candrakīrti claims that for ordinary beings, the first sense of convention eclipses the second and the third. As a result, far from understanding things as dependently arisen (the second sense) and dependently designated (the third), ordinary beings reify them as independently arisen, independent of designation:

> Confusion is *convention* because it conceals the nature; it fabricates all conditioned phenomena to appear as if they are real. The [Śākya]mūni [Buddha] declares those things to be conventional truths since conventionality is comprised of all created things.[370]

Confusion, Candrakīrti says, is the cognitive error that contaminates the cognitive processes of ordinary beings. Ordinary beings cannot cognize things without confusing conventional reality with intrinsic reality. But the mundane cognition of noble beings is not so afflicted, and the second and third senses prevail. Thus,

> anything that is regarded by the mundane conventions of ordinary beings as true amounts only to an untruth [judged against] the mundane cognition of noble beings, [which sees the same thing as] created and dependently arisen.[371]

Ordinary beings can't perceive something without reifying it. Noble beings, having broken the habit of reification, see things as having the nature of being *created* (Tib. *bcos ma*) and *unreal* (Tib. *bden pa ma yin pa*), just like a reflected image. The mundane convention of ordinary beings thus falls radically short of even the mundane convention of noble beings, which is free from confusion.

In his *Commentary on the Introduction to the Middle Way*, Candrakīrti illustrates this distinction by contrasting the *mere convention* (Tib. *kun rdzob tsam*) of noble beings with the *conventional reality* or *conventional truth* (Tib. *kun rdzob bden pa*) of ordinary beings. Childish ordinary beings, Candrakīrti says, are easily deceived, and the nature of things is deceptive. So deceived, they treat convention as a reality or truth unto itself. They treat conventionalities as though they were ultimate. On the other hand, noble beings, freed from afflictive perceptual confusion and acquainted with ultimate truth, recognize the conventional as it is: as *mere* convention. They recognize the deception for what it is and recognize phenomena as "dependently arisen, like the illusion."[372] Candrakīrti summarizes:

> That which is ultimate truth for ordinary beings is merely conventional for the noble beings cognitively engaged with appearances. Its nature, emptiness, is the ultimate truth for them [i.e., noble beings].[373]

Candrakīrti argues all noble beings are free from the gross confusion of ordinary beings. They do not confuse intrinsic reality with the absence of intrinsic reality, the substantial with the insubstantial, the permanent with the impermanent, self with nonself, reality with unreality, or substance with emptiness. Having directly realized emptiness, they have freed themselves from the tendency to reify. But, consistent with Mahāyāna orthodoxy, he argues that only a fully awakened being (*buddha*) is free from *all* cognitive confusion regarding the nature of two truths. In lesser noble beings—hearers, solitary buddhas, and bodhisattvas up to the eighth to tenth levels—subtle confusion of varying degrees remains.

Candrakīrti calls the subtle confusion that continues to afflict lesser noble beings "[nonafflictive] confusion that obstructs knowledge" (*jñeyāvaraṇa*, Tib. *shes bya'i sgrib pa*).[374] Nonafflictive confusion is a remnant of past conditioning, the latent imprints of countless lifetimes' worth of perceptual distortion. Though beings subject to nonafflictive confusion no longer reify things, they remain predisposed to the subtler misconceptions of dualistic appearance (Tib. *gnyis snang 'phrul ba'i bag chags*). They assume the existence of subtle dualities, even if they do not believe the components of the duality to be intrinisically real. Thus, although lesser noble beings have rid themselves of any reifying tendencies, they are not yet fully awakened. Their nonafflictive confusion presents a very subtle but very real cognitive limitation. The mundane cognition of these noble beings may directly comprehend all entities as merely conventional, as dependently arisen and illusory. But until they have uprooted nonafflictive confusion, they cannot directly realize the dependently arisen nature of dependent arising itself. Likewise, while the ultimate cognition of these noble beings may directly realize emptiness, until nonafflictive confusion is uprooted, they cannot directly realize the emptiness of emptiness.

On the other hand, awakened beings—i.e., buddhas—are permanently free from all cognitive limitations, nonafflictive confusion included. They are able to completely and exhaustively comprehend the reality of all things at all times:

> Reality as it is is the ultimate truth of awakened beings. It is ultimate truth, for it is nondeceptive. It is perceived directly by the awakened beings. Conventional truth, since it deceives, is not the ultimate truth.[375]

Here, Candrakīrti is arguing that the the mundane cognition of awakened beings, unlike that of lesser noble beings, directly knows the dependently arisen nature of dependently arisen entities, and hence knows conventional truth to be deceptive, to be *conventionally unreal.*[376]

"Dependent arising," Candrakīrti says, is simply the "definition of the reality of the mundane cognitive processes" (Tib. *'jig rten pa'i di kho na nyid kyi mtshan nyid*).[377] "Emptiness," he says in his commentary, citing Nāgārjuna's *Fundamental Verses on the Middle Way*,[378] is simply the "definition of the reality of the noble beings" (Tib. *'phags pa rnams kyi de kho na nyid kyi mtshan nyid*).[379] Awakened beings thus recognize the dependently arisen nature of dependent arising and the emptiness of emptiness. They recognize that the conventional domain—dependent arising—is mere convention, and that the ultimate domain—emptiness—is bereft of ultimate reality.

The two-tiered theory of illusion

We saw earlier that the way in which Candrakīrti treats illusion is quite distinct from his philosophical predecessors and plays a significant role in his presentation of the theory of the two truths. For Candrakīrti, *all* objects are like illusions in that they are partly real and partly unreal; even what is ordinarily held to be conventionally real is unreal in the final analysis. Accordingly, Candrakīrti presents a two-tiered theory of illusion in which *illusory* things are conventionally real and causally efficacious and *conventionally real* things are illusion-like. The ordinary distinction we make between illusion and conventional reality has its basis not in the world, but in epistemic capacity: while the mundane cognition of ordinary beings can perceive the unreality of illusions, they are blind to the unreality of conventionally real entities. A key passage on this point occurs in the *Commentary on the Introduction to the Middle Way*, in which Candrakīrti says:

> Although partly unreal, dependently arisen things such as reflected images and echoes do appear to those who possess cognitive confusion. So also appear entities such as forms—colors, thoughts, feelings, etc.—which are partly real. Intrinsic reality does not ever appear to the ones who possess cognitive confusion. This [i.e., intrinsic reality] and those that are conventionally unreal are, therefore, not conventional truths.[380]

Here, Candrakīrti presents us with four candidates for the status of conventional truth. Conventional truth may be considered (1) partly unreal entities (i.e., illusory objects), (2) partly real entities (i.e., nonillusory objects), (3) intrinsic reality, or (4) conventionally unreal entities. Candrakīrti rejects the latter two candidates outright, accepting only the conventional truth of the first two—the partly unreal and partly real—on the ground that they both appear to the mundane cognitive processes of ordinary, confused beings. We will deal with the candidates he rejects later on, but for now we'll focus only on those he accepts.

The first are *partly unreal* entities in the sense that they do not exist in the manner they appear to. Here, Candrakīrti is referring to conventionally illusory objects: a mirage that appears as a real oasis, a reflection that appears as an original image, an echo that is perceived as an original sound. This is the reason that the Buddhist philosophers we have previously examined exclude illusory objects from the domain of conventional truth. Candrakīrti takes a different approach, recognizing that they are partly unreal for the reason explained above: that they don't exist in the manner they appear makes them partly unreal. But the fact they exist at all—a fact proved by their appearance to mundane cognition—makes them conventionally partly real. And they appear because they are causally effective, the combined product of their necessary conditions. A reflected image, for instance, is the causal result of light travelling from its source to the retina via the original image and a reflective medium.

The second category, *partly real* entities, are so because they conventionally exist in the manner in which they appear to mundane cognition. Here, Candrakīrti is referring to conventionally real objects: colors, cognitions, feelings, and so on, objects whose appearance to mundane cognition accords with their conventional existence. But the fact that they appear to the distorted cognition of ordinary beings as something more than convention—as reality itself—makes them partly unreal. Absent that distortion, from the perspective of noble beings or the analytical perspective of ordinary beings their mere conventionality is revealed. Even conventionally real entities are *unreal* and *illusory*. They arise due to the same causal forces that govern the arising of illusory objects. The original image that reaches us without first visiting a reflective medium is just as dependently arisen as the one that does.

Thus for Candrakīrti, the ontological status of conventional illusions and conventionally real things are the same. Both are equally unreal, illusory, dependently arisen. The difference is simply one of perspective. The mundane cognition of ordinary beings is sufficient to detect the illusory nature of conventionally illusory objects, but the illusory nature of all objects requires more sophisticated cognition.

Having seen Candrakīrti's equation of illusion and conventional reality, we turn to his theoretical explanation of it. The crux of the matter is the ontological status of intrinsic reality: Is intrinsic reality conventionally real, a conventional truth? In contrast with the philosophical schools I have previously examined, most notably the school with which it is most closely philosophically related, the Svātantrika Madhyamaka, Candrakīrti answers this question in the negative. Intrinsic reality, he says, is not even conventionally real. In the passage I cited earlier, Candrakīrti listed intrinsic reality as one of the two candidates excluded from the domain of conventional truth. As he says in the *Commentary on the Introduction to the Middle Way*:

> This [intrinsic reality] and those that are conventionally unreal are, therefore, not conventional truths.[381]

We have previously seen that Candrakīrti holds that the mundane cognitions of ordinary beings habitually reify, investing all perceptual objects with intrinsic reality. This seems to pose a philosophical challenge for Candrakīrti, since he has accepted illusions as conventionally real on account of their appearance to mundane cognitions. I have argued that, according to Candrakīrti, illusions win conventional status on account of their appearance to mundane cognitions. Then the objection could be raised here: why does intrinsic reality not achieve the status of conventional truth? After all, it also appears to mundane cognitions. Candrakīrti addresses this problem in two ways. First, though he admits that things seem to mundane cognition to possess intrinsic nature, that doesn't warrant the conclusion that intrinsic nature is a reality:

> Mundane cognitive processes are not treated as epistemically reliable in any sense with reference to the [ultimate] reality. Nor is it the case that [ultimate] reality is undermined by the mundane cognitive processes.[382]

Mundane cognitions are constitutionally confused and are excluded from questions of ultimacy. This isn't a new argument, though, and while it might help settle the ultimate status of intrinsic reality, it doesn't settle the question of mundane cognitions' conventional status. The second line of argument is more decisive. Recall the reason Candrakīrti cites earlier for excluding the candidacy of intrinsic reality:

> Intrinsic reality (*svabhāva*) does not ever appear to the ones who possess cognitive confusion.[383]

Mundane cognitions may be excluded from questions of ultimacy, but they remain the arbiters of the conventional. What appears to mundane or conventional cognition simply is, we have seen, conventional reality. But, Candrakīrti says, intrinsic reality *never* objectively appears to that cognition. We might have a confused belief in intrinsic reality, but its root is not in mundane cognition: that reality *never* appears to it. Intrinsic reality, Candrakīrti says, never falls in the cognitive domain of ordinary beings. For Candrakīrti intrinsic reality is a fabrication apart from and after cognition. It is a conceptual construct we superimpose upon the nonintrinsic entities that appear to our mundane cognitions and constitute our conventional reality:

> Thus the framework that determines conventional truth has the force of confusion, an afflictive factor associated with the factors of cyclic existence.[384]

Intrinsic reality has no basis in the world itself, Candrakīrti argues; it is a conceptual fraud without any epistemic credentials. Hence it is not warranted even by ordinary cognitive processes.

Candrakīrti's epistemological claim, that intrinsic reality doesn't objectively appear to any cognition, even mundane cognition, is anchored on an ontological claim—that is, intrinsic reality doesn't appear because it *can't*. It is an ontological impossibility. Candrakīrti provides us the following grounds for rejecting any ontology based on intrinsic reality. The most obvious place where Candrakīrti defends this position is indeed his critique of the possibility of ontology based on the notion of intrinsic reality (*svabhāva*) and unique particularity (*svālakṣaṇa*), posited by Dignāga and Dharmakīrti, which was later embraced by the Svātantrika Madhyamaka as the defining characteristic of the conventional truth. In the first place, Candrakīrti denies the possibility that intrinsic reality is something that can be confined to the conventional domain. If it existed in either domain, it would have to exist in both, he reasons. Recall that the test for ultimate reality is that it can be found under refined critical analysis. And intrinsic reality—ontologically cordoned off and invulnerable to further critical analysis—is precisely the kind of thing that analysis searches for, and would be bound to find if it existed at all. It cannot be further broken into constituent components because it is primary, and it cannot be separated into its relationships of dependence because it is constitutionally independent. Were it to exist at all, even in the conventional domain, it would be the terminus of any analysis and thus we would be compelled to conclude that it is the ultimate nature of things, too.

And that, argues Candrakīrti, is an impossible conclusion for a Mādhyamika to reach, since the bedrock Madhyamaka position is that *nothing* is capable of resisting ultimate analysis. All things are empty, for the reasons we have previously examined—reasons that are common to both the Svātantrika Madhyamaka and Prāsaṅgika Madhyamaka. Intrinsic reality and emptiness mutually exclude each other; after all, emptiness simply is the emptiness of intrinsic reality. Thus, to grant intrinsic reality *any* existence is impossible without accepting the wholesale dismantlement of the Madhyamaka theory of emptiness. Candrakīrti states:

> If things exist in virtue of being unique particulars, then through negation of that [unique particularity] things would be destroyed, and emptiness would be the cause of its destruction. This is not the case, however, because things do not exist [that way].[385]

The corollary to this argument—that even a conventional intrinsic reality will violate the Mādhyamikas' conception of the ultimate—is that it will *also* violate the Mādhyamikas' conception of the conventional. That is, that the conventional is *dependently arisen*. Candrakīrti states:

> According to the view that asserts the intrinsic reality of entities, they would stay constant like intrinsic reality itself, because the intrinsic reality, by definition, is not possible to become another.[386]

To be intrinsically real is to be causally self-contained and ontologically self-defined. It rules out any possibility of change, and therefore any possibility of causal efficacy. Thus, if Mādhyamikas are to retain their signature doctrines of emptiness and dependent arising, then they must reject intrinsic reality in all forms, since it is by nature the opposite of emptiness and constitutionally incapable of arising dependently. Therefore, Candrakīrti argues, "from the point of view of either of the two truths there is none that arises as a unique particular,"[387] nothing that possesses intrinsic reality.

ULTIMATE TRUTH

We now turn to Candrakīrti's second thesis, his position on ultimate truth, which is that it is simply emptiness. Emptiness is causally efficacious because, lacking ultimate intrinsic nature, it is subject to the conditioned arising that is only possible of intrinsically empty things. Ultimate truth is therefore ultimately unreal—or, we might say, emptiness is always empty.

Before turning to the arguments by which Candrakīrti advances his position, some further background is in order. Following his discussion of conventional truth in *Commentary on the Introduction to the Middle Way*, Candrakīrti turns to ultimate truth. He begins by admitting that ultimate truth cannot be explicitly demonstrated on the ground that it is inexpressible; though it is knowable, it is not an entity *per se*. So, he promises only to approximate the phenomenological experience of the ultimate truth by way of a visual metaphor.[388] In our afflictive confusion, Candrakīrti reasons, we are like someone afflicted by myodesopsia, whose vision is obscured by optical "floaters," deposits in the vitreous humor of the eye. Someone with this condition will see floaters that aren't in the world, in the same way we see an intrinsic reality that is just as absent. The ultimate truth, then, is simply the absence of the cognitive obscuration. When we are not afflicted by myodesopsia, these floaters do not obscure our vision, and we see truly. When we are not afflicted by confusion, intrinsic reality does not obscure our vision, and we see the ultimate truth of things.[389] Those who see without obstruction are noble or awakened beings, and ultimate truth is simply their reality: reality as seen by those who see clearly.[390] Thus, the ultimate truth is not something that transcends reality, it is simply the characteristic of reality as it is (*etat tattvasya lakṣaṇaṃ*).[391] As we have seen, Candrakīrti expresses it thus:

> It is said that all things have two natures—that found by a perception of reality and [that found by a perception] of unreality. Objects of a perception of reality are things as they are.[392]

In his commentary, Candrakīrti expands this definition:

> Ultimate is the object whose nature is found by a particular exalted cognitive process of those who perceive reality. Such an object does not exist by virtue of its intrinsic objective reality (*svarūpatā*, Tib. *bdag gi ngo bo nyid*). This is the first nature, the object of the perception of reality is the way things really are.[393]

Candrakīrti's explanation here raises three important points. First, in saying that the nature of things "is found by a *particular* exalted cognitive process," he means that not all cognitive processes are capable of uncovering the ultimate truth. Only one is capable of such perception: the *analytical* mode. Second, in saying that the ultimate truth "does not exist by virtue of its *intrinsic objective reality*," he reminds us that the ultimate truth—the lack of intrinsic reality—*itself* lacks intrinsic reality. The ultimate truth is no more intrinsically real than the conventional truth; both lack intrinsic reality entirely. Finally, in saying that the ultimate truth is the first of the two natures of things found by perception of reality, he means that ultimate truth is the ultimate nature of all conventionally real things. All things have an ultimate nature that constitutes ultimate truth, just as they have conventional nature constituting conventional truth.

In commenting on Nāgārjuna's *Fundamental Verses on the Middle Way* (18.9) in *Clear Words*, Candrakīrti expands this further, listing five characteristics of ultimate reality. It is, he says:

1. Not able to be comprehended from others

By "not able to be comprehended from others" (*aparapratyaya*), Candrakīrti means that we have to come to a personal understanding of ultimate truth. The explanations and insights of others cannot substitute for personal insights; though immensely helpful, they alone cannot bring us to a full understanding of ultimate truth. That truth must be individually *experienced*. A person with unafflicted vision may describe the experience of such vision to another with afflicted vision, but until their affliction is actually resolved, that person's understanding of unafflicted vision remains essentially theoretical. In the same way, Candrakīrti argues, noble and awakened beings may sketch the ultimate truth to us ordinary beings conceptually, but until we attain the unobscured, nonconceptual cognitive processes of noble and awakened beings, the ultimate truth remains obscured to us.[394] It is only when we stop incessantly superimposing intrinsic reality that we actually see reality as it is.[395]

2. *Peaceful*

By "peaceful" (*śānta*), Candrakīrti means the way things really are is unobstructed and undisturbed by the error of perceived intrinsic reality.[396] In particular, Candrakīrti's term "peaceful" describes the freedom from the pathologically destructive habits of aversion, desire, and confusion, which are the cognitive and psychological tendencies that fuel epistemic error and mistaken belief about the intrinsic nature of things.

3. *Unfabricated by linguistic fabrications*

By "unfabricated by linguistic fabrications" (*prapañcair aprapañcitaṃ*), Candrakīrti means ultimate reality cannot be found in verbal expressions and in books, which are incapable of expressing the way things really are, ultimately. Although words may be perfectly capable of describing how things are conventionally, conventional truth is defined within the framework of linguistic convention.[397]

4. *Nonconceptual*

By "nonconceptual" (*nirvikalpa*), Candrakīrti means that ultimate truth cannot be fully conceptualized, and thus is free from the conceptualization of mental discursiveness. Conceptualization governs the conventional truth; there is no place for it in the ultimate.[398]

5. *Without distinctions*

Finally, the ultimate is "without distinctions" (*anānārtham*), by which Candrakīrti means that all things are ultimately alike and equal in their emptiness of intrinsic reality.[399] We can only make ultimate ontological distinctions on the basis of intrinsic reality, and absent it, no distinction is possible—there is just emptiness through and through.

Nevertheless, Candrakīrti says, the Buddha makes a pedagogical distinction, subclassifying the ultimate truth of emptiness according to that which it applies: to the emptiness of persons (*pudgalanairātmya*) or to the emptiness of phenomena (*dharmanairātmya*). He does so, Candrakīrti says, for the purpose of liberating all sentient beings,[400] who vary in disposition and capacity and therefore require equally varied instruction.[401] The realization of the nonself of persons leads to the individual liberation of the hearers and solitary buddhas. By directly realizing the interdependence and insubstantiality of the five aggregates that constitute the self, the underlying afflictive confusion and other defilements are overcome, and the very root of cyclic existence is cut.

Though hearers and solitary buddhas have exhaustive realization of the nonself of persons, they lack an exhaustive realization of the nonself of all other phenomena. This is the more demanding and total realization, and satisfies a more demanding goal: the total enlightenment of the bodhisattva. The realization of the nonself of both persons *and* phenomena removes both afflictive confusion and nonafflictive confusion—which is the subtle confusion we examined in the previous section, the penultimate obstacle to enlightenment.[402]

Having now briefly outlined Candrakīrti's position on the two truths, let us now turn to his defense of his position. I will focus on three arguments: (1) the not-self argument, (2) the emptiness argument, and (3) the emptiness of emptiness argument. We will address them in sequence.

1. The not-self argument: the unreality of the conventionally real self

The not-self argument demonstrates the self's lack of intrinsic nature both ultimately and conventionally. But a proper understanding of any refutation requires first understanding that which is being refuted—here, the self. And to do so, Candrakīrti says, we must first determine from where the presumption of self arises. Like all Buddhist philosophers, Candrakīrti says the presumption arises in relation to the five aggregates. Candrakīrti hews to the standard Buddhist line that the five aggregates exhaust the entire field of compounded phenomena. If a person is to be found, it can only be found in the aggregates, which contain and exhaust every possible configuration of personhood:

> Therefore there is no self different from the aggregates, for apart from the aggregates its conception cannot be established. Nor is it considered to be the mundane cognitive basis for clinging to an "I."[403]

There is, in effect, nothing more to a person than that constituted by the five aggregates, the raw materials of our very existence. Recall that the five aggregates are: (1) the form aggregate (*rūpa*), (2) the sensation or feeling aggregate (*vedanā*), (3) the perception aggregate (*saṃjñā*), (4) the disposition aggregate (*saṃskāra*), and (5) the consciousness aggregate (*vijñāna*).

The form aggregate constitutes our physical phenomenon, the basis for the entire physio-neurological structure of the person. Therefore sensory faculties—eyes, ears, nose, tongue, body, and mind—and their respective objects—visual objects, sounds, smells, tastes, tactile objects, and concepts or ideas—all belong to this aggregate. The sensation or feeling aggregate is exhaustively composed of the entire range of experiences, the sensations or feelings that are either physical or emotional/psychological as a result of the contact of six sense faculties with their respective sensory objects. The perception aggregate is exhaustively comprised of six perceptions that arise from the contact of the six sense faculties with the six sense objects, resulting in six sense consciousnesses. The primary function of this aggregate is to provide the conceptual evaluations through naming, discriminating, appropriating, and identifying the specific features of the objects. It is at this stage where the birth of the notion of self as "I," "me," and "mine" takes place. So from this arises dualistic notions such as thought and thinker, observer and observed, feeling and feeler, seeing and seer, experience and experiencer, and so forth. The dispositional aggregate exhausts all mental dispositions, ranging from the mental/emotional states (such as wholesome or unwholesome desires, urges, karmic drives, fears, insecurity, defensiveness, and expectations) to cognitive states (such as memories, mindfulness, intelligence, knowledge, and confusion). These psychological/cognitive internal drives arise in response to, and in reaction against, the conceptual judgments carried out through the perception aggregate. The consciousness aggregate is constitutive of the six consciousnesses arisen from the contact of sensory faculties with their respective objects.

Candrakīrti explains these aggregates concisely as follows:

> Form is characterized by color and shape; feeling naturally experiences; perception discriminates; dispositions predispose [mental, vocal, and physical actions]; the characteristic of consciousness is to directly perceive objects.[404]

The five aggregates are therefore the root of our conception of self. It is from our misapprehension of these aggregates that we form our misapprehension of a self. Though the aggregates are parts, we totalize them. Though they are fluid and impermanent, we eternalize them. Candrakīrti says:

> Seeing wisely that all afflictive defilements and misfortunes arise from objectifying the transient composites (*satkāyadṛṣṭi*, Tib. *'jig tshogs la lta ba*), and realizing that the self is the object of this view, the practitioner negates such a self.[405]

Here, Candrakīrti makes three important points. First, the sense of self stems from the reification of things that ought not to be reified: the transient and composite five aggregates. If there is a solid substantial self, it must be found among the aggregates, but the aggregates are the very opposite of substantial: they are ephemeral and momentary. Nevertheless, they are reified by identifying the aggregates either individually or collectively as a self: as "I," "me," or "mine."[406]

Second, "afflictive defilements" and the "misfortunes" that are their karmic result stem from our reification of the aggregates. Among the afflictive defilements referred to here are confusion, anger, hatred, ill-will, craving, and clinging. Among the misfortunes they give rise to are birth, aging, illness, and death. All suffering is the result of our afflictive emotions; all such emotions attach to the objects we create through reification; and all such objects are comprised of the five aggregates. To craft self and other from the aggregates is to carve up an interconnected world into spheres of identification and preference, in relation to which afflictive emotions may be generated. By reifying the aggregates, we engage the phenomological world in a way that only accumulates the causes of suffering.

Third, while the aggregates are the source of the misconception of self, they are also the source of the eradication of that misconception—the ultimate freedom. The route to the correct view does not avoid the incorrect view, but runs through it. It is by recognizing and negating the misconception, not ignoring it, that it is overcome. Candrakīrti says that practitioners attain the knowledge of reality pertaining to self or persons through the *negation and transcendence* of the misconceptions of a reified self. After all, the eradication of clinging to self is impossible without engaging with the aggregates, the very objects clung to.[407] If there is a possible basis for a substantial self, it must be found within the five aggregates, and it is by appreciating that such a basis cannot be found within them that we dismantle the misconceptions to which they give rise. This is only possible by searching exhaustively among the aggregates and finding nothing, not by neglecting to search. It is by this process of exhaustive analysis that one begins to dismantle the habit of reification that keeps one from the correct knowledge of nonself.

Candrakīrti develops his arguments against the personal self in great detail in chapter six of *Introduction to the Middle Way* and its commentary. One such argument, known as the "argument from the sevenfold analysis of a chariot" (Tib. *shing rta rnams bdun gyi rigs pa*), will suffice here, since it is in many ways a synthesis of Candrakīrti's arguments. Candrakīrti concludes that argument by saying:

> It is not plausible that the self is different from the aggregates, nor identical with them, nor dependent upon them.[408] The self does not own the aggregates. This is established in codependence with the aggregates.[409]

Candrakīrti argues that the self's lack of intrinsic reality is analogous to a chariot:

> We do not accept a chariot to be different from its own parts, nor to be identical [to its parts], nor to be in possession of them, nor is it in the parts, nor are the parts in it, nor is it the mere composite [of its parts], nor is it the shape [or size of those parts].[410]

The structure of the argument demonstrating the same lack of intrinsic reality for the self is, thus, as follows: Since the aggregates are exhaustive, if there is an intrinsically real self, it exists in relation with the aggregates. To extract an intrinsically real self from the aggregates requires following one of seven routes: that the self either (1) is distinct from, (2) is identical to, (3) possesses, (4) is within, (5) is contained within, (6) is composed of, or (7) is simply the shape of the aggregates. Candrakīrti rejects each of these in turn.

The first route, a self distinct from its aggregates, is the position held by the non-Buddhist Sāṃkhya philosophical school, which holds the self to be eternal, inactive, without qualities, a nonagent, and the partaker of all objects of knowledge.[411] This is an implausible position, Candrakīrti retorts:

> The self like this does not exist, for it is no more produced than the son of an infertile woman. Moreover, it is not plausible for it to be the basis of the conception of self. We do not accept such a self to exist even conventionally.[412]

Were it to so exist, Candrakīrti continues, a raft of absurd consequences would ensue: the self and the aggregates would exist without being related, meaning the self would remain unchanged while the body it inhabits and which is one of its bases of designation changes and decays. This consequence could only be avoided were the self visibly separate from the body, which is plainly not the case:

> Apart from the aggregates the self is not apprehended. If it were the case that self is different from the aggregates, then their existence could be apprehended separately. But such is not the case. Therefore the self does not exist distinct from the aggregates.[413]

Moreover a distinct self would entail moral nihilism, since it would shirk moral responsibility for the *karma* performed by its aggregates. The impossibility of their separateness also rules out proposing their mutual codependence, since a thesis of dependent relation presupposes distinct identities that relate, and such a possibility has been excluded.

The second route is a self that is identical to either all the aggregates or the single aggregate of mind.[414] From this alternative, Candrakīrti shows, absurdity also ensues. The chief absurdity, he says, is that an identity relationship between a thing that is singular, solid, and enduring (the self) and things that are manifold, transient, and momentary (the aggregates, or just the mental aggregate) is impossible without the identity of one subsuming rather than proving the other. Were the self and the aggregates indistinguishably one and the same, self would either be as manifold as the aggregates, or the aggregates would be as singular as the self; the self would be as causally conditioned, transient, and composite as the aggregates, or the aggregates as independent, unitary, and enduring as the self. To say that the aggregates bear the singular nature attributed to the self makes calling them "aggregates" at all nonsensical, but to say that the "self" bears the manifold, conditioned nature of the aggregates is to concede that the singular, intrinsic nature we are searching for cannot be found.

It is also to concede that such a self, one with the afflicted aggregates, would be annihilated with those aggregates at the moment of attaining nirvāṇa, and would, again, not reap the effects of its karma. A self identical with the aggregates performs the actions producing nirvāṇa and also its own demise; quite another self would be required to partake of the result itself, nirvāṇa.

For these reasons, Candrakīrti says, the self cannot be identical to the aggregates. The fact that the first two routes are blocked also rules out the third route—a relationship of possession or ownership—since it can only be reached by means of one of the former routes. A possessive relationship ordinarily presupposes a distinction between those that relate. It might be reasonable to say "Devadatta owns a cow," so long as Devadatta and the cow are separate entities. But it is not reasonable to say "the self owns the aggregates" when the possibility of their distinctness has, in the first alternative, already failed. Candrakīrti nevertheless allows the possibility of a possessive relationship between two things identified with each other, but that possibility fell with the second alternative. It might be reasonable to say "Devadatta owns a body" if the body can be identified with Devadatta. But it is not reasonable to say "the self own the aggregates" since the possibility of their identity has also been excluded. This route depends on the viability of one of the routes preceding it, and absent them, it bears no further consideration: neither distinct from nor identical to each other, we cannot say that the self owns the form.[415]

A similar fate befalls the next two routes—that the self exists within the aggregates or vice versa. Such a relationship presupposes the distinctness of those that relate to one another, and Candrakīrti's analysis of the second alternative has shown the impossibility of that distinctness. Therefore he says:

> The self does not exist in the aggregates and the aggregates do not exist in the self. If they exist distinctly, then such a relation can be plausible. But because no such distinctness exists, it is mere reification.[416]

His commentary reinforces this point, arguing that only distinct entities can reasonably comprise a container-contained relationship. We can meaningfully say, he argues, "there is yogurt in the bowl," because "bowl" and "yogurt" are distinct entities perceived in their respective roles of container and contained. But it is impossible for the two to have a container-contained relationship, given the impossibility of the distinctness of aggregate and self that has previously been demonstrated.[417]

The sixth route—that the self is the mere collection of the aggregates—is likewise blocked because it is simply the first failed route—that the self is distinct from the aggregates—rephrased. To say the self is the collection of the aggregates is simply to say the self *is* the collected aggregates. It is asserting the identity relationship already shown to be impossible under a different guise. Candrakīrti further adds that it is absurd for the appropriator—the self as the agent—and the appropriated—the five aggregates—to be identical, since the actor (self) and that which is acted on (aggregates) would be identical if this were the case. We would hence be forced to accept the identity of a pot and its potter, or of fuel and fire. It would be nonsensical to do so, and it is thus equally nonsensical to treat the appropriator and the appropriated as identical.[418]

The final alternative, that the self is found in the shape and form of the aggregates, is implausible because it is overly reductive. While it might be more plausible to reduce an inanimate object like a chariot to the shape of its composite parts, to do the same to the self would imply that the self is equally inanimate: a purely physical form, nothing more than its form aggregate. To relate the self to the aggregates by means of their shape and form is to discount the four nonphysical aggregates—consciousness, feeling, perception, and compositional factors—which lack any shape, color, size, or form of their own.[419] One has hardly successfully related the self to the *five* aggregates by abandoning all but one of them.

Having exhausted the only available routes by which one could arrive at an intrinsically real self, Candrakīrti concludes that no such self can be located or logically sustained. The aggregates are exhaustive, and were there an intrinsically real self, it would be found in relation to them. Of the seven possible relationships between self and aggregates we have explored, all fail. The first two lead to intolerable absurdities; the third depends on either of the two that fell before it; the fourth and fifth depend on the already fallen first; the sixth is simply the fallen first rephrased; and the seventh doesn't relate self to the aggregates but to a single aggregate, form—an absurd and unsatisfying result. Thus, Candrakīrti concludes that, both ultimately and conventionally, the self is empty of any intrinsic reality.

That it is empty of intrinsic reality even at the conventional level is not to say that it doesn't conventionally exist, nor that it cannot be conventionally effective. The self exists, but *nominally* rather than intrinsically: it is dependently designated on the basis of its aggregates just as a chariot is dependently designated on the basis of its parts.[420] Such a dependently designated self can, nevertheless, effectively serve as a conventionally real moral agent, just like a dependently designated chariot can effectively serve as a real mode of transport.[421] To be a moral agent, according to Candrakīrti, is to act in moral relation to others, and such a mode of existence not only does not require an intrinsic self, it demands its absence. Things that intrinsically exist do so in ontological isolation, and things that are isolated by nature cannot and do not relate. Moral relations are relations of causal interaction and interdependence, and so a merely conventional self, designated and dependent, is, in fact, the requisite moral agent.

2. *The emptiness argument: unreality of conventionally real phenomena*

Candrakīrti's second argument demonstrates phenomena's lack of intrinsic reality both conventionally and ultimately. In the previous section, an intrinsically real self required a viable model of relation with the aggregates; here, intrinsically real phenomena require a viable model of their causal production. As in the previous section, this is a demand that cannot be met. Candrakīrti's argument here is an extension of Nāgārjuna's famous tetralemma:

> Neither from itself nor from another,
> nor from both,
> nor without cause,
> does anything, anywhere, ever arise.[422]

Candrakīrti develops this argument in great detail in chapter six of *Introduction to the Middle Way* and its commentary. Here I will examine his overall strategy without particular attention to the argumentative details, many of which, we will notice, replicate arguments advanced in discussions of causality by schools previously examined. Candrakīrti's innovation is not so much the contents of his argument as the radical conclusion he uses it to prosecute: the utter absence of intrinsic reality.

If entities are intrinsically real, Candrakīrti argues, they must arise either causally or causelessly. Whereas to arise causelessly is a self-contained option, to arise causally contains three distinct options: to arise from itself, from another, or from both itself and another. Thus, we arrive at the four options of Nāgārjuna's tetralemma, the four routes to intrinsically real phenomena:

1) To arise from itself
2) To arise from another
3) To arise from both itself and another
4) To arise causelessly

As in the previous section, all routes are blocked. First, if entities arise from themselves, cause and effect would be identical and would exist simultaneously. The effect, already existent, need not be further caused. The cause is either redundant, or, if it insists on nevertheless acting, would simply begin an infinite regress, an unstoppable feedback loop of causation.[423] In short, a cause in which the effect already exists can only be unproductive or incapable of cessation, and both results are intolerable.

Second, if entities arise from another, the possibility of causal relation is discounted. If cause and effect are distinct from each other, there can be no *relation*—we already saw Candrakīrti's argument for the impossibility of a relation between distinct things—and causation without relation is hardly causation at all. Causation, properly understood, refers to observable, replicable relations between causes and effects of a certain type. Relation is what gives causation its utility—its predictive power and its soteriological value. Without relation, chaos ought to ensue; as Candrakīrti puts it:

> Anything could arise from anything, like a fire from pitch darkness; given that the cause and the effect would be distinct, all causes would be equally "another."[424]

And yet chaos is observably not the state of things. Seeds yield sprouts only of the same type; fire arises from a spark and fuel, not "pitch darkness." Without causal relation, the entire corpus of natural laws can be explained only as coincidence—a possibility so improbable as to be absurd.

The final two routes have been blocked by the arguments already advanced. The third, "from itself and another," would be prone to the faults of the previous two,[425] and I foreshadowed the problem with the fourth route, "from neither," in discussing the loss of causal relations involved in the second route—that is, the chaos objection. A world ungoverned by causal relations is a world of chaos, a world in which "anything could arise from anything."[426] This is observably, and thankfully, not the case. Thus, all four routes to the production of an intrinsically real entity are blocked.[427] Intrinsically real entities, incapable of being brought into existence, do not exist.

Again, Candrakīrti emphasizes that lacking intrinsic existence, even conventionally, is not tantamount to nonexistence. Though lacking intrinsic reality, barred from the four established routes by which it might be produced, things nevertheless arise, simply codependently, rather than intrinsically; ephemerally, rather than substantively. Candrakīrti summarizes:

> Entities do not arise causelessly, and they do not arise from causes like God. Nor do they arise out of themselves, nor from another, nor from both. They arise codependently.[428]

Things lack intrinsic reality, but they are still things, they still serve as functional objects of experience. In fact, these two features—lack of intrinsic reality and functionality—are, as in the previous section, not coincidences. They mutually entail each other. To be an object of experience requires *interacting* with the experiencer—it is a collaboration between the object cognized, the cognizer, and requisite conditions of cognition. Candrakīrti says:

> Empty entities such as reflections are not manifest without depending on collocations. In the same way, from an empty reflection, consciousness of that form can be seen to arise. In the same way, since all phenomena are empty, everything arises from emptiness.[429]

Intrinsically real things simply cannot interact; they cannot phenomenologically contribute to causal process. And so, merely conventional phenomena, designated and dependent, are in fact the requisite components of experience.

3. The emptiness of emptiness argument: unreality of ultimate reality

The previous two arguments show that both phenomena and persons are empty of intrinsic reality, ultimately and conventionally. Under analysis, no intrinsic reality can be found, either within or without.

The unfindability of intrinsic reality, of an ultimate, independent mode of existence, simply is the ultimate truth of things. That things instead exist in a conditional, dependent mode simply is the conventional truth of things.

But this begs a final possibility, which this, Candrakīrti's final argument, is aimed at rejecting. That is, if the absence of intrinsic reality is the very nature of all things, might we not claim that things' lack of intrinsic reality *is their very intrinsic nature*? Might we not claim that emptiness—the universal unfindability of an ultimate mode of existence—is in fact the ultimate mode of existence?

This, Candrakīrti argues, would be a grievous mistake, and his final argument is aimed at heading it off. He says:

> The emptiness of intrinsic reality of things is itself called by the wise "emptiness," and this emptiness also is considered to be empty of any intrinsic reality.[430]

The emptiness of that which is called "emptiness" is accepted as "the emptiness of emptiness" (*śūnyatāśūnyatā*). It is explained in this way for the purpose of controverting objectification of the emptiness as intrinsically real.[431]

Candrakīrti cites as textual support for this position the Buddha's subclassification of emptiness into "the sixteen emptinesses."[432] What these "emptinesses" have in common, he argues, is that each and every one is itself empty of intrinsic reality. Each one of these "emptinesses" is noneternal, not subject to disintegration, and totally lacking in intrinsic reality.[433] For instance:

> The eye is empty of eye[ness] because that is its reality. The ear, nose, tongue, body, and mind are also to be explained in this way . . . Because each of them is noneternal, not subject to disintegration, and their reality is nonintrinsic, [the emptiness of] the eye and the other sense faculties are accepted as possessing internal emptiness.[434]

The same holds, Candrakīrti argues, for the remaining "emptinesses"—the aforementioned emptiness of emptiness, and also the external emptiness (*bahirdhāśunyatā*), the internal-external emptiness (*adhyātmabahirdhāśunyatā*), the vast emptiness (*mahāśūnyatā*), the emptiness of the ultimately real (*paramārthaśūnyatā*), the emptiness of composite phenomena (*saṃskṛtaśūnyatā*), and the emptiness transcending the extremes (*atyantaśūnyatā*).

Moreover they must be this way, Candrakīrti argues in his commentary on the *Fundamental Verses on the Middle Way* (13.7), lest the doctrine of emptiness descend into absurdity. For instance, if emptiness were intrinsically, which is to say, *ultimately* real, that would render it quite distinct from conventional things, which are not ultimately real. And once again, Candrakīrti applies the now familiar argument that distinctness and relation are mutually exclusive. If emptiness existed intrinsically and that to which it applies did not, then the two would be quite distinct. The emptiness of the chariot and the empty chariot itself would be quite unrelated. And, if the chariot were empty of intrinsic reality, but its emptiness was not, we would have to posit two distinct and contradictory realities even for the one conventional object: a logically intolerable result. Thus, while emptiness is the ultimate truth of conventionally real entities, it is not, *and cannot be*, itself ultimately real. Everything, the ultimate truth included, is bereft of intrinsic reality.

The heart, and the major philosophical advance, of Candrakīrti's two truths theory is this total rejection of intrinsic reality. All things, conventionally and ultimately, are without intrinsic reality. This is the trademark nonfoundationalism of the Prāsaṅgika, and it underwrites their conception of the interrelation between the two truths—and the entire Buddhist project. It is a thing's emptiness of intrinisic reality that makes possible its dependent arising, its functionality. As Nāgārjuna's classic statement goes:

> To whomsoever emptiness makes sense,
> everything makes sense.

To whomsoever emptiness makes no sense,
nothing makes sense.[435]

Explaining this passage, Candrakīrti makes the following points:

> To whom the emptiness of intrinsic reality of all things makes sense, what we have been discussing makes sense. Why? Because we maintain emptiness to be dependent arising. Therefore for whomsoever emptiness makes sense, dependent arising makes sense.
>
> For whomsoever dependent arising makes sense, the four noble truths make sense. This is why it makes sense: only the dependently arisen suffers, but not that which is nondependently arisen. That which is dependently arisen is empty of intrinsic reality.
>
> Since there is suffering, there is an origin of suffering, a cessation of suffering, and meditation on the path. Since these exist, knowledge of suffering, elimination of the origin, cessation of suffering, and attainment of the path make sense. When knowledge of the truth of suffering and the like exists, effects also make sense.[436]

Candrakīrti goes on to argue that all mundane conventions—the Buddha, Dharma, Sangha, mundane, supramundane, the sacred, the profane, etc.—make sense because they are empty of intrinsic reality, which is simply to say they are dependently arisen. Candrakīrti's commentary on Nāgārjuna's *Fundamental Verses on the Middle Way* (24.14) concludes in these words:

> A special knowledge of all mundane and supramundane phenomena makes sense. Virtuous actions (*dharma*), vicious actions (*adharma*) and their fruits, and mundane ethical conventions also make sense. For this reason for whomsoever emptiness makes sense, everything makes sense. For whomsoever emptiness makes no sense, depen-

dent arising does not make sense. Hence nothing makes sense.[437]

CONCLUSION

As we have observed the Vaibhāṣika and Sautrāntika all attribute causal efficacy (*arthakriya*) to the *ultimate* intrinsic reality of simple atomic particles. Yogācāra on the other hand attributes causal efficacy to mental events. The Svātantrika Madhyamaka instead attributes causal efficacy to the *conventional* intrinsic reality of the unique particulars. The Prāsaṅgika Madhyamaka rejects all these positions, arguing that only what lacks all conventional *and* ultimate intrinsic reality can dependently arise, and that conventional truth is the field of dependent arising itself. Conventional truth, thus, is *always* intrinsically unreal; it lacks intrinsic reality not just ultimately (as the Svātantrika argue) but also conventionally. Hence that which is conventionally (or dependently) coarisen strictly does not arise ultimately.

Candrakīrti's defense of his nonfoundationalist theory of conventional truth is extensive and varied. By means of the two-nature theory, Candrakīrti argues that the two truths mirror the two natures of all conventionally real phenomena. Since each phenomenon possesses two natures, a complete knowledge of all phenomena requires epistemic collaboration between the two cognitive processes, mundane and exalted cognition. Candrakīrti's epistemic distinction has ontological implications: *mundane* convention is epistemically reliable, and such entities are conventionally real. *Nonmundane* convention is epistemically deceptive, and such entities are conventionally unreal.

The way in which Candrakīrti treats illusion is quite distinct and plays a significant role in his presentation of the theory of the two truths. Candrakīrti presents a two-tiered theory of illusion in which *illusory objects* are conventionally real and causally efficacious and *conventionally real objects* are themselves illusion-like. All objects are like illusions in that they are partly real and partly unreal; even what is ordinarily held to be conventionally real is unreal in the Madhyamaka analysis. The distinction is that while the mundane cognition of ordinary beings can appreciate the unreality of illusions, they cannot appreciate the unreality of conventionally real entities.

In contrast with the philosophical schools we have previously examined, intrinsic reality, he says, is not even conventionally real. Since all Mādhyamikas accept that emptiness is the ultimate truth, that emptiness and intrinsic reality mutually exclude each other, and that intrinsic reality cannot be confined to the conventional domain, then they must reject intrinsic reality in all its forms. Therefore, Candrakīrti says, "from the point of view of either of the two truths there is none that arises as a unique particular."[438]

The corrollary to this argument—that even a conventional intrinsic reality will violate the Madhyamaka conception of the ultimate—is that a conventional intrinsic reality *also* violates the Madhyamaka conception of the conventional. Being intrinsically real is to be causally self-contained and ontologically self-defined. It rules out any possibility of change, and therefore causal efficacy. Thus, if the Madhyamaka are to retain their signature doctrines of emptiness and dependent arising, then they must reject intrinsic reality in all forms since it is by nature the opposite of emptiness and incapable of dependent arising.

Candrakīrti defines ultimate truth as emptiness. He advances three key arguments to demonstrate that emptiness is the ultimate truth although it is ultimately unreal. First, by means of the not-self argument, Candrakīrti shows the unreality of the conventionally real person by demonstrating that persons are empty of any intrinsic reality. Second, by means of the emptiness argument, Candrakīrti explicitly shows the unreality of conventionally real phenomena by proving that all things are empty of any intrinsic reality. Third, by means of the emptiness of emptiness argument, Candrakīrti shows the unreality of ultimate reality (i.e., selflessness and emptiness) by showing that selflessness and emptiness are also ultimately empty of any intrinsic nature.

In the first argument, like all Buddhist philosophers, Candrakīrti says the presumption of self arises in relation to the five aggregates. Therefore the refutation must examine the nature and scope of the five aggregates. Candrakīrti holds the standard Buddhist line that the five aggregates exhaust the entire field of compounded phenomena. If a real self is to be found, it can only be found in the aggregates, which contain and exhaust every possible configuration of personhood.

However, after having embarked on this process of exhaustive analysis, Candrakīrti's argument from the sevenfold analysis of a chariot shows that the lack of intrinsic reality of the self is analogous to that of a chariot. He shows that the self is neither different from the five aggregates nor identical to the five aggregates, nor is the self in possession of the aggregates, nor is the self *in* the five aggregates, nor are the five aggregates in the self, nor is the self the mere composite of its aggregates, nor is the self the shape or size of the aggregates.[439]

Thus, Candrakīrti concludes that ultimately and conventionally, an intrinsically real self has no basis and is therefore unreal, empty of any intrinsic reality. That it is empty of any intrinsic reality even at the conventional level however is not to conclude that it doesn't conventionally exist, nor that it cannot be conventionally effective.

The self exists, but nominally rather than intrinsically: it is dependently designated on the basis of its aggregates just as a chariot is dependently designated on the basis of its parts.[440] And such a dependently designated self can effectively serve as a conventionally real moral agent, just like a dependently designated chariot can nevertheless effectively serve as a real mode of transport.[441] Moral relations are relations of causal interaction and interdependence, and so a merely conventional self, designated and dependent, is the requisite moral agent.

In the second argument, the emptiness argument, Candrakīrti demonstrates the unreality of conventionally real phenomena by means of appealing to the causal processes at work in producing these entities. According to this argument entities are not intrinsically real because they neither arise (1) from themselves, (2) nor from another, (3) nor from both, (4) nor causelessly.

Third, through the emptiness of emptiness argument Candrakīrti shows us even ultimate reality is empty of any intrinsic reality. Although the emptiness argument and the not-self argument show that all conventionally real phenomena and persons are empty of intrinsic reality, the two arguments do not show that ultimate reality, emptiness, or nonself *per se* are empty. And in the third argument Candrakīrti takes his nonrealism to a different level, in which even ultimate reality is not spared from any taint of realism.

Therefore, instead of following any model of the two truths theories of the preceding schools, Candrakīrti advances a complete nonfoundationalist theory of the two truths, which he defends against his foundationalist opponents. Fundamentally, Candrakīrti's theory of the two truths is that: (1) Conventional truth is dependent arising. Dependent arising is causally efficacious, and it is so because it lacks conventional intrinsic nature. Conventional truth is conventionally intrinsically unreal. (2) Ultimate truth is emptiness. Emptiness is causally efficacious, and it is so because it lacks ultimately intrinsic nature. Ultimate truth is ultimately intrinsically unreal. For Candrakīrti these two theses, although advanced separately, are mutually coextensive. That is, conventional truth and ultimate truth are compatible just as dependent arising and emptiness are compatible. There is no conflict between the two.

CHAPTER EIGHT

Implications on Contemporary Studies

Current philosophical studies reveal that the theory of two truths in Buddhist thought is not in any way directly equivalent to any of the Western philosophical conceptions of truth. Even when the two truths are approached semantically, the predominant practice in Western philosophy, the traditional Buddhist philosophers are not strict correspondence theorists and neither are they strictly coherentists. They are neither pragmatists nor realists, not even fictionalists or deflationary theorists in a strict Western philosophical sense. And yet the Buddhist notions of truth do share many aspects in common with Western philosophical treatments of truth. Hence Buddhist philosophers are putting forward some tentative proposals to articulate the relationship between Western philosophical theories of truth and Buddhist theories of truth.

Whereas the notion of truth in the Western analytical philosophy is predominantly concerned with the assessment of the syntactic and semantic structures of statements, reference, validity, etc., Buddhist philosophers traditionally do not advance the conception of propositional truth. Modern philosophical studies show that Buddhism is pluralistic about truth. Truth as a cluster-concept is dynamic and varies what it means extensively across different domains of discourse.

Truth may be what gets things right, what makes things work, what gives things their causal efficacy; truth may be what makes a statement true. Truth may be praxis-guiding discourse, the Way or the path in a soteriological sense; truth may be reality or things as they are in an ontological sense. Even then, truth for Buddhist philosophers principally assumes an epistemic notion. Truth is anything that is knowable and anything that knows, and any epistemic instrument—linguistic, empirical or phenomenological, reasoning—that makes knowing possible.[442]

THERAVĀDA

In Maria Heim's most recent study on Buddhaghosa, *The Voice of the Buddha: Buddhaghosa on the Immeasurable Words*, she proposes that Buddhaghosa's two truths distinction is "about different kinds of language or teachings; it is not an epistemological or ontological distinction."[443] According to Heim there has been a "rather a muted but still long standing scholarly tradition" that insists on the position that "the Pali Abhidhamma tradition at the canonical level is phenomenological rather than metaphysical in orientation."[444] Matthew Kapstein makes a similar argument in *Reason's Traces*, in which he argues there is a strong sense that the conception of truth in early Theravāda Buddhism is fundamentally phenomenological. Like Heidegger, who makes explicit the connection between truth as *alḗtheia*, "disclosure," and the "Being" of *Dasein* to be rediscovering the roots of the Pre-Socratic Greek experience of truth as *alḗtheia*, early Buddhism bridges the perceived gap between truth and ontology within the phenomenological framework. For the Buddha, as for Heidegger, truth is a disclosure or unconcealment (Greek *a-lḗtheia* = un-cover) through an "understanding" or insight (*jñāna*) of the lived experience.[445] Just as the symbolism of Plato's allegory of the cave, under Heidegger's treatment, identifies four stages in the career of the prisoner of the cave for whom truth discloses itself from concealed to unconcealed through existential stress, anxiety, fear, and freedom, for the Buddha the disclosure of truth unfolds in four stages. The concealment of truth (through ignorance, desire, and aversion) causes the concealment of the truth of suffering (*duḥkha*), of the origin of suffering, of freedom from suffering, and of the path; and the unconcealment of the truth (through true seeing and true reflection) removes that unconcealment, leading to immediate understanding of suffering, to abandoning the origin of suffering, to realizing the freedom from suffering, and to developing the path leading to the freedom from suffering—unleashing the freedom from existential stress.[446]

The Neo-Sthaviravāda school, founded by the fifth-century scholar Buddhaghosa, introduced into Theravāda the *kalāpa* theory—which roughly corresponds to the Sarvāstivāda ontological system of irreducible atoms (Pali: *dhammas)* or the theory of intrinsic nature (Pali: *sabhāva*). After that, dhamma theory, according to Yakupitiyage Karunadasa[447] and Noa Ronkin,[448] took off as an integral part of the Neo-Sthavirvāda philosophy. Consequently, as far as the treatment of the ultimate truth goes, there occurs a significant shift in the later Theravāda Abhidhamma, a shift I describe as embracing a version of ontological foundationalism and correspondence theory of truth. And in that sense, according to the Theravāda Abhidhamma, for a statement or epistemic process to be ultimately true, it must correspond to or arrive at the final possible reduction, immune to any further division as basic ontological facts, the irreducible phenomena (Pali: *dhammas*) that exist under their own power—that is to say, phenomena that possess intrinsic nature (Pali: *sabhāva*). This is not because we say, think, or truly apprehend that intrinsic nature is a phenomenon's essence; intrinsic nature is essential because it is immune to analysis, and that, Karunadasa says, is because it is foundational.[449]

Conventional truths for the Theravāda are accordingly deflationary truths that fail to meet the irreducible criteria of the ultimate, but conventional truths are pragmatic truths. Conventional truths include, therefore, all phenomena that are denoted by concepts and that are intuited as independent and stable, when analysis would prove of them quite the opposite. They are phenomena whose independent reality we accept without the analysis that would reveal theirs a provisional reality that we have a hand in conceptually constructing.[450]

VAIBHĀṢIKA

The Vaibhāṣika school, as represented in Vasubandhu's *Commentary on the Treasury of Abhidharma*, may be characterized as undertaking something like the project of *svabhāva* ontology akin to the Pali Abhidhamma, offering categories of what exists, asserting that only statements and cognition concerning entities with intrinsic nature (*svabhāva*) can belong to the final ontological category and therefore be ultimately real. This is because the Vaibhāṣika proponent is a robust panrealist, arguing that ultimate truth stands in direct correspondence with the semantic and epistemic realist conception of reality that consists of mind-independent spatial *svabhāvas*—meaning intrinsically real, irreducible spatial particles (e.g., atoms)—and temporal *svabhāvas*—or irreducible temporal units (e.g., instants of consciousness).[451] Hence the Vaibhāṣika's approach to ultimate truth can be described as a form of correspondence theory. That is, ultimate truth is a relational property involving a characteristic correspondence or congruence relation to ultimately real *svabhāvas*, in which *svabhāvas* play the role of genuine truthmakers and ultimately true statements play the role of genuine truthbearers. Thus, the statement "entities with intrinsic nature are ultimately real" is an ultimately true statement if it accurately represents the way that ultimately real entities may then be said to be ultimately true.[452]

Conventional truth, the Vaibhāṣika school claims, consists of statements and cognitions concerning things that consist only of mentally supervenient aggregates, reducible spatial wholes (such as a person, self, table, etc.), or reducible temporal continua (stream of consciousness, etc.). Since conventionally true statements denote collections, wholes, or continua such as a person, self, car, table, etc.—all of which are conventionally real, but only conceptually constructed fictions—they are ultimately unreal and possess only contingent natures, which are characteristics they borrow from elsewhere as opposed to an intrinsic nature. So no statement employing a linguistic concept of an aggregation can be ultimately true.[453] There is a sense that the Vaibhāṣika employ a weaker notion of correspondence theory, a deflationary kind, as an appropriate truth for the convention. After all, there is no denying that conventional truth genuinely leads to successful pragmatic purposes. In this sense, the conventional truth of the Vaibhāṣika appears to follow the pragmatic theory of truth. Vaibhāṣika proponents argue that linguistic truth expresses and applies strictly to conventional truth. Conventional truth, composite substances, and the lack of intrinsic nature are all equally fictitious, and thus linguistic truths apply to types of things that are unreal, reducible, derived, and constructed.[454]

SAUTRĀNTIKA

The Sautrāntika school, philosophical home to some of the most prominent Indian logicians and epistemologists, not surprisingly undertakes the project of epistemological foundationalism significantly diverging from the Vaibhāṣika's ontological foundationalism focus, even though both belong to the Abhidharma tradition and both adhere to the Abhidharma's ontological reductionism. The Sautrāntika hold epistemological or empiricistic foundationalism. The chief feature of this foundationalism is the line of Buddhist thought that Dignāga sets in motion and is promoted through the works of Dharmakīrti and his commentators, which as Dan Arnold aptly puts it, "remains wedded to a fundamentally causal account of knowledge and justification," conflating "causal explanation with the question of justification—the question of how one comes to believe something, with the normative question of why one should believe it."[455] The Sautrāntika thus adopt an epistemic notion of truth that we could describe as the view that, as Arnold says, "regards the truth of beliefs as somehow related to the fact of their being known."[456] The truthbearer in this account does not consist in its relationship to there being some kind of independent state of affairs that is the truthmaker, but rather to epistemic processes—beliefs, experience, cognitions, and discourses. Truth value, in this context, William P. Alston states in *A Realist Conception of Truth*, "is a matter of whether, or the extent to which, a belief is justified, warranted, rational, well grounded, or the like."[457]

Alternatively, the Sautrāntika could be said to advocate a pragmatist theory of truth. Accordingly, Dharmakīrti defines ultimate truth as ultimately existent (*paramārthasat*)—that which is ultimately causally efficacious—and conventional truth as fictionally existent (*saṃvṛtisat*)—that which is fictionally causally efficacious. Thus the Sautrāntika are fictionalist about conventional truth, believing that since conventional truths—universals or abstractions (*sāmānyalakṣaṇa*)—are true merely as conceptual fictions apprehended not by virtue of their own reality, but as abstract properties that are conceptually constructed and appear to be common to objects of a particular class. Conventional truths are therefore entirely fictional entities that are: (1) causally inept, (2) indistinct, (3) denotable by language, and (4) apprehendable by language and thought.[458] Conventional truths are mental fabrications that exist outside of the network of causation composed of momentary unique particulars. Eternal, they are both immune to change and unable to effect it. Universals are practically and cognitively inefficient; abstract properties do not contribute to the genuine welfare of beings, nor do they present anything but a uniform cognitive image, which bears no relation to its proximity to the perceiver.[459]

YOGĀCĀRA

Traditionally Yogācāra philosophy is interpreted as a form of epistemological idealism that asserts external reality is entirely false and fictional, while the truth is wholly consistent of mental properties, outside of which no corresponding states of affairs exist, given the external physical universe is a mentally constructed fiction. In this sense, Yogācāra is fictionalist about all physical entities. To the extent external entities are truths, they are so as they serve the pragmatic purpose of three forms of convention: (1) fabrication, (2) consciousness, and (3) a linguistic signifier. Respectively, a conventional truth is (1) fabricated by the conceptual mind, (2) apprehended in error by the dualistic consciousness, or (3) invested with meaning by its signifier. The Yogācāra treat the products of the three conventions as separate categories of conventional truth: the truths of fabrication, consciousness, and language.

Truths of fabrication and language are labelled imaginary phenomena, while truths of consciousness are labelled dependent phenomena.[460]

The Yogācāra view can also be interpreted as a version of phenomenology according to which the universe is entirely phenomenological in nature. All truths are reducible to our experience, like a dream or mirage in which all we seem to outwardly perceive has been produced inwardly. Yogācāra's phenomenological truth finds its expression in the theory of the three natures: (1) dependent nature; (2) imaginary nature; and (3) perfect nature. The first two natures account for conventional truth and the third nature ultimate truth. If dependent nature is "what appears" in one's experience, imaginary nature is experiencing phenomena "as they appear." If dependent nature is the appearance of experience itself, imaginary nature is the dualistic mode in which experience appears. That mode is "imaginary" because the dualistic appearance of experience is only an unreal conceptual fabrication. The perfect nature is thus phenomenological freedom from the imaginary nature—the dualistic experience—superimposed upon the nondual consciousness of the dependent nature. Freeing the imaginary nature from dependent nature yields nondual phenomenological awareness as the perfect nature, the ultimate truth. Since the imaginary nature is dualistic experience, the perfect nature in which it is absent is nondual experience.[461]

MADHYAMAKA

Madhyamaka does not hold a robust correspondence theory of truth, at least not the kind that allows a truthbearer to be true if it corresponds to some mind-independent truthmakers in the world. Madhyamaka philosophy offers a deflationary account of truth as it claims there can be no intrinsic nature whatsoever that we can consider an ultimate truthmaker; therefore, there can be no statement that we can consider to be an ultimate truthbearer. Even emptiness is itself empty of intrinsic nature. According to Mark Siderits's *Personal Identity and Buddhist Philosophy: Empty Persons*, "the only way in which a statement can be true [for the Madhyamaka school] is conventionally—by having the sort of truth that consists in conformity with the conventionally determined dictates of common sense."[462] Nāgārjuna and Candrakīrti, according to Jay Garfield's *Engaging Buddhism: Why It Matters to Philosophies*, are two of the first explicit defenders of an epistemological coherentism in the history of world philosophy.[463] That is, for Nāgārjuna and Candrakīrti, epistemic states (*pramāṇa*)—epistemic instruments, warrants, cognitions—as truthbearers may be true if they cohere with epistemic objects (*prameyas*), another set of truthbearers, in the sense that truthmakers are a different kind of truthbearers. Modern-day coherentists like Lawrence BonJour maintain that the warrant or justification of our beliefs is entirely a matter of their relation to our other beliefs, of their "belonging to a coherent web of mutually supporting beliefs."[464] So, Garfield says, Nāgārjuna and Candrakīrti are coherentists not because they defend the view in which "all beliefs are mutually supportive, but rather one according to which the warrant of mechanisms of attaining knowledge and the warrant of the beliefs they deliver are mutually supportive."[465] Their epistemological coherentism is concerned with how well the four valid epistemic resources—perception, inference, testimony and anology—and their respective epistemic objects hang together within the mundane epistemic convention to produce an ordered, coherent, and coordinated system of beliefs.[466]

But Tom Tillemans, in *How Do Mādhyamikas Think?*, has interpreted Candrakīrti to be a global error theorist, a panfictionalist who asserts conventional truth is only fiction or error (*bhrānta*, Tib. *'khrul ba*), and who rejects any commitment to truth or reality by assuming a type of "pretense or make-believe" position.[467] The implication, therefore, is that for Candrakīrti, there are no "genuine sources of knowledge" (*pramāṇas*), no reliable epistemic resources whatsoever.[468] According to Tillemans's view Candrakīrti accepts everything whatsoever that ordinary people say or believe to be true is indeed true at least conventionally.[469] On this reading, Candrakīrti's account of truth has been called a "dismal position," "duplication," "trivialization of the idea of truth," "dumbed-down truth," "easy-easy truth," and "hopelessly dismal" truth.[470]

Bhāvevika fuses the logico-epistemological pragmatism of the Sautrāntika concept of conventionality with Madhyamaka's deflationary account of ultimate truth. Hence Madhyamaka supplies the ultimate truth, Sautrāntika the conventional truth.[471] This means Bhāviveka is a pragmatist about conventional truth since the Sautrāntika-logician's pragmatic criterion of the truth—practical efficacy—is used to assess conventional truth, and he is deflationist about ultimate truth since he evaluates ultimate truth from the standpoint of the Madhyamaka. Bhāviveka thus argues that conventionally, all truths are intrinsically true (*svabhāvata*), for such truths are warranted to be true by the reliable nonanalytical epistemic resources. Ultimately, he argues, all truths are nonintrinsic truths, for such truths are warranted to be nonintrinsically true by the reliable analytical epistemic resource.

So, we see the theory of truth in Buddhist thought is not in any way directly equivalent to any of the Western philosophical conceptions of truth. Even approaching truth semantically, which is the predominant practice in Western philosophy, the traditional Buddhist philosophers are not strict correspondence theorists and neither are they strictly coherentists. They are neither pragmatists nor realists, not even fictionalist or deflationary theorists in a strict Western philosophical sense. And yet Buddhist notions of truth do share many aspects in common with Western philosophical treatments of truth. Tentatively we could describe early Buddhism—the Nikāya phase—as adopting truth as *alētheia*, phenomenological disclosure; Theravada Abhidhamma and Vaibhāṣika, a version of pragmatism about conventional truth and correspondence theory about ultimate truth; Sautrāntika, a pragmatism and epistemic notion of truth; Yogācāra, a type of fictionalism or phenomenology; and Madhyamaka, a deflationary theory. Nāgārjuna and Candrakīrti could be considered epistemological coherentists or even panfictionalists, and Bhāviveka a pragmatist about conventional truth, while a fictionalist about ultimate truth.

Notes

1 These teachings are found in the *Sūtra of the Wheel of Dharma* (*Dharmacakrasūtra, Chos 'khor rab to bskor ba'i mdo*).

2 Traditional Tibetan accounts maintain that these sūtras were originally taught by the Buddha Śākyamuni and later concealed in nonhuman abodes—the longest being the *Sūtra in One Billion Lines*, the *Sūtra in Ten Million Lines*, the *Sūtra in One Hundred Thousand Lines* (*Śatasāhasrikāprajñāpāramitā,* Toh 8), in *Twenty-Five Thousand Lines* (*Pañcaviṃśatisāhasrikāprajñāpāramitā*, Toh 9), and in *Eighteen Thousand Lines* (*Aṣṭādaśasāhasrikāprajñāpāramitā*, Toh 10). Nāgārjuna is said to have revealed some of these sūtras from the land of nāgas and initially propagated them in South India. Of these, Jinamitra, Prajñāvarman, and Yeshé Dé translated the *Daśasāhasrikāprajñāparamita* into Tibetan as *Shes phyin khri pa*; the Padmakara Translation Group translated it into English as *The Transcendent Perfection of Wisdom in Ten Thousand Lines* (Toh 11, Degé Kangyur, vol. 31, shes phyin, *ga*, 1b–91a and vol. 32, shes phyin, *nga*, 92b–397a. 84000: Translating the Words of the Buddha, 2018). Edward Conze (2017, 1–18) outlines the following four historical phases of the evolution of the sūtras within the Indian subcontinent: (1) the appearance of the medium-length *Sūtra in Eight Thousand Lines*, dated 100 BCE–100 CE; (2) the expansion of the longer versions in *One Billion Lines* and *Ten Million Lines*, dated 100–300 CE; (3) the contraction of the shorter versions into *Three Hundred Lines*, dated 300–500 CE; and (4) the appearance of various means for attainment (*sādhana*, Tib. *sgrub thabs*) associated with the female deity Prajñāpāramitā, dated 600–1200 CE. Cited in 84000, i.10.

3 About one hundred years after the Buddha's death (*mahāparinirvāṇa*), the monks of Vaiśālī allegedly violated the monastic code of conduct by adopting ten new practices. Consequently, a dispute arose between conservative and liberal monks over the matters related to the ten practices. This was the catalyst for the Second Council. According to the *Sri Lankan Chronicle* (*Mahāvaṃsa*), when the venerable Yaśas (P. Yasakākāṇḍakaputta) noticed that Vaiśālī monks were in breach of the *vinaya* precepts—they were receiving gold and silver offerings from the

lay devotees—he mobilized a congregation of seven hundred monks and presided over the Second Council. The position of the conservatives prevailed in the council, and the elders agreed to reject the ten practices. Vaiśālī monks did not accept the conservative ruling, however; they favored more flexibility in the monastic rules. The controversy resulted in the initial split of the early Buddhist order into two schools, the Sthaviravāda and the Mahāsaṅghika. The former agreed with the conservative ruling while the latter rejected it and founded the school that bears the name Mahāsaṅghika. The initial split into the Sthaviravāda and the Mahāsaṅghika schools that triggered the Second Council also led to further divisions. Eventually, according to the *Sri Lankan Chronicle*, as many as eighteen schools of Buddhist thought with varying doctrinal interpretations took shape. The Mahāsaṅghika lineage was the first to experience further breakaways. See Wilhelm Geiger, 1964, 26; Akira Hirakawa and Paul Groner, 1990, 80.

4 On the life of the Buddha, see Tārānātha's *Tāranatha's History of Buddhism in India* (1990); Akira Hirakawa and Paul Groner's *A History of Indian Buddhism* (1990); Bhikkhu Nyanamoli's *The Life of the Buddha* (1972); William W. Rockhill, Ernst Leumann, and Bunyiu Nanjio's *The Life of the Buddha and the Early History of His Order, Derived from Tibetan Works in the Bkah-Hgyur and Bstan-Hgyur, Followed by Notices on the Early History of Tibet and Khoten* (1884); Michael Carrithers' *The Buddha: A Very Short Introduction* (2001); Rupert Gethin's *The Foundations of Buddhism* (1998); Hans W. Schumann's *The Historical Buddha: The Times, Life and Teachings of the Founder of Buddhism* (2003); and Eugène Burnouf's *Introduction to the History of Indian Buddhism* (2015). For a good historical survey of the early development of Mahāyāna and its sūtras, see Nakamura 2007, 149–182.

5 This has been translated by the Dharma Translation Committee as *The Noble Great Vehicle Sūtra: Teaching the Relative and Ultimate Truths*. 84000: Translating the Words of the Buddha, 2014. Toh 179, Degé Kangyur, mdo sde, *ma*, 244b–266b.

6 *Pitāpūtrasamāgamasūtra*, Toh 60, dkon brtsegs, *nga*, 1–168a7: 'di ltar de bzhin gshegs pas kun rdzob dang don dam pa gnyis thugs su chud de/ shes par bya ba yang kun rdzob dang don dam pa 'dir zad do/.

7 Nāgārjuna, *Mūlamadhyamakakārikā* 24:8. dve satye samupāśritya buddhānāṃ dharmadeśanā / lokasaṃvṛtisatyaṃ ca satyaṃ ca paramārthataḥ //. Toh 3824, dbu ma, *tsa*, 20a.

8 Suzuki, 1999, 148–149. Cf. The Sanskrit text *Saddharmalaṅkāvatārasūtram* edited by L. P. Vaidya (1963). See 3.61: tatredamucyate / nayo hi dvividho mahyaṃ siddhānto deśanā ca vai / deśemi yā bālānāṃ siddhāntaṃ yogināmaham //. Cf. *Laṅkāvatārasūtra*, Toh 107, mdo sde, *ca*, 198a: blo gros chen po/ de ltar grub pai mtha'i tshul dang/ bstan pa'i mtshan nyid de la khyod dang byang chub sems dpa' sems dpa' chen po gzhan dag gis brtson par bya'o// de la 'di skad ces bya ste, nga yi tshul ni rnam gnyis te// grub pa'i mtha' dang bstan pa'o// byis pa rnams la brjod pa bshad// rnal 'byor can gyi grub mtha'o//.

9 Halbfass 1988, 267.

10 See Guy Newland's *The Two Truths in the Mādhyamika Philosophy of the Ge-Luk-Ba Order of Tibetan Buddhism* (1992) and Sonam Thakchoe's *The Two Truths Debate: Tsongkhapa and Gorampa on the Middle Way* (2007).

11 For more on the Samyé debate, see Dalton 2014, 69–71; van Schaik 2015, 113–131; and van Schaik 2011, 37–40. These works explore the complex political and historical backdrop of this debate.

12 Ruegg 2010, 22.

13 See Ruegg 2010, 22.

14 Thakchoe (2007) showcases the two truths controversy between Tsongkhapa and Gorampa.

15 Mādhava 2002, 19–25.

16 Shastri 1997, 15.

17 Nāgārjuna, *Śūnyatāsaptatikārikā* 1, Toh 3827, dbu ma, *tsa*, 24a: gnas pa'am skye 'jig yod med dam// dman pa'am mnyam dang khyad par can// sangs rgyas 'jig rten snyad dbang gis// gsung gi yang dag dbang gis min//.

18 Candrakīrti, *Catuḥśatakaṭīkā*, 13, Toh 3865, dbu ma, *ya*, 133a: de'i phyir gang dag rtog pa yod pa kho nas yod pa nyid dang/ rtog pa med par yod pa nyid med pa de dag ni gor ma chag par thag pa bsngogs pa la brtags pa'i sbrul ltar rang gi ngo bos ma grub par nges so//.

19 Nāgārjuna, *Yuktiṣaṣṭikākārikā* 34, Toh 3825, dbu ma, *tsa*, 21b: 'byung ba che la sogs bshad pa// rnam par shes su yang dag 'du// de shes pas ni 'bral 'gyur na// log par rnam brtags ma yin nam. Sanskrit text edited by B. Kumar (1993): mahābhūtādaya khyātā vijñāne nicayastathā / tajjñānena viyukttena mṛṣaiva na vikalpitam//.

20 Candrakīrti, *Yuktiṣaṣṭikāvṛtti* 34. Toh 3864, dbu ma, *ya*, 21b–22a: 'byung ba che la sogs bshad pa// rnam par shes su yang dag 'du// de shes pas ni 'bral 'gyur na// log par rnam [22a]// brtags ma yin nam// zhes bya ba smos so// rnam par shes pas dmigs pa gang gi rnam pa 'dzin cing skye ba'i dmigs pa de/ rnam par shes pa la rnam pa nye bar bsgrubs pa'i rang gi dngos po thob nas dngos po'i don gyi ngo bo nyid kyis 'byung ba chen po la sogs par yongs su brtags so// rnam par shes pa la 'ga' zhig gi rnam par ma bzhag pa la ni 'jig rten gyis yod pa nyid du rnam par gzhag mi nus te/ mo gsham gyi bu la sogs pa yang yod par thal bar 'gyur ba'i phyir ro// de bas na 'byung ba dang 'byung ba las gyur pa dang/ sems dang sems las byung ba dang/ sems dang ldan pa ma yin pa rnams ni rnam par shes pa'i rnam pa'i rgyu can yin pa'i phyir 'byung ba chen po la sogs pa gang dang gang bshad pa ci yang rung ba de dag thams cad ni rnam par shes par yang dag par 'du zhing khongs su chud do//.

21 Candrakīrti, *Yuktiṣaṣṭikāvṛtti* 5cd, dbu ma, *ya*, 7b: ci mya ngan las 'das pa yang kun rdzob kyi bden pa yin nam/ de de bzhin te/ 'khor bar yongs su rtog pa yod na mya ngan las 'das par yongs su rtog ste/ de gnyi ga yang 'jig rten gyi tha snyad yin pa'i phyir ro// de bas na bcom ldan 'das ma las gsungs pa/ tshe dang ldan pa rab 'byor mya ngan las 'das pa yang sgyu ma lta bu rmi lam lta bu'o zhes smra'am/ sh'a ri'i bu mya ngan las 'das pa bas ches lhag pa'i chos shig yod na yang sgyu ma lta bu'o zhes kho bo smra'o zhes 'byung ngo// gal te de 'khor bar rtog pa la ltos pa ma yin na de sgyu ma lta bur mi 'gyur ro// de bas na mya ngan las 'das pa yang kun rdzob kyi bden par yongs su brtags pa yin no//.

22 I-Tsing and Takakusu 1896, xvii–xviii.

23 While the the *Abhidharmajñānaprasthānaśāstra* is commonly recognized as the body of the Sarvāstivāda Abhidharmapiṭaka, the six supplements are identified as its limbs (*pāda*). This text is also called the *Aśtagrantha*, or "the eight chapters."

All chapters are attributed to the Sarvāstivāda teacher Kātyāyanīputra, who lived in the latter part of the first century BC. The *Abhidharmajñānaprasthānaśāstra* is now considered to be the youngest of all the canonical works of the Sarvāstivāda Abhidharmapiṭaka. The *Abhidharmajñānaprasthānaśāstra* was composed by Kātyāyanīputra and translated into Chinese by Xuanzang. It took him four years to complete this monumental translation task, which he started in early 657 and finished in 660. This is no doubt the largest and perhaps the most authoritative of the Sarvāstivādin Abhidharma books, hence it is the foundational text for all the later Sarvāstivāda treatises, including Vasubandhu's *Abhidharmokośa* and its commentary, and not surprisingly the modern academic study of Abhidharma, including in Tibetan Buddhism. In the Taishō edition of the Chinese canon, Xuanzang's translation is numbered 1544, found at T vol. 26, 918a. There exists an earlier translation of the text by Saṅghadeva and Zhu-fo-nian in CE 383, which is found at T 1543, T vol. 26, 771a. Since the original Sanskrit text was lost, it has been retranslated into Sanskrit from the Chinese version of Xuanzang by Santi Bhiksu Sastri in 1955, published as Kātyāyanīputra's *Abhidharmajñānaprasthānaśāstra: Retranslated into Sanskrit from Chinese Version of Hsuan Tsang by Santi Bhiksu Sastri* (1955). Apparently this text was not translated into Tibetan until recently. But in 2011 the first known Tibetan translation of this text appeared as Kātyāyanīputra's *Chos mngon pa byed brag tu bshad pa chen po* (*Abhidharmamahāvibhāṣa*), translated by Lobsang Chodak (Blo bzang chos grags).

24 Following Yaśomitra's *Sphuṭārthābhidharmakośavyākhyā* (1971, 11, 24–29, 25ff), the order of other six supplementary Sarvāstivāda Abhidharma treatises are: (1) *Prakaraṇapāda* by Vasumitra, (2) *Vijñānakāya* by Devaśarman, (3) *Dharmaskandha* of Śāriputra (or of Maudgalyāyana, according to the Chinese sources), (4) *Prajñaptibhāṣya* by Maudgalyāyana, (5) *Dhātukāya* by Pūrṇa (or of Vasumitra, according to the Chinese source), and (6) *Saṃgītiparyāya* by Mahākauṣṭhila (or of Śāriputra, according to the Chinese source). Cf. Bart Dessein's translation, *Saṃyuktābhidharmahṛdaya: Heart of Scholasticism with Miscellaneous Additions* (Dharmaśrī 1999, xxvii). Yaśomitra's enumerations differ from the other traditions, which offer another order and other authors. See Lamotte 1967, 202ff, cited in Dharmaśrī 1999, xxvii. Yaśomitra himself uses a different order elsewhere in Yaśomitra 1971, 9.12–14, 12.4ff. The Tibetans list the *Dharmaskandha* of Śāriputra first and the *Jñānaprasthāna* only as sixth; the Tibetans regard the former as the most important of all six supplementary texts, which incidentally is also the opinion of the Chinese colophon by Ching-mai (664 AD). See Takakusu 1905, 115.

25 The *Abhidharmakośa* identifies Buddhadeva (Sangs rgyas lha), Dharmatrāta (Chos skyob), Dharmasubhūti (Chos ldan rab 'byor), Ghoṣaka (Dbyangs sgrog), Vasumitra (Dbyigs bshes), and Kumāralāta (Gzhon nu len) as the four masters of the *Mahāvibhāṣa*. Vasumitra is the author of the *Pañcavastuka*. Ghoṣaka is the author of the *Abhidharmāmṛta*.

26 Based on what he calls "internal evidence," Stefan Anacker (1998, 144n40) proposes the view that there may have been three Vasumitras: (1) the old Vasumitra, author of the *Prakaraṇapāda* and of the *Dhātukāya* and probably of the *Saṅgītiśāstra*, the probable originator of the view of the mahābhūmika theory; (2) the Bhadanta Vasumitra, author of the *Paripṛcchā* and the *Pañcavastuka*, opposed

to the mahābhūmika theory, upholder of a subtle citta, forger of the most accepted theory regarding past and future events, cautioner of dogmatists, one of the "Great Masters" of the *Vibhāṣā*, and a truly great philosopher; (3) the latter Vasumitra, author of a commentary on the *Koṣa* and the *Samayabhedoparacanacakra*. The following texts are attributed to a Vasumitra: the *Prakaraṇapāda* (Taisho 1541, 1542) and the *Dhātukāya* (Taisho 1540), both among the six primary texts of Sarvāstivada Abhidharma; the *Saṅgītiśāstra* (Taisho 1549), the *Pañcavastuka* (Taisho 1556, 1557), the lost *Paripṛcchā*, and the *Samayabhedoparacanakcakra* (Taisho 2031, 2032).

27 Dharmaśrī 1999, xxv–xxvi; Anacker 1998, 146.

28 Vasubandhu, *Abhidharmakośabhāṣyam* 1.9ab. trans. Pruden, 1988–1990a, 63.

29 Ibid., 1.16; trans. Pruden, 1988–1990a, 74.

30 Ibid., 2.35–48; trans. Pruden, 1988–1990a, 206–254.

31 Ibid., 1.5, trans. Pruden, 1988–1990a, 59–61.

32 Ibid., 6.4: yatra bhinnena tadbuddhiranyāpohe dhiyā ca tat | ghaṭārthavatsaṃvṛtisat paramārthasadanyathā. Pruden (1988–1990c, 910–11) translates this passage slightly differently: "The idea of a jug ends when the jug is broken; the idea of water ends when, in the mind, one analyses the water. The jug and the water and all that resembles them, exist relatively. The rest exist absolutely." Cf. mngon pa, *khu*, 7ab: gang la bcom dang blo yis gzhan// bsal na de blo mi 'jug pa// bum chu bzhin du kun rdzob tu// yod de don dam yod gzhan no//.

33 Vasubandhu, *Abhidharmakośabhāṣya* 6.4; see Pruden (1991c, 910) for a slightly different translation of the passage:

> If the idea of a thing disappears when this thing is broken into pieces, then this thing has relative existence (*samvṛtisat*); for example, a jug: the idea of a jug disappears when it is reduced to pieces. If the idea of a thing disappears when this thing is dissipated, or broken to pieces, by the mind, then this thing should be regarded as having relative existence; for example, water. If we grasp and remember the *dharmas,* such as color, etc., in the water, then the idea of water disappears. These things—jug, clothes, etc., water, fire, etc.,—are given their different names from the relative point of view or conforming to conventional usage. Thus if one says, from the relative point of view, "There is a jug, there is water," one is speaking truly, and one is not speaking falsely. Consequently this is relatively true.

Toh 4090, mngon pa, *khu*, 7b: gang la cha shas su bcom na de'i blo mi 'jug pa de ni kun rdzob tu yod pa ste/ dper na bum pa lta bu'o/ de la ni gyo mor bcom na bum pa'i blo mi 'jug go// gang la blos chos gzhan bsal na de'i blo mi 'jug pa de yang kun rdzob tu yod pa yin par khong du chud par bya ste/ dper na chu lta bu'o/ de la ni blos gzugs la sogs pa'i chos bsal na chu'i blo mi 'jug go// de dag kho na la kun rdzob tu de'i ming du ba tags pa yin pas kun rdzob kyi dbang gis bum pa dang chu yod do zhes brjod pa ni bden pa kho na smras pa yin gyi/ brdzun pa ni ma yin pas de ni kun rdzob kyi bden pa yin no//.

34 Anacker 1998, 124.

35 Pūrṇavardhana, *Abhidharmakośaṭīkālakṣaṇānusāriṇī,* mngon pa, chu, 1b–347a.

36 Ibid., 155a: gang la bcom dang zhes bya ba 'de la dpe gnyis nye bar 'kod pa yin te/ 'jig pa gnyis nye bar bstan pa'i phyir ro/ bcom pas 'jig pa ni bum pa la sogs pa dag go/ blos 'jig pa gnyis ni chu la sogs pa dag ste/ bcom pas ro la sogs pa bsal ba mi 'thad pa'i phyir ro// rnam pa gcig tu na kun rdzob ni rnam pa gnyis te dbyebs kyi kun rdzob bum pa la sogs pa dang/ tshogs pa'i kun rdzob chu la sogs pa ste/ de'i phyir gnyis smras so/ yang na bum chu bzhin tu kun rdzob te/ zhes de gnyis bkod pa ni kun rdzob gnyis bstan pa'i phyir te/ bum pa la sogs pa yod pa rnams ni gyo mo la sogs pa dag la brten nas yod pas kun rdzob gzhan la rten pa'i kun rdzob yin la/ chu la sogs pa rnams ni gzugs la sogs pa la brten nas yod pas rdzas gzhan la rten pa'i kun rdzob yin no//.

37 Dignāga, *Abhidharmakoṣavṛttimarmadīpa,* mngon pa, ngu, 160b: de la kun rdzob gzhan la brten pa gang yin pa de ni 'jig pa yang srid la gzhan sel ba yang srid do/ rdzas gzhan la brten pa gang yin pa de la ni gzhan sel ba kho na srid kyi 'jig pa ni ma yin te/ rdul phra rab rdzas brgyad cha shas su bral bar mi nus so/.

38 Vasubandhu, *Abhidharmakośa* 3.18bd, mngon pa, *ku,* 7b: bdag med phung po tsam nyid do// nyon mongs las kyis mngon 'dus byas// srid pa bar ma'i rgyun gyis na// mar me bzhin du mngal du 'gro//. Sanskrit text edited by Pradhan 1967, 18: nātmāsti skandhamātraṃ tu kleśakarmābhisaṃskṛtam// antarābhavasaṃtatyā kukṣimeti pradīpavat //.

39 Vasubandhu, *Abhidharmakośabhāṣya* 3.18ad, trans. by Pruden, 1991b, 399; mngon pa, *ku,* 122b–123a: 'o na bdag ji lta bu zhig mi dgag ce na phung po tsam nyid do// gal te phung po tsam kho na la bdag ces 'dogs na de la ni dgag pa med do// de lta na 'o na phung po bdag nyid 'jig rten gzhan du 'pho'o zhes bya bar gyur to zhe na/ de dag ni mi 'pho ba'i phung po tsam ni/ nyon mongs las kyis mngon du byas// srid pa bar ma'i rgyun gyis na// mar me bzhin du mngal du 'gro// phung po rnams ni skad cig ma ste/ de dag la ni 'pho ba'i mthu med kyi nyon mongs pa rnams dang/ las rnams kyis yongs su bsgos pa'i phung po tsam gyis srid pa bar ma zhes bya ba'i rgyun gyis ma'i mngal du 'gro ste/ dper na mar me skad cig ma yin yang rgyun kyis yul gzhan du 'gro ba ta bu yin pas de ni nyes pa med do//.

40 *Dravya* is also a central concept in the Nyāya-Vaiśeṣika tradition. There is a fundamental distinction to be drawn between *dravya* as a "foundational entity" in the Sarvāstivāda and *dravya* as "substance" in the Nyāya-Vaiśeṣika tradition. According to the Nyāya-Vaiśeṣika, all objects of experience come under seven categories: (1) substance (*dravya*), (2) quality (*guṇa*), (3) action (*karma*), (4) universal (*sāmānya*), (5) particular (*viśeṣa*), (6) inherence (*samavāya*), and (7) nonexistence (*abhāva*). The most fundamental of the categories is undoubtedly substance. Substance denotes the objective reality of things, exists in and of itself, and is self-subsistent. Substance is the substrate of qualities and actions (present or potential) either in the relation of intimate union (*samavāyasaṃbandha*) or the future existence, antecedent negation (*prāgabhāva*). Substance is divided into two general categories: eternal and impermanent substances. Substance that depends on something else is noneternal, hence composite substances (*avayavidravya*) are dependent and impermanent. The eternal substances are simple, independent, and unique. Eternal substances are neither caused nor destroyed, whereas noneternal substances are caused and destroyed—not by themselves, but

by the force of something else. Substance is of nine kinds: earth (*pṛthivī*), water (*apas*), fire (*tejas*), air (*vāyu*), ether (*ākāśa*), time (*kāla*), space (*diś*), self (*ātman*), and mind (*manas*). The nine substances are all eternal and infinitesimal, and they form the basis for compound (*avayavidravya*) and destructible substances. See Agrawal 2001, 85–110.

41 Vasubandhu, *Abhidharmakośabhāśya* 1.5; trans. Pruden 1988–1990a, 59–60; cf. mngon pa, *ku*, 94a.

42 Ibid., 6.4; trans. Pruden, 1988–1990c, 910-11; mngon pa, *ku*, 214a: de las gzhan pa ni don dam pa'i bden pa ste/ gang la bcom yang de'i blo 'jug pa kho na yin la/ blos chos gzhan bsal yang de'i blo 'jug pa de ni don dam par yod pa yin te/ dper na gzugs lta bu'o/ de la ni rdul phra rab tu bcom yang rung/ blos ro la sogs pa'i chos bsal kyang rung gzugs kyi rang bzhin gyi blo 'jug pa nyid de/ tshor ba la sogs pa yang de bzhin du blta bar bya'o// de ni don dam par yod pa'i phyir don dam pa'i bden pa zhes bya'o//.

43 Pūrṇavardhana, *Abhidharmakośaṭīkālakṣaṇānusāriṇī*, mngon pa, *chu*, 155a: tshor ba la sogs pa la yang de bzhin du lta bar bya'o// zhes bya ba ni tshor ba dang 'du shes dang sems pa la sogs pa dag kyang tshogs pa kun rdzob tu yod pa yin // tshor ba la sogs pa re re ba ni rdzas su yod pa kho nar blta'o/ 'ji ltar zhe na/ tshor ba la sogs pa ni blos bsal nas kyang tshor ba'i rang bzhin gyi blor 'gyur bas tshor ba rdzas su yod pa yin no/ sems pa la sogs pa dag la yang de bzhin du sbyar bar bya'o//.

44 Priest, Siderits, and Tillemans 2011, 138.

45 See Fraser MacBride's "Truthmakers" in *The Stanford Encyclopedia of Philosophy*. https://plato.stanford.edu/archives/spr2019/entries/truthmakers.

46 Priest, Siderits, and Tillemans 2011, 136.

47 Ibid., 136.

48 See his *Exegesis on the Verses of Epistemology* (*Pramāṇavārttikapañjikā*).

49 See his *Commentary on the Pramāṇavārttika* (*Pramāṇavārttikaṭīkā*).

50 See his *Commentary on the Investigation of the Percept* (*Ālambanaparīkṣāṭīkā*), *Gloss on the Dose of Logical Reasoning* (*Hetubinduṭīkā*), *Gloss on the Dose of Reasoning* (*Nyāyabinduṭīkā*), and *Commentary of the Analysis of Relation* (*Sambandhaparīkṣāṭīkā*).

51 Dharmottara's epistemological works include: *Commentary on Ascertaining Epistemology* (*Pramāṇaviniścayaṭīkā*), *Commentary on Doses of Reasoning* (*Nyāyabinduṭīkā*), and *Establishing Momentariness* (*Kṣaṇabhaṅgasiddhi*).

52 Vasubandhu, *Abhidharmakośabhāśya* 2.43, Toh 4089, mngon pa, *ku*, 94a: reg bya med pa tsam ni nam mkha' yin te/ 'di ltar mun pa'i nang dag na thogs pa ma rnyed na nam mkha'o zhes zer to/ phra rgyas dang skye ba skyes pa 'gags nas so sor brtags pa'i stobs kyis gzhan mi skye ba ni so sor brtags pas 'gog pa yin no// so sor brtags pa med pa kho nar rkyen ma tshang bas mi skye ba ni so sor brtags pa ma yin pas 'gog pa ste dper na bar ma dor 'chi ba'i ris mthun pa lhag ma lta bu'o zhes zer ro//.

53 Ibid., 2.43, Toh 4089, mngon pa, *ku*, 94a: mdo sde pa rnams na re 'dus ma byas thams cad kyang rdzas su med pa kho na ste/ de ni gzugs dang tsor pa la sogs pa bzhin du rdzas gzhan du ni med do/ 'o na ci zhe na/ reg bya med pa tsam ni nam mkha' yin te/ 'di ltar mun pa'i nang dag na thogs pa ma rnyed na nam mkha'o zhes zer to/ phra rgyas dang skye ba skyes pa 'gags nas so sor brtags pa'i stobs kyis gzhan mi skye ba ni so sor brtags pas 'gog pa yin no/ so sor brtags pa med pa kho nar

rkyen ma tshang bas mi skye ba ni so sor brtags pa ma yin pas 'gog pa ste dper na bar ma dor 'chi ba'i ris mthun pa lhag ma lta bu'o zhes zer ro//.

54 Ibid., 1.14, Toh 4089, mngon pa, *ku*, 35b–36a: gal te spungs pa'i don phung po'i don yin na phung po rnams btags pa'i yod par 'gyur te/ rdzas sum 'dus pa yin pa'i phyir spungs pa dang gang zag bzhin no zhe na/ ma yin te/ rdzas kyi rdul phra rab gcig pu yang [36a] phung po yin pa'i phyir ro/.

55 Ibid., 1.12, Toh 4089, mngon pa, *ku*, 63a: rdzas brgyad ni 'byung ba chen po bzhi dag dang/ rgyur byas pa'i gzugs bzhi ste/ gzugs dang/ dri dang/ ro dang/ reg bya rnams so//.

56 Ibid., 1.14, Toh 4089, mngon pa, *ku*, 36a: de lta na gcig pu la spungs pa nyid med pas spungs pa'i don ni phung po'i don to zhes brjod par mi bya'o/.

57 Ibid., 4.2, Toh 4089, mngon pa, *ku*, 168a: de la ni reg bya dang lhan cig spyod pa'i phyir dran pa tsam yin gyi mngon sum du 'dzin pa ni ma yin gyi/ dper na me'i gzugs mthong nas de'i tsha ba dran pa 'byung ba dang/ me tog gi dri ma snams nas de'i kha dog gi dran pa 'byung ba bzhin no/.

58 Ibid., 4.2, Toh 4089, mngon pa, *ku*, 167b–168a: mdo sde pa rnams na re dbyibs ni rdzas su med de/ phyogs gcig gi sgor kha dog phal cher byung ba la gzugs ring por zhes 'dogs par byed/ de nyid la ltos nas nyung ngur byung ba la thung du zhes 'dogs par byed/ phyogs bzhir mang por byung ba la gru bzhi zhes 'dogs par byed/ thams cad du mnyam pa na lham pa zhes 'dogs par byed de/ thams cad kyang de dang 'dra'o// dper na mgal me phyogs gzhan gcig tu myur du 'dab chags par snang ba ni ring po'o snyam du shes la/ thams cad du snang na zlum po'o snyam du shes kyi dbyibs rdzas su gzhan yod pa ni ma yin pa bzhin no// gal te yod na ni/ gnyis gzung 'gyur/ mig gis mthong na yang ring po'o snyam du shes par 'gyur la/ lus kyi dbang po reg na yang shes par 'gyur bas 'di dbang po gnyis kyi gzung bar 'gyur bzhig na/ gzugs kyi / [168a] skye mched la ni gnyis kyis 'dzin pa med do zhes zer ro// yang na ji ltar reg bya la ring po la sogs par 'dzin pa ltar kha dog la yang de bzhin du yid ches par bya'o//.

59 Dharmakīrti, *Pramāṇavārttikakārikā* 2.3 (ed. Pandey 1989): arthakriyāsamartha yat tadatra paramārthasat / anyat saṃvṛtaisat proktam te svasāmānyalakṣaṇe//. Toh 4216, tshad ma, *ce*, 118b: don dam don byed nus pa gang// de 'dir don dam yod pa yin// gzhan ni kun rdzob yod pa ste// de dag rang spyi'i mtshan nyid bshad/. In the *Ālambanaparīkṣāvṛtti*, Dignāga (Toh 4206, tshad ma, *ce*, 92a) applies the concept of causal efficacy to define true cognition (*pramāṇa*): don byed nus pa'i dngos su gzhal ba'i phyir te tshad ma'ang yin no//. This same idea Dharmakīrti uses in the *Pramāṇavārttikakārikā* (1.1) to define true cognition; see Toh 4216, tshad ma, *ce*, 107b: tshad ma bslu med can shes pa// don byed nus par gnas pa ni// mi slu sgra las byung ba yang// mngon par 'dod pa ston phyir ro/.

60 The term *svalakṣaṇa* is variously rendered into English as "own-natured," "self-defining characteristic," "unique particular," "real particular," etc. Notice here a crucial distinction between this Sautrāntika and the Vaiśeṣika theory of particular (*viśeṣa*). The author of the *Vaiśeṣika Sūtra*, Kaṇāda (or Kāśyapa, ca. 300 BC), considers that the particulars reside in the ultimate substance and are dependent on the activity of thought (God) (*Vaiśeṣika Sūtra*, 1.2–4; see *A Sourcebook in Indian Philosophy*, 1989, 384). *The Padārthadharmasaṃgraha* by Praśastapāda (fourth century CE) and the *Nyāyakandalī* (991 CE) by Śridhara (translated by Ganga-

natha Jha, 1916) make the similar claim that particulars are brought into existence by the Supreme Lord, the Great Egg, the Four-Faced Brahmā, the Grandfather of all creatures who assigns various duties, enabling us to perceive things as different from one another. Praśastapāda, however, believes particulars to be an independent reality residing in eternal substances, distinguishing them from one another (*Padārthadharmasaṃgraha*, v. 40, cited in Radhakrishnan and Moore 1989, 399–401). Therefore unlike the Buddhist Sautrāntika, on the Vaiśeṣika account the particular does not have the sense of the particularity or individuality of composite objects; it means the particularity of eternal, indivisible, nonmaterial substances, such as atoms, the self, mind, space, and time. The Vaiśeṣika argue that the empirical objects are distinguished by means of the parts from which they are composed. In the course of analysis, we arrive at simple substances that no longer have any parts by means of which such distinctions can be made. Therefore we need to assume that these partless ultimate atomic substances have specific particularities that are both qualitatively and quantitatively distinct from each other. Therefore substances, time, space, ether, self, and mind all have their particulars, which are not qualities of classes or generalities, but only of individuals, which make them distinct from all others. At the atomic level these distinctive particulars reach the final ontological fact of being, beyond which we cannot go even logically. Only yogins are able to perceive the ultimate particulars in their simple forms.

61 Dharmakīrti, *Vādanyāya*, Toh 4218, tshad ma, *che*, 327ab: 'di ltar gang yod pa'am byas pa de thams cad mi rtag pa ste/ dper na bum pa la sogs pa lta bu'o// sgra yang yod pa'am byas pa 'o zhes bya ba lta bu'o//.

62 Ibid., *Pramāṇavārttikavṛtti*, Toh 4216, tshad ma, *ce*, 179a: dngos po'i mtshan nyid ni don byed nus pa yin pa'i phyir te/ nus pa brjod pa thams cad dang bral ba ni nye bar brjod pa med pa'i mtshan nyid yin no/.

63 Vasubandhu, *Abhidharmakośabhāṣya* 4.3a, Toh 4089, mngon pa, *ku*, 166b: 'gro min gang phyir 'dus byas ni// skad cig pa yin zhes bya ba brjod do// skad cig ces bya ba 'di ci zhe na/ bdag nyid du red ma thag tu 'jig pa'o// de 'di la yod pas na skad cig pa ste dbyug pa bzhin no//.

64 Ibid., 167a: rgyu med pa las 'ga' mi 'byung// gal te 'jig pa rgyu dang ldan pa zhig tu gyur na skye ba bzhin du 'ga' yang rgyu med pa las mi 'gyur ba zhig na skad cig ma blo dang sgra dang me lce dag 'jig pa rgyu med pa las byung ba yang mthong bas 'di rgyu la ltos pa ma yin no//. "We have said that disintegration, being a negative state, cannot be caused. We would further say that if disintegration is the effect of a cause, nothing would perish without a cause. If, like arising, disintegration proceeds from a cause, it would never take place without a cause. Now we hold that intelligence, a flame, or a sound, which are momentary, perish without their disintegration depending on a cause. Hence disintegration of the kindling, etc., is spontaneous."

65 Dharmakīrti, *Pramāṇavārttikakārikā*, Toh 4210, tshad ma, *ce*, 102a: dper na mi rtag nyid byas pa 'am// ma byas pas na mi 'jig bzhin// 'rgyu med phyir na 'jig pa na// rang gi ngo bos rjes 'brel nyid// dngos po ltos dang bcas rnams ni// nges par 'gyur ba med par mthong// de rgyu mang po yod na yang// 'ga' zhig la ni mi srid 'gyur//. See also Ibid., 178ab: da ni gang gis de skad du brjod par 'gyur ba byas pa gdon mi za bar mi rtag pa'o zhes ji ltar bshad par bya zhe na/ 'di ltar rgyu med

phyir na 'jig pa ni/ rang gi ngo bos rjes dngos po 'jig pa de'i ngo bo rgyu las ltos pa ma yin te/ rang gi rgyu kho na [178b] las 'jig pa'i dang can du 'byung ba'i phyir ro// de bas na gang cung zad byas pa de ni rang bzhin gyis 'jig pa'i ngang can yin no// ji ltar/ ltos dang bcas pa'i chos rnams ni// nges par 'gyur ba med par mthong// dngos po 'jig pa ni ltos pa med pa yin te// ltos pa dang bcas pa nyid yin na bum pa la sogs pa 'ga' zhig rtag par yang 'gyur ro// gal te 'jig pa rgyu mang po yod kyang de dag kyang rang gi rkyen la rag las nas nye ba yin pa'i phyir/ gdon mi za bar nye ba ma yin pas 'ga' zhig mi 'jig par yang 'gyur ro// rgyu rnams ni gdon mi za bar 'bras bu dang ldan pa ma yin te/ ma tshang ba dang gegs byed pa srid pa'i phyir ro// des na 'bras bu gnas med phyir// 'jig pa rgyu ldan smra rnams kyi// 'jig pa'i rgyu ni thams cad dag/ 'khrul pa nyid du bshad pa yin// zhes bya ba ni bar skabs kyi tsigs su bcad pa'o// de'i phyir dngos po de'i ngo bor 'gyur ba gzhan la ltos pa med pa de ni de'i ngo bor nges pa yin te/ rgyu tshogs pa tha mas rang gi 'bres bu bskyed pa la gegs byed pa mi srid pa bzhin no// gal te 'ga' zhig 'ga' zhig tu 'gyur ba la ltos pa med du zin kyang/ de'i ngo bor ma nges pa ma yin nam/ sa dang sa bon dang chu'i tshogs pa dag kyang res 'ga' myu gu bskyed pa'i phyir ro zhe na ma yin te/ der yang rgyu yongs su 'gyur ba la ltos pa'i phyir ro// de ltar dngos po ni 'ga' la yang ltos pa ma yin no// de la yang rgyu tshogs pa tha mas 'bras bu bskyed pa la bar du chod pa med pa gang yin pa de ni 'bras bu dang ldan pa nyid do// de la myu gu'i rgyu ni de nyid yin la/ yongs su 'gyur ba snga ma dag ni de'i don du yin no// der ni de la gegs byed par nus pa 'ga' yang yod pa ma yin no// zhes mang du bshad zin to//.

66 Dharmottara, *Nyāyabinduṭīkā,* Toh 4231, tshad ma, *we*, 36b–92a.

67 Dharmakīrti, *Pramāṇavārttikakārikā*, Toh 4210, tshad ma, *ce*, 96a: gang phyir dngos kun rang bzhin gyis// rang rang ngo bo la gnas phyir// mthun dngos gzhan gyi dngos dag las// ldog pa la ni brten pa can//. Sarve bhāvāḥ svabhāvena svasvabhāvayavasthiteḥ /svabhāvaparabhāvābhyāṃ yasmād vyāvṛttibhāginā ḥ//.

68 Ibid., 274b–275b: dngos po thams cad ni rang gi ngo bo la gnas pa can kho na yin no// de dag ni rang dang gzhan du 'dre bar mi byed de// de gzhan ma yin pa nyid du thal bar 'gyur ro// gang yang 'di dag gi rang bdag nyid du gyur pa'i ngo bo tha mi dad pa de ni de dag gi ma yin te/ de'i tshe de dag med pa'i phyir ro// de kho na yin par 'gyur te/ tha mi dad pa yin pa'i phyir dang/ de las ma gtogs pa tha dad pa yang med pa'i phyir ro// de nyid tha dad par ni 'gal ba'i phyir ro// de yang bdag nyid la rnam par gnas pas ma 'dres pa kho na yin no// don gzhan yang du ma dang 'brel du zin kyang de ni de dag gi spyi ma yin te/ de'i ngo bo ma yin pa'i phyir ro// gnyis nyid la sogs pa dang ldan pa dang/ 'bras bu'i rdzas dag la yang thal bar 'gyur ba'i phyir ro// 'brel pa can gzhan gyis kyang gzhan dag mtshungs pa ni ma yin gyi de dang ldan pa dag tu ni 'gyur te/ 'byung po'i mgul chings lta bu'o// shes pa tha mi dad pa'i yul yang ma yin te/ 'byung po bzhin no// blo ni de dag gi bdag nyid kho na bsre zhing spyi'i yul can du snang gi gcig dang 'brel ba can dag go zhes bya ba ni ma yin te/ 'byung po lta bu'o//.

69 Given that the Nyāya-Vaiśeṣika posits universals as eternal objective realities, they would exist regardless of whether particulars exist or not. Even if all individual fires go out of existence, the fire-ness would continue to exist.

70 Dharmakīrti, *Pramāṇavārttikakārikā*, Toh 4210, tshad ma, *ce*, 179a: don rnams kyi rang bzhin nges pa yang glo bur bar ni mi rigs te/ ltos pa med pa ni yul dang dus dang rdzas nges par mi 'thad pa'i phyir ro//.

71 Ibid., 274b: dngos po thams cad ni rang gi ngo bo la gnas pa can kho na yin no//.

72 Ibid., 231a: de'i yul ni rang gi mtshan nyid de/ don gang nye ba dang mi nye ba dag las shes pa la snang ba tha dad pa de ni rang gi mtshan nyid do// de nyid don dam par yod pa ste dngos po'i mtshan nyid ni don byed mtshan nyid kho na yin pa'i phyir ro//.

73 Dignāga, *Ālambanaparīkṣa*, Toh 4206, tshad ma, *ce*, 92a: rtog par shes pa'ang mngon sum ltar snang ngo// shes pa rnams kyi bum pa la sogs pa rtog pa skyes pa de mngon sum ltar snang yin te/ shes pa de la don rang gi mtshan nyid mi snang ba'i phyir ro/.

74 The four conditions of the sense consciousness are as follows. (1) The objective (or causal) condition (*hetupratyaya*) of sense consciousness is that which directly and chiefly gives rise to a sense consciousness bearing an image of that object. (2) The homogeneous and immediately preceding condition (*samanantarapratyaya*) of sense consciousness is that which directly and chiefly gives rise to a sense consciousness that is clear and knowing in nature. It is through this condition we bring out semantics (such as meanings, desires, and prejudices) to bear into mental consciousness. (3) The percept (or the intentional object) condition or observed object (*ālambanapratyaya*) of sense consciousness is that which directly and chiefly gives rise to a sense consciousness bearing an image similar to the object itself. This condition explains the nature of the intentional object. (4) The dominant condition (*adhipatipratyaya*) of sense consciousness is that which directly and chiefly gives rise to a sense consciousness enabling the apprehension of its intentional object.

75 The secondary minds or mental factors are said to number fifty-one and can be subdivided into six categories. (1) The *five all-accompanying mental factors* are intention, attention, contact, discernment, and sensation. These are also called "omnipresent" mental factors because they accompany every primary mental event. If one of them is missing, the primary mind will not be able to cognize its object. (2) The *five object-ascertaining mental factors* are aspiration, firm apprehension, mindfulness, concentration, and wisdom. Each apprehends and confirms the nature of the object involved. (3) The *eleven virtuous mental factors* are the mental factors that are all naturally moral, which means that they are virtuous through their own nature and not through the force of a specific motivation. They are confidence, humility, considerateness, nonattachment, nonhatred, nonignorance, enthusiastic effort, mental suppleness, conscientiousness, equanimity, and nonharm. (4) The *six root delusions* are the principal delusions from which all other secondary delusions arise. They are passionate lust, anger, arrogance, confusion, deluded scepticism, and deluded view. (5) The *twenty secondary delusions* are the ones that arise from the six root delusions. They are aggression, resentment, spite, jealousy, miserliness, concealment, pretense, denial, selfishness, harmfulness, inconsiderateness, shamelessness, dullness, distraction, mental excitement, scepticism, laziness, nonconscientiousness, deluded forgetfulness, and dullness. (6) The *four changeable mental factors* depend upon the motivation, and these mental factors can be virtuous, nonvirtuous, or ethically neutral—which is why they are called "changeable." They are sleep, regret, conception, and analysis.

76 Dharmakīrti, *Vādanyāya*, Toh 4218, tshad ma, *che*, 108b–109a: dngos po skad cig ma rnams ni rgyu'i gzhan dbang nyid yin no// de ni bsgom pa na yang dngos su grol ba'i phyir ma yin no// 'o na ci yin zhe na/ bdag med ltar rten yin/ bdag med pa

nyid mthong ba skye ba'i thabs yin te skad cig mar zad pa can gyi dngos po mi rtag pa rigs pas nges par byas bas mi rtag pa gang yin pa de ni rgyu'i gzhan dbang skad cig ma re rer 'jig pa can byed pa med par 'jug par 'gyur ro// de bas na 'di ni bdag gam bdag gi ma yin no zhes bsgoms pa na/ gang zag stong ba nyid du rtogs par 'gyur ro// stong pa nyid mthong ba las kyang nga dang nga'i zhes bya bar mthong ba med pas ga' zhig la yang rjes su chags pa'am/ 'ga' zhig las skyo ba med pa de ltar na/ 'khor ba'i 'ching ba las grol bar 'gyur ro// de bas na bdag med pa nyid mthong ba de ni/ stong nyid lta bas grol 'gyur gyi// mi rtag pa nyid la sogs pa bsgom pa lhag ma gang yinpa de dag thams cad de don yin/ stong pa nyid mthong ba'i 'bras bu can yin no//.

77 Dharmakīrti, *Pramāṇavārttikavṛtti*, Toh 4216, tshad ma, *ce*, 118b: gzhan ni kun rdzob yod pa ste/ de dag rang spyi'i mtshan nyid bshad//.

78 The term *sāmānyalakṣaṇa* has been variously translated as "generally characterized," "generally defined," "universal," or "generality."

79 Dharmakīrti, *Pramāṇavārttikavṛtti*, Toh 4216, tshad ma, *ce*, 179a: dngos po'i mtshan nyid ni don byed nus pa yin pa'i phyir te/ nus pa brjod pa thams cad dang bral ba ni nye bar brjod pa med pa'i mtshan nyid yin no/.

80 Dharmottara, *Nyāyabinduṭīkā*, Toh 4212, tshad ma, *we*, 45ab: rang gi mtshan nyid du nges pa de lta na yang de mthong ba nyid ni ma yin gang zhig rang gi mtshan nyid ma yin pa de ni spyi'i mtshan nyid yin no// rnam par rtog pa'i shes pas nges pa'i don ni nye ba dag las shes pa'i snang ba tha dad par mi byed do// 'di ltar sgro btags bar bya ba'i me ni sgro btags nas yod pa dang/ sgro btags nas nye ba dang ring bar gnas pa yin no// sgro btags pa de nye ba dang ring ba las ni shes pa'i snang ba tha dad pa med do// de bas na rang gi mtshan nyid las gzhan zhes bshad do//.

81 Dharmakīrti, *Pramāṇavārttikakārikā*, Toh. 4210, tshad ma, *ce*, 97ab: tha dad dngos rnams la brten nas// don gcig tu ni snang ba'i blo// gang gi rang gi ngo bo yis// gzhan gyi ngo bo sgrib byed pa// sgrib byed des bdag tha dad kyang// tha dad pa nyid bsgribs pa yis// dngos rnams ngo bo 'ga' zhig gis// tha dad min pa lta bur snang// 'de la bsam pa'i dbang gis na// spyi yod [97b] par ni rab tu bsgrags// de yis ji ltar kun brtags pa// de ni dam pa'i don du med//.

82 Ibid., *Pramāṇavārttikavṛtti*, Toh 4216, tshad ma, *ce*, 282a: rnam par rtog pa can gyi blo ni de dag las gzhan pa las ldog pa can gyi dngos po rnams la brten nas skye ba na/ rang [282b] gi bag chags kyi rang bzhin byed cing de dag gi ngo bo tha dad pa mi snang bar byas nas/ bdag nyid kyi rnam pa tha dad pa med pa zhen par byas te/ de rnams 'dres par kun du ston to// bsgrub par bya ba dang/ sgrub pa gcig pa can nyid kyis na gzhan las tha dad pa'i dngos po rnams dang/ rnam par rtog pa de'i bag chags kyi rang bzhin na de dag las skye ba can 'di de lta bur snang ba gang yin pa de yin no// da ni kun rdzob ste 'dis rang gi ngo bos gzhan gyi ngo bo sgrib pa'i phyir ro// de dag ni des tha dad pa bsgribs pas bdag nyid kyis tha dad kyang ngo bo 'ga' zhig gis tha mi dad pa bzhin du snang ngo// de bas na rjes su byed pa rnams kyi blo'i snang ba la blo la snang ba'i dngos po la rnam pa'i khyad par yongs su 'dzin pas phyi rol lta bur kun tu 'phro ba de dag kho na'i spyi yin bar brjod do//.

83 Matilal 1971, 45.

84 Dharmakīrti, *Nyāyabindu*, Toh 4212, tshad ma, *ce*, 231a: gzhan ni spyi'i mtsan nyid de/ de ni rjes su dpag pa'i yul yin no/. Sanskrit: anyat sāmānyalakṣaṇam /so 'numānasys viṣayaḥ //.

85 Hirakawa 1990, 243–46.

86 Harris 1991, 64–65.

87 Maitreya, *Dharmadharmatāvibhaṅgakārikā*, Toh 4023, sems tsam, *phi*, 50b–53b: 'di dag thams cad mdor bsdu na// rnam pa gnyis su shes bya ste// chos dang de bzhin chos nyid kyis// thams cad bsdus pa nyid phyir ro//.

88 Vasubandhu, *Vyākhyāyukti*, Toh 4061, sems tsam, *shi*, 94a: 'jig rten pa'i shes pa ma 'khrul ba'i yul dang/ 'jig rten las 'das pa'i shes pa'i yul la dgongs nas bden pa gnyis po kun rdzob kyi bden pa dang/ don dam pa'i bden par gsungs so//.

89 Many of the Yogācāra texts are now available in English translations. Stefan Anacker, in his *Seven Works of Vasubandhu: The Buddhist Psychological Doctor*, produced the translations of six seminal works of Vasubandhu on Yogācāra: *A Discussion on the Five Aggregates* (*Pañcaskandhakaprakaraṇa*), *A Discussion for the Demonstration of Action* (*Karmasiddhiprakaraṇa*), the *Twenty Verses* (*Viṃśatikā*), the *Thirty Verses* (*Triṃśikā*), *Commentary on the Separation of the Middle from the Extremes* (*Madhyāntavibhāgabhāṣya*), and the *Discernment of the Three Natures* (*Trisvabhāvanirdeśa*). Fernando Tola and Carman Dragonett's *Being as Consciousness: Yogācāra Philosophy of Buddhism* offers us excellent studies of the Yogācāra philosophy in addition to the translations of Dignāga's *Investigation about the Support of the Cognition* (*Ālambanaparīkṣāvṛtti*), Vasubandhu's the *Twenty Stanzas: The Demonstration of the Only Existence of Consciousness* (*Viṃśatikāvijñaptimātratāsiddhi*; alternatively *Twenty Verses*); and *Identifying the Three Natures* (*Trisvabhāvanindeśa*). Swati Ganguly's *Treatise in Thirty Verses on Mere Consciousness* provides a critical English translation of Xuanzang's Chinese version of the *Vijñaptimātratātriṃśikā* with notes from Dharmapāla's commentary in Chinese. Jay Garfield's *Empty Words: Buddhist Philosophy and Cross-Cultural Interpretation* has in it a study of the three natures and three naturelessnesses, a translation and commentary on Vasubandhu's *Trisvabhāvanirdeśa*.

90 Vasubandhu, *Viṃśatikā* 1: vijñaptimātramevaitadasadarthāvabhāsanāt/ yathā taimirikasyāsatkeśacandrādidarśanam//. Toh 4056, sems tsam, *shi*, 3a: 'di dag rnam par rig tsam nyid// yod pa ma yin don snang phyir// dper na rab rib can dag gis// skra zla la sogs med mthong bzhin//.

91 Ibid., Toh 4056, sems tsam, *shi*, 4a–10a.

92 Vasubandhu, *Trisvabhāvanirdeśa* 1: kalpitaḥ paratantraśca pariniṣpanna eva ca/ trayaḥ svabhāvā dhīrāṇāṃ gambhīrajñeyamiṣyate//. Toh 4058, sems tsam, *shi*, 10a: brtags dang gzhan gyi dbang dang ni// yongs su grub pa nyid dag ste// rang bzhin gsum po brtan rnams kyi// zab mo yi ni shes byar 'dod//.

93 Asaṅga, *Mahāyānasaṃgraha*, Toh 4048, sems tsam, *ri*, 13a: de la gzhan gyi dbang gi mtshan nyid gang zhe na/ gang kun gzhi rnam par shes pa'i sa bon can yang dag pa ma yin pa kun rtog pas bsdus pa'i rnam par rig pa'o/.

94 Vasubandhu, *Trisvabhāvanirdeśa* 2: yat khyāti paratantro . . . / pratyayādhīnavṛttitvāt . . . . Toh 4058, sems tsam, *shi*, 10a: rkyen gyi dbang gis 'jug pa dang . . . gang zhig snang de gzhan dbang ste . . . //.

95 *Ālayavijñāna* ("storehouse consciousness") is one of the most innovative and central ideas in Yogācāra idealism. The storehouse consciousness contains series of dispositions or subliminal impressions (*vāsanās*) of various kinds that manifest as the material resources for the representations in five sensory cognitions and the mental cognition (*manovijñāna*).

96 Vasubandhu, *Trisvabhāvanirdeśa* 2: 'sau yath khyāti sa kalpitaḥ /... kalpanāmātrabhāvataḥ//. Toh 4058, sems tsam, *shi*, 10a: brtags pa tsam gyi dngos yin pas// ... ji snang de kun brtags pa yin//.

97 *Saṃdhinirmocanasūtra*, H 109, mdo sde, *ca*, 35b: de bzhin nyid rnam par dag pa'i dmigs pa gang lags pa de ni yongs su grub pa'i mtshan nyid lags te/ de la brten nas bcom ldan 'das chos rnams kyi don dam pa'i ngo bo nyid ma mchis pa de nyid las gcig 'dogs par mdzad lags so//.

98 Vasubandhu, *Trisvabhāvanirdeśa* 3: tasya khyāturyathākhyānaṃ yā sadāvidyamānatā/ jñeyaḥ sa pariniṣpannasvabhāvo 'nanyathātvataḥ//. Toh 4058, sems tsam, *shi*, 10a: gang snang de yi ji ltar snang// rtag tu med pa gang yin de// gzhan du 'gyur med ces bya bas// yongs su grub pa'i rang bzhin yin//.

99 Ibid., 4cd: tasya kā nāstitā tena yā tatrādvayadharmatā //. Toh 4058, sems tsam, *shi*, 10a: de la de med gang yin pa// de nyid de yi gnyis med chos//.

100 Maitreya, *Madhyāntavibhāgakārikā*. Toh 4021, sems tsam, *phi*, 41a: stong pa nyid ni mdor bsdu na// de bzhin nyid dang yang dag mtha'// mtshan ma med dang don dam dang // chos kyi dbyings ni rnam grangs so// gzhan min phyin ci log ma yin// de 'gog 'phags pa'i spyod yul dang // 'phags pa'i chos kyi rgyu yi phyir// rnam grangs don te go rims bzhin//.

101 Vasubandhu, *Viṃśakārikāvṛtti* 10, Toh 4057, sems tsam, *shi*, 6b: gang byis pa rnams kyis chos rnams kyi rang bzhin kun brtags pa'i bdag nyid des de dag bdag med kyi sangs rgyas kyi yul gang yin pa brjod du mad pa'i bdag nyid kyis ni med pa ma yin no //.

102 Ibid., 33, Toh 4057, sems tsam, *shi*, 8b: gang gi tshe de'i gnyen po 'jig rten las 'das pa rnam par mi rtog pa'i ye shes thob nas sang par gyur pa de'i tshe de'i rjes las thob pa dag pa 'jig rten pa'i ye shes de mngon du gyur nas yul med par ji lta ba bzhin du khong du chud de de ni mtshungs so //.

103 Ibid., 10: tathā pudgalanairātmyapraveśo hi anyathā punaḥ/ deśanā dharmanairātmyapraveśaḥ ... // Toh 4057, sems tsam, *shi*, 3b: de ltar gang zag bdag med par// 'jug par 'gyur ro gzhan du yang// bstan pas chos la bdag med par// 'jug 'gyur... //.

104 Vasubandhu, *Triṃśikākārikā* 3.25: dharmāṇāṃ paramārthaśca sa yatastathatāpi saḥ/ sarvakālaṃ tathābhāvāt saiva vijñaptimātratā//. Toh 4055, sems tsam, *shi*, 3b: chos kyi don gyi dam pa'ang de// 'di ltar de bzhin nyid kyang de// dus rnams kun na'ang de bzhin nyid // de nyid rnam par rig pa tsam//.

105 Sthiramati, *Triṃśikābhāṣya*, Toh 4064, sems tsam, shi, 169ab: dam pa ni 'jig rten las 'das pa'i ye shes te/ bla na med pa'i phyir ro// de'i don ni dam pa'o// yang na nam mkha' ltar thams cad du ro gcig pa dang / dri ma med pa dang mi 'gyur ba'i chos yongs su grub pa ste/ don dam pa zhes bya 'o//.

106 Maitreya, *Madhyāntavibhaṅgakārikā*, Toh 4021, sems tsam, *phi*, 42b: don dang thob dang sgrub pa ni// don dam rnam pa gsum du 'dod//.

107 Vasubandhu, *Triṃśikākārikā* 23: trividhasya svabhāvasya trividhāṃ niḥsvabhāvatām/ sandhāya sarvadharmāṇāṃ deśitā niḥsvabhāvatā//. Toh 4055, sems tsam, *shi*, 2b: ngo bo nyid ni rnam gsum gyi// ngo bo nyid med rnam gsum la// dgongs nas chos rnams thams cad ni// ngo bo nyid med bstan pa yin//.

108 Ibid., 24, Toh 4055, sems tsam, *shi*, 2b: dang po pa ni mtshan nyid kyis// ngo bo nyid med gzhan pa yang// de ni rang nyid mi 'byung bas// ngo bo nyid med gzhan yin no//.

109 Sthiramati, *Triṃśikābhāṣya*, Toh 4064, sems tsam, *shi*, 169a: dang po pa ni kun du brtags pa'i ngo bo nyid de/ de ni mtshan nyid kyis ngo bo nyid med pa ste/ de'i mtshan nyid ni brtags pa'i phyir ro// gzugs kyi mtshan nyid ni gzugs su yod pa'o// tshor ba'i mtshan nyid ni myong ba'o zhes bya ba la sogs pa ste/ de dag rang gi ngo bo med pas nam mkha'i me tog bzhin du rang gi ngo bo med pa'o//.

110 Ibid., 169a: gzhan pa yang zhes bya ba ni gzhan gyi dbang gi ngo bo nyid do// de ni sgyu ma bzhin du rkyen gzhan gyis skyes pa'i phyir rang gi dngos po med do// 'di ltar yang ji ltar snang ba de bzhin du de la skye ba med de/ de'i phyir skye ba ngo bo nyid med pa zhes bya'o//.

111 Ibid., 169a: di ltar yongs su grub pa'i ngo bo nyid de ni gzhan gyi dbang gi bdag nyid chos thams cad kyi don dam pa ste/ de'i chos nyid yin pas de'i phyir yongs su grub pa'i ngo bo nyid ni don dam pa ngo bo nyid med pa ste/ yongs su grub pa ni dngos po med pa'i ngo bo nyid kyi phyir ro//.

112 Vasubandhu, *Trisvabhāvanirdeśa* 26, Toh 4058, sems tsam, *shi*, 11a: rang bzhin gsum po de dag ni// dmigs med gnyis med mtshan nyid de// shin tu med dang de bzhin med// de dngos med pa'i rang bzhin no//. Sanskrit: trayo 'pyete svabhāvā hi advayālambalakṣaṇāḥ/ abhāvādatathābhāvāt tadabhāvasvabhāvataḥ //.

113 Maitreya, *Madhyāntavibhaṅgakārikā*, Toh 4021, sems tsam, *phi*, 41a: stong pa nyid ni mdor bsdu na// de bzhin nyid dang yang dag mtha'// mtshan ma med dang don dam dang // chos kyi dbyings ni rnam grangs so// gzhan min phyin ci log ma yin// de 'gog 'phags pa'i spyod yul dang // 'phags pa'i chos kyi rgyu yi phyir// rnam grangs don te go rims bzhin//.

114 Vasubandhu, *Triṃśikākārikā* 1d–2abc: 'sau pariṇāmaḥ sa ca tridhā // vipāko mananākhyaśca vijñaptirviṣayasya ca . . . // Toh 4055, sems tsam, *shi*, 1a: gyur pa de yang rnam gsum ste// rnam par smin dang ngar sems dang // yul la rnam par rig pa'o//.

115 Ibid., 2cd: tatrālayākhyaṃ vijñānaṃ vipākaḥ sarvabījakam//. Toh 4055, sems tsam, *shi*, 1b: de la kun gzhi rnam shes ni // rnam smin sa bon thams cad pa //.

116 Ibid., 17c–18, Toh 4055, sems tsam, *shi*, 3b: mngon sum blo ni rmi sogs bzhin// de yang gang tshe de yi tshe// khyod kyi don de mi snang na// de ni mngon sum ji ltar 'dod// dper na der snang rnam rig bzhin// bshad zin de las dran par zad// rmi lam mthong ba yul med par// ma sad bar du rtogs ma yin// gcig la gci gi dbang gis na// rnam par rig pa phan tshun des// sems ni gnyid kyis non pas na// de phyir rmi dang 'bras mi mtshungs/.

117 Buddhist philosophical schools (Vaibhāṣika and Sautrāntika) and Hindu philosophical schools (Sāṃkhya-Yoga, Nyāya-Vaiśeṣika, Pūrva Mīmāṃsā) claim that the atoms of the physical objects are ultimately real and argue, in contrast with Yogācāra, that in perception we have either the external objects as the basis of our mental representations or that we directly perceive the external objects as the presentative.

118 Vasubandhu, *Viṃśatikākārikā* 2: na deśakālaniyamaḥ santānāniyamo na ca/ na ca kṛtyakriyā yuktā vijñaptiryadi nārthataḥ//. Toh 4055, sems tsam, *shi*, 3a–4b: gal te rnam rig don min na// yul dang dus la nges med cing// sems kyang nges med ma yin la// bya ba byed pa'ang mi rigs 'gyur//.

119 Ibid., *Viṃśakārikāvṛtti*, Toh 4057, sems tsam, *shi*, 4a–4b.

120 Ibid., *Viṃśatikākārikā* 3: deśādiniyamaḥ siddhaḥ svapnavat pretavatpunaḥ/ santānāniyamaḥ sarvaiḥ pūyanadyādidarśane//. Toh 4055 Degé Tengyur, sems tsam, *shi,* 4b: yul la sogs pa nges 'grub ste// rmi 'dra'o sems kyang nges pa med// yi dags bzhin te thams cad kyis// klung la rang la sogs mthong bzhin//.

121 Dignāga, *Ālambanaparīkṣāvṛtti* 1, Toh 4205, tshad ma, *ce,* 86a: gang dag mig la sogs pa'i rnam par shes pa'i dmigs pa phyi rol gyi don yin par 'dod pa de dag ni de'i rgyu yin pa'i phyir rdul phra rab dag yin pa'am der snang ba'i shes pa skye ba'i phyir de 'dus pa yin par rtog grang na//.

122 Ibid., 86b: 'dus pa ni de lta yang ma yin te/ rdzas su med phyir zla gnyis bzhin// dbang po mtshang ba'i phyir zla ba gnyis mthong ba ni der snang ba nyid yin du zin kyang de'i yul ma yin no// de bzhin du rdzas su yod pa ma yin pa nyid kyis rgyu ma yin pa'i phyir 'dus pa dmigs pa ma yin no//.

123 Vasubandhu, *Viṃśatikākārikā* 13: paramāṇorasaṃyoge tatsaṅghāte 'sti kasya saḥ/ na cānavayavatvena tatsaṃyogād na sidhyati//. Toh 4055, sems tsam, *shi,* 3b: rdul phran sbyor ba med na ni// de 'dus yod pa de gang gis// cha shas yod pa ma yin pas// de sbyor mi grub ma zer cig//.

124 Ibid., 12: saṭkena yugapadyogātparamāṇoḥ ṣaḍaṃśatā/ ṣaṇṇāāṃ samānadeśatvātpiṇḍaḥ syādaṇumātrakaḥ//. Toh 4055, sems tsam, *shi,* 3b: drug gis cig car sbyar ba na// phra rab rdul cha drug tu 'gyur// drug po dag ni go gcig na// gong bu rdul phran tsam du 'gyur//.

125 Ibid., 11: na tadekaṃ na cānekaṃ viṣayaḥ paramāṇuśaḥ/ na ca te saṃhatā yasmātparamāṇurna sidhyati//. Toh 4055, sems tsam, *shi,* 3b: de ni gcig na'ang yul min la// phra rab rdul du du ma'ang min// de dag 'dus pa 'ang ma yin te// /di ltar rdul phran mi 'grub phyir//.

126 Dignāga, *Ālambanaparīkṣāvṛtti* 5. Dignāga gives two defining criteria for the intentional object: (1) An intentional object is an "object when its own nature is apprehended with certainty by the cognition, and so that (the cognition) arises having it as its representation." Toh 4205, tshad ma, *ce,* 86a: yul zhes bya ba ni shes pas gang gis rang gi ngo bo nges par 'dzin pa yin te de'i rnam par skye ba'i phyir ro//. (2) "An object, which produces a cognition that appears under its own representations, is just the intentional object, because it is said to be the determining condition of the arising (of the cognition)." Tshad ma, *ce,* 86b: don gang zhig rang snang ba'i rnam par rig pa bskyed pa de ni dmigs pa yin par rigs te/ 'di ltar de ni skya ba'i rkyen nyid du bshad pas so//.

127 Among these are the *One Hundred Thousand Verses of the Perfect Wisdom Sūtra* (*Śatasāhasrikāprajñāpāramitā*), present in Sanskrit, Chinese, and Tibetan manuscripts; the *Twenty-Five Thousand Verses of the Perfect Wisdom Sūtra* (*Pañcaviṃśatiprajñāpāramitā*), which has some passage-fragments preserved in Sanskrit, though it is available in Chinese and Tibetan translation; and the *Eighteen Thousands Verses of the Perfect Wisdom Sūtra* (*Aṣṭādaśasāhasrikāprajñāpāramitā*), of which no complete Sanskrit version exists, only the portions of Gilgit manuscripts that have been edited.

128 Nāgārjuna's *Mūlamadhyamakakārikā* is known to have at least eight Indian commentaries, four of which are preserved in Tibetan translation—the commentary by Buddhapālita known simply as the *Buddhapālitavṛtti*, Bhāviveka's *Lamp of Wisdom* (*Prajñapradīpa*), Candrakīrti's *Clear Words* (*Prasannapadā*), and a

commentary called the *Akutobhaya*—and four that are not preserved in Tibetan translation by Devaśarman, Guṇamati, Guṇaśrī, and Sthiramati.

Several English translations of the *Mūlamadhyamakakārikā* are available: Jay Garfield's *The Fundamental Wisdom of the Middle Way* (1995), David Kalupahana's *Mūlamadhyamakakārikā of Nāgārjuna: The Philosophy of the Middle Way* (1991), and Mark Siderits and Shōryū Katsura's *Nāgārjuna's Middle Way: Mūlamadhyamakākarikā* (2013).

129 The Sanskrit text cited here is based on the edition by Yoshiyasu Yonezawa in "Vigrahavyāvartanī, Sanskrit Transliteration and Tibetan Translation," *Journal of Naritasan Institute for Buddhist Studies*; input by K. Wille (Göttingen, Germany).

130 The tradition attributes dozens of treatises to Nāgārjuna, and his more well-known writings on Madhyamaka philosophy have received the most attention and appreciation from modern scholarship. Christian Lindtner's *Master of Wisdom: Writings of the Buddhist Master Nāgārjuna* (1986) includes translations and studies of the *Lokātītastava*, *Acintyastava*, *Bodhicittavivaraṇa*, *Yuktṣaṣṭikā*, *Śūnyatāsaptati*, *Vyavahārasiddhi*, and *Bodhisaṃbhāra*[*ka*].

131 Nāgārjuna, *Mūlamadhyamakakārikā* 24.8: dve satye samupāśritya buddhānāṃ dharmadeśanā/ lokasaṃvṛtisatyaṃ ca satyaṃ ca paramārthataḥ//. Toh 3824, dbu ma, *tsa*, 14b–15a: sangs rgyas rnams kyis chos bstan pa// bden pa gnyis la yang dag brten// 'jig rten kun rdzob bden pa dang// dam pa'i don gyi bden pa'o//.

132 Ibid., 24.9: ye 'nayorna vijānanti vibhāgaṃ satyayordvayoḥ/ te tattvaṃ na vijānanti gambhīraṃ buddhaśāsane//. Toh 3824, dbu ma, *tsa*, 15a: gang dag bden pa de gnyis kyi// rnam dbye rnam par mi shes pa// de dag sangs rgyas bstan pa ni// zab mo'i de nyid rnam mi shes//.

133 Ibid., 24.10: vyavahāramanāśritya paramārtho na deśyate/ paramārthamanāgamya nirvāṇaṃ nādhigamyate//. Toh 3824, dbu ma, *tsa*, 15a: tha snyad la ni ma brten par// dam pa'i don ni bstan mi nus// dam pa'i don ni ma rtogs par// mya ngan 'das pa thob mi 'gyur//.

134 Although the Yogācāra school formally emerged only after Nāgārjuna, its view was quite prevalent in his time.

135 Nāgārjuna also devotes a great deal of energy to rejecting the positions of the Brahmanical systems, particularly of Nyāya-Vaiśeṣika and Sāṃkhya-Yoga, on both metaphysical and epistemological grounds. All the theories of truth and knowledge advanced in these systems from his Madhyamaka point of view are too rigid to be of any significant use. His criticisms of these schools however are beyond the purview of this book.

136 Nāgārjuna, *Mūlamadhyamakakārikā* 24.14: sarvaṃ ca yujyate tasya śūnyatā yasya yujyate/ sarvaṃ na yujyate tasya śūnyaṃ yasya na yujyate//. Toh 3824, dbu ma, *tsa*, 15a: gang la stong pa nyid rung ba// de la thams cad rung bar 'gyur/ gang la stong nyid mi rung ba// de la thams cad rung mi 'gyur//.

137 Ibid., 24.18: yaḥ pratītyasamutpādaḥ śūnyatāṃ tāṃ pracakṣmahe/ sā prajñaptirupādāya pratipatsaiva madhyamā//. Toh 3824, dbu ma, *tsa*, 15a: rten cing 'brel bar 'byung ba gang // de ni stong pa nyid du bshad// de ni brten nas gdags pa ste// de nyid dbu ma'i lam yin no//.

138 Ibid., 24.19: apratītya samutpanno dharmaḥ kaścinna vidyate/ yasmāttasmādaśūnyo hi dharmaḥ kaścinna vidyate//. Toh 3824, dbu ma, *tsa*, 15a: gang phyir rten

'byung ma yin pa'i chos 'ga' yod pa ma yin pa// de phyir stong pa ma yin pa'i// chos 'ga' yod pa ma yin no//.

139 Ibid., *Śūnyatāsaptatikārikā* 68, Toh 3827, dbu ma, *tsa*, 24a–27a: dngos kun rang bzhin stong pas na// de bzhin gshegs pa mtshungs med pas// rten cing 'brel par 'byung ba 'di// dngos po rnams sun ye bar bstan//.

140 Nāgārjuna, *Vigrahavyāvartanī* 71, Toh 3828, dbu ma, *tsa*, 29a: gang la stong pa nyid srid pa// de la don rnams thams cad srid// gang la stong nyid mi srid pa// de la ci yang mi srid do//.

141 Ibid., 72: yaḥ śūnyatāṃ pratītyasamutpādaṃ madhyamāṃ pratipadam/ anekārthāṃ nijagāda praṇamāmi tam apratimaṃ tu buddhim iti//. Toh 3828, dbu ma, *tsa*, 29a: gang zhig stong dang rten 'byung dag 'dbu ma'i lam du don gcig par// gsung mchog mtshungs pa med pa yi// sangs rgyas de la phyag 'tsal lo//.

142 Nāgārjuna, *Yuktiśastikakārikā* 6: nirvāṇaṃ ca bhavaś caiva dvayam etan na vidyate/ parajñānaṃ bhavasyaiva nirvāṇam iti kathyate//. Toh 3825, dbu ma, *tsa*, 20b: srid pa dang ni mya ngan 'das// gnyis po 'di ni yod ma yin// srid pa yongs su shes pa nyid// mya ngan 'das shes bya bar brjod//. Sanskrit citations are from fragments of Nagarjuna's *Yuktiśastikakārikā* text input by Richard Mahoney.

143 Bhāvaviveka and Bhavya are two other ways to spell his name. See Eckel 2008, 88, and Lindtner 1995, 37–65.

144 Nāgārjuna, *Mūlamadhyamakakārikā* 1.1: na svato nāpi parato na dvābhyāṃ nāpy ahetutaḥ/ utpannā jātu vidyante bhāvāḥ kva cana ke can//. Toh 3824, dbu ma, tsa, 1a: bdag las ma yin gzhan las min// gnyis las ma yin rgyu med min// dngos po gang dag gang na yang // skye ba nam yang yod ma yin//.

145 Buddhapālita, *Buddhapālitamūlamadhyamakavṛtti*, Toh 3842, dbu ma, *tsa*, 161b: de la re zhig dngos po rnams bdag gi bdag nyid las skye ba med de/ de dag gi skye ba don med pa nyid du 'gyur ba'i phyir dang / skye ba thug pa med par 'gyur ba'i phyir ro// 'di ltar dngos po bdag gi bdag nyid du yod pa rnams la yang skye ba dgos pa med do// gal te yod kyang yang skye na nam yang mi skye bar mi 'gyur bas de yang mi 'dod de/ de'i phyir re zhig dngos po rnams bdag las skye ba med do//.

146 Bhāviveka, *Prajñāpradīpamūlamadhyamakavṛtti*, Toh 3853, dbu ma, *tsha*, 49ab: de ni rigs pa ma yin te/ gtan tshigs dang dpe ma brjod pa'i phyir dang/ gzhan gyis smras pa'i nyes pa ma bsal pa'i phyir dang / glags yod pa'i tshig yin pa'i phyir te/ skabs kyi don las bzlog pas bsgrub par bya ba dang / de'i chos bzlog pa'i don mngon pas dngos po rnams gzhan las skye bar 'gyur ba dang / skye ba 'bras bu dang bcas pa nyid du 'gyur ba dang / skye ba thug pa yod par 'gyur ba'i phyir mdzad [49b] pa'i mtha' dang 'gal bar 'gyur ro//.

147 Ibid., 49a: 'dir sbyor ba'i tshig tu 'gyur ba ni don dam par nang gi skye mched rnams bdag las skye ba med par nges te/ yod pa'i phyir dper na shes pa yod pa nyid bzhin no//.

148 Ibid., 1.1, Toh 3853, dbu ma, *tsha*, 48b: dpe ni bsgrub par bya ba dang / sgrub pa'i chos kyi dbang gis te bsgrub par bya ba dang / sgrub pa'i chos grags pa dang ldan pa'i chos can gyi dpe yin pa'i phyir ro//.

149 Jñānagarbha, *Satyadvayavibhaṅgavṛtti* 19, Toh 3882, dbu ma, *sa*, 9b–10a.

150 Bhāviveka, *Prajñāpradīpamūlamadhyamakavṛtti*, Toh 3853, dbu ma, *tsha*, 49a: 'dir sbyor ba'i tshig tu 'gyur ba ni don dam par nang gi skye mched rnams bdag las skye ba med par nges te/ yod pa'i phyir dper na shes pa yod pa nyid bzhin no//.

151 Bhāviveka, *Madhyamakahṛdayakārikā* 3.26, Toh 3855, dbu ma, *dza*, 4b: 'dir ni sa la sogs pa dag/ don dam par na 'byung ba yi// ngo bo nyid min byas phyir dang // rgyu ldan sogs phyir shes pa bzhin//.

152 Candrakīrti, *Prasannapadā*, Toh 3860, dbu ma, 'a, 5b: skyon 'di dag thams cad ni rigs pa ma yin par kho bo cag gis mthong ngo//.

153 Ibid., 6a: dbu ma pa yin na ni rang gi rgyud kyi rjes su dpag par bya ba rigs pa yang ma yin te/ phyogs gzhan khas blangs pa med pa'i phyir ro//. Sanskrit (Vaidya 1960), 1.16b: na ca mādhyamikasya sataḥ svatantramanumānaṃ kartuṃ yuktaṃ pakṣāntarāṃayupagamābhāvāta//.

154 Ibid., 8a: phal cher thal ba sgrub pa kho na'i sgo nas gzhan gyi phyogs sel bar mdzad do// ci skye slob dpon gyi ngag rnams ni don gyi ngag yin pa'i phyir don chen po nyid yin pas sbyor ba du ma'i rgyu nyid du rtogs na ni/ slob dpon sangs rgyas bskyangs kyi ngag dag kyang ci'i phyir de ltar yongs su mi rtog/ 'on te sbyor ba'i ngag [8b] rgyas par rjod par byed pa gang yin pa 'di ni 'grel pa mkhan po rnams kyi lugs yin no zhe na/ de yang yod pa ma yin te/ rtsod pa bzlog pa'i 'grel pa mdzad pa na/ slob dpon gyis kyang sbyor ba'i ngag ma gsungs pa'i phyir ro//.

155 Bhāviveka, *Prajñāpradīpamūlamadhyamakavṛtti*, Toh 3853, dbu ma, *tsha*, 49a: 'dir sbyor ba'i tshig tu 'gyur ba ni don dam par nang gi skye mched rnams bdag las skye ba med par nges te/ yod pa'i phyir dper na shes pa yod pa nyid bzhin no//.

156 Candrakīrti, *Prasannapadā*, Toh 3860, dbu ma, *'a*, 8b: gzhan yang rtog ge ba 'dis bdag nyid rtog ge'i bstan bcos la shin tu mkhas pa tsam zhig bstan par 'dod pas, dbu ma pa'i lta ba khas len bzhin du yang rang rgyud kyi sbyor ba'i ngag brjod pa gang yin pa de ni ches shin tu nyes pa du ma'i tshogs kyi gnas su rtogs te/ ji ltar zhe na /de la re zhig gang 'di skad du 'dir sbyor ba'i tshig tu 'gyur ba ni/ don dam par na nang gi skye mched rnams bdag las skye ba med par nges te/ yod pa'i phyir dper na shes pa yod pa nyid bzhin no zhes smras pa yin no//.

157 Ibid., 8b: 'dir don dam pa zhes bya ba'i khyad par ci'i phyir nye bar bkod pa yin/ gal te 'jig rten gyi kun rdzob tu skye bar khas blangs pa dgag par bya ba ma yin pa'i phyir dang/ 'gog na yang khas blangs pas gnod par thal bar 'gyur ba'i phyir ro zhe na/ 'di ni rigs pa ma yin te/ bdag las skye ba ni kun rdzob tu yang khas ma blangs pa'i phyir ro//.

158 Ibid., 9a: gang las de la ltos nas kyang khyad par 'bras bu dang bcas par 'gyur ba 'jig rten las kyang bdag las skye bar mi rtogs te/ 'jig rten pas ni bdag dang gzhan las zhes bya ba de lta bu la sogs pa'i rnam par spyod pa 'jug pa med par byas nas/ rgyu las 'bras bu 'byung ngo zhes bya ba 'di tsam zhig rtogs pa yin no// slob dpon yang de ltar rnam par gzhag pa mdzad pa yin te/ de'i phyir rnam pa thams cad du khyad par don med pa nyid do zhes bya bar nges so//.

159 Ibid., 8b–9a: gzhan gyi lugs la ltos te khyad par du byas so zhe na/ de yang rigs pa ma yin te/ de dag gi rnam par gzhag pa ni kun rdzob tu yang khas blangs pa med pa'i phyir ro// bden pa gnyis phyin ci ma log par [9a] mthong ba las nyams pa'i mu stegs pa dag ji srid du gnyi ga'i sgo nas 'gog pa de srid du yon tan nyid yin par rtogs so// de ltar na gzhan gyi gzhung la ltos te khyad par brjod pa yang rigs pa ma yin no//.

160 Kamalaśīla, *Madhyamakāloka*, Toh 3887, dbu ma, *sa*, 152a: ngo bo nyid 'di ni rnam pa gnyis ka yang don dam par mi rung ste/ de'i phyir chos thams cad ngo bo nyid 'dis don dam par ngo bo nyid med pa yin gyi/ kun rdzob p'i ngo bo nyid kyang med pa'i phyir ni ma yin no// de med na ni kun nas nyon mongs pa dang rnam par byang ba'i chos rnam par gzhag par yang mi 'gyur te//.

161 Jñānagarbha, *Satyadvayavibhaṅgakārikā* 18–19, Toh 3881, dbu ma, *sa*, 2b: rgol ba gnyis ka'i shes pa la// ji tsam snang ba'i cha yod pa// de tsam de la brten nas ni// chos can chos la sogs par rtog/ de tshe rjes su dpag pa 'byung// gang gi tshe na gzhan na min// de bas rigs pa smra ba rnams// de skad smra la su zhig 'gog/ gal te rigs pa'i stobs kyis na// kun rdzob tu yang mi skye dang // de bden de yi phyir na ni// ji ltar snang bzhin yin par gsungs// ji ltar rang bzhin ngo bo'i phyir// 'di la dpyad pa mi 'jug go//.

162 Ibid., *Satyadvayavibhaṅgavṛtti* 19, Toh 3882, dbu ma, *sa*, 9b–10a: rjes su dpag pa dang rjes su dpag par bya ba 'di tha snyad kyi rgol ba dang / phyir rgol ba dag gi blo'i bdag nyid la snang ba'i chos can dang chos dang dpe nyid du rnam par gzhag par 'byung gi// chos can dang chos la sogs pa gnyi ga la ma grub pa nyid kyis rjes su dpag pa 'byung ba mi rung ba'i phyir gzhan na ni ma yin te/ gzhung lugs tha dad pa la gnas pa rnams ni gang la yang blo mtshungs pa nyid med pa'i phyir ro// chos can de lta bu la gnas pa [10a] rnams ni gtan tshigs la sogs pa de lta bu kho nas yang dag par na yod dam med ces sems par byed par khas blang bar bya'o//.

163 Candrakīrti, *Madhyamakāvatāra* 6.36–38, Toh 3861, dbu ma, *'a*, 205b–206a: de nyid skabs su rigs pa gang zhig gis// [206a] bdag dang gzhan las skye ba rigs min pa'i// rigs des tha snyad du yang rigs min pas// khyod kyi skye ba gang gis yin par 'gyur// dngos po stong pa gzugs brnyan la sogs pa// tshogs la ltos rnams ma grags pa yang min// ji ltar der ni gzugs brnyan sogs stong las // shes pa de yi rnam pa skye 'gyur ltar// de bzhin dngos po thams cad stong na yang // stong nyid dag las rab tu skye bar 'gyur// bden pa gnyis su'ang rang bzhin med pa'i phyir// de dag rtag pa ma yin chad pa'ang min//.

164 Jñānagarbha, *Satyadvayavibhaṅgakārikā* 25, Toh 3882, dbu ma, *sa*, 2b: rtsod ngan grags pa kha cig ni// yang dag par dngos ma skyes pa// mo gsham bu la sogs bzhin du// kun rdzob tu yang mi skye zer//.

165 Ibid., *Satyadvayavibhaṅgavṛtti* 25, Toh 3882, dbu ma, *sa*, 11ab: de ni rigs pa ma yin te [11b] 'jig rten gnod sogs srid pa'i phyir//.

166 Ibid., 11ab: yang dag skye ba bkag pa yis// yang dag par na skye med 'dod//.

167 Candrakīrti, *Catuḥṣatakaṭīkā* 13.311, Toh 3865, dbu ma, *ya*, 201b: kho bo cag gi rnam par dpyod pa don rang bzhin tshol ba lhur byed pa nyid kyi phyir ro// kho bo cag ni 'dir dngos po rnams rang gi ngo bos grub pa 'gog gi mig la sogs pa byas shing rten cing 'brel par 'byung ba'i las kyi rnam par smin pa nyid ni mi 'gog pa'o// de'i phyir de yod pas gang zhig rnam par smin pa nyid du bsnyad pas mig la sogs pa yod pa nyid do//.

168 Ibid., 15.360. Toh 3865, dbu ma, *ya*, 225a: rten cing 'brel par 'byung ba ni ji lta ba bzhin mthong ba na sgyu ma byas pa lta bur 'gyur gyi mo gsham gyi bu lta bu ni ma yin no// gal te rnam par dpyod pa 'dis skye ba rnam pa thams cad du bkag pa las 'dus byas skye ba med par bstan par 'dod na ni de'i tshe sgyu ma lta bu nyid du mi 'gyur gyi mo gsham gyi bu la sogs pa dag gis nye bar gzhal bar 'gyur ba zhig na/ rten cing 'brel par 'byung ba med par thal bar 'gyur ba'i 'jigs pas de dag dang bstun par mi byed kyi/ de dang mi 'gal ba sgyu ma la sogs pa dag dang ni mi byed do//.

169 Ibid., 15.375. Toh 3865, dbu ma, *ya*, 229a: de'i phyir de ltar yongs su dpyad pa na dngos po rnams kyi rang bzhin 'grub par mi 'gyur bas so so nas dngos po rnams la sgyu ma lta bu de nyid lhag ma lus par 'gyur ro//.

170 Bhāviveka, *Madhyamakahṛdayakārikā* 5.15. Toh 3856, dbu ma, *dza*, 20b: gal te gzung bar snang 'dod pas// gzugs blo yang dag ma yin na// des na gtan tshigs 'khrul 'gyur zhing// dam bcas pa yang nyams par 'gyur//.

171 Bhāviveka, *Tarkajvālā* 5.15. Toh 3856, dbu ma, *dza*, 204ab: 'khrul zhes bya ba ni 'gal zhes bya ba'i tha tshig ste/ 'di ltar gzugs kyi blo ni gzung bar snang bar snang ba nyid du rjes su dpag pa yang dag pa ma yin pa snang ba nyid du rjes su dpag pa yang dag pa ma yin pa nyid kyis yang dag pa bsal ba'i phyir chos can gyi ngo bo nyid log par bsgrub pas 'gal lo// 'dir dam bcas pa ni gzugs kyi blo yang dag pa ma yin pa'o// 'di la gzugs kyi blo gang yin pa de ji ltar na yang dag pa ma yin par 'gyur te/ [204b] mngon sum dang/ lung dang/ 'jig rten la grags pas gzugs kyi blo yang dag pa nyid yin par yang dag pa nyid ma yin pa bsal ba'i phyir rjes su dpag pa dang 'gal lo//.

172 *Daśabhūmikasūtra,* chap. 31, 1.448. Trans. by Roberts, 2021.

173 Ibid., 1.493. Trans. by Roberts, 2021.

174 Bhāviveka, *Madhyamakahṛdayakārikā* 5.17, Toh 3855, dbu ma, *dza*, 20b: sems tsam du ni dmigs pa dang// gzugs la sogs pa mi 'dzin na// khas blangs pa dang grags pa yis// dam bcas pa la gnod par 'gyur//.

175 Ibid., 5.18, Toh 3855, dbu ma, *dza*, 20b: de ltar snang ba skye ba'i phyir// rmi lam gzugs sogs blo bzhin du// gzugs la sogs pa don med par// rnam par shes zhes byar mi rung//.

176 Ibid., *Madhyamakahṛdayavṛttitarkajvālā* 5.18, Toh 3855, dbu ma, *dza*, 20b: zhes bya ba ni thog ma med pa'i dus nas gzung ba dang 'dzin pa'i bag chags kyis bsgos pa'i shes pa dang ldan pa'i mig gis rmi lam na mthong ba nyid kyi gzugs la sogs pa dag mthong ba yin gyi ma mthong ba ma yin te/ rmi lam la sogs pa'i rnam par shes pa dag ni dmigs pa dang bcas pa nyid yin te/ sngon mthong ba la sogs pa mngon bar brjod pa'i phyir dran pa la sogs pa bzhin no// dmus long gi mig gi mthug tan nyams pa la yang tshe rabs gzhan na mthong ba'i bag chags kyi shugs kyis rmi lam na kha dog dang dbyibs tha dad pa'i gzugs du ma dag snang bar 'gyur bas de'i shes pa de la yang dmigs pa med pa ma yin te/ 'di ltar bzang skyong dmus long des rmi lam na shes pa dang ldan pa'i mig gis gzugs de dag mthong ste/ sha'i mig gis ni ma yin no zhes gsungs pa lta bu'o// shes pa'i mig gis ni chos la dmigs pa'i phyir rmi lam la sogs pa'i rnam par shes pa yang dmigs pa dang bcas pa nyid yin pas khyed cag gi sgrub pa la dpe med pa'i skyon nyid du 'gyur ro// gzugs la sogs pa'i don gyi dngos po sel bar byed pa'i phyir yul la skur pa 'debs pa nyid kyang yin no//.

177 Bhāviveka, *Madhyamakahṛdayakārikā* 5.19, Toh 3855, dbu ma, *dza*, 20b: gang phyir rmi lam la sogs pa'i// rnam shes chos la dmigs pa'i phyir// de phyir dpe yang med pa dang // yul la skur pa 'debs par 'gyur//.

178 In contrast, Bhāviveka's *Madhyamakaratnapradīpa* (Toh 3854, dbu ma, *tsha*, 259b–289a) has the term "convention" taken as the word of the Buddha to mean "unfixed" and "misleading," hence conventional reality is explained as "analogous to a reflection of the moon in the water." (Ibid., 260b: bcom ldan 'das kyi zhal nas kun rdzob ces bya ba ni mi brtan pa dang / gyo ba'o// de'i bden pa ni chu zla lta bu'o/.) "Convention," he says, "comes to mean all evident phenomena, the visual form and so forth. They are truths, for the perspective of the ordinary beings warrants their reality and that they constitute the incontrovertible linguistic convention." (Ibid., 260b: kun rdzob ces bya ba ni gzugs la sogs pa ji ltar snang

ba'i dngos po'o// de nyid bden pa ste tshu rol mthong ba'i ngo la tshad ma yin pa'i phyir dang / 'jig rten gyi tha snyad phyin ci ma log pa'o//.) The *Madhyamakaratnapradīpa* (259b–289a) explains conventional truth under two categories. The first is conventional truth that merely appears, which consists of things such as cataracts, spinning wheels, the double moons, reflection of the moon in water, the city of *gandharvas*, dreams, illusions, mirages, tricks, echoes, images in the mirror, shadows, water bubbles, rainbows, light, and so forth. (Ibid., 260a: de la dang por kun rdzob kyi bden pa rnam par gzhag pa ni/ skra shad bal gyi 'khor lo dang // zla gnyis chu yi zla ba dang // dri za'i grong khyer rmi lam dang// sgyu ma smig rgyu sbrul pa dang // brag ca me long gzugs brnyan dang // grib ma chu bur dbang po'i gzhu// glog la sogs pa'i dngos po ni// snang ba tsam gyis kun rdzob yin//.) Conventional truths that "merely appear" are those phenomena that are causally inefficacious although they appear to be one. A mirage for instance does not quench one's thirst even though it appears to be water. The second is "real conventional truth" which, according to Bhāviveka, is "conventional truth for the short-sighted," or reality for ordinary beings. Real conventionality is analogous to the aggregates of the plantain tree whose identity is presupposed by nonanalytical experience of ordinary beings. However, unlike conventionality that simply appears, real conventionality is causally produced and functionally efficient phenomena. (Ibid., 260a: chu shing gi ni phung po bzhin// ma brtags nyams dga'i mtshan nyid can// rgyu las skyes dang don byed nus// tshu rol mthong ba'i kun rdzob yin/.) Hence included under this classification are all the objects and cognitions that are *real conventional truths*. The real conventional truths are nevertheless all *ultimately* false or unreal, appear to be reality under the influence of the confusion that is akin to the sight of falling hairs or the objects and the cognitions in dreams. Bhāviveka states: "The works of us Mādhyamika hold that all external and internal phenomena are false, conditioned, illusion-like, and dream-like, even conventionally" (Ibid., 260a: bdag cag dbu ma pa'i gzhung gis phyi dang nang gi chos thams cad kun rdzob nyid du yang brdzun pa dang/ bcos ma dang/ sgyu ma lta bu dang/ rmi lam lta bur 'dod de //). The objects and the sensory organs are nonfoundational, hence consciousness is also nonfoundational as it has its base in the nonfoundational objects and the sensory organs, and it is a composite of the multitude of phenomena such as the mind and the mental factors (Ibid., 260ab: yul dang dbang po rdzas med pas shes pa yang rdzas med de/ yul dang dbang po rdzas med pa la gnas pa'i shes pa yang rdzas su grub pa med de/ gzhi rdzas med pa dang/ sems dang sems las byung ba dag kyang mang po 'dus pas rdzas su grub pa med de/).

179 Bhāviveka, *Tarkajvālā* 3.8, Toh 3856, dbu ma, *dza*, 56a: kun rdzob ces bya ba ni gzugs la sogs pa'i dngos po kun rnam par 'byed pa'i don gyis te / 'jig rten gyi tha snyad phyin ci ma log pa'o // de nyid bden pa ste/ rnam par gzhag pa thams cad la 'gro ba'i tshad ma yin pa'i phyir ro//.

180 Ibid., 55b: mtshan nyid ces bya ba ni chos rnams kyi mtshan nyid ni rang dang spyi'i bye brag las rnam pa gnyis te/ de la rang gi mtshan nyid ni dngos po rang gi ngo bo spyod yul dang ldan pa rnam par rtog pa med pa'i shes pas nges par gzung bar bya'o// spyi'i mtshan nyid ni rjes su dpog pa'i shes pa rnam par rtog pa can gyis rtogs par bya ba'o//.

181 Ibid., 56b: de la chos rnams kyi rang gi mtshan nyid ni gzugs su rung ba dang / myong ba dang/ mtshan mar 'dzin pa dang / mngon par 'du byed pa dang/ rnam par shes par byed pa la sogs pa'o//.

182 Ibid., 56b–57a: yang rang [57a] gi mtshan nyid ni sngon po dang ser po dang ring po dang/ thung ngu la sogs pa dang gzugs dang sgra la sogs pa'o//.

183 Ibid., 56b: spyi'i mtshan nyid ni mi rtag pa dang sdug bsngal ba dang stong pa dang / bdag med pa la sogs pa'o//.

184 His *Madhyamakaratnapradīpa* takes a different stance that is almost identical to Candrakīrti's position in some respects, especially regarding the fact that he does not explicitly state anywhere the notion that conventional truths are unreal even on the level of convention. This text though does state: "The works of us Mādhyamika hold that all external and internal phenomena are false, conditioned, illusion-like, and dream-like, even conventionally" (Toh 3854, dbu ma, *tsha*, 260a).

185 Bhāviveka, *Tarakjvālā* 3.141, Toh 3856, dbu ma, *dza*, 93b: bdag nyid yod pa nyid dang dngos po nyid ces bya ba de dag ni kun rdzob pa yin te/ de dag la brten nas byung ba ni don dam par ngo bo nyid med pa nyid yin te/ bdag dang gzhan dang gnyi ga dang rgyu med pa las rnam pa thams cad du skye ba med pa'i phyir/ skye ba med pa'i mi mthun pa'i phyogs skye ba med pas// mi mthun phyogs ni med pa'i phyir//.

186 Ibid., 3.152, Toh 3856, dbu ma, *dza*, 96a: 'o na dngos po rnams kyi ngo bo nyid sra ba dang gsher ba dang/ tsha ba dang g-yo ba nyid la sogs pa dag snang bzhin pa nyid ma yin nam zhe na/ bshad pa de dag kun rdzob kyi bden pa'i tshul gyis gzhan sel ba'i ngo bo nyid tsam la brten nas yod par zad de// don dam pa ni ma yin no//.

187 Bhāviveka, *Madhyamakahṛdayakārikā* 3.171, Toh 3855, dbu ma, *dza*, 10a: bum pa la sogs skye ba dag// byis pa'i blo dang mthun mthong ba// gang phyir de ni mi 'gog pas// de phyir ji skad smras skyon med//.

188 Bhāviveka, *Tarkajvālā* 3.17, Toh 3856, dbu ma, *dza*, 99b–100a: ces bya ba ni bum pa la sogs pa'i skye ba bdag dang gzhan dang gnyi ga dang rgyu med pa dang / yod pa dang med pa la sogs pa dpyad pa dang bral ba sgyu ma dang smig rgyu dang / dri za'i grong khyer la sogs pa'i skye ba snang ba lta bu'i byis pa'i skye bo'i blo dang mthun par mthong ba de ni kun [100a] rdzob kyi tshul du yod pas byis pa'i blo dang mthun par mthong ba de ni ma bkag ste/ 'di ltar don dam pa'i blo rtog pa'i skyon gyi dri ma ma lus pa spong par bzod pas brtags na mi rigs par bstan pas de'i phyir mngon sum dang grags pa'i gnod pa ji skad smras pa'i skyon med do//.

189 Ibid., 3.172, Toh 3856, dbu ma, *dza*, 12b: de ni don dam nyid du na// bdag las ma yin gzhan las min// gnyis las ma yin rgyu med min// yod med ma yin gzhan ma yin// sred med dbang phyug skyes bu dang// gtso bo rdul phran la sogs pa'i// rgyu las skyes dang gsal bya yi// dngos po 'ga' yang yod ma yin//.

190 Ibid., 3.155, Toh 3856, dbu ma, *dza*, 96a: 'dir rang gi sde pa dag gis smras pa/ khyod kyi dngos po rnams gzhan las skye ba 'gog par byed pa ni khas blangs pa nyams te/ bcom ldan 'das kyis mdo sde las/ rgyu'i rkyen dang / dmigs pa'i rkyen dang / de ma thag [96b] pa'i rkyen dang / bdag po'i rkyen zhes bya ba rkyen bzhi po dag bka' stsal te/ de la rgyu'i rkyen ni lhan cig 'byung ba'i rgyu dang skal ba mnyam pa'i rgyu dang mtshungs par ldan pa'i rgyu dang/ kun du 'gro ba'i rgyu dang/ rnam par smin pa'i rgyu zhes bya ba rgyu lnga po dag go// dmigs pa'i rkyen ni chos thams cad do// de ma thag pa'i rkyen ni sems dang sems las byung ba 'gags ma thag pa

rnams las dgra bcom pa'i sems tha ma ma gtogs pa'o// bdag po'i rkyen ni byed pa'i rgyu ste// de ltar rkyen bzhi po gzhan du gyur pa de dag las dngos po rnams skye bar 'gyur ro zhes gsungs pa'i phyir ro zhe na . . . //.

191 Bhāviveka, *Madhyamakahṛdayakārikā* 3.155, Toh 3855, dbu ma, *dza*, 96b: rgyu la sogs pa rkyen gzhan las // skye ba kun rdzob tha snyad len // de phyir khas blangs gnod pa med // de dag yang dag nyid ma yin//.

192 The *Madhyamakaratnapradīpa* makes a similar point. See Toh 3854, dbu ma, *tsha*, 276ab: kun rdzob kyi bden par [276b] snang ba'i phreng ba 'di dag thams cad khas blangs pas de dag la skur ba btab pa yang ma yin no// yang don dam par zhes dam bcas pa/ de dag gis gnod par yang mi 'gyur te/ 'di ltar mngon sum gyis kyang mi gnod do// yul rnams log pa yin pa'i phyir dang / dbang po rnams blun pa'i phyir dang / mthong ba la sogs pa'i nus pa med bzhin du rab rib can la skra dang / sbrang bu dang/ khab 'dzag pa la sogs pa snang ba lta bu dang brag ca la sogs pa grag pa ltar mngon sum yang mngon pa'i nga rgyal yin pas de'i phyir gang la ci zhig mngon sum du gyur nas des gnod par 'gyur/ de bas na mngon sum gyi gnod pa med do//.

193 Cf. Bhāviveka makes the same point in the *Madhyamakaratnapradīpa*. See Toh 3854, dbu ma, *tsha*, 276b: rjes su dpag pas kyang gnod pa med do// don dam par 'ga' yang grub pa med pas so// grags pas kyang gnod pa med de/ gang gi phyir 'jig rten ni me shes pa'i ling thog gis mdongs pa yin pas don dam pa dpyad pa'i skabs su de ni nor bu rin po che brtag pa'i skabs su dmus long ma gtogs pa bzhin du 'jig rten pa skabs 'dir mi gtogs pas grags pa'i gnod pa med do//.

194 In the *Madhyamakaratnapradīpa* the author writes: "We Mādhyamika make no claim of the things whatsoever to be made known, not even a dimension of the atomic particle divided into one hundred thousand times, for [everything is] primordially unproduced akin to the son of an infertile woman. For instance, when asked, 'Which one is your son?' an infertile woman, given that she does not have any son, could not respond by saying either 'this' or 'that.' Both responses would be fallacious as they each imply having a son. Therefore we Mādhyamika," says Bhāviveka, "make no claim of things, akin to what you claim, neither of existence nor of nonexistence from the perspective of the transcendent cognition. This is so since all phenomena are unproduced and unexpressible." Dbu ma, *tsha*, 273b: bdag cag dbu ma pa la ni khas blang bar bya ba'i dngos po ni rdul phra rab 'bum du gshags pa'i tshad kyang bstan du med do// khas blangs pa yid dngos po ni// phra rab tsam yang yod min te// gdod nas skye ba med pa'i phyir// mo gsham gyi ni bu bzhin no// dper na bud med mo gsham la// khyod kyi bu ni gang yin dris// de la de ni yod min pas// smra bar nus pa ma yin no// de bas na bdag cag dbu ma pa'i shes rab kyi mdun na yod pa dang med pa la sogs pa'i dngos po khyed kyi 'dod pa lta bu ci yang med de/ chos thams cad skye ba med cing brjod du med pa'i phyir ro//.

195 Bhāviveka, *Tarkajvālā*, Toh 3856, dbu ma, *dza*, 55a. Here, he is commenting on verse 3.7 of the *Madhyamakahṛdayakārikā*, which reads: "A cognition of the conventionally real is one that accords with the understanding of the real conventionality." Dbu ma, *dza*, 40b: shes rab kyi blo gros de yang kun rdzob dang don dam pa'i bden pa gnyis la ltos nas rnam pa gnyis su 'dod do// de la re zhig yang dag pa'i kun rdzob shes pa ni dag pa 'jig rten pa'i ye shes zhes bya ba yin te/ yang dag pa'i don rtogs pa'i rjes su mthun pa'i phyir yang dag pa'i kun rdzob shes pa yin no//.

196 Ibid., *Madhyamakahṛdayakārikā* 3.12–13, Toh 3855, dbu ma, *dza*, 4a: yang dag kun rdzob rnams kyi skas// med par yang dag khang pa yi// steng du 'gro bar bya ba ni// mkhas la rung ba ma yin no// de nyid khang bzangs thog 'dzeg pa// yang dag kun rdzob them pa'i skas// med par rung ba ma yin pa// gang gi phyir ba de phyir ro//. I did not include the last line of verse 3.13 in the translation; the first three lines basically reiterate the same point Bhāviveka makes in 3.12.

197 Bhāviveka, *Tarkajvālā* 3.271, Toh 3856, dbu ma, *dza*, 126a: rnam par mi rtog pa zhes bya ba ni mngon sum gyi mtshan nyid yin pas rtog pa dang rjes su dran pa'i rnam par rtog pa dag mi 'jug pa'i phyir ro//.

198 Ibid., 60a: min zhes bya ba ni dgag pa ston pa'i sgra ste/ ma yin zhes bya bar sbyar ro// gang zhig ci zhig ma yin zhe na/ sa la sogs pa dag don dam par na 'byung ba'i ngo bo nyid ni ma yin no zhes bya bar sbyar ro//.

199 Ibid., 60a: don dam par zhes sam bcas pa'i khyad par yod pa'i phyir khas blangs pa dang mngon sum dang grags pa'i gnod pa med do// gang gi phyir bcom ldan 'das kyis bden pa gnyis bka' stzal pa/ de la kun rdzob tu ni chos rnams kyi ngo bo nyid dang / mtshan nyid rnam par gzhag pa yang mdzad la/ don dam par ni ngo bo nyid med par gsungs te . . . //.

200 Ibid., 3.26. Toh 3855, dbu ma, *dza*, 59ab: don dam pa zhes bya ba la don zhes bya ba ni shes bar bya ba yin pa'i phyir don te/ brtag par bya ba dang go bar bya ba zhes bya ba'i tha tshig go// dam pa zhes bya ba [59b] ni mchog ces bya ba'i tshig gi sgra yin te/ don dam pa zhes bsdu ba ni de don yang yin la dam pa yang yin pas don dam pa'o// yang na dam pa'i don te rnam par mi rtog pa'i ye shes dam pa'i don yin pas dam pa'i don to/ yang na don dam pa dang mthun pa ste don dam pa rtogs pa dang rjes su mthun pa'i shes rab la don dam pa de yod pas don dam pa dang mthun pa'o//. Cf. the *Madhyamakaratnapradīpa* makes very similar point in dbu ma, *tsha*, 260b: don dam pa'i bden pa zhes bya ba ni stong pa nyid bco brgyad do zhes gsungs so// de'i dgongs pa 'di yin te . . . don zhes bya ba ni brtag par bya ba dang / go bar bya ba'o// dam pa ni mchog go// yang na don yang yin la/ dam pa yang yin pas don dam pa'o// yang na dam pa'i don te ye shes dam pa'i don yin pas na dam pa'i don to// bden pa ni mi slu ba'o//.

Ultimate truth is emptiness (*śūnyatā*) since emptiness is the "truth" (*satya*, Tib. *bden pa*), for it is "incontrovertible (*avisaṃvādi*, Tib. *mi slu ba*) and is also the "ultimate," in three senses of the word as Bhāviveka's etymological analysis reveals: (1) Emptiness is the "domain" (*artha*, Tib. *don*) in the sense of being "an object to be analyzed" (*parīkṣaṇīya*, Tib. *brtag par bya ba*) or an "object to be understood" (*pratipādya*, Tib. *go bar bya ba*); it is the "ultimate" (*param*, Tib. *dam pa*) in the sense of it being the final or definitive. (2) Emptiness is the "ultimate domain" (*paramārtha*, Tib. *don dam pa*) in the sense that it is the domain of engagement that is also the ultimate. Or else (3) emptiness is the "ultimate domain" in the sense that it is the domain of the ultimate cognition or ultimate knowledge (Tib. *ye shes dam pa*). See Donald Lopez's *A Study of Svātantrika* (1987, 135–36) for further discussion on this topic.

201 Bhāviveka, *Prajñāpradīpamūlamadhyamakavṛtti* 24.8, Toh 3853, dbu ma, *tsha*, 228a: don dam par ni de don kyang yin la/ dam pa yang yin pas don dam pa'am/ rnam par mi rtog pa'i ye shes dam pa'i don yin pas/ don dam pa ste/ de kho na gzhan las shes pa ma yin pa la sogs pa'i mtshan nyid do// don dam pa nyid bden pa

yin pas/ don dam pa'i bden pa ste/ de dus thams cad dang rnam pa thams cad du de bzhin du gnas pa'i phyir ro// rnam par mi rtog pa'i ye shes de'i yul can yang yul med pa'i tshul gyis don dam pa ste/ de la don dam pa yod pa'i phyir ro// de 'gog pa dang rjes su mthun pa skye ba med pa la sogs pa bstan pa dang/.

202 Bhāviveka, *Tarkajvālā* 3.26, Toh 3855, dbu ma, *dza*, 59ab.

203 Ibid., *Prajñāpradīpamūlamadhyamakavṛtti* 24.8, Toh 3853, dbu ma, *tsha*, 228a: thos pa dang/ bsams pa dang/ bsgoms pa las byung ba'i shes rab kyang don dam pa ste/ don dam pa rtogs pa'i thabs kyi phyir phyin ci ma log pa'i phyir ro//.

204 Ibid., *Tarkajvālā* 3.26, Toh 3856, dbu ma, *dza*, 60b: don dam pa ni rnam pa gnyis te/ de la gcig ni mngon par 'du byed pa med par 'jug pa 'jig rten las 'das pa zag pa med pa spros pa med pa'o// gnyis pa ni mngon par 'du byed pa dang bcas par 'jug pa bsod nams dang ye shes kyi tshogs kyi rjes su mthun pa dag pa 'jig rten pa'i ye shes zhes bya ba spros pa dang bcas pa ste/.

205 Ibid., *Madhyamakahṛdayakārikā*, 3.27, Toh 3855, dbu ma, *dza*, 4b: sa ni sra ba'i ngo bo min// 'byung ba nyid phyir rlung bzhin no// sa yis las ni 'dzin ma yin// byas pa nyid phyir chu bzhin no//.

206 Ibid., *Tarkajvālā* 3.27, Toh 3856, dbu ma, *dza*, 61b: gang gi phyir chu dang me dang rlung las logs shig nas zhes bya ba 'ga' yang yod pa ma yin te/ 'dus pa'i ngo bo nyid dag las sa'i mtshan nyid logs shig tu bkar te bstan par ni ji ltar yang mi nus la/ las kyi bye brag kyang de bzhin pas de'i phyir ngo bo nyid yod pa ma yin no//.

207 Ibid., 3.29, Toh 3856, dbu ma, *dza*, 63ab: sa la sogs pa ni rdzas su yod pa ma yin te/ chu la sogs pa'i tshogs pa'i yan lag ma [63b] gtogs par sa zhes bya ba dmigs su med pa'i phyir ro// gang tshogs pa'i yan lag ma bzung na gzung du med pa de ni rdzas su yod pa ma yin te/ dper na nags tshal bzhin no// shing dha ba dang seng ldeng dang/ palāśa la sogs pa ma gtogs par nags tshal zhes bya ba gzung du med pa bzhin no// 'dus pa la ni nags tshal zhes tha snyad gdags su rung ngo//.

208 Ibid., 3.28, Toh 3856, dbu ma, *dza*, 62a: gang gi phyir de dag gi rdul phra rab kyang 'dus pa'i ngo bo nyid de/ sa dang chu dang me dang rlung dang gzugs dang dri dang ro dang reg pa zhes bya ba rdzas brgyad 'dus pa yin pas de'i phyir gang gis so so la ngo bo nyid dang las rnam par gzhag par bya ba'i mtshan nyid 'ba' zhig pa ni gang la ci yang med la/ las 'ba' zhig pa yang gang la ci yang med do//. For more on this argument see Bhāviveka, *Madhyamakahṛdayakārikā* 3.248–250, dbu ma, *dza*, 13a and *Tarkajvālā* 3.248–250, dbu ma, *dza*, 119a.

209 Ibid., 3.30, Toh 3856, dbu ma, *dza*, 62a: de dag thams cad la sra ba dang gsher ba dang tsha ba dang yang ba nyid yod pas de dag gi rang gi mtshan nyid 'ba' zhig pa rnam par gzhag pa ni bstan par dka'o/.

210 Ibid., 3.29, Toh 3856, dbu ma, *dza*, 61b: ngo bo nyid ces bya ba ni byas pa ma yin pa dang/ 'gyur ba med pa yin pas sus kyang nam yang gzhan du bsgyur bar mi nus pa'i phyir ro//.

211 Ibid., *Madhyamakahṛdayakārikā* 3.33, Toh 3855, dbu ma, *dza*, 5a: gang phyir gzugs ni don dam du// mig gi dbang po'i gzung ba min// bsags phyir dper na sgra bzhin dang // 'byung las gyur phyir de nyid bzhin//.

212 Ibid., *Tarkajvālā* 3.33, Toh 3856, dbu ma, *dza*, 65ab: zhes bya ba la mig gi yul gyi gzugs ni don dam par na mig gi dbang po'i gzung ba ma yin no zhes dam bca'o// . . . [65b] . . . ci'i phyir zhe na/ bsags pa'i phyir te/ rdzas brgyad bsags pa'i phyir te dper na sgra bzhin no zhes bya bar sbyar ro// yang na 'byung ba las gyur pa'i phyir

dper na sgra de nyid bzhin te/ gzugs dang sgra gnyi ga bsags pa dang 'byung ba las gyur pa nyid yin par 'dra bzhin du gzugs ni mig gi yul yin la/ sgra ni ma yin no zhes bya ba'i gtan tshigs kyi khyad par med pa'i phyir ro zhes bya ba'i tha tshig go//.

213 Ibid., *Madhyamakahṛdayakārikā* 3.33, Toh 3855, dbu ma, *dza*, 4b: sa la sogs pa yul gyi blo [5a] de yang rdzas yod ma yin 'dod// rgyu dang bcas phyir 'jig pa'i phyir// nags tshal la sogs blo bzhin no//. Cf. Bhāvaviveka, *Tarkajvālā* 3.33, Toh 3856, dbu ma, *dza*, 63b: gang gi phyir sa la sogs pa rdzas su yod pa ma yin pa de'i phyir de'i yul can gyi blo gros kyang rdzas su yod pa ma yin te/ rgyu yod pa'i phyir dang/ 'jig pa'i phyir nags tshal gyi blo bzhin pas de'i phyir. . . /.

214 Ibid., *Madhyamakahṛdayakārikā*, 3.43, Toh 3855, dbu ma, *dza*, 5a: mig gi dbang po don dam du// gzugs la lta ba ma yin te// sems dang sems byung las gzhan phyir// dper na ri bo'i dbang po bzhin// yang na mig ni don dam du// gzugs la lta ba ma yin te// rnam shes dngos med mi skye'i phyir// pags pa dag la sogs pa bzhin//.

215 Ibid., *Tarkajvālā* 3.43, Toh 3856, dbu ma, *dza*, 66b: gal te mig de la blta ba'i mthu yod par gyur na ni gnyid log pa dang myos pa dang shi ba la sogs pa'i gnas skabs dag dang/ mun khung dang dus thams cad du yang thams cad mthong bar 'gyur ro// gal te mi mthong na ni de la blta ba yod pa ma yin no zhes bya bar tshad ma rnam par bzhag go//.

216 Ibid., 3.43, Toh 3856, dbu ma, *dza*, 66b–67a: gal te rnam par shes pas mthong ngo zhe na ni dmus long gis kyang gzugs mthong bar thal bar 'gyur ro// gal te mig ma nyams pas yid kyis mthong ngo zhe na ni de lta na mig byed pa po nyid ma yin par 'gyur ro// gal te [67a] rnam par shes pa dang bcas pa'i mig gis mthong ngo zhe na de ni kun rdzob tu kun kyang 'dod pa kho na yin te/ de la yang mig 'ba' zhig byed pa po ma yin gyi mthong ba ni gzugs dang snang ba dang nam mkha' dang yid la byed pa tshogs pa la rag lus pa'i phyir/ des na mig 'ba' zhig byed pa po nyid yin par bstan dka'o//.

217 Bhāviveka, *Madhyamakahṛdayakārikā* 3.10–11, Toh 3855, dbu ma, *dza*, 4a: rtog pa'i dra ba ma lus pa// dgag pa sgrub par byed pa dang// zhi dang so so rang rig dang// rnam rtog med cing yi ge med// gcig nyid tha dad nyid bral dang// mkha' ltar dri med de nyid la// 'jug pa med pas 'jug pa yi// shes rab don dam shes pa yin//.

218 Bhāviveka, *Tarkajvālā* 3.35, Toh 3856, dbu ma, *dza*, 56a: rtog pa'i dra ba ma lus pa dgag pa sgrub par byed pa ni chos kyi de bzhin nyid yin te/ rtag pa dang/ mi rtag pa dang / yod pa dang/ med pa dang/ ther zug dang / chad pa la sogs pa rtog pa'i dra ba ma lus pa sel bar byed pa'i ngang tshul can yin pa'i phyir ro// zhi ba ni spros pa thams cad las yang dag par 'das pa'o// so so rang rig pa ni gzhan las shes pa ma yin pa'o// rnam rtog med pa ni rtog pa la sogs pa'i rnam par rtog pa med pa'o// yi ge med pa ni brjod pa'i yul ma yin pa'o// gcig pa nyid dang tha dad pa nyid dang bral ba ni de nyid dang gzhan nyid dang / gnyi ga nyid dang gnyi ga ma yin pa nyid du brjod par bya ba ma yin pa'o// mkha' ltar dri ma med pa ni nam mkha' sprin gyi rim pa dang bral ba ltar dri ma med pa'o//.

219 Ibid., 56a: . . . ji skad smos pa'i rnam pa de dag lta bu'i chos kyi de nyid la 'jug pa med pas 'jug pa ni snang ba med cing 'jug pa med pa nyid de'i 'jug pa yin pa'i phyir te/ de lta bu'i shes rab ni don dam pa shes pa yin par shes par bya ste/ ji skad du mthong ba med pa ni de nyid mthong ba'o zhes gsungs pa lta bu'o//.

220 Bhāviveka, *Madhyamakahṛdayakārikā* 3.26, Toh 3855, dbu ma, *dza*, 4b: 'dir ni sa la sogs pa dag/ don dam par na 'byung ba yi// ngo bo nyid min byas phyir dang // rgyu ldan sogs phyir shes pa bzhin//.

221 Jñānagarbha, Satyadvayavibhaṅgakārikā 3, Toh 388, dbu ma, sa, 1a: kun rdzob dang ni dam pa'i don// bden gnyis thub pas gsungs pa la// ji ltar snang ba 'di kho na// kun rdzob gzhan ni cig shos yin//.

222 Ibid., *Satyadvayavibhaṅgavṛtti* 3, Toh 3882, dbu ma, *sa*, 4a: ji ltar ba lang rdzi mo la sogs pa yan chad kyis mthong ba de ltar kun rdzob tu bden pa rnam par gnas kyi yang dag par ni ma yin te/ mthong ba dang mthun par dngos po'i don nges par 'dzin pa'i phyir ro//.

223 Śāntarakṣita, *Satyadvayavibhaṅgapañjika* 2, Toh 3883, dbu ma, *sa*, 17b: kun rdzob tu bum pa la sogs pa bden par rnam par gnas kyi de kho na nyid du ni ma yin te/ rigs pas dpyad na bum par mi rung ngo zhes bya ba'i tha tshig go//.

224 Jñānagarbha, *Satyadvayavibhaṅgakārikā* 5, Toh 3881, dbu ma, *sa*, 1a: ji ltar snang ba'i dngos por ni// rnam par gnas par mi rung ste// shes pa'i dngos po thams cad la// ji lta bur yang snang mi 'gyur//.

225 Ibid., 7, Toh 3881, dbu ma, *sa*, 4ab: yod med dngos po mkhyen pa po// kun mngon mkhyen pas gang ma gzegs// de yi dngos po ci 'dra zhig// shin tu zhib pa'i lta bas dpyod//.

226 Ibid., *Satyadvayavibhaṅgavṛtti* 4, Toh 3882, dbu ma, *sa*, 4ab: don dam pa ni [4b] ji ltar snang ba bzhin du rnam par gnas pa med de/ thams cad mkhyen pa'i mkhyen pa nyid la yang mi snang ba'i phyir ro// de nyid kyi phyir mdo sde las 'ga' yang mthong ba med pa ni de kho na mthong ba zhes gsungs so//.

227 Ibid., *Satyadvayavibhaṅgakārikā* 4, Toh 3881, dbu ma, *sa*, 1a: slu ba med pas rigs pa ni// don dam yin te kun rdzob min// de ltar mi slu min phyir te// ji ltar snang ba de nyid bden//.

228 Ibid., *Satyadvayavibhaṅgavṛtti* 4, Toh 3882, dbu ma, *sa*, 1a: don dam pa ni kun rdzob kyi bden pa ma yin te/ tshig tha ma khong nas dbyung ba'i phyir ro// ci'i phyir zhe na / de ltar mi slu min phyir te/ de ji ltar shes pa'i bdag nyid la gnas pa de ltar rigs pas mi rung ba'i phyir ro//.

229 Ibid., 4, Toh 3882, dbu ma, *sa*, 4a: don dam par bden pa ni don dam pa'i bden pa ste/ de ni rigs pa'i rjes su 'gro ba can gyi bden pa nyid ces bya ba'i tha tshig go// gang gi phyir/ slu ba med pas rigs pa ni don dam yin te/ rigs pa'i stobs kyis don la nges pa ni slu bar mi 'gyur te/ de'i phyir tshul gsum pa'i rtags kyis bskyed pa'i rtogs pa gang yin pa de ni dam pa yang yin la/ don yang yin pas don dam pa'o// des gtan la phab pa'i don kyang don dam pa ste/ mngon sum la sogs pa bzhin du brjod do//.

230 Ibid., *Satyadvayavibhaṅgakārikā* 12, Toh 3881, dbu ma, *sa*, 1b: snang du 'dra yang don byed dag/ nus pa'i phyir dang mi nus phyir// yang dag yang dag ma yin pas// kun rdzob kyi ni dbye ba byas//.

231 Ibid., *Satyadvayavibhaṅgavṛtti* 12, Toh 3882, dbu ma, *sa*, 6b: yang kun rdzob ni rnam pa gnyis su bstan te/ . . . shes pa gsal ba'i rnam pa snang ba can du 'dra yang/ ji ltar snang ba bzhin du don byed pa la slu ba dang mi slu ba yin par nges par byas nas chu la sogs pa dang smig rgyu la sogs pa dag 'jig rten gyis yang dag pa dang yang dag pa ma yin par rtogs so// dngos su na gnyis ni ngo bo nyid med pa nyid du ngo bo nyid mtshungs pa kho na'o// ji ltar snang ba bzhin du ni rnam par gnas so// don byed pa la slu ba dang mi slu ba yang ji ltar grags pa kho na bzhin te/ de yang ngo bo nyid med pa'i phyir ro//.

232 Ibid., *Satyadvayavibhaṅgakārikā* 8ab, Toh 3881, dbu ma, *sa*, 2a: brtags pa'i don gyis dben gyur pa// dngos tsam brten nas skyes pa ste//.

233 Ibid., 21ab, Toh 3881, dbu ma, *sa*, 2b: ji ltar rang bzhin ngo bo'i phyir// 'di la dpyad pa mi 'jug go// rnam par dpyod pa byed na don// gzhan du song bas gnod par 'gyur//.

234 Ibid., *Satyadvayavibhaṅgavṛtti* 8, Toh 3882, dbu ma, *sa*, 5b: brtags pa'i don ni yang dag par skye ba la sogs pa dang / rnam par shes pa snang ba dang/ gtzo bo dang 'byung ba'i yongs su 'gyur ba la sogs pa ste/ de dag gis dben pa'o//.

235 Ibid., *Satyadvayavibhaṅgakārikā* 8cd, Toh 3881, dbu ma, *sa*, 2a: yang dag kun rdzob shes par bya// yang dag ma yin kun brtags yin//.

236 Ibid., *Satyadvayavibhaṅgavṛtti* 8c, Toh 3882, dbu ma, *sa*, 5b: yang dag par skye ba la sogs pa ni mi snang ste/ ji lta bur yang rung ba'am/ grub pa'i mtha' la brten nas sgro btags pa 'ba' zhig tu zad do// de lta ma yin na ni rtsod pa med par thal ba kho nar 'gyur ro// rgol ba dang phyir rgol ba'i shes pa la snang ba'i cha la ni rtsod pa su yang med do// rtsod par byed na ni mngon sum la sogs pas gnod par 'gyur ro//. Cf. Śāntarakṣita, *Satyadvayavibhaṅgapañjikā* 8c, Toh 3883, dbu ma, *sa*, 24a: yang dag par skye ba la sogs pa ni mi snang ste zhes bya ba smos so// gal te mi snang na ji ltar sgro btags pa yin zhe na/ ji lta bu'ang rung ba'am/ grub pa'i mtha' la brten nas sgro btags pa 'ba' zhig tu zad do zhes bya ba smos so// ji lta bu'ang rung zhes bya ba ni thog ma med pa'i dus nas log par yongs su brtags pa'i dbang gis te/ de ni de lta'o// de lta ma yin na ni yang dag par skye ba la sogs pa snang bar gyur pa de dag la/ rtsod pa med par thal ba kho nar 'gyur ro// ci'i phyir zhe na/ rgol ba dang phyir rgol ba'i shes pa la snang ba'i cha la ni rtsod pa su yang med do zhes bya ba smos so// gal te 'di lta bu'i cha la brgya la rtsod par byed do zhe na/ rtsod par byed na ni mngon sum la sogs pas gnod par 'gyur ro zhes bya ba smos so//.

237 Jñānagarbha, *Satyadvayavibhaṅgavṛtti* 8c, Toh 3882, dbu ma, *sa*, 5b: de ni 'di skad du gang dag bstan bcos gyis brtan por byas pa'i blo dang ldan pa de dag la yang ji ltar byis pa la snang bde bzhin du bum pa la sogs pa snang ba gang yin pa de ni yang dag pa'i kun rdzob kyi bden pa'o//.

238 Ibid., 8d, Toh 3882, dbu ma, *sa*, 5b: yang dag par skye ba la sogs pa gang yin pa de ni rtog pa'i bzos sbyar ba ste/ de ni yang dag pa ma yin pa'i kun rdzob kyi bden pa'o//.

239 Ibid., 8, Toh 3882, dbu ma, *sa*, 5b: dngos po tsam gang yin pa ni ji ltar snang ba bzhin du don byed nus pa'i phyir ro// rgyu dang rkyen rnams la brten nas skyes pa de ni yang dag pa'i kun rdzob kyi bden pa yin par shes par bya ste// 'di ltar byis pa yan chad kyi shes pa la mthun par don ji snyed rgyu las snang ba de ni yang dag pa'i kun rdzob yin par rigs te/ shes pa la snang ba dang mthun par dngos po gnas pa'i phyir ro//.

240 Śāntarakṣita's commentary explicitly make mention of those whose mind is fixated by the influence of any philosophical system. See Śāntarakṣita, *Satyadvayavibhaṅgapañjikā* 8, Toh 3883, dbu ma, *sa*, 23b: su dag dang mthun zhe na/ byis pa yan chad ces bya ba smos te/ mkhas pa rnams nas bzung ste/ byis pa'i bar du zhes bya ba'i tha tshig go// de ni 'di skad du gang dag bstan bcos gyis brtan por byas pa'i blo dang ldan pa de dag la yang ji ltar byis pa la snang bde bzhin du bum pa la sogs pa snang ba gang yin pa de ni yang dag pa'i kun rdzob kyi bden pa'o//.

241 Jñānagarbha, *Satyadvayavibhaṅgakārikā* 21, Toh 3881, dbu ma, *sa*, 2b: ji ltar snang bzhin ngo bo'i phyir// 'di la dpyad pa mi 'jug go// rnam par dpyod pa byed na don// gzhan du song bas gnod par 'gyur//.

242 Śāntarakṣita also holds this position—that conventionally real phenomena must not be subjected to ultimate analysis—in *Madhyamakālaṃkārakārikā* 63, Toh 3883, dbu ma, *sa*, 70a: ji skad bshad pa'i rigs pa dag gis/ dngos po thams cad ni brtag mi bzod pa'i phyir ma brtags na nyams dga' ba kho na'i bdag nyid kyi ngo bo 'dzin te/ sgyu ma'i glang po che dang rta dang mi la sogs pa bzhin no//. This thesis that conventionally real phenomena must not be subjected to ultimate analysis is also found in Prajñākaramati's *Commentary on the Difficult Points of Engaging an Awakened Life* (*Bodhicaryāvatārapañjikā*, Toh 3872, dbu ma, *la*, 41b–288a), in which he states that mere causality (*idaṃpratyayatāmātraṃ*) satisfies only when it is not analyzed (*avicāramanohara*), like a dream, magic, or a reflection. Kamalaśīla makes the same claim in his *Madhyamakālaṃkārapañjikā* 63, Toh 3886, dbu ma, *sa*, 11a: gang dag la ma brtags gcig pun dga' ba yod pa de dag la de skad ces bya ste/ ma brtags pa nyid ce na dga'o zhes bya ba'i tha tsig go// yang dag pa'i kun rdzob ces bya ba ni ji ltar grags pa bzhin nye bar brtags pa'i phyir ro// grags pa las 'das te rtogs pa dper na dbang phyug la sogs par rtogs pa gang yin pa de ni log pa'i kun rdzob [115b] yin no//.

243 Śāntarakṣita, *Satyadvayavibhaṅgapañjikā* 14, Toh 3883, dbu ma, *sa*, 2ab: du mas gcig gi dngos mi byed// du mas du ma byed ma yin// gcig gis du ma'i [2b] dngos mi byed// gcig gis gcig byed pa yang min//. "Many do not produce one, many do not produce many, one does not produce many, and one does not produce one."

244 Ibid., 21ab, Toh 3883, dbu ma, *sa*, 38a: ma brtags na nyams dga' ba yin pa'i phyir ro// kun rdzob 'di la dpyad pa ste// brtag pa mi 'jug go// 'di la ji skad bshad pa'i dpyad ci rgyu dang 'bras bu'i dngos po kun rdzob pa/ shes pa rnam pa dang bcas pas shes sam zhes bya ba dang / de bzhin du 'di ji ltar 'do/ ci du mas gcig byas sam/ 'on te du ma byas zhes bya ba la sogs pa de ni gnas med de rten med do// ci'i phyir zhe na/ 'di ltar ji [39a] skad bshad pa'i rnam bar dpyod par byed pa yin na ni/ gnod pa de tshar gcad pa'i gnas su 'gyur ro// ci'i phyir zhe na/ don gzhan du song bas te/ skabs yin pa'i don bor na rtsod pa gzhan la brten pa'i phyir zhes bya ba'i tha tshig go//.

245 Jñānagarbha, *Satyadvayavibhaṅgavṛtti*, 21cd, Toh 3882, dbu ma, *sa*, 10b: dpyod par byed pa la ni 'gog par byed do// gal te dpyad par byas te ma rung na ma rung du zad do // ji ltar snang ba'i ngo bo'i kun rdzob pa la brten nas de la dpyod pa byed pa ni don gzhan du 'gro ba'i phyir gnod pa 'ba' zhig tu zad do//.

246 Ibid., *Satyadvayavibhaṅgakārikā* 23, Toh 3881, dbu ma, *sa*, 2b: brtags pa gzhi dang bcas pa ni// 'ga' yang gang la'ang mi snang ngo// shing la sogs pa 'di yang ni// gzhi la ltos pa ma yin nyid//.

247 Ibid., *Satyadvayavibhaṅgavṛtti* 23, Toh 3882, dbu ma, *sa*, 10b–11a: shing la sogs pa gdags pa'i rgyu ni yal ga la sogs pa yin la/ de'i yang gzhan yin te/ rim gyis rdul phra rab kyi bar du yin la/ de yang phyogs tha dad pas dpyad na med pa kho na yin na/ shing la sogs pa gdags pa'i rgyu dngos po yod pa de lta ga la yod/ de lta bas na ji ltar snang ba 'di kho na yin gyi/ gang la yang rgyu dngos po yod pa kho na la ltos nas 'jug pa ni ma yin zhes khas blang bar bya'o// gal te kun rdzob gzhi la ni // ltos gyur de lta yin na ni// dngos 'gyur yang na khyod kyi gzhi// de ltar kun rdzob mi 'gyur te//.

248 Candrakīrti's *Clear Words* (*Mūlamadhyamakavṛttiprasannapadā* 24.8) uses a similar etymology where he first defines *saṃvṛti* as "ignorance" (*avidyā*, Tib. *ma rig pa*), which is equivalent to Jñānagarbha's interpretation in verse 15. Candrakīrti alternatively adds two other definitions of *saṃvṛti* as "mutual interdependence"

(*parasparasambhavana*, Tib. *phan tshun brten pa*), emphasizing the causal dependency thesis, and as "verbal conventions" (*saṃketa*, Tib. *rda*). According to Franklin Egerton's *Buddhist Hybrid Sanskrit Dictionary* (1953), Pāḷi and Sanskrit sources indicate that this third definition occurs prior to the other two. And according to Eckel 1987, 136, Jñānagarbha's definition of *saṃvṛti* as "ignorance" or "concealment of reality" has taken priority.

249 Jñānagarbha, *Satyadvayavibhaṅgavṛtti* 15ab, dbu ma, *sa*, 9a: blo gang zhig gis sam blo gang zhig la yod na yang dag pa sgrib par byed pa 'jig rten na grags pa de lta bu ni kun rdzob tu bzhed de/.

250 Vaidya 1963, 135: bhāvā vidhanti saṃvṛtyā paramārthe na bhāvakāḥ/ niḥsvabhāveṣu yā bhrāntis tat satyaṃ saṃvṛtir bhavet//.

251 Jñānagarbha, *Satyadvayavibhaṅgavṛtti* 15, Toh 3882, dbu ma, *sa*, 9a: mdo las ji skad du/ dngos rnams skye ba kun rdzob tu// dam pa'i don du rang bzhin med// rang bzhin med la 'khrul pa gang// de ni yang dag kun rdzob 'dod//.

252 Ibid., *Satyadvayavibhaṅgakārikā* 16, Toh 3881, dbu ma, *sa*, 2b: dam pa'i don du ma skyes pa// tshig don de ni rigs pa yi// rjes su 'brangs nas skye ba med// gzhan la'ang de bzhin sbyar bar gyis//.

253 Ibid., *Satyadvayavibhaṅgavṛtti* 16, Toh 3882, dbu ma, *sa*, 9b: ji ltar 'di sbyar ba de bzhin du yang dag par na med do// yang dag par na stong ngo zhes bya ba la sogs pa 'di dag la yang rigs pa'i lam gyi rjes su 'brangs na yod pa ma yin zhing de dag la stong pa nyid ma yin pa med ces bya ba la sogs pa sbyar bar bya'o// pha rol rnams kyis dngos rnams kyi// skye sogs rigs lam brten pa can// 'dod pa dag ni 'gog byed de// des na 'di la ci zhig gnod//.

254 Ibid., *Satyadvayavibhaṅgakārikā* 17, Toh 3881, dbu ma, *sa*, 2b: kun rdzob de bzhin nyid gang yin// de nyid dam pa'i don phyir bzhed// tha dad min phyir rigs de yang// ji ltar snang ba bzhin du gnas//.

255 Ibid., 19, Toh 3881, dbu ma, *sa*, 10a: 'jig rten gyi kun rdzob kyang gzhan la/ don dam pa yang gzhan pa ni ma yin gyi/ 'jig rten gyi kun rdzob kyi de bzhin nyid gang yin pa de nyid don dam pa'i de bzhin nyid yin no zhes gsungs so//.

256 Ibid., 18–19, Toh 3881, dbu ma, *sa*, 2b: rgol ba gnyis ka'i shes pa la// ji tsam snang ba'i cha yod pa// de tsam de la brten nas ni// chos can chos la sogs par rtog/ de tshe rjes su dpag pa 'byung// gang gi tshe na gzhan na min// de bas rigs pa smra ba rnams// de skad smra la su zhig 'gog/ gal te rigs pa'i stobs kyis na// kun rdzob tu yang mi skye dang // de bden de yi phyir na ni// ji ltar snang bzhin yin par gsungs// ji ltar rang bzhin ngo bo'i phyir// 'di la dpyad pa mi 'jug go//.

257 Ibid., *Satyadvayavibhaṅgavṛtti* 19, Toh 3882, dbu ma, *sa*, 9b–10a: rjes su dpag pa dang rjes su dpag par bya ba 'di tha snyad kyi rgol ba dang/ phyir rgol ba dag gi blo'i bdag nyid la snang ba'i chos can dang chos dang dpe nyid du rnam par gzhag par 'byung gi// chos can dang chos la sogs pa gnyi ga la ma grub pa nyid kyis rjes su dpag pa 'byung ba mi rung ba'i phyir gzhan na ni ma yin te/ gzhung lugs tha dad pa la gnas pa rnams ni gang la yang blo mtshungs pa nyid med pa'i phyir ro// chos can de lta bu la gnas pa [10a] rnams ni gtan tshigs la sogs pa de lta bu kho nas yang dag par na yod dam med ces sems par byed par khas blang bar bya'o//.

258 Ibid., *Satyadvayavibhaṅgakārikā* 12, Toh 3881, dbu ma, *sa*, 1b: snang du 'dra yang don byed dag/ nus pa'i phyir dang mi nus phyir// yang dag yang dag ma yin pas// kun rdzob kyi ni dbye ba byas//.

259 Ibid., 8ab, Toh 3881, dbu ma, *sa*, 2a: brtags pa'i don gyis dben gyur pa// dngos tsam brten nas skyes pa ste//.

260 Ibid., 21ab, Toh 3881, dbu ma, *sa*, 2b: ji ltar rang bzhin ngo bo'i phyir// 'di la dpyad pa mi 'jug go// rnam par dpyod pa byed na don// gzhan du song bas gnod par 'gyur//.

261 Although the Tibetan canon attributes this text, the *Commentary on Distinguishing the Two Truths* (*Satyadvayavibhaṅgapañjikā*), to Śāntarakṣita—who is the author of the *Verses on the Ornament of the Middle Way* (*Madhyamakālaṃkāra*)—the identity of the commentator is called into question by Tsongkhapa. In his *Speech of Eloquence,* often called *Essence of Eloquence* (*Legs bshad snying po*), Tsongkhapa says that it could have been written by someone with the same name or someone who borrowed that name, but it could not be the author of works such as the *Madhyamakālaṃkāra*. He offers two reasons. The first is based on a comparison of the opening section of the *Satyadvayavibhaṅgapañjikā* with the opening section of Kamalaśīla's *Subcommentary on the Compendium of Reality* (*Tattvasaṃgrahapañjikā*). Given that Śāntarakṣita was his teacher, Kamalaśīla would be unlikely to disagree with his philosophical views. However, Kamalaśīla refutes the *Subcommentary* author's explanation of the purpose (*prayojana*) of the text's composition in his commentary on the *Tattvasaṃgraha*, which makes it unlikely his teacher could have written the text. Tsongkhapa's second point has to do with the substance of the text. This author of the *Satyadvayavibhaṅgapañjikā* (see 24ab) approves the literal meaning of Jñānagarbha's statement claiming that both subject and object are imagined natures (*parikalpitasvabhāva*) and do not exist as they appear (*yathādarśana*) to perception, but this is denied by common sense realism. If the subcommentator agrees to this, he would seem to accept the position of Bhāviveka's Sautrāntika-Svātantrika system rather than Śāntarakṣita's Yogācāra-Svātantrika. For a detailed analysis on these two points, see Eckel 1987, 27–31, and Blumental 2004, 29–30.

262 Śāntarakṣita, *Madhyamakālaṃkārakārikā* 23, Toh 3884, dbu ma, sa, 56a: sems tsam la ni brten nas su// phyi rol dngos med shes par bya// tshul 'dir brten nas de la yang// shin tu bdag med shes par bya//.

263 Ibid., 24, Toh 3884, dbu ma, *sa*, 56a: tshul gnyis shing rta zhon nas su// rigs pa'i srab skyogs 'ju byed pa// de dag de phyir ji bzhin don// theg pa chen po pa nyid 'thob//. This passage, as Blumenthal 2004, 172, correctly observes, is the most commonly cited from the entire text and sums up the final major development of Indian Buddhist philosophy, the synthesis of the Buddhist logical tradition of the Sautrāntika with two major trends in Mahāyāna: Yogācāra and Madhyamaka. Changkya Rölpai Dorjé's *Ornament of the Philosophical Systems* (1989, 254–255) makes the point that Yogācāra-Svātantrika Madhyamaka only adopts Yogācāra's account of the conventional truth, but not its account of the ultimate truth, and it rejects, even conventionally, Yogācāra's claim that consciousness and nondual reality are ultimately real. If Changkya's argument is correct, which I think it is, then we need to be specific about the two systems in question; otherwise, readers may be led to think that the Yogācāra-Svātantrika Madhyamaka takes on board the entire system of Yogācāra idealism.

264 Kamalaśīla, *Madhyamakāloka* 73, Toh 3887, dbu ma, *sa*, 233ab: skye ba med pa la sogs pa yang dag [233b] pa'i tshad mas kun tu gtan la phab cing sgro ma btags pa gang yin pa de ni don dam pa'i bden pa zhes bya'o//.

265 Ibid., 74, Toh 3887, dbu ma, *sa*, 233b: 'di ltar chos dang gang zag la bdag med pa'i mtshan nyid kyi ngo bo de kho na nyid ni rigs pa dang ldan pas dam pa yin zhing don kyang de yin te/ don du gnyer ba rnams kyi sgrib pa spang bar bya ba'i ched du don du gnyer bar bya ba yin pa'i phyir dang / ye shes dam pa phyin ci ma log pa'i don te yul yin pa'i phyir don dam pa zhes bya'o// 'jig rten las 'das pa'i ye shes de'i yul can gang yin pa de yang tshig gi don gzhan du sbyor ba'i sgo nas der tha snyad gdags so// thos pa dang / bsams pa dang / bsgoms pa las byung ba'i shes rab de'i rjes su mthun pa gang yin pa de yang gdags pas de skad du brjod do//.

266 Ibid., 62–64, Toh 3887, dbu ma, *sa*, 229a: sgyu ma'i skyes bu la sogs pa de nyid la rnam par shes pa ma 'khrul pa can dag gis gzhag pa'i ngo bo ji lta ba de bzhin du dngos po thams cad la yang dag pa'i tshad ma yongs su gtan la phab pa'i ngo bo gang yin pa de ni don dam pa'i bden pa yin no//. For a Sansktrit reconstruction of this passage, see Penpa Dorjee's *Ācārya Kamalaśīla's Madhyamakāloka* (2001, 130).

267 Kamalaśīla's *Madhyamakāloka* uses a qualifying term in its negation of the possibility of arising from another: "Arising from another is, ultimately, incoherent. The arising of all entities is, therefore, strictly false, though it has its appeal when it is not analyzed, like the arising of illusions." Toh 3887, dbu ma, *sa*, 198a: don dam par gzhan las kyang skye bar rigs pa ma yin no// de'i phyir dngos po rnams kyi skye ba 'di thams cad ni sgyu ma 'byung ba bzhin du ma brtags na dga' ba ste brdzun pa kho na yin no//. He goes on: "To the extent that the arising of all things is ultimately strictly unacceptable, to that extent conditions and so forth do not arise, they remain unestablished. Therefore in reality, there is no entity that would be finally another." Ibid., 198b: de'i phyir gang gi tshe dngos po thams cad don dam par gzhan las skye ba mi 'thad pa kho na yin pa de'i tshe rkyen la sogs pa yang ma skyes pa'i phyir ma grub pa yin pas yang dag par na gang la sgra 'di mthar thug par 'gyur pa gzhan du gyur pa'i dngos po ni ci yang med do//.

268 Kamalaśīla, *Madhyamakāloka* 26, Toh 3887, dbu ma, *sa*, 190a: gang dag don dam par rang dang/ gzhan dang/ gnyi ga las skye ba dang / rgyu med pa las skye ba dang bral ba de dag ni yang dag par na ngo bo nyid med pa yin te/ dper na nam mkha'i padma la sogs pa lta bu'o/ rang dang gzhan gyis yang dag par yod par smras pa'i dngos po thams cad kyang de dang 'dra ba kho na yin no//.

269 Etymologically, the Sanskrit term *svataḥ* (Tib. *bdag*) means "from self" while *utpāda* (Tib. *skyes*) means "to bring forth," "to produce," or "to give rise to." Therefore the compound Sanskrit term *svataḥ utpāda* (Tib. *bdag skyes*) literally comes to mean "self-caused" or "self-produced." The causal theory formulated on the basis of this view is therefore variously described by scholars as the theory of "self-causation" (Garfield 1995, 105; Kalupahana 1991, 106), "spontaneous production" (Huntington and Wangchen 1989, 158), and "self-production" (Huntington and Wangchen 1989, 168). This causal theory is also characterized as the *satkāryavāda* (Sharma 1960, 151; Misra 2004, 99).

270 Richard King (1999, 217) and C. Sharma (1960, 256) identify the Vedānta school among those who hold the same position, even though the Sāṃkhya is regarded as

its chief proponent. The Sāṃkhya and the Vedānta schools nevertheless disagree concerning the nature of causality. For the Sāṃkhya, both the cause and the effect are real, whereas for the Vedānta only the cause is real; the effect is merely the appearance of the cause. Another issue that distinguishes the two schools is the issue of the first cause. The former holds the primacy of the unconscious primordial material *prakṛti* (one of the two ultimate realities constituted by three qualities), which, according to the school, drives the evolution and the dissolution of the psycho-physical world, whereas the latter holds the primacy of the conscious primordial *brahman* (the ultimate reality associated with its potency *māyā*) is seen as responsible for the creation, preservation, and destruction of the world. See Padhi and Padhi 2005, 195.

271 Organ 1975, 201.

272 Sharma 1960, 151.

273 Īśvara Kṛṣṇa's *Sāṁkhyakārikā* (1995, 15–16) advances the following arguments in its attempt to prove the existence of the *prakṛti* as the primordial cause of the universe: (1) All the manifest things—all the products of the universe—are finite and dependent, whereas no limited thing can serve itself as the ultimate cause; hence it has to be nonfinite and nondependent. (2) All the entities possess certain common and homogeneous characteristics that are capable of causing pleasure, pain, and indifference. It follows that they must originate from a single ultimate source composed of three *guṇas*—positive, negative, and neutral qualities. (3) All the manifest entities, being themselves effects, lack causal efficacy, and thus presuppose the existence of *prakṛti*, the active causal principle (*śakti*). (4) All manifest objects are effects, and the effects are different from the cause because in the process of evolution, the effects are the manifestations and the causes are not manifested. The effects, therefore, point to the cause wherein all the effects are potentially contained. (5) Finally, all the manifest things have a unity in terms of being defined in ordinary space and time, thus suggesting one nonspatial and nontemporal cause. These five arguments are the Sāṃkhya's proofs for the existence of the primordial *prakṛti*. Though the *prakṛti* is the primal cause of the universe, the Sāṃkhya claim, it does not by itself complete the function of creating the universe. The *prakṛti* depends upon the pure consciousness, *puruṣa*, to initiate the process of evolution.

274 Kamalaśīla, *Madhyamakāloka* 26, Toh 3887, dbu ma, *sa*, 190a: 'di ltar re zhig grangs can la sogs pa gang dag rgyu nyid 'bras bu'i bdag nyid du rnam par gnas so zhes rjod par byed cing / dngos po rnams rang kho na las skye bar nye bar brjod pa de dag ni thang cig rig pa ma yin pa kho na ste/ dngos po yod pa dang med pa ni bdag nyid kyi rgyu nyid du mi 'thad pa'i phyir te/ 'di ltar dngos pos bdag nyid skyed na grub pa'am/ ma grub pa zhig skyed par 'gyur grang na/ de la re zhig ma grub pa ni mi skyed de/ de ni de'i tshe med pa'i phyir ci zhig gang gi skyed pa por 'gyur/ mo gsham gyi bu la sogs pa bdag nyid kyi ngo bo yongs su ma grub pa ni rang gi ngo bo nyid skyed par nus pa ma yin no/ . . .

275 Ibid., 190a: grub pa yang skyed par byed pa ma yin te/ bye brag med pa nyid kyis de'i bdag nyid kyang grub pa'i phyir ci zhig gang gis bskyed par 'gyur/ gang zhig grub na gang ma grub pa de ni de'i ngo bo nyid du rigs pa ma yin te/ ha cang thal bar 'gyur ba'i phyir ro//.

276 Ibid., 190a: phan gdags par bya ba dang/ phan 'dogs par byed pa nyid dag yin na bskyed par bya ba dang/ skyed par byed pa'i dngos por rigs kyi/ ngo bo [190b] nyid de grub na phan gdags par bya ba'i ngo bo phra rab kyang cung zad med pa'i phyir 'di ji ltar na bskyed par bya ba nyid du 'gyur//. Interestingly, Kamalaśīla seems to be defending the use of the Prāsaṅgika's *reductio* style argument in this context and criticizes the Svātantrika's probative styled argument. Although without naming the names, he paraphrases Bhāviveka's critique of Buddhapālita and argues that the former failed to understand the significance of the *reductio* argument of the latter. "Some scholars [i.e., Buddhapālita, Candrakīrti, etc.] pose a reductio argument: 'It is incoherent for the internal domains (*ādhyātamikāyatanāni*) to arise from themselves, for they exist, even so, as consciousness that already exists.' [Responding] to this argument some [i.e., Bhāviveka, etc.] who do not appreciate the meaning of this *reductio*, assert 'this [argument is invalid since] its example remains established, and the reason adduced is contradictory.' This [criticism] arose due to the faults of those who fail to understand [the *reductio* argument]. Here only with the intention really to reveal mutual contradictions in others [i.e., the Sāṃkhya's claim], [Buddhapālita, etc.,] employs consciousness and so forth that others regard as existents. Apart from this, they do not accept anything real from their own standpoint." Kamalaśīla, *Madhyamakāloka* 26, Toh 3887, dbu ma, *sa*, 190b: de nyid kyi phyir mkhas pa rnams kyis nang gi skye mched ni rang las skye bar rigs pa ma yin te/ yod pa'i phyir shes pa yod pa bzhin no zhes thal bar bsgrub pa 'di nye bar brjod pa 'dir thal ba'i don mi shes pa kha cig 'di la dpe ma grub pa nyid dang gtan tshigs 'gal ba nyid rjod par byed pa gang yin pa de ni de dag gis yongs su ma shes pa'i nyes pa kho na yin te/ 'di ltar gzhan dag la phan tshun 'gal ba yang dag par brjod par 'dod pas pha rol la grub pa shes pa yod pa la sogs pa kho na rjes su zlos pa yin gyi/ bdag nyid la yang dag par grub pa'i dngos po la cung zad kyang mi 'dod par thal bar byed pa ma yin no// shes pa yod pa yang gzhan dag la yang dag par ma grub pa ma yin no// de'i phyir dpe ma grub pa nyid kyang ma yin la// gtan tshigs 'gal ba nyid kyang ma yin te/ rang gi rgyud kyis rtag pa dang/ gcig pa nyid kyi rnam grangs ngo bo bsgrub pa la/ de lta bu'i gtan tshigs dang dpe ma grub pa'i phyir ro// de ni gzhan dag phan tshun ma 'brel ba nyid du brjod pa ni bsnyad pa tsam zhig brjod par 'dod par zad kyi/ rang gi rgyud kyis dngos po'i chos rab tu sgrub pa ni ma yin no// de rab tu sgrub na de la 'gal ba nyid brjod par rigs te/ de la ni gtan tshigs dang dpe dag rab tu ma grub pa'i phyir de brjod pa 'brel pa med pa kho na yin no//. Note, Bhāviveka also criticizes Buddhapālita in his *Prajñāpradīpa* (Toh 3853, dbu ma, *tsha*, 49a) as as follows: de ni rigs pa ma yin te/ gtan tshigs dang dpe ma brjod pa'i phyir dang/ gzhan gyis smras pa'i nyes pa ma bsal pa'i phyir dang/ glags yod pa'i tshig yin pa'i phyir te/ skabs kyi don las bzlog pas bsgrub par bya ba dang/ de'i chos bzlog pa'i don mngon pas dngos po rnams gzhan las skye bar 'gyur ba dang/ skye ba 'bras bu dang bcas pa nyid du 'gyur ba dang/ skye ba thug pa yod par 'gyur ba'i phyir mdzad [49b] pa'i mtha' dang 'gal bar 'gyur ro//. For Kamalaśīla's detailed critique of self-causation, see *Madhyamakāloka*, Toh 3888, dbu ma, *sa*, 199a–199a on causation from another and 199a–202b on causeless arising.

277 Etymologically, the Sanskrit term *parata* (Tib. *gzhan*) means "other" while *utpāda* (Tib. *skyes*) means "to bring forth," "to produce," or "to give rise to." So the sense of

the compound Sanskrit term *parata utpāda* comes to mean "arising from another" according to Tsongkhapa Lobzang Dragpa (2006, 67), "production from another" according to Huntington and Wangchen (1989, 158), and "external causation" according to Kalupahana (1991, 107).

278 Kamalaśīla, *Madhyamakāloka*, Toh 3888, dbu ma, *sa*, 198b: grangs can gtso bo dbang phyug dang bcas par smra ba gang dag dngos po rnams gtso bo dbang phyug dang bcas pa las skye bar nye bar brjod pa na rang dang gzhan las de nye bar [199a] brjod pa de dag gi phyogs ni so sor bshad pa'i nyes pas sun phyung ba'i phyir rigs pa ma yin pa nyid do//.

279 Śaṃkara (788–820), the founder of the nondualistic Vedānta, characterizes *Brahman* as *advaitam*, or "nondual." He claims that at best we can say what *Brahman* is not, and not what it is. Brahman is transempirical, hence described as *nirguṇa* ("unqualified"), as opposed to *saguṇa* ("qualified"), since *guṇas* qualify the object and the Absolute is not an object. Śaṃkara argues that the logical, cosmological, and moral arguments all point to something larger than the finite. The effort to be free from the limits of the finite implies that consciousness, the finite itself, is not real. There has to be a basis for the whole universe. This obliges Śaṃkara to posit the existence of *Brahman*, otherwise our whole structure of knowledge and experience, he claims, tumbles to pieces. See Radhakrishnan 1998b, 536.

280 The eleventh-century Viśiṣṭādvaita philosopher Rāmānuja attempted to synthesize absolutism with personal theism. This attempt took shape for the Vaiśṇava school with Viṣṇu, Śaiva school with Śiva, and Śākta school with Śākti. Rāmānuja's metaphysical view is called "nondualism qualified by difference" (Viśiṣṭādvaita). He argues that God, the Absolute, is an organic unity, an identity that is qualified by difference. God is a concrete whole (*viśiṣṭa*) that is constituted by the interrelated, interdependent, and subordinate elements (*viśeṣaṇas*) and the immanent and controlling spirit (*viśeṣya*). According to Rāmānuja there are three categories of ultimate reals: matter (*acita*), souls (*cita*), and God (Īśvara). Although all three are equally real, the first two are said to be absolutely dependent on God. Both matter and souls are in themselves substances, yet in relation to God, they become his attributes (*prakāra*). In Rāmānuja's account of God, there are three key principles: (1) God is identified with the Absolute; (2) God is the immanent controller (*antaryāmī*), the qualified substance (*prakārī*) who is in himself changeless and the unmoved mover of the world process; and (3) God is transcendent, the perfect personality, with a divine body (*aprākṛtadehaviśiṣṭa*). The first two principles about God are derived from the interpretation of the Upaniṣad, while the third theistic principle comes from the Bhāgavata influence on Rāmānuja. See Radhakrishnan 1998b, 50.

281 Kamalaśīla, *Madhyamakāloka*, Toh 3887, dbu ma, *sa*, 192a: gzhan las kyang ma yin te/ 'di ltar de las dngos po skye bar 'gyur na rtag pa'am mi rtag pa'i ngo bo zhig las 'gyur grang na/ re zhig rtag pa las ni tha snyad du yang da rigs pa ma yin te/ de ni rim dang rim ma yin pa dag gis don byed par mi 'thad pa'i phyir ro// rgyu nus pa thogs pa med par yod pa yang 'bras bu res 'ga' mi skye bar mi 'gyur la/ 'bras bu rgyu ma tshang ba med pa yang res 'ga' mi 'byung bar mi 'gyur na gang gi phyir rim gyis de'i don bya ba byed par 'gyur te/ gzhan dag gis khyad par du byar med pa ni de la [192b] ltos par mi 'thad pa'i phyir ro//.

282 Ibid., 192a: lhan cig byed pa'i rgyu dang 'brel ba'i rang bzhin rjes su 'brang na ni de dang 'dra ba lhan cig byed pa rnams kyang rtag tu rjes su 'brang bar thal ba yin no// ji ste rjes su mi 'brang na ni de'i rtag pa nyid nyams par 'gyur ro// de'i phyir 'di yang lhan cig byed pa'i rkyen la ltos pa ma yin no// rgyu rtag pa la rag las te skye ba'i 'bras bu yang rkyen gzhan las ltos pa ma yin te/ de ni med pa'i phyir ro//.

283 Ibid., 192b–193a: des na rgyu rim can ma yin pa las kyang 'bras bu rim dang ldan pa mi 'gal ba kho na'o snyam du sems na/ de ni rigs pa ma yin te/ 'bras bu rgyu'i chos thams cad kyi rjes su byed par ni mi smra'o// 'on kyang re zhig gdon mi za bar 'bras bu rgyu la yod pa'i rjes su 'gro ba dang/ ldog pa'i rjes su byed par ni 'gyur dgos te/ rgyu dang 'bras bu'i dngos po'i rgyu ni 'di tsam du zad pa'i phyir ro// 'bras bu 'ga' yang dngos po rtag pa la yod pa'i ldog [193a] pa'i rjes su byed pa ni med de/ rtag pa la ldog pa med pa'i phyir ro// de lta ma yin na ni mi rtag pa kho nar 'gyur gyi/ rtag pa ni ma yin no// rjes su 'gro ba'i rjes su byed pa yang ma yin te/ de ma tshang ba med par nye yang res 'ga' 'bras bu mi skye ba'i phyir ro// gang zhig gang la yod pa'i rjes su byed pa 'gro ba dang ldog pa dag gis rjes su mi byed pa de ni de'i 'bras bur rigs pa ma yin te/ ha cang thal bar 'gyur ba'i phyir ro// 'bras bu yod pa ni ltos par rigs pa yang ma yin te/ de ni bdag nyid thams cad kyis grub zin pas thams cad la re ba med pa'i phyir ro// de ltar na re zhig rtag pa la rim gyis don byed pa'i mthu rigs pa ma yin no//.

284 Ibid., 193ab: cig car yang ma yin te/ de'i don byed pa'i rang bzhin de lta bu zhig yang rjes su 'brangs na 'bras bu'i skyed pa dang 'bral bar mi rung ba'i phyir ro/// ji ste mi 'bral na ni de'i rtag pa nyid nyams pa yin no// 'on te yang 'di'i nus pa'i rang bzhin dus phyis kyang rjes su 'brang mod kyi/ 'on kyang re zhig des 'bras bu thams cad sngar bskyed zin pa gang yin pa de ni yang bskyed par nus pa ma yin pa kho na ste// de ni skyes zin pa'i phyir ro// gzhan de dang 'dra ba gang yin pa de ci ste mi skyed ces brgal zhing brtag par 'os pa yang ma yin te/ de la des mi nus pa'i phyir ro// nus pa yin na ni sngar bskyed zin pa kho nar 'gyur ro snyam du sems na/ de ni rigs pa ma yin te/ des sngar bskyed zin pa'i 'bras bu mi skyed du chug kyang/ 'on kyang 'di'i skyed par nus pa'i rang bzhin rjes su 'brang ba ni rnam par nyams par 'gyur te/ gang zhig gang gi tshe gang skyed par mi byed pa ni de'i tshe de la mthu thogs pa med pa yin no zhes brjod par rigs pa ma yin no// de'i phyir 'di ni sngar yang dus phyis bzhin du skyed par byed pa ma yin pa kho nar 'gyur te/ skyed par byed pa ma yin pa'i gnas skabs dang khyad par med pa'i phyir ro// 'dis dus phyis kyang sngon bzhin du skyed par byed pa nyid du yang 'gyur ro// de lta ma yin na chos 'gal ba dang ldan pa'i phyir 'di'i gcig pa nyid rnam par nyams [193b] par 'gyur ro// de lta bas na de cig car don byed pa yang ma yin no// rim dang cig car dag las ma gtogs pa gang gis na don bya ba byed par 'gyur ba'i rnam pa gzhan yang yod pa ma yin te// de dag ni phan tshun yongs su gcod pa rnam par bcad pa med na med pa nyid kyis phan tshun spangs te gnas pa'i mtshan nyid dag gang yang rung ba zhig dgag pa gzhan sgrub pa med na med pa yin pa'i phyir ro// de ltar na re zhig gzhan rtag pa las skye bar rigs pa ma yin no//.

285 Ibid., 193b: mi rtag pa las kyang ma yin te/ 'di ltar mi rtag pa ni dngos po skad cig mar gnas pa'i chos can kho na yin par rigs te/ bskal par gnas pa ni khyad par med pas sngon bzhin du phyis kyang 'jig par mi rung ba'i phyir ro// de'i phyir 'bras bu skye ba na 'das pa las 'gyur te/ dper na bye brag tu smra ba rnams kyis rnam par smin pa'i rgyu 'das pa las kyang 'bras bu nye bar brjod pa'am/ ma 'ongs pa las te

dper na/ de dag nyid kyis ma 'ongs pa'i skye ba yang bskyed par bya ba skyed par byed pa yin no zhes nye bar brtags pa lta bu'am . . . //.

286 Ibid., 193b: de la re zhig 'das pa las zhes bya ba ni rigs pa ma yin te/ 'das pa ni med pa'i phyir ro// de las skye bar khas len na ni 'di rgyu med pa nyid du yang 'gyur ro// 'di ltar 'das pa zhes bya ba ci la bya/ gang rang gi ngo bo las nyams pa yin grang/ de lta ma yin na de lta bzhin du ma nyams pa'i bdag nyid yin pa'i phyir ji ltar 'das par 'gyur/ nyams pa'i ngo bo nyid gang yin pa de yang rang gi ngo bo yod pa ma yin pa'i phyir ji ltar 'bras bu nye bar skyed par 'gyur te/ don byed pa ni rang gi ngo bo la rag las pa'i phyir ro//. For Kamalaśīla's detailed discussion on this argument, see *Madhyamakāloka*, Toh 3887, dbu ma, *sa*, 193b–194b.

287 Ibid., 194b–195a: ma 'ongs pa las kyang ma yin te/ de yang 'das pa bzhin du med pa'i [195a] phyir te 'di ltar bdag nyid du ma red pa'i phyir ma 'ongs pa zhes bya ba na de lta bu nam mkha'i padma dang 'dra ba gang yin pa de las ni 'bras bu skye bar rigs pa ma yin no//. For Kamalaśīla's detailed discussion on this argument, see *Madhyamakāloka*, Toh 3887, dbu ma, *sa*, 195a.

288 Ibid., 194b–195a: dus mnyam pa ni ma yin te 'bras bu skye ba'i sngon rul na rgyu yang ri bong gi rva bzhin du med pa nyid kyis nus par mi rung ba'i phyir ro// gang gi tshe rgyu bdag nyid kyi dngos por red pa nyid kyis nus pa yin pa de'i tshe ni 'bras bu yang de dang dus mnyam par yod pa nyid kyis grub pa kho na yin pas de la de cung zad kyang mi byed pa'i phyir ro// rgyur tha snyad gdags pa yang rigs pa ma yin te/dper na 'bras bur mngon par 'dod pa de nyid rgyu ma yin pa bzhin no// de lta ma yin na rgyu dang 'bras bu dag mchol pa kho nar 'gyur ro// dus tha dad pa zhes bya ba'i phyogs kyang ma yin te/ 'di ltar gal te 'bras bu sngon gyi dus na yod pa yin na de lta na ni ma 'ongs pa kho na las 'byung bar 'gyur te/ de yang rigs pa ma yin par sngar bstan zin to//.

289 The Jaina causal thesis is steeped in the doctrine known as *anekāntavāda*—meaning "many-sided" or "not one-sided" position. This doctrine developed partly due to Jaina's response to the rise of various competing ethical claims in Indian philosophy. This doctrine partly reflects Jainism's metaphysical perspective, which views reality as always multidimensional and having infinite characteristics, of which many often appear to be contradictory. The theory of *anekāntavāda* with its twin approaches to reality—partial viewpoints (Nayavāda) and conditioned viewpoints (Syādvāda)—stresses the coexistence of conflicting viewpoints. It argues that the universe is constituted by conflicting pairs, like ignorance and wisdom, pleasure and pain, life and death, self and other. For more on these issues in the Jaina tradition, see Sagarmal Jain's *Jaina Literature and Philosophy: A Critical Approach* (1999); Nathmal Tatia's *Studies in Jaina Philosophy* (1951), and Sāgaramala Jaina and Śrīprakāśa Pāṇḍeya's *Multi-Dimensional Application of Anekāntavāda* (1999).

290 Kamalaśīla, *Madhyamakāloka*, Toh 3887, dbu ma, *sa*, 199a: gzhan gang dag res 'ga' rang dga'i dbang gis gnyi ga las skye bar brjod par 'gyur ba de dag kyang nyes pa gnyi gas sun phyung ba'i phyir bstsal ba kho na yin no//.

291 A major problem for the researchers on this school is almost all original texts were lost. The only extant and authentic text attributed to this school is the *Tattvopaplavasiṃha* by Jayarāśī Bhaṭṭa (ca. 600 CE), found only in the 1930s. K. K. Mittal offers us the following list of texts, which he argues are the secondary sources from

which we are informed about Cārvāka philosophy: Śāntarakṣita's *Tattvasaṃgraha*, Candrakīrti's *Madhyamakāvatāra*, Mādhavācārya's *Sarvadarśanasaṃgraha*, Haribhadra Suri's *Ṣaḍdarśana Samuccaya*, the *Sarvasiddhāntasārasaṁgraha* attributed to Śaṃkarācārya, Mādhava Sarasvati's *Sarvadarśanakaumudi*, *Rāmāyana*, *Mahābhārata*, *Padamapurāṇa*, *Viṣṇupurāṇa*, *Manusmṛti*, Kauṭīlīya's *Arthaśāstra*, *Bārhaspatya-Arthaśāstra*, Vātsyāna's *Kāmasūtra*, the *Brahmasūtra*, and *Bhāskara Bhāśya* (Mittal 1974, 24–25). All these secondary Cārvāka sources have recently been compiled under a single volume, Debiprasad Chattopadhyaya's *Cārvāka, Lokāyata: An Anthology of Source Materials and Some Recent Studies* (2006). From these resources we can understand that the heterodox school of the Cārvāka is the only school in Indian philosophy that denies the validity of karma and rebirth. See Tatia 1951, 220. This school is also known as the Lokāyata for "it holds that only this world (*loka*) exists and there is no beyond" (Radhakrishnan and Moore 1957, 227). It argues that sensual pleasure is the only end of human existence, and it rejects the afterlife and accepts the dissolution of the body as the liberation that brings everything to an end. The Cārvāka school accepts only perception as valid knowledge and rejects the epistemic authority of inference and the scriptures. That which cannot be directly perceived, it claims, does not exist.

292 Kamalaśīla, *Madhyamakāloka*, Toh 3887, dbu ma, *sa*, 199a: gzhan dag ni tsher ma la sogs pa rno ba la sogs pa'i dpes dngos po thams cad yang dag par rgyu med pa kho nar skye bar nye bar brjod de//.

293 Ibid., 199a: de la de dag gi dngos po rnams rgyu med par skye ba don dam pa par bsgrub par bya ba la dpe ma grub ste/ don dam pa par chos thams cad ma skyes pa'i phyir ro// gtan tshigs la sogs pa sgyu ma la sogs pa bzhin du gnas pa ma brtags na dga' ba ji ltar grags pa ma bkag pa'i phyir skye ba med par smra ba la ni mngon sum la sogs pa'i gnod pa med do//.

294 Ibid., 199a: de kun rdzob par bsgrub par bya ba la yang ma grub pa nyid de/ 'di ltar tsher ma la sogs pa rang gi sa bon la sogs pa las 'byung bar mngon sum 'dis rnam par nges la/ de nyid kyis de dag gi rno ba la sogs pa yang nges pas gang yang rgyu med par skye ba med do//.

295 Ibid., 199ab: sa bon dang myu gu la sogs pa rgyu dang 'bras bu'i dngos po yang 'jig [199b] rten na mngon sum kho nar grub pa'i phyir/ dam bcas pa la mngon sum gyis gnod pa yang yin la/ gzhan dag la gtan tshigs las bsgrub par bya ba la nges par skye bar khas blangs pa'i phyir rang gi tshig dang 'gal ba yang yin no// de lta ma yin na gtan tshigs sbyor ba don med pa kho nar 'gyur ro//.

296 Ibid., 199b: dam bcas pa tsam gyis ni 'dod pa'i don 'grub pa ma yin te/ thams cad kyis thams cad 'grub par thal bar 'gyur ba'i phyir ro// de lta bas na rgyu med par smra ba 'di ni tha snyad du yang mngon sum la sogs pas gnod pa'i phyir mkhas pa rnams kyis thag bsrings te spang bar bya ba nyid do//.

297 Ibid., 199a: rgyu med pa nyid yin na ni khyad par med pa'i phyir tsher ma la sogs pa dag la rno ba la sogs pa nges par mi 'gyur te/ de'i phyir thams cad kyang thams cad kyi bdag nyid du 'gyur ro//.

298 An earlier version of the neither-one-nor-many argument appears in the work of Śrīgupta, Jñānagarbha's teacher who is himself recognized to be Śāntarakṣita's teacher. Śrīgupta advances the argument as follows: "In reality everything, both inside and out, is empty, because it is neither one nor many, like a reflection." See

Eckel 1987, 22. Similarly Jetāri, Dharmakīrti, and others employ this argument; see Blumenthal 2004, 61.

299 Śāntarakṣita, *Madhyamakālaṃkārakārikā* 1, Toh 3884, dbu ma, *sa*, 53a: bdag dang gzhan smras dngos 'di dag// yang dag tu na gcig pa dang // du ma'i rang bzhin bral ba'i phyir// rang bzhin med de gzugs brnyan bzhin//.

300 Space and time are two of the nine substances recognized by the Nyāya-Vaiśeṣika, which also include earth (*pṛthivī*), water (*apas*), fire (*tejas*), air (*vāyu*), ether (*ākāśa*), time (*kāla*), space (*diś*), self (*ātman*), and mind (*manas*). Yet the notion of time, the Nyāya-Vaiśeṣika claim, is not associated with the other substances because none of them can be a binding link between objects or events and the sun. However other substances are attributed to time. See *Vaiśeṣikasūtra* 1.1.4–6, cited in Radhakrishnan and Moore 1989, 387.

301 *Vaiśeṣikasūtra* 5.2.21–23, cited in Radhakrishnan and Moore 1989, 394.

302 Śāntarakṣita, *Madhyamakālaṃkārakārikā* 10, Toh 3884, dbu ma, *sa*, 53a.

303 Ibid., 58b: nam mkha' la sogs pa phyogs tha dad pa'i shing la sogs pa dang 'brel pa de dag gi gcig dang 'brel ba'i rang bzhin gang yin pa de nyid gzhan dang 'brel pa can yang yin na ni des na de dang 'brel ba'i phyir de gcig pu'i bdag nyid yin pa bzhin du gzhan yang de dang tha dad ma yin par 'gyur ro//.

304 Gyaltsab Jé, *Dbu ma rgyan gyi brjed byang*, in Blumenthal 2004, 62–65.

305 Śāntarakṣita, *Madhyamakālaṁkārakārikā* 2, Toh 3884, dbu ma, *sa*, 53a: 'bras bu rim can nyer sbyor bas// rtag rnams gcig pu'i bdag nyid min// 'bras bu re re tha dad na// de dag rtag las nyams par 'gyur//.

306 Ibid., *Madhyamakālaṃkāravṛtti* 2, Toh 3885, dbu ma, *sa*, 57b: gcig pu'i bdag nyid du mi rigs te/ de dag gi 'bras bu rnams kyang cig car du 'byung bar 'gyur ba'i phyir ro// 'bras bu rnams ni rgyu ma tshang na shol gyi/ gang gi tshe rgyu'i nus pa thogs pa med par gyur pa de'i tshe/ de dag la shol ba srid par ga la 'gyur/ shol na ni de la yod pa'i rjes su 'gro ba dang / ldog pa'i rjes su mi byed pa'i phyir/ 'di dag de'i 'bras bur ga la 'gyur//. See Ibid., 57ab, for more on his critique of the Sāṃkhya school, and Blumenthal 2004, 62–65, for the analysis of the arguments and for the formulation of the arguments in Gyaltsab Jé's explanation of the text.

307 Śāntarakṣita only identifies his opponents as Buddhist and does not specify any particular school, whereas Kamalaśīla's *Madhyamālaṃkārapañjikā*, according to Blumenthal (2004, 66), specifies them as Vaibhāṣika since they assert three uncompounded and eternal entities. See the next endnote for details. Following Kamalaśīla on this point, Gyaltsab Jé, in his *Note of Reminder on the Ornament of the Middle Way*, explicitly mentions the Vaibhāṣika view in connection with three uncompounded entities (Blumenthal 2004, 321).

308 Vasubandhu, *Abhidharmakośabhāṣya*, Toh 4090, mngon pa, *ku*, 94a: reg bya med pa tsam ni nam mkha' yin te/ 'di ltar mun pa'i nang dag na thogs pa ma rnyed na nam mkha'o zhes zer to/ phra rgyas dang skye ba skyes pa 'gags nas so sor brtags pa'i stobs kyis gzhan mi skye ba ni so sor brtags pas 'gog pa yin no// so sor brtags pa med pa kho nar rkyen ma tshang bas mi skye ba ni so sor brtags pa ma yin pas 'gog pa ste dper na bar ma dor 'chi ba'i ris mthun pa lhag ma lta bu'o zhes zer ro//.

309 Śāntarakṣita, *Madhyamakālaṃkārakārikā* 3, Toh 3884, dbu ma, *sa*, 53a: bsgoms las byung ba'i shes pa yis// shes bya 'dus ma byas smra ba'i// lugs la'ang gcig min de dag ni// rim can shes dang 'brel phyir ro//.

310 Ibid., 4, Toh 3884, dbu ma, *sa*, 53a: rnam shes snga mas shes bya ba'i// rang bzhin rjes su 'brang na ni// shes pa snga ma'ang phyi mar 'gyur// phyi ma'ang de bzhin snga mar 'gyur//.

311 Ibid., *Madhyamakālaṃkāravṛtti* 4, Toh 3885, dbu ma, *sa*, 57b: de lta ma yin na rnam par shes pa snga mas shes par bya ba 'dus ma byas kyi rang bzhin ni phyi ma'i dus na'ang yod la/ rnam par shes pa snga ma ni med pa dang / de bzhin du shes pa phyi mas shes par bya ba ni snga na yod la/ shes pa phyi ma ni med do zhes bya ba nyams par 'gyur ro//.

312 Ibid., *Madhyamakālaṃkārakārikā* 5, Toh 3884, dbu ma, *sa*, 53a: sngon dang phyi ma'i gnas rnams su// de yi ngo bo mi 'byung na// 'dus ma byas de shes pa bzhin// skad cig 'byung bar shes par bya//.

313 Ibid., 7, Toh 3884, dbu ma, *sa*, 53a: skad cig pa rnams 'di dag tu// rang dbang 'byung bar 'dod na ni// gzhan la ltos pa med pa'i phyir// rtag tu yod pa'am med par 'gyur /.

314 Ibid., *Madhyamakālaṃkāravṛtti* 9, Toh 3885, dbu ma, *sa*, 53b; it simply says "others claim" (Tib. *pha rol gyi khas blangs*), whereas Gyaltsab Jé, according to Blumenthal 2004, 324, does explicitly identify the Vātsīputrīya to hold this view. Also, see Blumenthal 2004, 71, for the same point.

315 Ibid., *Madhyamakālaṃkārakārikā* 9, Toh 3884, dbu ma, *sa*, 53a: skad cig skad cig ma yin par// gang zag bstan du mi rung bas// gcig dang du ma'i rang bzhin dang// bral bar gsal bar rab tu shes//.

316 Ibid., *Madhyamakālaṃkāravṛtti* 9, Toh 3885, dbu ma, *sa*, 58ab: skad cig par gyur na ni du ma'i rang bzhin du 'gyur te/ skad cig re re la [58b] yang rang bzhin gzhan dang gzhan 'byung ba'i phyir ro// skad cig ma yin na ni rtag tu bstan pa gcig pu'i ngo bo yin pa'i phyir gcig pu'i rang bzhin du 'gyur ro// gnyi ga ltar yang brjod du med na ni tshegs med par gcig dang du ma'i rang bzhin gyis stong pa nyid du grub bo//.

317 See Blumenthal 2004, 73–74.

318 Śāntarakṣita, *Madhyamakālaṃkārakārikā* 10, Toh 3884, dbu ma, *sa*, 53a: bsgribs dang ma bsgribs dngos sogs phyir// rags pa rnams kyang gcig pu min//.

319 See Blumenthal 2004, 326 (for Gyaltsab Jé): bum pa chos can/ gcid tu me bden par thal/ bsgribs ma bsgrib so rdas la brten pa'i 'gal 'du/ gyo mi gyo sogs bya ba la brten pa'i 'gal 'du/ mtshon gyis bsgyur ma bsgyur sogs yod tan la brten pa'i 'gal 'du sogs gsum dang ldan pa'i phyir//. Also Changkya Rölpai Dorjé frames the argument stressing the three contradictions (1989, 267). See Blumenthal 2004, 74–76, for a discussion on this argument.

320 Śāntarakṣita, *Madhyamakālaṃkārakārikā* 11–12ab, Toh 3884, dbu ma, *sa*, 53a: 'byar ba dang ni bskor ba'am// bar med rnam par gnas kyang rung// dbus gnas rdul phran rdul gcig la// bltas pa'i rang bzhin gang yin pa// rdul phran gzhan la lta ba yang// de nyid gal te yin brjod na//.

321 Ibid., 12cd, Toh 3884, dbu ma, *sa*, 53a: de lta yin na de lta bu// sa chu la sogs rgyas 'gyur ram//.

322 Ibid., 13, Toh 3884, dbu ma, *sa*, 53a: rdul [53b] phran gzhan la lta ba'i ngos// gal te gzhan du 'dod na ni// rab tu phra rdul ji lta bur// gcig pu cha shas med par 'gyur// rdul phran rang bzhin med grub pa// de phyir mig dang rdzas la sogs// bdag dang gzhan smras mang po dag rang bzhin med par mngon pa yin//.

323 Gyaltsab Jé 2004, 326: phyogs bcu'i dbus na gnas pa'i rdul phran chos can/ shar rdul dang phyogs bzhan dgu'i rdul go sa tha dad med par thal/ khod kyi shar la blta ba'i ngos de dang khyod phyogs bzhan dgu'i rdul la lta ba'i ngo gcig yin pa'i phyir/ 'rang bzhin dod na/ sa'i dkyil 'rang bzhin khor la sogs pa'i rags pa rgyas pa mi srid par thal/ 'rang bzhin dod pa'i phyir/ blta ba'i ngos so so sor 'rang bzhin dud na/ de chos can/ ca med kyi gcig min par thal/ phyogs bcu'i rdul la blta ba'i khyod kyi ngos me 'dra ba bcu yod pa'i phyir//.

324 Śāntarakṣita, *Madhyamakālaṃkārakārikā* 61, Toh 3884, dbu ma, *sa*, 55a: dngos po gang gang rnam dpyad pa// de dang de la gcig nyid med// gang la gcig nyid yod min pa// de la du ma nyid kyang med//.

325 Ibid., *Madhyamakālaṃkāravṛtti* 61, Toh 3885, dbu ma, *sa*, 68a: pha rol dang bdag gi lta ba'i rjes su 'brang ba dag gis khas blangs pa rtag pa dang/mi rtag pa dang/ khyab pa dang/ cig shos dang / rdul dang / rags pa dang / shes bya dang / shes pa la sogs pa so sor tha dad pa'i dngos po gang la gcig pur brtags na de la de ltar brtags pa de'i tshe/ brtag pa'i khur lci ba bzod pa phra rab tsam yang med do// gang gcig pa'i rang bzhin du mi 'thad pa de du ma'i bdag nyid du khas blangs pa ni rigs pa ma yin pa nyid de/ 'di ltar du ma ni gcig bsags pa'/.

326 Ibid., *Madhyamakālaṃkārakārikā* 62, Toh 3884, dbu ma, *sa*, 55a: gcig dang du ma ma gtogs par// rnam pa gzhan dang ldan pa yi// dngos po mi rung 'di gnyis ni// phan tshun spangs te gnas phyir ro//.

327 Ibid., *Madhyamakālaṃkāravṛtti* 62, Toh 3885, dbu ma, *sa*, 69b: gcig pu'i bdag nyid dang/ du ma'i bdag nyid ni phan tshun spangs te gnas pa'i mtshan nyid yin pas phung po gzhan sel to// de bas na rnam pa gzhan du gzhag pa'i dngos po med pa'i phyir 'di la ldog pa mi ldog pa med do//.

328 For more detail on Śāntarakṣita's views on the pervasion of the neither-one-nor-many argument, see Blumenthal 2004, 137–139.

329 Śāntarakṣita, *Madhyamakālaṃkāravṛtti* 91, Toh 3885, dbu ma, *sa*, 79a: de ltar byas na stug po bkod pa dang/ dgongs pa nges par 'grel pa la sogs pa las 'byung ba thams cad dang mthun pa yin no// lang kar gshegs pa las/ phyi rol gzugs ni yod ma yin// rang gi sems ni phyi rol snang// zhes bstan pa 'di yang legs par bshad pa yin no snyam du sems so//. For a further discussion on this point see Blumenthal 2004, 167–171.

330 Śāntarakṣita, *Madhyamakālaṃkārakārikā* 91, Toh 3885, dbu ma, *sa*, 56a: rgyu dang 'bras bur gyur pa yang// shes pa 'ba' zhig kho na ste// rang gi grub pa gang yin pa// de ni shes par gnas pa yin//.

331 Ibid., *Madhyamakālaṃkāravṛtti* 91, Toh 3885, dbu ma, *sa*, 79a: de ni shes par gnas pa yin [79a] rang gis grub pa'i ngo bor na shes pa'i ngo bo gzhan rtog pa med do// rang gis grub pa'i rang bzhin yang rmi lam dang sgyu ma la sogs pa'i gzugs bzhin no// gzugs la sogs pa phyi rol du 'dod pa rnams shes pa las gud na yod par bzhugs na yang mig la sogs pa bzhin du dus mnyam pa dang mi mnyam pa'i tshe na rab tu nye ba'i rgyu med pas rig par mi 'grub bo// de lta bas na de dag myong ba ni tha dad pa ma yin pa'i sngon po la sngon po la sogs pa'i rnam pa myong ba ste/myong ba'i ngo bo yin pas rmi lam dang sgyu ma la sogs pa'i gzugs myong ba bzhin no//.

332 Ibid., 79a: gal te shes pa'i rnam pa bskyed pa'i don gzhan zhig 'bras bu las gud na yod par rjes su dpog na/ de lta na yang mngon sum du grub par ma gyur gyi rjes su

dpag par zad do// de lta na yang 'di med par grub ste/ de ma thag pa'i rkyen nges par yod pa dang/ rdul phra mo la sogs pa bkag pa'i phyir ro//.

333 Ibid., *Madhyamakālaṃkārakārikā* 63, Toh 3884, dbu ma, *sa*, 55a: de phyir dngos po 'di dag ni// kun rdzob pa nyid mtshan nyid 'dzin// gal te 'di dag don 'dod na// de la bdag gis ci zhig bya//. See also Kamalaśīla, *Madhyamakāloka*, 62–64.

334 Ibid., 64, Toh 3884, dbu ma, *sa*, 55a: ma brtags gcig pu nyams dga' zhing// skye dang 'jig pa'i chos can pa// don byed pa dag nus rnams kyis// rang bzhin kun rdzob pa yin rtogs// brtag pa ma byas nyams dga' ba'ang// bdag rgyu snga ma snga ma la// brten nas phyi ma phyi ma yi// 'bras bu de 'dra 'byung ba yin// de phyir kun rdzob rgyu med na// rung min zhes pa'ang legs pa yin// gal te 'di yi nyer len pa// yang dag yin na de smros shig/ dngos po kun gyi rang bzhin ni// rigs pa'i lam gyi rjes 'brang ba// [55b] gzhan dag 'dod pa sel bar byed//.

335 Ibid., *Madhyamakālaṃkāravṛtti* 63, Toh 3885, dbu ma, *sa*, 70a: ji skad bshad pa'i rigs pa dag gis/ dngos po thams cad ni brtag mi bzod pa'i phyir ma brtags na nyams dga' ba kho na'i bdag nyid kyi ngo bo 'dzin te/ sgyu ma'i glang po che dang rta dang mi la sogs pa bzhin no//. Kamalaśīla, *Madhyamakālaṃkārapañjikā* 63, Toh 3886, dbu ma, *sa*, 11a: gang dag la ma brtags gcig pun dga' ba yod pa de dag la de skad ces bya ste/ ma brtags pa nyid ce na dga'o zhes bya ba'i tha tsig go// yang dag pa'i kun rdzob ces bya ba ni ji ltar grags pa bzhin nye bar brtags pa'i phyir ro// grags pa las 'das te rtogs pa dper na dbang phyug la sogs par rtogs pa gang yin pa de ni log pa'i kun rdzob [115b] yin no//. Śāntarakṣita, *Madhyamakālaṃkāravṛtti* 63, Toh 3884, dbu ma, *sa*, 70a: ji skad bshad pa'i rigs pa dag gis/ dngos po thams cad ni brtag mi bzod pa'i phyir ma brtags na nyams dga' ba kho na'i bdag nyid kyi ngo bo 'dzin te/ sgyu ma'i glang po che dang rta dang mi la sogs pa bzhin no//. Kamalaśīla, *Madhyamakālaṃkārapañjikā* 63, Toh 3886, dbu ma, *sa*, 11a: gang dag la ma brtags gcig pun dga' ba yod pa de dag la de skad ces bya ste/ ma brtags pa nyid ce na dga'o zhes bya ba'i tha tsig go// yang dag pa'i kun rdzob ces bya ba ni ji ltar grags pa bzhin nye bar brtags pa'i phyir ro// grags pa las 'das te rtogs pa dper na dbang phyug la sogs par rtogs pa gang yin pa de ni log pa'i kun rdzob [115b] yin no//.

336 Kamalaśīla, *Madhyamakāloka* 73, Toh 3888, dbu ma, *sa*, 233a: dngos po'i ngo bo don dam pa pa ni med kyang gzugs la sogs pa ma brtags na grub pa dag la ji tsam du skye ba la sogs par sgro btags pa gang yin pa de ni kun rdzob kyi bden pa zhes bya bar rnam par bzhag la //.

337 Śāntarakṣita, *Madhyamakālaṃkārakārikā* 8, Toh 3884, dbu ma, *sa*, 53a: don byed nus pa ma yin la// de 'dod brtags pas ci zhig bya// ma ning gzugs bzang mi bzang zhes// 'dod ldan rnams kyis brtags ci phan//. Blumenthal argues that this is one of the areas that reveals part of the enormous debt Śāntarakṣita owes Dignāga and Dharmakīrti, as they categorize objects into (1) universals, which are characterized as being permanent, conceptually constructed, conventionally real, and causally inefficacious, and (2) unique particulars, which are characterized as impermanent, nonconceptual, ultimately real, and causally efficacious (2004, 70). Śāntarakṣita borrows this from Dharmakīrti's *Pramāṇavārtika* 1.211, and so does Kamalaśīla in his *Sarvadharmāsvabhāvasiddhi* (Toh 3889, dbu ma, *sa*, 298b).

338 Śāntarakṣita, *Madhyamakālaṃkāravṛtti* 64, Toh 3885, dbu ma, *sa*, 58a: de bas na mkhas pa rnams kyis ni don byed nus pa la dngos po'i mtshan nyid ces smra'o//.

339 Ibid., 8, Toh 3885, dbu ma, *sa*, 58a: de bas na mkhas pa rnams kyis ni don byed nus pa la dngos po'i mtshan nyid ces smra'o// dngos po rnam pa de lta bu la/ gang zag dang chos la bdag med pa la sogs pa ston cing de las bzlog pa sgro btags pa'i ngo bo ni dgag par byed de/ skyes bu'i don ces brjod pa 'bras bu 'byung ba ni 'di nyid la rag las pa'i phyir ro//.

340 Kamalaśīla, *Madhyamakālaṃkārapañjikā* 64, Toh 3884, dbu ma, *sa*, 115ab: yang dag pa'i kun rdzob ces bya ba ni ji ltar grags pa bzhin nye bar brtags pa'i phyir ro// grags pa las 'das te rtogs pa dper na dbang phyug la sogs par rtogs pa gang yin pa de ni log pa'i kun rdzob [115b] yin no//.

341 Śāntarakṣita, *Madhyamakālaṃkāravṛtti* 8, Toh 3885, dbu ma, *sa*, 58a: de ltar na dngos po yul thams cad bdag med pa la sogs par ma bstan to snyam du ma sems shig/ thams cad ces bya ba'i sgra ni brjod par 'dod pa'i don ma lus pa la brjod pa'i phyir te/ brjod par 'dod pa ni don byed nus pa'i dngos po thams cad do//.

342 Ibid., 58a: don byed nus pa ni skad cig pa nyid du nges so// gzhan ni rim dang cig shos kyi don byed par mi 'thad pa'i phyir ro//.

343 Kamalaśīla, *Madhyamakāloka* 62–64, Toh 3888, dbu ma, *sa*, 229a: sgyu ma'i skyes bu la sogs pa bzhin du dngos po thams cad la rnam par shes pa 'khrul pa'am/ ma 'khrul pas rnam par gzhag pa'i ngo bo nyid kyis go rims bzhin du bden pa gnyis rnam par dbye ba rnam par gzhag ste/ 'di ltar sgyu ma'i skyes bu la sogs pa la 'khrul pa'i rnam par shes pa dang ldan pa'i mi dag gis gzhag pa'i ngo bo ji lta ba de bzhin du dngos po thams cad la yang brdzun pa'i rnam pa can gyi shes pas sgro btags pa'i ngo bo gang yin pa de ni kun rdzob kyi bden pa'o zhes tha snyad gdags la//. We may compare Kamalaśīla's definition of conventional truth with his definition of ultimate truth, which reads: "The nature of any entity established through a reliable cognition (*saṃyak pramāṇa*, Tib. *yang dag pa'i tshad ma*) is ultimate truth. It is akin to a nature posited by those who do not have erroneous cognitions of the reality of illusory persons and the like." Ibid., 229a: sgyu ma'i skyes bu la sogs pa de nyid la rnam par shes pa ma 'khrul pa can dag gis gzhag pa'i ngo bo ji lta ba de bzhin du dngos po thams cad la yang dag pa'i tshad ma yongs su gtan la phab pa'i ngo bo gang yin pa de ni don dam pa'i bden pa yin no//. For a Sanskrit reconstruction of this text, see Dorjee 2001, 130.

344 Ibid., 229a: ri bong gi rva bzhin du gtan med pa'i ngo bo nyid kyang ma yin te/ ma brtags na dga' ba'i rnam par snang ba'i phyir ro// ri bong gi rva bzhin du gtan med pa'i ngo bo nyid kyang ma yin te/ ma brtags na dga' ba'i rnam par snang ba'i phyir ro//.

345 Ibid., 22–24, Toh 3888, dbu ma, *sa*, 228ab: kun rdzob ni ri bong gi rva bzhin du thams cad med pa'i ngo bo yang ma yin no// 'o na ci zhe na/ dngos po yang dag pa ngo bo nyid med pa dag la yang de las bzlog pa'i rnam par sgro 'dogs par 'khrul pa'i blo gang yin pa de ni kun rdzob ces bya ste/ [228b] 'di 'am 'dis de kho na nyid kun tu sgrib pa lta bur byed 'gegs pa lta bur byed pa'i phyir ro//.

346 *Laṅkāvatārasūtra* 10:429: bhāva vidhyanti saṁvṛtya paramārthe na bhāvakāḥ// niḥsvabhāveśu bhrāntistatastyaṃ saṃvṛti bhavet//. Toh 107, mdo sde, *ca*, 174ba: dngos rnams skye ba kun rdzob tu// dam pa'i don du rang bzhin med// rang bzhin med la 'khrul pa gang// de ni yang dag kun rdzob 'dod// ces gsungs so//.

347 Kamalaśīla, *Madhyamakāloka* 75, Toh 3888, dbu ma, *sa*, 142b–143a: gzhan yang gal te kun rdzob dang don dam pa dag gcig par 'dod na ni/ de'i tshe bden pa gnyis su rnam par gzhag par ji ltar 'gyur te gnyis las gang yang rung ba zhig dor dgos pa

kho nar 'gyur ro// 'on te tha dad na ni de'i tshe gnyi ga yang so sor grub pa'i phyir dngos po nyid [143a] du thal bar 'gyur ro// ji ste tha dad pa dang tha dad pa ma yin pa'o zhe na/ gcig la phan tshun 'gal ba 'di gnyis su ji ltar 'gyur/ de nyid kyi phyir tha dad pa yang ma yin/ tha dad pa ma yin pa yang ma yin no zhes bya ba'i phyogs 'di yang rigs pa ma yin te/ 'gal ba'i phyir ro// 'di ltar tha dad pa dang tha dad pa ma yin pa phan tshun spangs te gnas pa'i mtshan nyid 'di dag ni gang yang rung ba zhig dgag pa cig shos bsgrub pa med na med pa yin no// de ni de'i tshe dgag par yang ji ltar nus te/ sgrub pa dang dgag pa dag cig car gcig la 'gal ba'i phyir ro//.

348 Ibid., 234a: de kho na nyid kyis don gyi mtshan nyid kyi don dam pa dang / 'dus byas kyi mtshan nyid kyi kun rdzob dang lhan cig/ cig pa yang ma yin zhing tha dad par yang mi 'dod de . . . //.

349 *Saṃdhinirmocanasūtra*, Toh 106, mdo sde, *ca*, 7a.

350 Kamalaśīla, *Madhyamakāloka* 75, Toh 3888, dbu ma, *sa*, 234a: gal te don dam pa'i mtshan nyid 'du byed dag las gzhan ma yin par gyur na ni de'i tshe so so'i skye bo thams cad bden pa mthong bar 'gyur te/ de'i phyir thams cad mya ngan las 'das pa'am/ sangs rgyas nyid thob par 'gyur zhing ji ltar 'dus byas kyi mtshan nyid kun nas nyon mongs pa'i mtshan nyid du gyur pa de bzhin du don dam pa yang kun nas nyon mongs pa'i mtshan nyid du 'gyur la/ ji ltar don dam par 'du byed thams cad la khyad par med pa de bzhin du 'du byed kyi mtshan nyid thams cad kyang khyad par med par 'gyur ba zhig na/ 'du byed thams cad ni mtshan nyid tha dad pa'i phyir khyad par med pa yang ma yin no// rnal 'byor pa rnams kyi don ji ltar thob pa la sogs pa'i 'og tu don dam pa tshol ba yang rung bar mi 'gyur te/ de lta bas na don dam pa'i mtshan nyid ni 'du byed dag las gzhan ma yin pa yang ma yin no//. For the Sanskrit restoration of the passage, see Dorjee 2001, 137.

351 Ibid., 234ab: gzhan pa yang ma yin no// de lta ma yin na bden pa mthong ba rnams kyi 'du byed kyi mtshan ma zil gyis mi non par 'gyur te/ de'i phyir rnal 'byor pa 'du byed kyi mtshan ma zil gyis mi [?] non pas mtshan ma'i 'ching ba las ma grol bar yang 'gyur la/ mtshan ma'i 'ching ba las [234b] ma grol bas gnas ngan len gyi 'ching ba las kyang ma grol bar 'gyur ro// de las ma grol ba ni mya ngan las 'das pa grub pa dang/ bde ba bla na med pa yang rtogs par mi 'gyur ro// gzhan yang gal te don dam pa'i mtshan nyid 'du byed kyi mtshan nyid dag las gzhan yin na de'i tshe don dam pa'i mtshan nyid 'du byed dag gi spyi'i mtshan nyid du yang mi 'gyur la/ don dam pa'i mtshan nyid 'du byed dag bdag med pa tsam dang/ ngo bo nyid med pa tsam du yang mi 'gyur la/ kun nas nyon mongs pa dang rnam par byang ba'i mtshan nyid dus gcig tu mtshan nyid so sor grub par yang 'gyur ro// de bas na don dam pa'i mtshan nyid ni dung la sogs pa'i dkar po nyid la sogs pa bzhin du 'du byed rnams dang de nyid dang/ gzhan nyid dag tu brjod par bya ba ma yin pa nyid do zhes gsungs pa lta bu'o//. For the Sanskrit restoration of this passage, see Dorjee 2001, 137–138.

352 Ibid., 234b: dngos po kho na la de nyid dang gzhan nyid kyi rnam par rtog pa srid pa'i don dam pa spyi'i mtshan nyid ni dngos po'i ngo bo med pa'i phyir de nyid dang / gzhan nyid dag tu brjod par bya ba ma yin pa kho na ste/ dngos po yod na de nyid dang gzhan nyid du rtogs pa srid par 'gyur gyi/ dngos po'i ngo bo nyid med pa dag la de mi srid pa nyid pas 'gal ba med pa kho na'o//.

353 Ibid., 234b: ye shes kyi bdag nyid kyi don dam pa ni sgyu ma la sogs pa dang khyad par med pa'i phyir yang dag pa'i kun rdzob kyi ngo bo nyid kyang yin la/ de kho

na nyid rtogs pa dang mthun pa'i phyir don dam pa'i ngo bo nyid kyang yin pas ltos pa'i bye brag gis gcig la gnyis ka'i ngo bo nyid kyang mi 'gal lo//. Kamalaśīla reiterates the same point in *Madhyamakāloka* 75, Toh 3888, dbu ma, *sa*, 234b: ye shes kyi bdag nyid kyi don dam pa yang kun rdzob dang lhan cig de bzhin nyid kyi mtshan nyid kyi don dam pa'i rnam par gcig pa nyid du 'dod pa kho na ste/....

354 Śāntarakṣita, *Madhyamakālaṃkārakārikā* 63, Toh 3884, dbu ma, *sa*, 55a; as cited in Kamalaśīla, *Madhyamakāloka* 62–64: de phyir dngos po 'di dag ni// kun rdzob pa nyid mtshan nyid 'dzin// gal te 'di dag don 'dod na// de la bdag gis ci zhig bya//.

355 Śāntarakṣita, *Madhyamakālaṁkārakārikā* 64, Toh 3884, dbu ma, *sa*, 55ab: ma brtags gcig pu nyams dga' zhing// skye dang 'jig pa'i chos can pa// don byed pa dag nus rnams kyis// rang bzhin kun rdzob pa yin rtogs// brtag pa ma byas nyams dga' ba'ang// bdag rgyu snga ma snga ma la// brten nas phyi ma phyi ma yi// 'bras bu de 'dra 'byung ba yin// de phyir kun rdzob rgyu med na// rung min zhes pa'ang legs pa yin// gal te 'di yi nyer len pa// yang dag yin na de smros shig/ dngos po kun gyi rang bzhin ni// rigs pa'i lam gyi rjes 'brang ba// [55b] gzhan dag 'dod pa sel bar byed//.

356 Based on Candrakīrti's refutation of Bhāviveka's interpretation of Nāgārjuna's *Mūlamadhyamakakārikā*, Candrakīrti is usually dated approximately thirty years after Bhāviveka. However, if a text attributed to Bhāviveka titled *Madhyamakaratnapradīpa* has any truth to it, it calls this theory into question. Interestingly the text clearly names Bhāviveka as the author, who is the same person who authored the *Tarkajvālā*. Moreover, his references to Candrakīrti are also explicit. Both these points are substantiated in the statement from Bhāviveka that reads: "For the detailed meaning [of atomic theory] see *Pañcaskandha*[*prakaraṇa*], composed by Ācārya Candrakīrti; my own composition [*Madhyamakahṛdayavṛtti*] *Tarkajvālā*, and the like." *Madhyamakaratnapradīpa*, dbu ma, *tsha*, 266b: 'di'i don rgyas par slob dpon zla ba grags pa'i zhal snga nas mdzed [?] pa'i dbu ma phung po lnga ba dang/ bdag gis bkod pa rtog ge 'bar ba la sogs par blta bar bya'o//. Also see the following references made to Candrakīrti (Ibid., 271a): "After paying homage to Ārya Nāgārjuna, Ārya Āryadeva, [and] Candrakīrti, and in accordance with the works of these immaculates, I will engage with the two truths." 'phags pa klu sgrub 'phags pa'i lha// zla ba grags par phyag byas nas// rje btsun dag gi gsung bzhin du// bden pa gnyis la 'jug par bya/. Cf. Ibid., dbu ma, *tsha*, 275b, 277b, 280b.

357 Huntington 1989, 74; Ames 1993, 44; Dreyfus and McClintock 2003, 128. I agree that Candrakīrti has no debt whatsoever to the Pramāṇavāda, or metaphysicians, however disagree with the conclusion that Candrakīrti's epistemology project meets its dead end after the refutation of foundationalism. I maintain that Candrakīrti's refutation of foundationalism is only a means to demonstrate the efficacy of the anti-foundationalist Prāsaṅgika account of *pramāṇa*. See Garfield 2011, 23–39; Thakchoe 2012a, 93–124; and Thakchoe 2012b, 427–52, which also make the same point with reference to the uses of inference in the Prāsaṇgika school.

358 Candrakīrti, *Madhyamakāvatāra* 6.23, Toh 3861, dbu ma, *'a*, 205a: dngos kun yang dag brdzun pa mthong ba yis// dngos rnyed ngo bo gnyis ni 'dzin par 'gyur// yang dag mthong yul gang de de nyid de// mthong ba brdzun pa kun rdzob bden par gsungs//.

359 Ibid., *Madhyamakāvatārabhāśya* 6.23, Toh 3862, dbu ma, *'a*, 253a: de la don dam pa ni yang dag par gzigs pa rnams kyi ye shes kyi khyad par gyi yul nyid kyis bdag gi ngo bo rnyed pa yin gyi/ rang gi bdag nyid kyis grub pa ni ma yin te/ 'di ni ngo bo gcig yin no//.

360 Ibid., 253a: 'di na bden pa gnyis kyi rang gi ngo bo phyin ci ma log par mkhyen pa sangs rgyas bcom ldan 'das rnams kyis/ 'du byed dang myu gu la sogs pa nang dang phyi rol gyi dngos po thams cad kyi rang gi ngo bo rnam pa gnyis nye bar bstan te/ 'di lta ste/ kun rdzob dang don dam pa'o//.

361 Ibid., *Madhyamakāvatāra* 6.24, Toh 3861, dbu ma, *'a*, 205a: mthong ba brdzun pa'ang rnam pa gnyis 'dod de// dbang po gsal dang dbang po skyon ldan no// skyon ldan dbang can rnams kyi shes pa ni// dbang po legs gyur shes ltos log par 'dod//.

362 Ibid., *Prasannapadā* 24.8, Toh 3860, dbu ma, *'a*, 163a: 'jig rten gyi kun rdzob ni 'jig rten gyi kun rdzob bo zhes 'jig rten kun rdzob ces gang las de ltar khyad par du byed pa 'jig rten ma yin pa'i kun rdzob kyang yod dam zhe na/ 'di ni dngos po ji ltar gnas pa rjes su brjod pa yin gyi/ 'dir dpyad pa de mi 'jug go//.

363 Ibid., *Madhyamakāvatārabhāśya* 6.25, Toh 3862, dbu ma, *'a*, 253b: til mar dang chu dang me long dang brag phug la sogs pa nas brjod pa'i sgra la sogs pa rnams dang/ nyi ma'i 'od zer yul dang dus khyad par can dang nye bar gyur pa la sogs pa rnams ni dbang po [254a] la gnod pa'i rkyen phyi rol na yod pa yin te/ de dag ni dbang po la gnod par byed pa nang na yod pa dag med par/ gzugs brnyan dang brag ca dang smig rgyu la chu la sogs par 'dzin pa'i rgyur 'gyur ro// de bzhin du mig 'khrul mkhan la sogs par rab tu sbyar ba'i sngags dang sman la sogs pa dag kyang shes par bya'o/.

364 Ibid., *Madhyamakāvatārabhāśya* 6.25, Toh 3862, dbu ma, *'a*, 254a: yid kyi gnod par byed pa ni de dag dang yang dag pa ma yin pas byas pa'i grub pa'i mtha' la sogs pa dag dang / rjes su dpag pa ltar snang bdag ste/ rmi lam la sogs pa rnams kyi rnam par gzhag pa ni 'chad par 'gyur ro//.

365 Ibid., *Prasannapadā* 24.8, Toh 3860, dbu ma, *'a*, 163ab: rnam pa gcig tu na/ rab rib dang ling tog sngon po dang/ mig [163b] ser la sogs pas dbang po nyams pas mthong ba phyin ci log la gnas pa de dag ni 'jig rten ma yin te/ de dag gi kun rdzob gang yin pa de ni/ 'jig rten kun rdzob bden pa ma yin pas// 'jig rten kun rdzob bden pa dang// zhes de las khyad par du byas so//.

366 Ibid., *Madhyamakāvatārabhāśya* 6.25, Toh 3862, dbu ma, *'a*, 254a: de'i phyir de ltar 'jig rten gyis dbang po la gnod pa'i rkyen ji skad du bshad pa med par dbang po drug car gyis gzung bar bya ba'i don rtogs pa de ni 'jig rten nyid las bden pa yin gyi 'phags pa la ltos nas ni ma yin no// gzugs brnyan la sogs pa gang zhig dbang po rnams la gnod pa yod pa na yul gyi ngo bo nyid du snang ba de ni 'jig rten nyid la ltos nas log pa yin no//.

367 Ibid., *Madhyamakāvatāra* 26, Toh 3861, dbu ma, *'a*, 205b: mi shes gnyid kyis rab bskyod mu stegs can// rnams kyis bdag nyid ji bzhin brtags pa dang // sgyu ma smig rgyu sogs la brtags pa gang // de dag 'jig rten las kyang yod min nyid//.

368 See Garfield 1995, 297, for a brief reflection on the three distinct meanings. Newland 1992, 77–89, also offers a reading of the Geluk school's presentation of the three meanings of *saṃvṛti*.

369 Candrakīrti, *Prasannapadā* 24.8, Toh 3860, dbu ma, *'a*, 163a: kun nas sgrib pas na kun rdzob ste/ mi shes pa ni dngos po'i de kho na nyid la kun nas 'gebs par byed

pa'i phir kun rdzob ces bya'o/ yang na phan tshun brten pas na kun rdzob ste/ phan tshun brten pa nyid kyis na zhes bya ba'i don to/ yang na kun rdzob ni brda ste/ 'jig rten gyi tha snyad ces bya ba'i tha tshig go/ de yang brjod pa dang brjod bya dang/ shes pa dang shes bya la sogs pa'i mtshan nyid can no//.

370 Ibid., *Madhyamakāvatāra*, 6.28, Toh 3861, dbu ma, *'a*, 205b: gti mug rang bzhin sgrib phyir kun rdzob ste// des gang bcos ma bden par snang de ni// kun rdzob bden zhes thub pa des gsungs te// bcos mar gyur pa'i dngos ni kun rdzob tu'o//. Huntington's (1989, 160) translation of this stanza problematically equates the first *kun rdzob* and the latter *kun rdzob*, treating both as having the same meaning, and thus unambiguously renders both with what he describes as the "screen," a Tibetan equivalent of *sgrib byed*. On my reading of Candrakīrti, however, only the first sense of *kun rdzob* is identified as "confusion" or "ignorance" and thus has the connotation of *sgrib byed*—meaning concealer or screen. Since ordinary beings are under the spell of this form of *kun rdzob*—confusion—the first sense of *kun rdzob* eclipses the second and the third senses. As a result, far from understanding things as dependently arisen (the second sense) and dependently designated (the third sense), ordinary beings reify them as independently produced, independent of designation. However, noble beings are free from the first sense of *kun rdzob*, because they have been liberated from confusion or ignorance and thus are no longer under its spell—the *sgrib byed*. As a result, they are able to understand things as dependently arisen (the second sense) and dependently designated (the third sense).

371 Candrakīrti, *Madhyamakāvatārabhāśya* 6.28, Toh 3862, dbu ma, *'a*, 254b: kun rdzob des gang zhig bden par snang zhing rang bzhin med bzhin du rang bzhin du so sor snang ba de ni 'jig rten phyin ci log tu gyur pa'i kun rdzob tu bden pas 'jig rten gyi kun rdzob kyi bden pa ste/ de ni bcos ma rten cing 'brel bar 'byung ngo//.

372 Ibid., 255a: de la nyan thos dang / rang sangs rgyas dang / byang chub sems dpa' nyon mongs ba can gyis gzigs pa spangs pa/ 'du byed gzugs brnyan la sogs pa'i yod pa nyid dang 'dra bar gzigs pa rnams la ni bcos ma'i rang bzhin gyi bden pa ma yin te/ bden par mngon par rlom pa med pa'i phyir ro//.

373 Ibid., 255a: byis pa rnams la ni slu bar byed pa yin la/ de las gzhan pa rnams la ni sgyu ma la sogs pa ltar rten cing 'brel par 'byung ba nyid kyis kun rdzob tsam du 'gyur ro//.

374 Ibid., 255a: de yang shes bya'i sgrib pa'i mtshan nyid can ma rig pa tsam kun du spyod pa'i phyir/ snang ba dang bcas pa'i spyod yul can gyi 'phags pa rnams la snang gi// snang ba med pa'i spyod yul mnga' ba rnams la ni ma yin no// sangs rgyas rnams la ni chos thams cad rnam pa thams cad du mngon par rdzogs par byang chub pa'i phyir/ sems dang sems las byung ba'i rgyu ba gtan log par 'dod pa yin no//.

375 Ibid., 255a: sangs rgyas rnams kyi don dam pa ni rang bzhin nyid yin zhing/ de yang slu ba med pa nyid kyis don dam pa'i bden pa yin la/ de ni de rnams kyi so so rang gis rig par bya ba yin no// kun rdzob kyi bden pa ni slu bar byed pa nyid kyi phyir don dam pa'i bden pa ma yin no //.

376 Nāgārjuna, *Mūlamadhyamakakārikā* 18.10, Toh 3824, dbu ma, *tsa*, 11a: gang la brten te gang 'byung ba// de ni re zhig de nyid min// de las gzhan pa'ang ma yin phyir// de phyir chad min rtag ma yin//. "Whatever arises dependently from something is neither identical to that thing nor different from it. Therefore it is neither annihilated nor permanent."

377 Candrakīrti, *Prasannapadā* 18.10, Toh 3860, dbu ma, *'a*, 121a: 'jig rten pa'i de kho na nyid kyi mtshan nyid kyi dbang du byas nas brjod par bya ste / . . . .

378 Nāgārjuna, *Mūlamadhyamakakārikā* 18.9, Toh 3824, dbu ma, *tsa*, 11a: gzhan las shes min zhi ba dang // spros pa rnams kyis ma spros pa// rnam rtog med don tha dad med// de ni de nyid mtshan nyid do//.

379 Candrakīrti, *Prasannapadā* 18.9, Toh 3860, dbu ma, *'a*, 121a: de ltar na re zhig 'phags pa rnams kyi de kho na nyid kyi mtshan nyid yin no//.

380 Ibid., *Madhyamakāvatārabhāśya* 6.28, Toh 3862, dbu ma, *'a*, 254b–255a: brten nas 'byung ba gzugs brnyan dang brag ca la sogs pa cung zad cig ni brdzun yang ma rig pa dang ldan pa rnams la snang la/ sngon po la sogs pa gzugs dang sems dang tshor ba la sogs pa cung zad cig ni bden par snang ste/ rang bzhin ni ma rig pa dang ldan pa rnams la rnam pa thams cad du mi snang ngo// de'i phyir de dang gang zhig kun rdzob tu yang brdzun pa kun rdzob [255a] kyi bden pa ma yin no// de ltar na re zhig srid pa'i yan lag gis yongs su bsdus pa nyon mongs pa can gyi ma rig pa'i dbang gis kun rdzob kyi bden pa rnam par gzhag go//.

381 Ibid., 254b–255a: rang bzhin ni ma rig pa dang ldan pa rnams la rnam pa thams cad du mi snang ngo// de'i phyir de dang gang zhig kun rdzob tu yang brdzun pa kun rdzob [255a] kyi bden pa ma yin no// de ltar na re zhig srid pa'i yan lag gis yongs su bsdus pa nyon mongs pa can gyi ma rig pa'i dbang gis kun rdzob kyi bden pa rnam par gzhag go//.

382 Ibid., 256b: de kho na nyid kyi skabs su 'jig rten rnam pa thams cad du tshad ma ma yin zhing/ de kho na nyid kyi skabs su 'jig rten gyi gnod pa yang ma nyin no //.

383 Ibid., 254b–255a: rang bzhin ni ma rig pa dang ldan pa rnams la rnam pa thams cad du mi snang ngo//.

384 Ibid., 255a: de ltar na re zhig srid pa'i yan lag gis yongs su bsdus pa nyon mongs pa can gyi ma rig pa'i dbang gis kun rdzob kyi bden pa rnam par gzhag go//.

385 Ibid., *Madhyamakāvatāra* 6.34, Toh 3861, dbu ma, *'a*, 205b: gal te rang gi mtshan nyid brten 'gyur na/ de la skur pas dngos po 'jig pa'i phyir/ stong nyid dgnos po 'jig pa'i rgyu 'gyur na/ de ni rigs med de phyir dngos yod min/.

386 Ibid., *Catuḥṣatakaṭīkā*, Toh 3865, dbu ma, *ya*, 159b: rang bzhin dang bcas par smra ba'i ltar na ni rang bzhin la gzhan du 'gyur ba nyid mi srid pa'i phyir rang bzhin ji lta ba bzhin du rtag par nges par thal bar 'gyur ro/.

387 Ibid., *Madhyamakāvatārabhāśya* 6.36, Toh 3862, dbu ma, *'a*, 205b: de'i phyir rang gi mtshan nyid kyi skye ba ni bden pa gnyis char du yang yod pa ma yin no/. I think Candrakīrti has in his mind Bhāviveka, a Mādhyamika who is committed to *svalakṣaṇa* ontology. Dan Arnold, however, thinks it is Dignāga who is in Candrakīrti's sight: "The latter point (i.e., that this sense of svalakṣaṇas does not obtain from the point of view of either of the two truths) neatly expresses Candrakīrti's contention that Dignāga's account of our epistemic practices is not only not ultimately, but not even conventionally valid" (Arnold 2005, 428).

388 Candrakīrti, *Madhyamakāvatārabhāśya* 6.29, Toh 3862, dbu ma, *'a*, 255a: de'i phyir de ltar kun rdzob kyi bden pa bstan nas/ don dam pa'i bden pa bstan par 'dod pas de ni brjod du med pa'i phyir dang shes pa'i phyir yul ma yin pa nyid kyi phyir dngos su bstan par mi nus pas/ nyan par 'dod pa sems la rang gis myong ba nyid du de'i rang bzhin gsal bar bya ba'i phyir dpe bshad pa/.

389 Ibid., *Madhyamakāvatāra* 6.29, Toh 3861, dbu ma, *'a*, 205b: rab rib mthu yis skra shad la sogs pa'i// ngo bo log pa gang zhig rnam brtags pa// de nyid bdag nyid gang du mig dag pas// mthong de de nyid de bzhin 'dir shes kyis//.

390 Ibid., *Prasannapadā* 18.9, Toh 3860, dbu ma, *'a*, 121a: de ltar na re zhig 'phags pa rnams kyi de kho na nyid kyi mtshan nyid yin no//.

391 Nāgārjuna, *Mūlamadhyamakakārikā* 18.9, Toh 3824, dbu ma, *tsa*, 11a: gzhan las shes min zhi ba dang // spros pa rnams kyis ma spros pa// rnam rtog med don tha dad med// de ni de nyid mtshan nyid do//.

392 Candrakīrti, *Madhyamakāvatāra* 6.23, Toh 3861, dbu ma, *'a*, 205a: dngos kun yang dag brdzun pa mthong ba yis// dngos rnyed ngo bo gnyis ni 'dzin par 'gyur// yang dag mthong yul gang de de nyid de// mthong ba brdzun pa kun rdzob bden par gsungs//.

393 Ibid., *Madhyamakāvatārabhāṣya* 6.23, Toh 3862, dbu ma, *'a*, 253ab: de la don dam pa ni yang dag par gzigs pa rnams kyi ye shes kyi khyad par gyi yul nyid kyis bdag gi ngo bo rnyed pa yin gyi/ rang gi bdag nyid kyis grub pa ni ma yin te/ 'di ni ngo bo gcig yin no//.

394 Ibid., *Prasannapadā* 18.9, Toh 3860, dbu ma, *'a*, 119b: de la 'di la gzhan las shes pa yod pa ma yin pas na gzhan las shes min te/ gzhan gyis bstan pas rtogs par bya ba ma yin gyi/ rang nyid kyis rtogs par bya ba yin no zhes bya ba'i don to// ji ltar rab rib can dag gis skra shad la sogs pa'i ngo bo phyin ci log mthong ba na/ rab rib med pas bstan du zin kyang/ rab rib med pa ltar skra shad la sogs pa'i rang gi ngo bo ma mthong ba'i tshul gyis rtogs par bya ba ji ltar gnas pa bzhin rtogs par mi nus kyi/ 'o na ci zhe na/ rab rib med pas bstan pa las 'di ni phyin ci log yin no zhes bya ba 'di tsam zhig tu ni rtogs par 'gyur la/ gang gi tshe rab rib sel ba'i mig sman bskus pas rab rib med par gyur pa de'i tshe ni skra shad la sogs pa'i rang gi ngo bo de ma rtogs pa'i tshul gyis rtogs par 'gyur ba de bzhin du/ 'phags pa rnams sgro btags pa'i sgo nas de kho na nyid ston mod kyi de lta na yang de tsam gyis 'phags pa ma yin pa rnams kyis de'i rang gi ngo bo rtogs par mi 'gyur la / . . . .

395 Ibid., 119b–120a: gang gi tshe stong pa nyid phyin ci ma log par lta ba ma rig pa'i rab rib [120a] sel bar byed pa'i mig sman gyis blo'i mig dag la bskus par gyur pa na/ de kho na nyid kyi ye shes skyes par gyur pa de'i tshe de kho na nyid de ma rtogs pa'i tshul gyis rang nyid kyis rtogs par 'gyur te/ de ltar na dngos po rnams kyi rang gi ngo bo gzhan las shes pa ma yin pa de ni de kho na nyid do//.

396 Ibid., 120a: de ni zhi ba'i rang bzhin te/ rab rib med pas skra shad ma mthong ba ltar rang bzhin dang bral ba yin no zhes bya ba'i don to//.

397 Ibid., 120a: de nyid kyi phyir de ni spros pa rnams kyis ma spros pa'o// spros pa ni ngag ste don rnams spro bar byed pa'i phyir ro// spros pa rnams kyis ma spros pa ni ngag dag gis ma brjod pa'o zhes bya ba'i tha tshig go//.

398 Ibid., 120a: de ni rnam par rtog pa med pa yang yin te/ rnam par rtog pa ni sems kyi rgyu ba yin na/ de dang bral ba'i phyir de kho na nyid de ni rnam par rtog pa med pa yin no//.

399 Ibid., 120a: 'di la don tha dad pa yod pas na// don tha dad pas te don so so ba'o// don tha dad pa med pa ni don tha dad pa min pa ste// don so so ba ma yin pa zhes bya ba'i don to //.

400 Ibid., *Madhyamakāvatāra* 6.179, Toh 3861, dbu ma, *'a*, 213a: bdag med 'di ni 'gro ba rnams dgrol phyir// chos dang gang zag dbye ba rnam gnyis gsungs//. Also

see *Madhyamakāvatārabhāśya* 6.179: bdag med pa 'di ni mdor bsdus nas rnam pa gnyis su gsungs te/ chos kyi bdag med pa dang gang zag gi bdag med pa'o// yang ci'i phyir bdag med pa rnam pa gnyis nye bar bstan zhe na/ bshad pa/ 'gro ba rnam dgrol phyir te/ bdag med pa rnam pa gnyis po 'di ni bcom ldan 'das kyis 'gro ba rnam par dgrol bar bya ba'i don du nye bar bstan to//.

401 Ibid., 213a: bdag med 'di ni 'gro ba rnams dgrol phyir// chos dang gang zag dbye ba rnam gnyis gsungs// de ltar ston pas slar yang 'di nyid ni// gdul bya rnams la phye ste rnam mang gsungs//.

402 Ibid., *Madhyamakāvatārabhāśya* 6.179, Toh 3862, dbu ma, *'a*, 213a: de la gang zag gi bdag med pa ni rang sangs rgyas rnams dang / nyan thos rnams rnam par dgrol bar bya ba'i phyir bstan la byang chub sems dpa' rnams rnam pa thams cad mkhyen pa nyid thob pas rnam par dgrol bar bya ba'i phyir ni gnyi ga bstan to// nyan thos dang rang sangs rgyas rnams kyis kyang rten cing 'brel par 'byung ba rkyen nyid 'di pa tsam mthong mod kyi/ de lta na yang de dag la chos kyi bdag med pa yongs su rdzogs par sgom pa med de/ khams gsum na spyod pa'i nyon mongs pa spong ba'i thabs tsam zhig ni yod do// de dag la gang zag gi bdag med pa ma lus par sgom pa ni yod par rnam par gzhag go//.

403 Ibid., *Madhyamakāvatāra* 6.124, Toh 3861, dbu ma, *'a*, 210a: de phyir phung po las gzhan bdag med de// phung po ma gtogs de 'dzin ma grub phyir// 'jig rten ngar 'dzin blo yi rten du yang // mi 'dod de rig min . . . //.

404 Ibid., 6.202–203ab, Toh 3861, dbu ma, *'a*, 214a: gzugs ni gzugs rung mtshan nyid can// tshor ba myong ba'i bdag nyid can// 'du shes mtshan mar 'dzin pa ste// 'du byed mngon par 'du byed pa'o// yul la so sor rnam rig pa// rnam shes rang gi mtshan nyid do// phung po sdug bsngal rang mtshan nyid// khams kyi bdag nyid sbrul gdug 'dod //.

405 Ibid., 6.120, Toh 3861, dbu ma, *'a*, 210a: nyon mongs skyon rnams ma lus 'jig tshogs la// lta las byung bar blo yis mthong gyur zhing // bdag ni 'di yi yul du rtogs byas nas// rnal 'byor pa yis bdag ni 'gog par byed//.

406 Ibid., *Madhyamakāvatārabhāśya* 6.120, Toh 3862, dbu ma, *'a*, 292ab: de la 'jig tshogs la lta ba ni nga dang nga'i snyam pa de [292b] lta bu'i rnam par zhugs pa shes rab nyon mongs pa can no //.

407 Ibid., 292b: de yang bdag gis bdag med pa nyid khong du chud pa las spong par 'gyur bas thog mar rnal 'byor pas bdag kho na 'gog par byed do// de bkag pa las 'jig tshogs la lta ba yang spangs par gyur na nyon mongs pa dang/ skyon ma lus par ldog pas na bdag rnam par dpyad pa na thar pa sgrub pa'i thabs yin te/ de'i phyir gang zhig 'jig tshogs la lta pa'i dmigs par gyur pa bdag ces bya ba 'di ci zhig ces rnal 'byor pa je thog mar bdag kho na rnam par dpyod par byed do //.

408 The "basis" (*skandhadhāra*, Tib. *phung po rten*) at issue is a compound that exposes the implausibility of self as both the container (*ādhāra*, Tib. *rten*) and the contained (*adheya*, Tib. *brten pa*).

409 Candrakīrti, *Madhyamakāvatāra* 6.150, Toh 3861, dbu ma, *'a*, 221b: 'dzin rten ni dngos po min// phung las gzhan min phung po'i ngo bo min// phung po rten min 'di ni de ldan min// 'di ni phung po rnams brten 'grub par 'gyur//.

410 Ibid., 6.151, Toh 3861, dbu ma, *'a*, 221b: shing rta rang yan lag las gzhan 'dod min// gzhan min ma yin de ldan yang min zhing // yan lag la min yan lag dag der min// 'dus pa tsam min dbyibs min ji bzhin no//.

411 Ibid., 6.121, Toh 3861, dbu ma, *'a*, 210a: za po rtag dngos byed po min pa'i bdag// yon tan bya med mu stegs rnams kyis brtags// ded bye cung zad cung zad la brten nas// mu stegs can rnams lugs ni tha dad 'gyur//. The Vaiśeṣika claims that mind, pleasure, misery, desires, hatred, effort, virtue and nonvirtue, energy, and so on are the properties of the self, according to *Madhyamakāvatārabhāśya* 6.121, Toh 3862, dbu ma, 294a: 'a ji ltar grangs can pa dag gis de ltar khas blangs pa de bzhin du/ de'i dbye ba cung zad cung zad la brten nas mu stegs can rnams kyi lugs tha dad par 'gyur te/ 'di lta ste bye brag pa rnams ni/ blo dang/ bde ba dang / sdug bsngal dang/ 'dod pa dang / sdang ba dang / 'bad pa dang/ chos dang / chos ma yin pa dang / bya ba'i shugs te/ bdag gi yon tan dgu smra bar byed do//.

412 Ibid., *Madhyamakāvatāra* 6.122, Toh 3861, dbu ma, *'a*, 210a: mo gsham bu ltar skye ba dang bral phyir// de ltar gyur pa'i bdag ni yod min zhing // 'di ni dar 'dzin rten du'ang mi rigs la// 'di ni kun rdzob tu yang yod mi 'dod//.

413 Ibid., *Madhyamakāvatārabhāśya* 6.124, Toh 3862, dbu ma, *'a*, 195a: de'i phyir phung po las tha dad par bdag yod pa ma yin te/ de dag ma gtogs par bdag ma bzung ba'i phyir ro// gal te phung po las tha dad par yod na ni/ de'i tshe so sor grub par bzung bar 'gyur ba zhig na de ltar ni ma yin pas// de'i phyir phung po las gzhan bdag med de// phung po ma gtogs de 'dzin ma drub phyir//.

414 Ibid., 6.126, Toh 3862, dbu ma, *'a*, 295b: phung po las gzhan bdag grub med pa'i phyir// bdag lta'i dmigs pa phung po kho na'o// gang gi phyir ji skad bshad pa'i rigs pas phung po las tha dad pa'i bdag ma grub pa de'i phyir/ phung po dag las gzhan pa'i bdag grub pa med pa'i phyir/ 'jig tshogs la lta ba'i dmigs pa ni phung po dag kho na yin no// de'i phyir bdag ni phung po tsam kho na yin no zhes zer ro// phyogs 'di ni rang gi sde pa 'phags pa mang pos bkur ba pa rnams kyi yin no// de las kyang/ kha cig bdag lta'i rten du phung po ni// lnga char yang 'dod kha cig sems gcig 'dod// kha cig dag ni gzugs dang tshor ba dang 'du shes dang 'du byed dang rnam par shes pa zhes bya ba phung po lnga char yang 'jig tshogs la lta ba'i dmigs par 'dod cing bdag tu mngon par zhen pa 'di yang de la yin no zhes smra ste/.

415 Ibid., 6.143, Toh 3862, dbu ma, *'a*, 302a: phung po dang ldan pa nyid kyang bdag la ji ltar yod pa ma yin pa de ltar bstan pa'i phyir bshad pa/ bdag ni gzugs ldan mi 'dod gang phyir bdag/ yod min de phyir ldan don sbyor ba med// gzhan ni gnag ldan gzhan min gzugs ldan na// bdag ni gzugs las de nyid gzhan nyid med// bdag phung po rnams de nyid dang gzhan nyid yin pa ni sngar bkag zin la/ ldan pa'i skyon yang lha sbyin gzugs dang ldan no zhes bya ba de ni tha mi dad pa nyid la dmigs la/ ba lang dang ldan no zhes bya ba ni tha dad pa yin na/ de nyid dang gzhan nyid de dag ni gzugs bdag la yod pa ma yin pas bdag gzugs dang ldan no zhes bya ba 'di yang mi srid do//.

416 Ibid., *Madhyamakāvatāra* 6.142, Toh 3861, dbu ma, *'a*, 111a: phung po bdag yod ma yin bdag la yang// phung po de rnams yod min gang phyir 'dir// gzhan nyid yod na rtog pa 'dir 'gyur na// gzhan nyid de med de phyir 'di rtogs pa'o //.

417 Ibid., *Madhyamakāvatārabhāśya* 6.142, Toh 3862, dbu ma, *'a*, 302a: gzhan nyid yod na ni rten dang brten pa'i dngos por rigs par 'gyur te/ dper na 'khar gzhong na zho yod do zhes bya ba lta bu'o// 'khar gzhong dang zho gnyis ni 'jig rten na gzhan nyid yin pa na rten dang brten pa'i dngos po mthong ngo// phung po rnams ni de ltar bdag las tha dad pa ma yin la bdag kyang phung po rnams las tha dad pa ma yin pas de gnyis la rten dang brten pa'i dngos po yod pa ma yin no//.

418 Ibid., 6.137, Toh 3862, dbu ma, *'a*, 300ab: len po rang nyer len gcig rigs dngos min// ci'i phyir zhe na/ de ltar na las byed po gcig nyid 'gyur/ 'dir nye bar len par byed pas na len po ste byed pa po yin la nye bar blangs pa na nye bar len pa ste las so// 'dir nye bar len pa po ni bdag yin la/ nye bar len pa ni phung po lnga rnams yin no// de la gal te gzugs la sogs pa tshogs pa tsam zhig bdag yin na ni de'i tshe byed pa po dang las gcig tu 'gyur na/ 'di ni 'dod pa yang ma yin te/ 'byung ba dang rgyur byas pa'i gzugs dag dang bum [300b] pa dang rdza mkhan dag kyang gcig nyid du thal bar 'gyur ba'i phyir ro//.

419 Ibid., 6.136, Toh 3862, dbu ma, *'a*, 300a: ci ste 'phang lo la sogs pa tshogs pa tsam nyid ni shing rta ma yin te/ 'o na ci zhe na/ gang gi tshe 'phang lo la sogs pa rnams dbyibs khyad par can dang ldan par gyur pa de'i tshe shing rta'i ming rnyed par 'gyur ro// de bzhin du gzugs la sogs pa rnams kyi bkod pa tsam bdag yin no snyam na/ de yang yod pa ma yin no// ci'i phyir zhe na/ dbyibs she na/ de gzugs can la yod phyir/ khyod la de dag nyid bdag cis 'gyur gyi// sems sogs tshogs ni bdag nyid 'gyur min te// ci'i phyir zhe na/ gang phyir de dag la dbyibs yod ma yin/ gzugs can ma yin pa'i phyir ro snyam du bsams pao//.

420 Ibid., *Madhyamakāvatāra* 6.158, Toh 3861, dbu ma, *'a*, 212b: de ni de nyid du'am 'jig rten du// rnam pa bdun gyis 'grub 'gyur min mod kyi// rnam dpyad med par 'jig rten nyid las 'dir// rang gi yan lag brten nas 'dogs pa yin//.

421 Ibid., 6.159, Toh 3861, dbu ma, *'a*, 212b: de nyid yan lag can de cha shas can// shing rta de nyid byed po zhes 'gror bsnyad// skye bo rnam la lenpo nyid du 'grub// 'jig rten grags pa'i kun rdzob ma brlag cig//.

422 Nāgārjuna, *Mūlamadhyamakakārikā* 1, Toh 3861, dbu ma, *tsa*, 1a: bdag las ma yin gzhan las min// gnyis las ma yin rgyu med min// dngos po gang dag gang na yang// skye ba nam yang yod ma yin//.

423 Candrakīrti, *Madhyamakāvatārabhāśya* 6.8–9, Toh 3862, dbu ma, *'a*, 204a: de ni de las 'byung na yon tan 'ga' yang yod ma yin// skyes par gyur pa slar yang skye bar rigs pa'ang ma yin nyid// skyes zin slar yang skye bar yongs su rtog par 'gyur na ni// myu gu la sogs rnams kyi skye ba 'dir rnyed mi 'gyur zhing // sa bo srid mthar thug par rab tu skye ba nyid du 'gyur//.

424 Ibid., 6.14, Toh 3862, dbu ma, *'a*, 204b: gzhan la brten nas gal te gzhan zhig 'byung bar 'gyur na ni// 'o na me lce las kyang mun pa 'thug po 'byung 'gyur zhing// thams cad las kyang thams cad skye bar 'gyur te gang gi phyir// skyed par byed pa ma yin ma lus la yang gzhan nyid mtshungs//.

425 Ibid., 6.98, Toh 3862, dbu ma, *'a*, 209a: gnyis las skye ba'ang rigs pa'i ngo bo ma yin gang gi phyir// bshad zin nyes pa de dag thog tu 'bab pa yin phyir ro// 'di ni 'jig rten las min de nyid du yang 'dod min te// gang phyir re re las ni skye ba 'grub pa yod ma yin//.

426 Ibid., 6.99, Toh 3862, dbu ma, *'a*, 209a: gal te rgyu med kho nar skye bar lta zhig 'gyur na ni// de tshe mtha' dag rtag tu thams cad las kyang skye 'gyur zhing// 'bras 'byung ched du 'jig rten 'di yi sa bon la sogs ni// brgya phrag dag gi sgo nas sdud par byed par yang mi 'gyur//.

427 Ibid., 6.104, Toh 3862, dbu ma, *'a*, 209a: gang gi phyir na bdag dang gzhan dang gnyis ka las skye dan// rgyu la ma ltos yod pa min pas dngos rnams rang bzhin bral//.

428 Ibid., *Madhyamakāvatāra* 6.114, Toh 3861, dbu ma, *'a*, 209b: gang phyir rgyu med pa dang dbang phyug gi/ rgyu la sogs dang bdag gzhan gnyis ka las// dngos rnams skye bar 'gyur ba ma yin pa// de phyir brten nas rab tu skye bar 'gyur//.

429 Ibid., *Madhyamakāvatārabhāśya* 6.37–38ab, Toh 3862, dbu ma, *'a*, 206a: dngos po stong pa gzugs brnyan la sogs pa/ tshogs la ltos rnams ma grags pa pa yang min/ ji ltar der ni gzugs brnyan sogs stongs las/ shes pa de yi rnam par skye 'gyur ltar/ de bzhin dngos po thams cad stong na yang/ stong nyid dag las rab tu skye bar 'gyur//.

430 Ibid., *Madhyamakāvatāra* 6.185, Toh 3861, dbu ma, *'a*, 213b: chos rnams rang bzhin med pa nyid// mkhas pas stong pa nyid ces bsnyad// stong nyid de yang stong nyid kyi// ngo bos stong par 'dod pa yin//.

431 Ibid., 6.186, Toh 3861, dbu ma, *'a*, 213b: stong nyid ces bya'i stong nyid gang// stong nyid stong nyid du 'dod de// stong nyid dngos po'i blo can gyi// 'dzin pa bzlog phyir gsungs pa yin//.

432 Ibid., 6.180, Toh 3861, dbu ma, *'a*, 213a: spros dang bcas par stong pa nyid// bcu drug bshad nas mdor bsdus te// slar yang bzhir bshad de dag ni// theg chen du yang bzhed pa yin//.

433 Ibid., 6.181, Toh 3861, dbu ma, *'a*, 2213b: ther zug gnas pa ma yin dang // 'jig pa ma yin nyid kyi phyir// mig la sogs pa drug pa yi// rang bzhin med nyid gang yin pa// de ni nang stong nyid du 'dod//.

434 Ibid., 6.181, Toh 3861, dbu ma, *'a*, 213ab: gang phyir de yi rang bzhin de// yin phyir mig ni mig gis stong// de bzhin rna ba sna dang lce// lus [213b] dang yid kyis bsnyad par bya//.

435 Nāgārjuna, *Mūlamadhyamakakārikā* 24.14, Toh 3824, dbu ma, *tsa*, 15a: gang la stong pa nyid rung ba/ de la thams cad rung bar 'gyur/ gang la stong nyid me rung ba/ de la thams cad mi rung 'gyur/

436 Candrakīrti, *Prasannapadā* 24.14, Toh 3860, dbu ma, *'a*, 166a: gang la dgnos po thams cad rang bzhin gyis stong pa nyid 'de rung ba de la ji skad smras pa de dag thams cad rung bar 'gyur ro// ji ltar zhe na/ gang gi phyir kho bo cag ni rten cing 'brel par 'byung ba stong pa nyid ces smra ste/ de'i phyir/ gang la stong pa nyid 'de rung ba de la rten cing 'brel bar 'byung a rung la/ rang la rten cing 'brel bar 'byung ba rung ba de la 'phags pa'i bden pa bzhi rnams rung bar 'gyur ro// ji ltar zhi na/ gang gi rten cing 'brel bar 'byung ba nyid sdug bsngal du 'gyur gyi/ rten cing 'brel bar mi 'byung ba ni ma yin no/ de ni rang bzhin med pas stong par 'gyur ro// sdug bsngal yod na ni sdug bsngal kun 'byung ba dang/ sdug bsngal 'gog pa dang/ sdug bsngal 'gog par 'dro ba'i lam rung bar 'gyur ro/ de'i phyir sdug bsngal yongs su shes pa dang / kung 'byung spang pa dang / 'gog pa mngon du bya ba dang / lam bsgom par yang rung ngo/ sdug bsngal la sogs pa'i bden pa yongs su shes ba la sogs pa yod na ni 'bras bu rnams rung bar 'gyur ro//.

437 Ibid., 166b: 'jig rten pa dang 'jig rten las 'das pa'i chos thams ca khyad par du rtogs pa thams cad kyang rung la/ chos dang chos ma yin pa dang / de'i 'bras bu dang / 'jig rten pa'i tha snyad dag kyang rung bar 'gyur ro// de'i phyir de ltar na/ gang la stong pa nyid rung ba de la thams cad rung bar 'gyur ro// gang la stong pa nyi mi rung ba de la rten cing 'brel bar 'byung ba nyid med pas/ thams cad mi rung bar 'gyur ro//.

438 Candrakīrti, *Madhyamakāvatārabhāśya* 6.36, Toh 3862, dbu ma, *'a*, 118: de'i phyir rang gi mtshan nyid kyi skye ba ni bden pa gnyis char du yang yod pa ma yin no/.

439 Ibid., *Madhyamakāvatāra* 6.151, Toh 3861, dbu ma, *'a*, 221b: shing rta rang yan lag las gzhan 'dod min// gzhan min ma yin de ldan yang min zhing // yan lag la min yan lag dag der min// 'dus pa tsam min dbyibs min ji bzhin no//.

440 Ibid., 6.158, Toh 3861, dbu ma, *'a*, 221b: de ni de nyid du'am 'jig rten du// rnam pa bdun gyis 'grub 'gyur min mod kyi// rnam dpyad med par 'jig rten nyid las 'dir// rang gi yan lag brten nas 'dogs pa yin//.

441 Ibid., 6.159, Toh 3861, dbu ma, *'a*, 221b: de nyid yan lag can de cha shas can// shing rta de nyid byed po zhes 'gror bsnyad// skye bo rnam la lenpo nyid du 'grub// 'jig rten grags pa'i kun rdzob ma brlag cig//.

442 Kapstein 2001, 213.

443 Heim 2018, 138.

444 Ibid., 138.

445 Heidegger 2001, 256–257.

446 Kapstein 2001, 213.

447 Karunadasa 1996, 4–5.

448 Ronkin 2005, 110.

449 Karunadasa 1996, 5, and Ronkin 2005, 110–112.

450 Anuruddha 2000, 23.

451 Thakchoe 2011b, 1.2; Gold 2016, 177–210; Arnold 2005, 17–22; Garfield 2015, 59–60.

452 Arnold 2005, 21; The Cowherds 2011, 136; Siderits 2011, 168.

453 Arnold 2005, 21; Siderits 2011, 168.

454 Arnold 2005, 21–22; Garfield 2015, 79–80; The Cowherds 2016, 136–37.

455 Arnold 2005, 16.

456 Arnold 2005, 50.

457 Alston 1996, 189–190; cf. Arnold 2005, 22–31, and The Cowherds 2016, 136–37.

458 Thakchoe 2011b, 2.1.

459 Garfield 2015, 48–51; Arnold 2012, 116–158.

460 Thakchoe 2017a, 3.1.

461 Garfield 2015, 175–213, and Thakchoe 2017a, 3.1–2.

462 Siderits, 2003, 182–3; cf. The Cowherds 2015, 143.

463 Garfield 2015, 235.

464 Lemos 2007, 78.

465 Garfield 2011, 28.

466 Garfield 2015, 235.

467 Tillemans 2016, 4–5.

468 Tillemans 2016, 4.

469 Tillemans 2016, 47.

470 Tillemans, 2016, 5.

471 The Cowherds 2011, 142.

References and Bibliography

ABBREVIATIONS

H Lhasa edition
N Narthang edition
Q Peking edition
Toh Tohoku Catalogue number, the first complete catalogue of the Tibetan Buddhist Canon (Degé Kangyur and Degé Tengyur), published in 1934

KANGYUR

Conze, Edward, ed. 1993. *Perfect Wisdom: The Short Prajñāpāramitā Texts*. Totnes: Buddhist Publishing Group.
——, ed. 1973. *The Perfection of Wisdom in Eight Thousand Lines and Its Verse Summary*. Wheel Series 1. Bolinas: Four Seasons Foundation; distributed by Book People, Berkeley.
——, ed. 1975. *The Large Sutra on Perfect Wisdom, with the Divisions of the Abhisamayālaṅkāra*. Berkeley: University of California Press.
Descent into Lanka Sūtra. Laṅkāvatārasūtra. 'Phags pa lang kar gshegs pa'i theg pa chen po'i mdo. Toh 107, Degé Kangyur, vol. 49, mdo sde, *ca*, 56a1–191b7.

Discourse on the Meeting of the Father and the Son. Pitāpūtrasamāgamasūtra. Yab sras mjal ba'i mdo. Toh 60, Degé Kangyur vol. 42, dkon brtsegs, *nga*, 1–168a7.

Discourse on Samsaric Migration. Bhavasaṃkrāntisūtra. 'Phags pa srid pa 'pho ba zhes bya ba theg pa chen po'i mdo. N 211, Narthang Kangyur vol. 63, mdo sde, *tsa*, 279b6–282b2. Toh 226, Degé Kangyur, vol. 63, mdo sde, *dza*, 175a6–177a3.

Mahāratnakūṭadharmaparyāyaśatasāhasrikagranthe Trisaṃvaranirdeśaparivartasūtra. 'Phags pa dkon mchog brtsegs pa chen po'i chos kyi rnam grangs stong phrag brgya pa las, sdom pa gsum bstan pa'i le'u zhes bya ba theg pa chen po'i mdo. H 45, Lhasa Kangyur vol. 35, dkon brtsegs, *ka*, 1b1–68b3.

The Sūtra of the Wheel of Dharma. Dharmacakrasūtra. Chos 'khor rab to bskor ba'i mdo. Toh 337, Degé Kangyur vol. 72, mdo sde, *sa*, 275a–277a. Translated by Dharmachakra Translation Committee, 2018. 84000: Translating the Words of the Buddha.

Suzuki, Daisetz Teitaro, trans. 1999. *The Laṅkāvatāra Sūtra: A Mahāyāna Text.* Delhi: Motilal Banarsidass Publishers.

The Teaching of Akṣayamati. Akṣayamatinirdeśasūtra. Blo gros mi zad pas bstan pa zhes bya ba theg pa chen po'i mdo. H 176, Lhasa Kangyur vol. 60, mdo sde, *pha*, 122b5–270b1. Toh 175, Degé Kangyur vol. 60, mdo sde, *ma*, 79a–174b. Translated by Jens Braarvig and David Welsh, 2020. 84000: Translating the Words of the Buddha.

Teaching the Relative and Ultimate Truths. Samvṛṭiparamārthasatyanirdeśa. Kun rdzob dang don dam pa'i bden pa bstan pa'i mdo. Toh 179, Degé Kangyur vol. 60, mdo sde, *ma*, 244b–266b. Translated by the Dharmachakra Translation Group, 2016. 84000: Translating the Words of the Buddha.

The Ten Bhūmis. Daśabhūmika. Sab cu pa'i mdo. Toh 44–31, Degé Kangyur vol. 36, phal chen, *kha*, 166.a–283a. Translated by Peter Alan Roberts, 2022, *The Ten Bhūmis Chapter from the Mahāvaipulya Sūtra "A Multitude of Buddhas."* 84000: Translating the Words of the Buddha.

Unraveling the Intent Sūtra. Saṃdhinirmocanasūtra. 'Phags pa dgongs pa nges par 'grel pa. H 109, Lhasa Kangyur vol. 51, mdo sde, *ca*,

1b1–87b7. Toh 106, Degé Kangyur vol. 49, mdo sde, *tsha*, 1b–55b. Translated by the Buddhavacana Translation Group, 2021. 84000: Translating the Words of the Buddha.

Vaidya, P. L., trans. 1963. *Saddharmalaṅkāvatārasūtram*. Darbhanga, Bihar: The Mithila Institute of Post Graduate Studies and Research in Sanskrit Learning.

HISTORY

Allen, Charles. 2011. *The Buddha and Dr Führer: An Archaeological Scandal*. City unknown: Haus Publishing.

Butön Rinchen Drub (Bu ston Rin chen grub). 2013. *Butön's History of Buddhism in India and Its Spread to Tibet: A Treasury of Priceless Scripture*. Translated by Lisa Stein and Ngawang Zangpo. The Tsadra Foundation Series. Boston: Snow Lion.

———. 1931. *History of Buddhism (Chos 'byung): Jewelery of Scripture and The History of Buddhism in India and Tibet*. Heidelberg: In kommission bei O. Harrassowitz.

Burnouf, Eugène. 2015. *Introduction to the History of Indian Buddhism*. Translated by Katia Buffetrille and Donald S. Lopez. Chicago: The University of Chicago Press.

Carrithers, Michael. 2001. *The Buddha: A Very Short Introduction*. Oxford: Oxford University Press.

Dalton, Jacob. 2014. "Bsam yas Debate." In *Encyclopedia of Buddhism*, edited by Robert Buswell, 69–71. New York: Thompson Gale.

Aśoka. 1993. *The Edicts of King Asoka: An English Rendering*. Translated by Shravasti Dhammika. The Wheel Publication 386/387. Kandy: Buddhist Publication Society.

Doniger, Wendy. 2010. *The Hindus: An Alternative History*. New York: Penguin Books.

Fa-Hsien. 1965. *A Record of Buddhistic Kingdoms: Being an Account of the Chinese Monk Fa-Hsien of His Travels in India and Ceylon (A.D. 399-414): Translated and Annotated with a Corean Recession of the Chinese Text*. Translated by James Legge. New York: Dover.

Geiger, Wilhelm, trans. 1964. *Mahāvaṃsa: The Great Chronicle of Ceylon*. London: Oxford University Press.

Gethin, Rupert. 1998. *The Foundations of Buddhism*. Oxford: Oxford University Press.

Gombrich, Richard. 1990. "Recovering the Buddha's Message." In *The Buddhist Forum, Vol. 1 Seminar Papers 1987–1988*, 5–20. London: School of Oriental and African Studies, University of London.

Halbfass, Wilhelm. 1990. *India and Europe: An Essay in Philosophical Understanding*. Albany: State University of New York Press.

Hirakawa, Akira, and Paul Groner. 1990. *A History of Indian Buddhism: From Śākyamuni to Early Mahāyāna*. Asian Studies at Hawaii, no. 36. Honolulu: University of Hawaii Press.

Hsün-Tsang. 1969. *His-Yu-Chi. Translated as Si-Yu-Ki: Buddhist Records of the Western World*. Translated by Samuel Beal. Delhi: Munshiram Manoharala.

I-ching. 1966. *A Record of the Buddhist Religion as Practised in India and the Malay Archipelago (A.D. 671–695)*. Translated by J. Takakus. Delhi: Munshiram Manoharala.

Keay, John. 1992. *India Discovered*. London: Collins.

Law, B. B., trans. 1959. *Dīpavaṃsa: Chronicle of the Island of Ceylon or A Historical Poem of the 4th Century A.D.* Ceylon: Saman Press.

McCrindle, J. W. 1877. *Ancient India as Described by Megasthenês and Arrian*. Bombay: Thacker and Co.

Nakamura, Hajime. 2007. *Indian Buddhism: A Survey with Bibliographical Notes*. Delhi: Motilal Banarsidass.

Nyanamoli, Bhikkhu. 1972. *The Life of the Buddha*. Kandy, Sri Lanka: Buddhist Publication Society.

Rāhula, Walpola. 1974. *What the Buddha Taught*. New York: Grove Press.

Rockhill, William Woodville, Ernst Leumann, and Bunyiu Nanjio. 1884. *The Life of the Buddha and the Early History of His Order, Derived from Tibetan Works in the Bkah-Hgyur and Bstan-Hgyur, Followed by Notices on the Early History of Tibet and Khoten*. London: Trübner.

Ruegg, David Seyfort. 2010. *The Buddhist Philosophy of the Middle: Essays on Indian and Tibetan Madhyamaka*. Boston: Wisdom Publications.

Schumann, Hans Wolfgang. 2003. *The Historical Buddha: The Times, Life and Teachings of the Founder of Buddhism*. Edited by Maurice O'C. Walshe. Delhi: Motilal Banarsidass.

Aung, Shwe Zan, and Carolyn Rhys Davids, trans. 1915. *Kathāvathu: The Point of Controversy*. London: Pali Text Society.

Stone, Susan Carol. 2012. *The Kosambi Intrigue: A Tale in the Time of the Buddha*. Charlottesville, VA: This Breath Press.

Tārānātha. 1990. *Tāranātha's History of Buddhism in India*. Edited by Debiprasad Chattopadhyaya. Translated by Lama Chimpa and Alaka Chattopadhyaya. Delhi: Motilal Banarsidass.

Thapar, Romila. 2004. *Early India: From the Origins to AD 1300*. Berkeley, CA: University of California Press.

van Schaik, Sam. 2011. *Tibet: A History*. New Haven: Yale University Press.

———. 2015. *Tibetan Zen: Discovering a Lost Tradition*. Boston: Snow Lion.

THERAVĀDA

Anuruddha, Ācariya. 2000. "Abhidhammatha Sangaha." In *A Comprehensive Manual of Abhidhamma of Ācariya Anuruddha: Pāli Text, Translation & Explanation Guide*. Edited by Bhikkhu Bodhi. Seattle: BPS Pariyatti Editions.

Bodhi, Bhikkhu, ed. 1985. *The Dhammapada: The Buddha's Path of Wisdom*. Translated from the Pali by Acharya Buddharakkhita. Introduction by Bhikkhu Bodhi. Kandy, Sri Lanka: Buddhist Publication Society.

———, trans. and ed. 2005. *In the Buddha's Words: An Anthology of Discourses from the Pāli Canon*. Boston: Wisdom Publications.

———, trans. 2000. *The Connected Discourses of the Buddha: A New Translation of the Saṃyutta Nikāya*. Boston: Wisdom Publications.

——, ed. 2000. *A Comprehensive Manual of Abhidhamma: The Abhidhammattha Sangaha of Ācariya Anuruddha*. Seattle: BPS Pariyatti Editions.

Bodhi, Bhikkhu, and Bhikkhu Ñāṇamoli, trans. 1995. *The Middle Length Discourses of the Buddha: A Translation of the Majjhima Nikāya*. Boston: Wisdom Publications.

Bhikkhu, Thanissaro, trans. 1997. *Dhammapada: A Translation from the Pali*. www.accesstoinsight.org.

Buddhaghosa. 1950. *Paramatthamañjūsā, Visuddhimagga Aṭṭhakathā Mahā ṭikā*. Pali Text Society's edition. London: Harvard University Press.

Buddhaghosa. 2001. *The Path of Purification* (*Visuddhimagga*). Translated by Bhikkhu Ñāṇamoli. Taipei: The Corporate Body of the Buddha Education Foundation.

Dhamma, U Rewata, and Bhikkhu Bodhi. 2000. *Introduction and Explanatory Guide to the Abhidhammattha Sangaha of Ācariya Anuruddha*. Seattle: BPS Pariyatti Editions.

Dhammapāla, Ācariya. 1909. *Paramatthamañjūsā: Commentary to the Visuddhimagga* (*Visuddhimaggamahā-ṭīkā*). Colombo: Vidyodaya edition.

Heim, Maria. 2018. *Voice of the Buddha: Buddhaghosa on the Immeasurable Words*. New York: Oxford University Press.

Ireland, John D., trans. 1997. *The Udāna and the Itivuttaka: The Classics from the Pāli Canon*. Kandy, Sri Lanka: Buddhist Publication Society.

Karunadasa, Yakupitiyage. 1996. *The Dhamma Theory: Philosophical Cornerstone of the Abhidhamma*. Wheel Publication 412/413. Kandy, Sri Lanka: Buddhist Publication Society.

——. 2006. "Theravāda Version of the Two Truths." Presentation to Korean Conference of Buddhist Studies. http://www.skb.or.kr/2006/down/papers/094.pdf.

Ñānamoli, Bhikkhu, trans. 2001. *The Path of Purification: A Translation of Visuddhimagga by Bhadanācariya Buddhaghosa*. Taipei, Taiwan: The Corporate Body of the Buddha Educational Foundation.

Rhys Davids, Caroline A. F., trans. 1900. *Dhammasaṅgaṇī as a Buddhist Manual of Psychological Ethics of the Fourth Century BC*. London: The Royal Asiatic Society.

Thera, Narada, trans. 1993. *The Dhammapada: Pāli Text & Translation with Stories in Brief and Notes*. Taipei, Taiwan: The Corporate Body of the Buddha Educational Foundation.

Walleser, Max, ed. 1973. *Manoratha pūraṇī: Buddhaghosa's Commentary on the Aṅguttaranikāya*. London: Pali Text Society.

ABHIDHARMA

Anacker, Stefan. 1998. *Seven Works of Vasubandhu: The Buddhist Psychological Doctor*. Delhi: Motilal Banarsidass.

Asaṅga. 2001. *Abhidharmasamuccaya: The Compendium of the Higher Teaching*. Translated by Walpola Rāhula and Sara Boin-Webb. Fremont, CA: Asian Humanities Press.

Balslev, Anindita Niyogi. 1983. *A Study of Time Indian Philosophy*. Wiesbaden: Otto Harrassowitz.

Changkya Rölpai Dorjé (Lcang skya Rol pa'i rdo rje). 1989. *Ornament of the Philosophical Systems. Grub mtha' thub bstan lhun po'i mdzes rgyan*. Xiling: Mtsho sngon mi rigs par khang. In *Beautiful Adornment of Mount Meru: A Presentation of Classical Indian Philosophy*. Translated by Donald S. Lopez. Somerville, MA: Wisdom Publications, 2019.

Dharmaśrī (Dharmarāta or Dharmaśreṣṭhin). 1999. *Saṃyuktābhidharmahṛdaya: Heart of Scholasticism with Miscellaneous Additions*. Translated by Bart Dessein. Buddhist Tradition Series, vols. 33–35. Delhi: Motilal Banarsidass Publishers.

Dignāga. *Commentary on the Abhidharmakośa: The Lamp Illuminating the Central Issues. Abhidharmakośavṛttimarmapradīpa. Chos mngon pa'i mdzod kyi 'grel pa gnad kyi sgron me*. Toh 4095, Degé Tengyur, mngon pa, *nyu*, 95b1–214a7.

Jampaiyang, Chim. 2019. *Ornament of Abhidharma: A Commentary on Vasubandhu's Abhidharmakośa*. Translated by Ian James Coghlan. Somerville, MA: Wisdom Publications.

Kātyāyanīputra. 1955. *Abhidharmajñānaprasthānaśāstra (Ye shes la 'jugpa)*. Translated by Śānti Bhikṣu Śāstrī. Calcutta: Visva-Bharati.

——. 2011. *The Great Commentary: Mahāvibhāṣya. Chos mngon pa bye brag tu bshad pa chen po*. Translated by Lobsang Chodak (Blo bzang chos grags). Lhasa: Krung go'i bod kyi shes rig dpe skrun khang.

Pūrṇavardhana. *Commentary on the Abhidharmakośa: Following the Defining Characteristics. Abhidharmakośaṭīkālakṣaṇānusāriṇī. Chos mngon pa'i mdzod kyi 'grel bshad mtshan nyid kyi rjes su 'brang ba*. Toh. 4093, Degé Tengyur, mngon pa, *cu*, 1b1–347a7; *chu*, 1b1–322a7; *nyu*, 214b1–237a2.

Sanghabhadra. *Commentary on the Abhidharmakośa. Abhidharmakośaśāstrakārikābhāṣya. Chos mngon pa mdzod kyi bstan bcos kyi tshig le'ur byas pa'i rnam par bshad pa*. Toh 4091, Degé Tengyur, mngon pa, *khu*, 95b1–266a7.

Sthiramati. *The Great Commentary on the Commentary of the Abhidharmakośa. Abhidharmakośabhāṣyaṭīkātattvārtha. Chos mngon pa mdzod kyi bshad pa'i rgya cher 'grel pa, don gyi de kho na nyid*. Toh 4421, Degé Tengyur, sna tshogs, *tho*, 1b1–426a7; *do*, 1b1–387a7.

Vasubandhu. 1967. *Abhidharmakośabhāṣyam*. Edited by Prahlad Pradana. Patna, India: K.P. Jayaswal Research Institute.

——. 1988–1990a. *Commentary on the Treasure of Knowledge (Abhidharmakośabhāṣyam)*. Translated by Louis de La Vallée Poussin. Vol. 1. Berkeley, CA: Asian Humanities Press.

——. 1988–1990b. *Commentary on the Treasure of Knowledge (Abhidharmakośabhāṣyam)*. Translated by Louis de La Vallée Poussin. Vol. 2. Berkeley, CA: Asian Humanities Press.

——. 1988–1990c. *Commentary on the Treasure of Knowledge (Abhidharmakośabhāṣyam)*. Translated by Louis de La Vallée Poussin. Vol. 3. Berkeley, CA: Asian Humanities Press.

——. 1988–1990d. *Commentary on the Treasure of Knowledge (Abhidharmakośabhaṣyam)*. Translated by Louis de La Vallée Poussin and Leo M. Pruden. Vol. 4. Berkeley, CA: Asian Humanities Press.

——. *Commentary on the Verses on the Treasury of Abhidharma. Abhidharmakośabhāṣya. Chos mngon pa'i mdzod kyi bshad pa.* Toh 4090, Degé Tengyur, mngon pa, *ku*, 26a1–258a7; *khu*, 1b1–95a7.

——. *Verses on the Treasury of Abhidharma. Abhidharmakośakārikā. Chos mngon pa'i mdzod kyi tshig le'ur byas pa.* Toh 4089, Degé Tengyur, mngon pa, *ku*, 1b1–25a7.

Vasumitra. *The Wheel of the Development of Schismatic Doctrines. Samayabhedoparacanacakra. Gzhung lugs kyi bye brag bkod pa'i 'khor lo.* Toh 4138, Degé Tengyur, 'dul ba, *su*, 141a5–147a2.

Vasumitra and Xuanzang. 1988. "Samayabhedoparacanacakra (The Cycle of the Formation of the Schismatic Doctrines)." In *Taishō Shinshū Daizōkyō*, Vol. 49, No. 2031, edited by Junjirō Takakusu. Tokyo: Taishō Shinshū Daizōkyō Kankōkai.

Yaśomitra. *Commentary on the Abhidharmakośa. Abhidharmakośaṭīkā. Chos mngon pa'i mdzod kyi 'grel bshad.* Toh 4092, Degé Tengyur, mngon pa, *gu*, 1b1–330a7; *ngu*, 1b1–333a7.

——. 1971. *Clear-Meaning Exegesis on the Abhidharmakośa Commentary. Sphuṭārthābhidharmakośavyākhyā.* Vol. 1 & 2, edited by U. Wogihara. Tokyo: Sankibo Buddhist Book Store.

SAUTRĀNTIKA

Devendrabuddhi. *Exegesis on the Verses of Epistemology. Pramāṇavārttikapañjikā. Tshad ma rnam 'grel gyi dka' 'grel.* Toh 4217, Degé Tengyur, tshad ma, *che*, 1b1–326b4.

Dharmakīrti. *Analysis of Relations. Sambandhaparīkṣā. 'Brel pa brtag.* Toh 4214, Degé Tengyur, tshad ma, *ce*, 255a2–256a2.

——. *Ascertaining Epistemology. Pramāṇaviniścaya. Tshad ma rnam par nges pa.* Toh 4211, Degé Tengyur, tshad ma, *ce*, 152b1–230a7.

——. *Commentary on Analysis of Relations. Sambandhaparīkṣāvṛtti. 'Brel pa brtag pa'i 'grel pa.* Toh 4215, Degé Tengyur, tshad ma, *ce*, 256a2–261a7.

——. *Commentary on Verses of Epistemology. Pramāṇavārttikavṛtti. Tshad ma rnam 'grel gyi 'grel pa.* Toh 4216, Degé Tengyur, tshad ma, *ce*, 261b1–365a7.

——. *Dose of Logical Reasoning. Nyāyabindu. Rigs pa'i thigs pa.* Toh 4212, Degé Tengyur, tshad ma, *ce*, 231b1–238a6.

——. *Doses of Reasoning. Hetubindu. Gtan tshigs kyi thigs pa.* Toh 4213, Degé Tengyur, tshad ma, *ce*, 238a7–255a1.

——. *Establishing the Other Continuum. Saṃtānāntarasiddhi. Rgyud gzhan grub pa.* Toh 4219, Degé Tengyur, tshad ma, *che*, 355b5–359a7.

——. *The Logic of Debate. Vādanyāya. Rtsod pa'i rigs pa.* Toh 4218, Degé Tengyur, tshad ma, *che*, 326b4–355b5.

——. *Verses on Epistemology. Pramāṇavārttikakārikā. Tshad ma rnam 'grel gyi tshig le'ur byas pa.* Toh 4210, Degé Tengyur, tshad ma, *ce*, 94b1–151a7.

Dharmottara. *Commentary on Ascertaining Epistemology: Chapters 1–2. Pramāṇaviniścayaṭīkā. Tshad ma rnam par nges pa'i 'grel bshad (le'u dang po dang gnyis pa).* Toh 4227, Degé Tengyur, tshad ma, *tshe*, 1b1–178a3.

——. *Commentary on Ascertaining Epistemology: Chapter 3. Pramāṇaviniścayaṭīkā. Tshad ma rnam par nges pa'i 'grel bshad (le'u gsum pa).* Toh 4227, Degé Tengyur, tshad ma, *tshe*, 1b1–178a3.

——. *Commentary on Doses of Reasoning. Nyāyabinduṭīkā. Rigs pa'i thigs pa'i rgya cher 'grel pa.* Toh 4231, Degé Tengyur, tshad ma, *we*, 36b2–92a2.

——. *Proof of Momentariness. Kṣaṇabhaṅgasiddhi. Skad cig ma 'jig pa grub pa.* Toh 4253, Degé Tengyur, tshad ma, *zhe*, 249b4–259a5.

Dignāga. *Analysis of the Three Times. Trikālaparīkṣā. Dus gsum brtag pa.* Toh 4207, Degé Tengyur, tshad ma, *ce*, 87b2–88b5.

——. *Commentary on the Compendium of Epistemology. Pramāṇasamuccayavṛtti. Tshad ma kun las btus pa'i 'grel pa.* Toh 4204, Degé Tengyur, tshad ma, *ce*, 14b1–85b7.

——. *Commentary on Investigation of the Percept. Ālambanaparīkṣāvṛtti. Dmigs pa brtag pa'i 'grel pa.* Toh 4206, Degé Tengyur, tshad ma, *ce*, 86a5–87b2.

——. *Compendium of Epistemology. Pramāṇasamuccaya. Tshad ma kun las btus pa zhes bya ba'i rab tu byed pa.* Q 5700, Peking Tengyur, vol. 130, tshad ma, *ce*, 1a1–13a5.

——. *Investigation of the Percept. Ālambanaparīkṣā. Dmigs pa brtag pa.* Toh 4205, Degé Tengyur, tshad ma, *ce*, 86a1–86a5.

——. *The Wheel of Logical Reasoning. Hetucakraḍamaru. Gtan tshigs kyi 'khor lo gtan la dbab pa.* Toh 4209, Degé Tengyur, tshad ma, *ce*, 93a1–93a7.

Dignāga, and Śaṅkarasvāmin. *The Gate for Engaging in Logical Reasoning. Nyāyapraveśa. Tshad ma rigs par 'jug pa.* Q 5706, Peking Tengyur, tshad ma, *ce*, 180b2–184b6, vol. 130, pp. 74–76.

Dreyfus, Georges. 1997. *Recognizing Reality: Dharmakīrti's Philosophy and Its Tibetan Interpretations.* Albany: State University of New York Press.

Duckworth, Douglas, et al. 2016. *Dignāga's Investigation of the Percept: A Philosophical Legacy in India and Tibet.* New York, NY: Oxford University Press.

Matilal, Bimal Krishna. 1971. *Epistemology, Logic and Grammar in Indian Philosophical Analysis.* The Hague: Mouton.

Śākyabuddhi. *Commentary on the Pramāṇavārttika. Pramāṇavārttikaṭīkā. Tshad ma rnam 'grel gyi 'grel bshad.* Toh 4220, Degé Tengyur, tshad ma, *je*, 1b1–328a7; *nye*, 1b1–282a7.

Vinītadeva. *Commentary of the Analysis of Relation. Sambandhaparīkṣāṭīkā. 'Brel pa brtag pa'i rgya cher bshad pa.* Toh 4236, Degé Tengyur, tshad ma, *zhe*, 1b1–21b3.

——. *Commentary on the Investigation of the Percept. Ālambanaparīkṣāṭīkā. Dmigs pa brtag pa'i 'grel bshad.* Toh 4241, Degé Tengyur, tshad ma, *zhe*, 175a3–187b5.

——. *Gloss on the Dose of Logic. Hetubinduṭīkā. Gtan tshigs kyi thigs pa rgya cher 'grel pa.* Toh 4234, Degé Tengyur, tshad ma, *we*, 100b3–181a7.

——. *Gloss on the Dose of Reasoning. Nyāyabinduṭīkā. Rigs pa'i thigs pa'i rgya cher 'grel pa.* Toh 4230, Degé Tengyur, tshad ma, *we*, 1b1–36b2.

YOGĀCĀRA

Anacker, Stefan. 2002. *Seven Works of Vasubandhu: The Buddhist Psychological Doctor.* Delhi: Motilal Banarsidass Publishers Private Limited.

Asaṅga. *The Bodhisattva Grounds: The Grounds of the Yogins. Yogācārabhūmaubodhisattvabhūmi. Rnal 'byor spyod pa'i sa las byang chub sems dpa'i sa.* Toh 4037, Degé Tengyur, sems tsam, *wi,* 1b1–213a7.

———. 2016. *The Bodhisattva Path to Unsurpassed Enlightenment: A Complete Translation of the Bodhisattvabhūmi.* Translated by Artemus B. Engle. Boulder: Snow Lion.

———. *Commentary on the Treatise on the Supreme Continuum of the Mahāyāna. Mahāyānottaratantraśāstravyākhyā. Theg pa chen po rgyud bla ma'i bstan bcos rnam par bshad pa.* Toh 4025, Degé Tengyur, sems tsam, *phi,* 74b1–129a7.

———. *Commentary on the Unraveling the Intent Sūtra. Āryasaṃdhinirmocanabhāṣya. 'Phags pa dgongs pa nges par 'grel pa'i rnam par bshad pa.* Toh 3981, Degé Tengyur, mdo 'grel, *ngi,* 1b1–11b5.

———. *Compendium of the Abhidharma. Abhidharmasamuccaya. Chos mngon pa kun las btus pa.* Toh 4049, Degé Tengyur, sems tsam, *ri,* 1b1–77a7; 44b1–120a7.

———. *Compendium of the Mahāyāna. Mahāyānasaṃgraha. Theg pa chen po bsdus pa.* Toh 4048, Degé Tengyur, sems tsam, *ri,* 1b1–43a7.

———. *Concise Establishing of the Grounds of the Yogins. Yogācārabhūmi viniścayasaṃgrahanī. Rnal 'byor spyod pa'i sa rnam par gtan la dbab pa bsdu ba.* Toh 4038, Degé Tengyur, sems tsam, *zhi,* 1b1–289a7; *zi,* 1b1–127a4.

———. *Illumination of Meditation. Dhyānadīpopadeśa. Bsam gtan gyi sgron ma zhes bya ba'i man ngag.* Toh 4073, Degé Tengyur, sems tsam, *hi,* 120b2–126b7.

———. *The Grounds of the Yogins: The Compendium of the Basis. Yogācārabhūmauvastusaṃgrahaṇī. Rnal 'byor spyod pa'i sa las gzhi bsdu ba.* Toh 4039, Degé Tengyur, sems tsam, *zi,* 127a4–335a7.

———. *The Grounds of the Yogins. Yogācārabhūmaubhūmivastu. Rnal 'byor spyod pa'i sa las dngos gzhi sa mang po.* Toh 4035, Degé Tengyur, sems tsam, *tshi*, 1b1–283a7.

———. *The Śravaka Grounds: The Grounds of the Yogins. Yogācārabhūmauśrāvakabhūmiḥ. Rnal 'byor spyod pa'i sa las nyan thos kyi sa.* Toh 4036, Degé Tengyur, sems tsam, *dzi*, 1b1–195a7.

Changkya Rölpai Dorjé (Lcang skya Rol pa'i rdo rje). 1989. *Ornament of the Philosophical Systems. Grub mtha' thub bstan lhun po'i mdzes rgyan.* Xiling: Mtsho sngon mi rigs par khang. In *Beautiful Adornment of Mount Meru: A Presentation of Classical Indian Philosophy.* 2019. Translated by Donald S. Lopez. Somerville, MA: Wisdom Publications.

Gung Thang Könchok Tenpai Dolmé. 2016. "Ornament for Dignāga's Thought in Investigation of the Percept (Dmigs pa brtag pa'i 'grel pa phyogs glang dgongs rgyan)." In *Dignāga's Investigation of the Percept: A Philosophical Legacy in India and Tibet*, translated by Douglas Duckworth, et al. New York, NY: Oxford University Press, 112–17.

Maitreya. *An Analysis of the Jewel Disposition: A Treatise on the Ultimate Continuum of the Mahāyāna. Mahāyānottaratantraśāstraratnagotravibhāga. Theg pa chen po rgyud bla ma'i bstan bcos.* Toh 4024, Degé Tengyur, sems tsam, *phi*, 54b1–73a7.

———. *Distinguishing Between Phenomena and Reality. Dharmadharmatāvibhāga. Chos dang chos nyid rnam par 'byed pa.* Toh 4022, Degé Tengyur, sems tsam, *phi*, 46b1–49a6.

———. *Ornament of the Mahāyāna Sūtra. Mahāyānasūtrālaṃkārakārikā. Theg pa chen po mdo sde'i rgyan zhes bya ba'i tshig le'ur byas pa.* Toh 4020, Degé Tengyur, sems tsam, *phi*, 1b1–39a4.

———. *Separating the Middle from the Extremes. Madhyāntavibhāga. Dbus dang mtha' rnam par 'byed pa'i tshig le'ur byas pa.* Toh 4021, Degé Tengyur, sems tsam, *phi*, 40b1–45a6. In *Middle Beyond Extremes: Maitreya's Madhyāntavibhāga with Commentaries by Khenpo Shenga and Ju Mipham.* 2007. Translated by Dharmachakra Translation Committee. Ithaca, N.Y: Snow Lion.

——. *Verses on Distinguishing between Phenomena and Reality. Dharmadharmatāvibhaṅgakārikā. Chos dang chos nyid rnam par 'byed pa'i tshig le'ur byas pa.* Toh 4023, Degé Tengyur, sems tsam, *phi*, 50b1–53a7.

——. *Commentary on Transmigration through Existences. Bhavasaṃkrāntiṭīkā. Srid pa 'pho ba'i ṭī ka.* Toh 3841, Degé Tengyur, dbu ma, *tsa*, 151b7–158a7.

Mipham, Ju, and Khenpo Shenga. 2013. *Distinguishing Phenomena from Their Intrinsic Nature: Maitreya's Dharmadharmatāvibhaṅga with Commentaries by Khenpo Shenga and Ju Mipham.* Translated by Dharmachakra Translation Committee. London: Snow Lion.

Powers, John, trans. 1995. *Wisdom of Buddha: The Saṃdhinirmocana Sūtra.* Berkeley: Dharma Publications.

Sthiramati. *Commentary on the Separation of the Middle from the Extremes. Madhyāntavibhāgaṭīkā. Dbus dang mtha' rnam par 'byed pa'i 'grel bshad.* Toh 4032, Degé Tengyur, sems tsam, *bi*, 189b2–318a7.

——. *Commentary on the Sūtrālaṃkāra. Sūtrālaṃkāravṛttibhāṣya. Mdo sde rgyan gyi 'grel bshad.* Toh 4034, Degé Tengyur, sems tsam, *mi*, 1b1–283a7; *tsi*, 1b1–266a7.

——. *Commentary on the Thirty Verses. Triṃśikābhāṣya. Sum cu pa'i bshad pa.* Toh 4064, Degé Tengyur, sems tsam, *shi*, 146b2–171b6.

——. *Specifically on the Discussion of the Five Aggregates. Pañcaskandhaprakaraṇavibhāṣā. Phung po lnga'i rab tu byed pa bye brag tu bshad pa.* Toh 4066, Degé Tengyur, sems tsam, *shi*, 195b6–250a7.

Vasubandhu. *A Chapter on the Five Aggregates. Pañcaskandhaprakaraṇa. Phung po lnga'i rab tu byed pa.* Toh 4059, Degé Tengyur, sems tsam, *shi*, 11b4–17a7.

——. *Commentary on Distinguishing Phenomena and Reality. Dharmadharmatāvibhāgavṛtti. Chos dang chos nyid rnam par 'byed pa'i 'grel pa.* Toh 4028, Degé Tengyur, sems tsam, *bi*, 27b1–38b6.

——. *Commentary on the Separation of the Middle from the Extremes. Madhyāntavibhāgabhāṣya. Dbus dang mtha' rnam par 'byed pa'i 'grel pa.* Toh 4027, Degé Tengyur, sems tsam, *bi*, 1b1–27a7.

——. *Commentary on Sūtrālaṃkārabhāṣya. Sūtrālaṃkārabhāṣya. Mdo sde'i rgyan gyi bshad pa.* Toh 4026, Degé Tengyur, sems tsam, *phi*, 129b1–260a7.

——. *Commentary on the Twenty Verses. Viṃśatikāvṛtti. Nyi shu pa'i 'grel pa.* Toh 4057, Degé Tengyur, sems tsam, *shi*, 4a3–10a2.

——. *A Discussion for the Demonstration of Action. Karmasiddhiprakaraṇa. Las grub pa'i rab tu byed pa.* Toh 4062, Degé Tengyur, sems tsam, *shi*, 134b2–145a6.

——. *Identifying the Three Natures. Trisvabhāvanirdeśa. Rang bzhin gsum nges par bstan pa.* Toh 4058, Degé Tengyur, sems tsam, *shi*, 10a3–11b4.

——. *The Principles of Exegesis. Vyākhyāyukti. Rnam par bshad pa'i rigs pa.* Toh 4061, Degé Tengyur, sems tsam, *shi*, 29a2–134b2.

——. *The Thirty Verses. Triṃśikākārikā. Sum cu pa'i tshig le'ur byas pa.* Toh 4055, Degé Tengyur, sems tsam, *shi*, 1b1–3a3.

——. *The Twenty Verses. Viṃśikākārikā. Nyi shu pa'i tshig le'ur byas pa.* Toh 4056, Degé Tengyur, sems tsam, *shi*, 3a4–4a2.

——. *The Eight Categories of the Principles of Exegesis. Vyākhyāyuktisūtrakhaṇḍaśata. Rnam par bshad pa rigs pa'i mdo sde'i dum bu brgya.* Toh 4060, Degé Tengyur, sems tsam, *shi*, 17b1–29a2.

Vinītadeva. *Commentary on the Thirty Verses. Triṃśikāṭīkā. Sum cu pa'i 'grel bshad.* Toh 4070, Degé Tengyur, sems tsam, *hi*, 1b1–63a7.

——. *A Discussion on the Commentary on the Twenty Verses. Prakaraṇa viṃśatikāṭīkā. Rab tu byed pa nyi shu pa'i 'grel bshad.* Toh 4065, Degé Tengyur, sems tsam, *shi*, 171b7–195b5.

MADHYAMAKA

Āryadeva. *Four Hundred Verses. Catuḥśatakaśastrakārikā. Bstan bcos bzhi brgya pa zhes bya ba'i tshig le'ur byas pa.* Toh 3846, Degé Tengyur, dbu ma, *tsha*, 1b–18a.

Nāgārjuna. *Affirming through Engaging with the Three Natures. Svabhāvatrayapraveśasiddhi. Rang bzhin gsum la 'jug pa'i sgrub pa.* Toh 3843, Degé Tengyur, dbu ma, *tsa*, 281a–282b.

———. *Akutobhaya: Commentary on the Fundamental Verses of the Middle Way. Mūlamadhyamakavṛttyakutobhaya. Dbu ma tsa ba'i 'grel ba ga las 'jigs med*. Toh 3829, Degé Tengyur, dbu ma, *tsa*, 29b–99a.

———. *Commentary on Rebutting Disputes. Vigrahavyāvartanīvṛtti. Rtsod pa bzlog pa'i 'grel pa*. Toh 3832, Degé Tengyur, dbu ma, *tsa*, 121a–137a.

———. *Commentary on the Seventy Verses on Emptiness. Śūnyatāsaptativṛtti. Stong nyid bdun bcu pa'i 'grel pa*. Toh 3831, Degé Tengyur, dbu ma, *tsa*, 110a–121a.

———. *Commentary on the Verses on the Essence of Dependent Origination. Pratītyasamutapādahṛdayavyākhyāna. Rten cing 'brel bar 'byung ba'i snying po'i rnam par bshad pa*. Toh 3837, Degé Tengyur, dbu ma, *tsha*, 146b–149a.

———. *Crushing the Categories. Vaidalyaprakaraṇa. Zhib mo rnam 'thag*. Toh 3826, Degé Tengyur, dbu ma, *tsa*, 22b–24a; Toh 3930, Degé Tengyur, dbu ma, *tsa*, 99b–110a.

———. *Fundamental Verses on the Middle Way. Mūlamadhyamakakārikā. Dbu ma rsta wa shes rab tshig le'ur byas pa*. Toh 3824, Degé Tengyur, dbu ma, *tsa*, 1b–19a.

———. 1960. *Madhyamakaśāstra of Nāgārjuna*. Edited by P. L. Vaidya. Darbhanga, Bihar: The Mithila Institute of Post Graduate Studies and Research in Sanskrit Learning.

———. *Rebutting the Disputes. Vigrahavyāvartanīkārikā. Rtsod pa bzog pa'i tshig le'ur byas pa*. Toh 3828, Degé Tengyur, dbu ma, *tsa*, 27a–29a.

———. *Seventy Verses on Emptiness. Śūnyatāsaptatikārikā. Stong pa nyid bdun bcu pa'i tshig le'ur byas pa*. Toh 3827, Degé Tengyur, dbu ma, *tsa*, 24a–27a; Pedurma 118, 1606–1779.

———. *Sixty Verses on Reasoning. Yuktiṣaṣṭikā. Rigs pa drug cu pa*. Toh 3825, Degé Tengyur, dbu ma, *tsa*, 20b–22b.

———. *Stages of Meditation. Bhāvanākrama. Bsgom pa'i rim pa*. Toh 3908, Degé Tengyur, dbu ma, *ki*, 1b–4a.

———. *Transmigration through Existences. Bhavasaṃkrānti. Srid pa 'pho ba*. Toh 3840, Degé Tengyur, dbu ma, *tsa*, 151a–151b.

———. *Verses on the Essence of Dependent Origination. Pratītyasamu-*

tapādahṛdayakārikā. Rten cing 'brel bar 'byung ba'i snying po'i tshig le'ur byas pa. Toh 3836, Degé Tengyur, dbu ma, *tsha*, 146b–146b.

Vasubandhu. *The Extensive Commentary on the Diamond Sūtra. Prajñāpāramitāvajracchedikāsaptārthaṭīkā. Shes rab kyi pha rol tu phyin pa rdo rje gcod pa'i don bdun gyi rgya cher 'grel pa.* Toh 3816, Degé Tengyur, shes phyin, *ma*, 178a5–203b7.

Yonezawa, Yoshiyasu. 2008. "Vigrahavyāvartanī, Sanskrit Transliteration and Tibetan Translation." *Journal of Naritasan Institute for Buddhist Studies* 31: 209–333.

SVĀTANTRIKA MADHYAMAKA

Avakokitavrata. *Grand Commentary on the Wisdom Lamp. Prajñāpradīpaṭīkā. Shes rab sgron me rgya cher 'grel ba.* Toh 3859, Dege Tengyur, dbu ma, *wa*, 1b1–287a7; *zha*, 1b1–338a7; *za*, 1b1–341a7.

Bhāviveka (Bhavya). *Blaze of Reasoning: Commentary on the Essence of the Middle Way. Madhyamakahṛdayavṛttitarkajvālā. Dbu ma snying po'i 'grel pa rtog gi 'bar ba.* Toh 3856, Degé Tengyur, dbu ma, *dza*, 40b–329b.

——. *Verses on the Essence of the Middle Way. Madhyamakahṛdayakārikā. Dbu ma snying po.* Toh 3855, Degé Tengyur, dbu ma, *dza*, 1b–40b.

——. *Condensed Meaning of the Middle Way. Madhyamakārthasaṃgraha. Dbu ma'i don bsdus pa.* Toh 3857, Degé Tengyur, dbu ma, *dza*, 329b–330a.

——. *Jewel Lamp of the Middle Way. Madhyamakaratnapradīpa. Dbu ma rin po che'i sgron ma.* Toh 3854, Degé Tengyur, dbu ma, *tsha*, 259b–289a.

——. *Wisdom Lamp: Commentary on the Fundamental Verses of the Middle Way. Prajñāpradīpamūlamadhyamakavṛtti. Dbu ma rtsa ba'i 'grel ba shes rab sgron ma.* Toh 3853, Degé Tengyur, dbu ma, *tsha*, 45b–259b.

Gyaltsab Jé (Rgyal tshab Rje). 2004. *A Note of Reminder on the Ornament of the Middle Way* (*Dbu ma rgyan gyi brjed byang*). In *The Ornament of the Middle Way: A Study of the Madhyamaka Thought of Śāntarakṣita*, by James Blumenthal, 323–40. Ithaca, NY: Snow Lion Publications.

Jayānanda. *Commentary on Introduction to the Middle Way. Madhyamakāvatāraṭīkā. Dbu ma la 'jug pa'i 'grel bshad.* Toh 3870, Degé Tengyur, dbu ma, *ra*, 1b–365a.

——. *Hammer of Reasoning. Tarkamudgarakārikā. Rtog gi tho ba'i tshig le'ur byas pa.* Toh 3869, Degé Tengyur, dbu ma, *ya*, 374b–375a; Pedurma 118, 1876–1879.

Jñānagarbha. *Commentary on Distinguishing the Two Truths. Satyadvayavibhaṅgavṛtti. Bden pa gnyis rnam par 'byed pa'i 'grel pa.* Toh 3882, Degé Tengyur, dbu ma, *sa*, 3b–15b. In *Jñānagarbha's Commentary on the Distinction Between the Two Truths: An Eighth Century Handbook of Madhyamaka Philosophy.* 1992. Translated by Malcolm David Eckel. Delhi: Motilal Banarsidass.

——. *Distinguishing the Two Truths. Satyadvayavibhaṅgakārikā. Bden pa gnyis rnam par 'byed pa'i tshig le'ur byas.* Toh 3881, Degé Tengyur, dbu ma, *sa*, 1b–3b.

——. *Yogic Path. Yogabhāvanāmārga. Rnal 'byor bsgom pa'i lam.* Toh 3909, Degé Tengyur, dbu ma, *ki*, 4a–6a.

Kamalaśīla. *Commentary on the Difficult Points of the Verses on the Ornament of the Middle Way. Madhyamakālaṃkārapañjika. Dbu ma rgyan gyi dka' 'grel.* Toh 3886, Degé Tengyur, dbu ma, *sa*, 84a–133b.

——. *Demonstrating All Phenomena Lack Intrinsic Nature. Sarvadharmāsvabhāvasiddhi. Chos thams cad rang bzhin med par grub pa.* Toh 3889, Degé Tengyur, dbu ma, *sa*, 273a–291a.

——. *Illuminating the Middle Way. Madhyamakāloka. Dbu ma snang ba.* Toh 3887, Degé Tengyur, dbu ma, *sa*, 133b–244a.

——. *Illuminating Reality As It Is. Tattvāloka. De kho na nyid snang ba.* Toh 3888, Degé Tengyur, dbu ma, *sa*, 244b–273a.

——. *Subcommentary on the Compendium of Reality. Tattvasaṃgrahapañjikā. De kho na nyid bsdus pa'i dka' 'grel.* Toh 4267, Degé Tengyur, tshad ma, *ze*, 133b1–363a7; *'e*, 1b1–331a7.

Śāntarakṣita. *Commentary on the Verses on the Ornament of the Middle Way . Madhyamakālaṃkāravṛtti. Dbu ma rgyan gyi 'grel pa.* Toh 3885, Degé Tengyur, dbu ma, *sa*, 56b–84a.

——. *Commentary on the Difficult Points of Distinguishing the Two Truths. Satyadvayavibhaṅgapañjika. Bden pa gnyis rnam par 'byed pa'i dka 'grel.* Toh 3883, Degé Tengyur, dbu ma, *sa*, 15b–52b.

——. *The Compendium of Verses on Reality. Tattvasaṃgrahakārikā. De kho na nyid bsdus pa'i tshig le'ur byas pa.* Toh 4266, Degé Tengyur, tshad ma, *ze*, 1b1–133a6.

——. 1986. *The Tattvasaṅgraha of Śāntarakṣita: With the Commentary of Kamalaśīla.* Translated by Ganganatha Jha. Delhi: Motilal Banarsidass.

——. *Verses on the Ornament of the Middle Way. Madhyamakālaṃkārakārikā. Dbu ma rgyan gyi tshig le'ur bhas pa.* Toh 3884, Degé Tengyur, dbu ma, *sa*, 56b–84a.

PRĀSAṄGIKA MADHYAMAKA

Atiśa Dīpaṃkaraśrījñāna. *Commentary on Illuminating the Path of Awakening. Bodhimārgapradīpapañjikā. Byang chub lam gyi sgron ma'i dka' 'grel.* Toh 3948, Degé Tengyur, dbu ma, *khi*, 241a4–293a4.

——. *Illuminating the Path of Awakening. Bodhipathapradīpa. Byang chub lam gyi sgron ma.* Toh 3947, Degé Tengyur, dbu ma, *khi*, 238a6–241a4.

——. *Introduction to the Two Truths. Satyadvayāvatāra. Bden pa gnyis la 'jug pa.* Toh 3902, Degé Tengyur, dbu ma, *a*, 72a–73a.

——. *The Pith Instruction on Madhyamaka. Madhyamakopadeśa. Dbu ma'i man ngag.* Toh 4468, Degé Tengyur, jo bo'i chos chung, *pho*, 6b5–7b3.

Buddhapālita. *Buddhapālita: Commentary on the Fundamental Verses of the Middle Way. Buddhapālitamūlamadhyamakavṛtti. Dbu ma rtsa ba'i 'grel ba buddhapālita.* Toh 3842, Degé Tengyur, dbu ma, *tsa*, 158b–281a. In *Buddhapālita's Commentary on Nāgārjuna's Middle Way: Buddhapālita-Mūlamadhyamaka-Vṛtti*. 2021. Translated into English by Ian Coghlan. New York: The American Institute of Buddhist Studies and Wisdom Publications.

Candrakīrti. *Clear Words Commentary on the Fundamental Verses of the Middle Way. Mūlamadhyamakavṛttiprasannapadā. Dbu ma rtsa ba'i 'grel pa tshig gsal ba*. Toh 3860, Degé Tengyur, dbu ma, *'a*, 1b1–200a.

——. *Commentary on the Four Hundred Verses. Catuḥśatakaṭīkā. Bzhi brgya pa'i rgya cher 'grel pa*. Toh 3865, Degé Tengyur, dbu ma, *ya*, 30b6–239a7.

——. *Commentary on Introduction to the Middle Way. Madhyamakāvatārabhāṣya. Dbu ma la 'jug pa'i bshad pa*. Toh 3862, Degé Tengyur, dbu ma, *'a*, 22b–348a.

——. *Commentary on the Seventy Verses on Emptiness. Śūnyatāsaptativṛtti. Stong nyid bdun cu pa'i 'grel pa*. Toh 3867, Degé Tengyur, dbu ma, *ya*, 267a1–336b7; Pedurma 118, 1606–1780.

——. *Commentary on the Sixty Verses on Reasoning. Yuktiṣaṣṭikāvṛtti. Rigs pa drug cu pa'i 'grel pa*. Toh 3864, Degé Tengyur, dbu ma, *ya*, 1b1–30b6; Pedurma 118, 934–1008.

——. *Discussion on the Five Aggregates. Pañcaskandhaprakaraṇa. Phung po lnga'i rab tu byed pa*. Toh 3866, Degé Tengyur, dbu ma, *ya*, 239b1–266b7; Pedurma 118, 1534–1600.

——. *Introduction to the Middle Way. Madhyamakāvatāra. Dbu ma la 'jug pa*. Toh 3861, Degé Tengyur, dbu ma, *'a*, 201b1–219a7.

——. *Seventy Ways of Taking the Three Refuges. Triśaraṇagamanasaptati. Gsum la skyabs su 'gro ba bdun cu pa*. Toh 3971, Degé Tengyur, dbu ma, *gi*, 251a1–253b2.

Śāntideva. *Engaging an Awakened Life. Bodhicaryāvatāra. Byang chub sems dpa'i spyod pa la 'jug pa*. Toh 3871, Degé Tengyur, dbu ma, *la*, 1b1–40a7.

CONTEMPORARY STUDIES

Alston, William P. 1996. *A Realist Conception of Truth*. Ithaca, NY: Cornell University Press.

Ames, William L. 1993. "Bhāvaviveka's Prajñāpradīpa: A Translation of Chapter One: 'Examination of Causal Conditions' (Pratyaya)." *Journal of Indian Philosophy* 21: 209–259.

———. 1986. "Buddhapālita's Exposition of the Madhyamaka." *Journal of Indian Philosophy* 14: 313–348.

Arnold, Dan. 2012. *Brains, Buddhas, and Believing*. New York: Columbia University Press.

———. 2005. *Buddhists, Brahmins, and Beliefs: Epistemology in South Asian Philosophy of Religion*. New York: Columbia University Press.

Balslev, Anindita Niyogi. 1983. *A Study of Time in Indian Philosophy*. Wiesbaden: Otto Harrassowitz.

Blumenthal, James. 2004. *The Ornament of the Middle Way: A Study of the Madhyamaka Thought of Śāntarakṣita*. Ithaca, NY: Snow Lion Publications.

Brunnholzl, Karl, trans. 2015. *When the Clouds Part: The Uttaratantra and Its Meditative Tradition as a Bridge between Sutra and Tantra*. Boston: Snow Lion.

Chatterjee, Ashok Kumar. 1999. *The Yogācāra Idealism*. Delhi: Motilal Barnarsidass Publishers Private Limited.

Cowherds, The. 2011. *Moonshadows: Conventional Truth in Buddhist Philosophy*. New York: Oxford University Press.

———. 2016. *Moonpaths: Ethics and Emptiness*. Oxford: Oxford University Press.

Dorjee, Penpa. 2001. *Ācārya Kamalaśīla's Madhyamakāloka* (*Restored Sanskrit Text from the Tibetan Version*). Sarnath: Central Institute of Higher Tibetan Studies.

Dreyfus, Georges, and Sara McClintock, eds. 2003. *The Svātantrika–Prāsaṅgika Distinction: What Difference Does a Difference Make?*. Boston: Wisdom Publications.

Eckel, Malcolm David. 1987. *Jñāngarbha's Commentary on the Distinction Between the Two Truths: An Eighth Century Handbook of Madhyamaka Philosophy*. New York: State University of New York Press.

——. 2008. *Bhāviveka and His Buddhist Opponents*. Cambridge: Harvard University Press.

Gaṇi, K. J., et al. 1950. *Śramaṇa Bhagavān Mahāvīra: Gaṇadharavāda, Vol. 3*. Ahmedabad: Śri Jaina Siddhanta Society.

Garfield, Jay L., trans. 2002. *Empty Words: Buddhist Philosophy and Cross-Cultural Interpretation*. Oxford: Oxford University Press.

——. 2015. *Engaging Buddhism: Why It Matters to Philosophies*. Oxford: Oxford University Press.

——. 1995. *The Fundamental Wisdom of The Middle Way: Nāgārjuna's Mūlamadhyamkakārikā*. New York: Oxford University Press.

——. 2011. "Taking Conventional Truth Seriously: Authority Regarding Deceptive Reality." In *Moonshadows: Conventional Truth in Buddhist Philosophy*. Edited by the Cowherds. Oxford: Oxford University Press, 23–39.

Garfield, Jay L., and Sonam Thakchoe. 2011. "Identifying the Object of Negation and the Status of Conventional Truth: Why the *dGag Bya* Matters So Much to Tibetan Mādhyamikas." In *Moonshadows: Conventional Truth in Buddhist Philosophy*. Edited by the Cowherds. New York: Oxford University Press, 73–87.

Garfield, Jay L., John Powers, and Sonam Thakchoe. 2016. "Introduction to Summary of the Essence: A Commentary on Investigation of the Percept." In *Dignāga's Investigation of the Percept: A Philosophical Legacy in India and Tibet*. Translated by Douglas Duckworth, et al. New York, NY: Oxford University Press, 169–74.

Garfield, Jay, and Jan Westerhoff, eds. 2015. *Madhyamaka and Yogācāra: Allies or Rivals?* Oxford: Oxford University Press.

Goetz, Stewart, and Charles Taliaferro, eds. 2021. *The Encyclopedia of Philosophy of Religion*. Hoboken, NJ: Wiley-Blackwell.

Gold, Jonathan C. 2015. *Paving the Great Way: Vasubandhu's Unifying Buddhist Philosophy*. New York: Columbia University Press.

Grupp, Jeffrey. 2005. "The R-theory of Time, or Replacement Presentism: The Buddhist Philosophy of Time." *The Indian International Journal of Buddhist Studies*, vol. X, 6: 51-121. B.J.K. Institute of Buddhist and Asian Studies. Varanasi: Aditya Shyam Trust.

Harris, Ian Charles. 1991. *The Continuity of Madhyamaka and Yogācāra in Indian Mahāyāna Buddhism*. Leiden, NY: E.J. Brill.

Heidegger, Martin. 2001. *Being and Time*. Translated by John Macquarrie and Edward Robinson. Cambridge, MA: BlackWell.

Huntington, C. W., and Geshe Namgyal Wangchen. 1989. *The Emptiness of Emptiness: An Introduction to Early Indian Mādhyamika*. Honolulu: University of Hawaii Press.

Husserl, Edmund. 1914. *Ideas for a Pure Phenomenology and Phenomenological Philosophy. First Book: General Introduction to Pure Phenomenology*. Cambridge, MA: Hackett Publishing Company.

Jain, Sagarmal. 1999. *Jaina Literature and Philosophy: A Critical Approach*. Varanasi: Pārśvanātha Vidyāpītha.

Jayatilleke, K. N. 1963. *Early Buddhist Theory of Knowledge*. London: George Allen and Unwin.

Jestun Lobsang Nyima (Dga' shar nyagri shar chos rin po che rje tsun Blo bzang Nyi ma). 2003. *An Outline of the Two Truths: The Pinnacle of All the Positions. Bden pa bnyis kyi spyi'i don rnam pa bshad pa bzhed tshul kun gyi za ma tog*. Mundgod: Gashar Nyagre Kangtsen Education Project.

Kalupahan, David. 1966. "Sarvāstivāda and Its Theory of 'Sarvam Asti.'" Sri Lanka: *University of Ceylon Review* 24: 94–105.

——. 1991. *Mūlamadhyamakakārikā of Nāgārjuna: The Philosophy of the Middle Way*. Delhi: Motilal Banarsidass Publishers Pvt. Limited.

Kapstein, T. Matthew. 2001. *Reason's Traces: Identity and Interpretation of Indian and Tibetan Buddhist Thought*. Boston: Wisdom Publications.

King, Richard. 1999. *An Introduction to Hindu and Buddhist Thought*. Edinburgh: Edinburgh University Press.

La Vallée Poussin, Louis de. 1988–1990. "Introduction." In *Abhidharmakośyam of Vasubandhu*. Translated by Leo M. Pruden. Berkeley, CA: Asian Humanities Press.

Lemos, Noah. 2007. *An Introduction to the Theory of Knowledge*. Cambridge: Cambridge University Press.

Lindtner, Christian. 1986. *Master of Wisdom: Writings of the Buddhist Master Nāgārjuna*. Oakland, CA: Dharma Press.

Lopez, Donald S. 1987. *A Study of Svātantrika*. New York: Snow Lion Publications.

Lusthaus, Dan. 2002. *Buddhist Phenomenology: A Philosophical Investigation of Yogācāra Buddhism and the Ch'eng Wei-shih lun*. New York: RoutledgeCurzon.

MacBride, Fraser. 2019. "Truthmakers." In *The Stanford Encyclopedia of Philosophy (Spring 2019 Edition)*. Edited by Edward N. Zalta. https://plato.stanford.edu/archives/spr2019/entries/truthmakers.

Matilal, Bimal K. 1971. *Epistemology, Logic and Grammar in Indian Philosophical Analysis*. The Hague: Mouton.

McGovern, William. 1895. *A Manual of Buddhist Philosophy*. London: Kegan Paul, Trench, Trübner & Co.

Mittal, K. K. 1974. *Materialism in Indian Thought*. New Delhi: Munshiram Manoharlal Publishers Pvt. Ltd.

Mookerjee, Satkari. 1935. *The Buddhist Philosophy of Universal Flux*. Delhi: Motilal Banarsidass Publishers.

Nāgārjuna. 2018. *Crushing the Categories* (*Vaidalyaprakaraṇa*). Translated by Jan Westerhoff. New York: American Institute of Buddhist Studies and Wisdom Publications.

Newland, Guy. 1992. *The Two Truths*. Ithaca, NY: Snow Lion Publications.

Ngawang Dendar (Ngag dbang Bstan dar). 2016. "Beautiful String of Pearls: A Commentary on Investigation of the Percept (Dmigs pa brtag pa'i 'grel pa mu tig 'phreng mdzes)." In *Dignāga's Investigation of the Percept: A Philosophical Legacy in India and Tibet*. New York: Translated by Douglas Duckworth, et al. Oxford University Press, 131–68.

Organ, T. W. 1975. *Western Approaches to Eastern Philosophy*. Athens: Ohio University Press.

Padhi, B., and M. Padhi. 2005. *Indian Philosophy and Religion*. New Delhi: D. K. Printworld (P) Limited.

Ronkin, Noa. 2005. *Early Buddhist Metaphysics: The Making of a Philosophical Tradition*. New York: RoutledgeCurzon.

Ruegg, David Seyfort. 1990. "On the Authorship of Some Works Ascribed to Bhāvaviveka/Bhavya." In *Earliest Buddhism and Madhyamaka*. Edited by Ernst Steinkellner. Vienna: Österreinchischen Akademie der Wissenschaften, 59–71.

——. 2010. *The Buddhist Philosophy of the Middle: Essays on Indian and Tibetan Madhyamaka*. Boston: Wisdom Publications.

Schubring, Walter. 1962. *The Doctrine of the Jainas*. Delhi: Motilal Banarsidass.

Sharma, C. 1960. *A Critical Survey of Indian Philosophy*. London: Rider and Company.

Siderits, Mark. 2003. *Personal Identity and Buddhist Philosophy: Empty Persons*. Burlington, VT: Ashgate Publishing Company.

——. 2007. *Buddhism as Philosophy: An Introduction*. Cambridge: Ashgate Publishing Limited.

——. 2011. "Is Everything Connected to Everything Else? What the Gopīs Know." In *Moonshadows: Conventional Truth in Buddhist Philosophy*. Edited by The Cowherds. New York: Oxford University Press.

Sinha, B. M. 1983. *Time and Temporality in Sāṃkhya-Yoga and Abhidharma Buddhism*. New Delhi: Munshiram Manoharlal Publishers.

Srivastava, Nirapma. 2004. *Dualistic Philosophy of Descartes and Sāṃkhya*. Lucknow: New Royal Book Company.

Stcherbatsky, Theodore. 1970. *The Central Conception of Buddhism and the Meaning of the Word "Dharma."* Delhi: Indological Book House.

Shcherbatskoi, Fëdor I. 1970. *The Conception of Buddhist Nirvāṇa: With Sanskrit Text of Madhyamaka-Kārikā*. Delhi: Motilal Banarsidass.

Takakusu, Junjirō. 1905. "The Abhidharma Literature, Pāli and Chinese." In *Journal of the Royal Asiatic Society* 37, 160–162.

———. 1920. "Sarvāstivādins." In *Encyclopaedia of Religion and Ethics, vol. 11*. Edited by James Hastings. Edinburgh: T&T Clark, 198–200.

Takakusu, Junjirō, and Watanabe Kaigyoku, eds. 1924–1934. *Taishō Revised Tripiṭaka*. Tokyo: Taishō Issaikyō Kankokai.

Tatia, Nathmal. 1951. *Studies in Jaina Philosophy*. Varanasi: P.V. Research Institute.

Thabkhas, Yeshes. 2016. "Summary of the Essence: A Commentary on Investigation of the Percept." In *Dignāga's Investigation of the Percept: A Philosophical Legacy in India and Tibet*. Translated by Douglas Duckworth, et al. New York: Oxford University Press, 175–213.

Thakchoe, Sonam. 2017. "Candrakīrti on Deflated Episodic Memory: Response to Endel Tulving's Challenge." *Australasian Philosophical Review* 1 (4): 432–38. https://doi.org/10.1080/24740500.2017.1411150.

———. 2003. "'The Relationship between the Two Truths': A Comparative Analysis of Two Tibetan Accounts." *Contemporary Buddhism* 4 (2): 111–27. https://doi.org/10.1080/1463994032000162947.

———. 2004. "How Many Truths? Are There Two Truths or One in the Tibetan Prāsaṅgika Madhyamaka?" *Contemporary Buddhism* 5 (2): 121–41. https://doi.org/10.1080/1463994042000291547.

———. 2005. "'Transcendental Knowledge' in Tibetan Mādhyamika Epistemology." *Contemporary Buddhism* 6 (2): 131–52. https://doi.org/10.1080/14639940500435638.

———. 2007a. "Philosophy of Vipassana Meditation: Appreciating the Rational Basis of the Insightful Meditation." *Journal of Rare Buddhist Texts Research Unit* 43 (1): 63–100.

———. 2007b. "Status of Conventional Truth in Tsong Khapa's Mādhyamika Philosophy." *Contemporary Buddhism* 8 (1): 31–47. https://doi.org/10.1080/14639940701295070.

———. 2007c. *The Two Truths Debate: Tsongkhapa and Gorampa on the Middle Way*. Boston: Wisdom Publications.

——. 2008. "Gorampa on the Objects of Negation: Arguments for Negating Conventional Truths." *Contemporary Buddhism* 9 (2): 265–80. https://doi.org/10.1080/14639940802556594.

——. 2011a. "Prāsaṅgika Epistemology in Context." In *Moonshadows: Conventional Truth in Buddhist Philosophy*. Edited by The Cowherds. New York: Oxford University Press, 39–55.

——. 2011b. "The Theory of Two Truths in India." In *Stanford Encyclopaedia of Philosophy*. Edited by Edward N. Zalta, 1–45.

——. 2011c. "The Theory of Two Truths in Tibet." In *Stanford Encyclopaedia of Philosophy*. Edited by Edward N Zalta, 1–25. https://plato.stanford.edu/archives/sum2022/entries/twotruths-tibet.

——. 2012a. "Candrakīrti's Theory of Perception: A Case for Non-Foundationalist Epistemology in Madhyamaka." *Acta Orientalia Vilnensia* 11 (1): 93–124.

——. 2012b. "Prāsaṅgika's Semantic Nominalism: Reality Is Linguistic Concept." *Journal of Indian Philosophy* 40 (4): 427–52. https://doi.org/10.1007/s10781-012-9160-5.

——. 2013. "Prāsaṅgika Epistemology: A Reply to Stag Tsang's Charge Against Tsongkhapa's Uses of Pramāṇa in Candrakīrti's Philosophy." *Journal of Indian Philosophy* 41 (5): 535–61. https://doi.org/10.1007/s10781-013-9186-3.

——. 2015. "Reification and Nihilism: The Three Nature Theory and Its Implications." In *Madhyamaka and Yogācāra: Allies or Rivals?*. Edited by Jay L. Garfield and Jan Westerhoff. New York: Oxford University Press, 72–110.

——. 2016. "The Prāsaṅgika Ethics of Momentary Disintegration (Vināśa Bhāva): Causally Effective Karmic Moments." In *Moonpaths: Ethics and Emptiness*. Edited by The Cowherds. New York: Oxford University Press, 159–82.

——. 2018a. "Svātantrika Madhyamaka Metaphysics: Bhāvaviveka's Conception of Reality." In *History of Indian Philosophy*. Edited by Purusottama Bilimoria. New York: Routledge, 343–50.

——. 2018b. "The Two Truths in Madhyamaka: Jnānagarbha', History of Indian Philosophy." In *History of Indian Philosophy*. Edited by Purusottama Bilimoria. Routledge History of World Philosophies. New York: Routledge, 351–59.

——. 2019. "Buddhist Philosophy of Mind: Nāgārjuna's Critique of Mind-Body Dualism from His Rebirth Arguments." *Philosophy East and West* 69 (3): 807–27. https://doi.org/10.1353/pew.2019.0064.

Thakchoe, Sonam, Malcolm David Eckel, Jay L. Garfield, et al. 2016. *Dignāga's Investigation of the Percept: A Philosophical Legacy in India and Tibet*. New York: Oxford University Press.

Thakchoe, Sonam, and Julien Tempone Wiltshire. 2019. "Madhyamaka Philosophy of No-Mind: Taktsang Lotsāwa's On Prāsaṅgika, Pramāṇa, Buddhahood and a Defense of No-Mind Thesis." In *Journal of Indian Philosophy* 47 (3): 453–87.

Tillemans, J. F. Tom. 2016. *How Do Mādhyamikas Think? And Other Essays on the Buddhist Philosophy of the Middle*. Boston: Wisdom Publications.

——. 2008. *Materials for the Study of Āryadeva, Dharmapāla, and Candrakīrti: The Catuḥśataka of Āryadeva, Chapters XII and XIII with the Commentaries of Dharmapāla and Candrakīrti*. Delhi: Motilal Banarsidass Publishers.

Tola, Fernando, and Carmen Dragonette. 2004. *Being as Consciousness: Yogācara Philosophy of Buddhism*. Delhi: Motilal Banarsidass Publishers.

Westerhoff, Jan. 2009. *Nāgārjuna's Madhyamaka: A Philosophical Introduction*. Oxford: Oxford University Press.

——. 2013. "Abhidharma Philosophy." In *The Oxford Handbook of World Philosophy*. Edited by Jay L. Garfield and William Edelglass. Oxford: Oxford University Press, 193–204.

——. 2018. *The Golden Age of Indian Buddhist Philosophy*. Oxford: Oxford University Press.

Yakherds, The. 2021. *Knowing Illusion*. 2 vols. New York: Oxford University Press.

BRAHMANICAL AND HINDU STUDIES

Āchārya, Mādhava. 2002. *The Sarva-Darśana-Saṃgraha, or, Review of the Different Systems of Hindu Philosophy.* Translated by Edward B. Cowell and Archibald Edward Gough. London: Routledge. https://www.taylorfrancis.com/books/e/9781136389177.

Agrawal, Madan Mohan. 2001. *Six Systems of Indian Philosophy: The Sūtras of Six Systems With English Translation, Transliteration and Indices.* Delhi: Chaukhamba Sanskrit Pratishthan.

Chatterjee, Satischandra. 2015. *The Nyaya Theory of Knowledge: A Critical Study of Some Problems of Logic and Metaphysics.* New Delhi: Rupa Publications India Private Limited.

Chattopadhyaya, Debiprasad, ed. 2006. *Cārvāka, Lokāyata: An Anthology of Source Materials and Some Recent Studies.* New Delhi: Indian Council of Philosophical Research.

Dasti, Matthew, and Stephen Phillips. 2017. *The Nyaya-Sutra: Selections with Early Commentaries.* Indianapolis: Hackett Publishing Company.

Īśvara Kṛṣṇa. 1995. *Sāṁkhyakārikā of Īśvara Kṛṣṇa.* Translated by Swami Virupakshananda. Madras: Advaita Ashrama.

Jha, Mahamahopadhyaya Ganganatha, trans. 1916. *The Padārtha-dharma-Saṃgraha of Praśastapāda with the Nyāyakandalii of Śridhara.* Allahabad: E. J. Lazarus & Co.

——. 2004. *The Samkhya-Tattva-Kaumudi: Vacaspati Misra's Commentary on the Samkhya-Karika.* Varanasi: Chaukhambha Sanskrit Pratishthan.

Jain, Sagarmal. 1999. *Jaina Literature and Philosophy: A Critical Approach.* Varanasi: Pārśvanātha Vidyāpītha.

Jaina, Sāgaramala, and Śrīprakāśa Pāṇḍeya, eds. 1999. *Multi-Dimensional Application of Anekāntavāda.* Varanasi: Pārśwanātha Vidyāpīṭha and Navin Institute of Self-development.

Kaṇāda (or Kāśyapa). 1989. "*Vaiśeṣika.*" In *A Sourcebook in Indian Philosophy.* Edited by Sarvepalli Radhakrishnan and Charles A. Moore. Princeton: Princeton University Press.

Mittal, K. K. 1974. *Materialism in Indian Thought.* New Delhi: Munshiram Manoharala.

Padhi, Bibhu, and Minakshi Padhi. 2005. *Indian Philosophy and Religion: A Reader's Guide*. New Delhi: D. K. Printworld.

Radhakrishnan, Sarvepalli, ed. 1998a. *Indian Philosophy, Volume 1*. New Delhi: Oxford University Press.

——. 1998b. *Indian Philosophy, Volume 2*. New Delhi: Oxford University Press.

——. 2003. *The Principal Upaniṣads*. New Delhi: HarperCollins India.

Radhakrishnan, Sarvepalli, and Charles A. Moore, eds. 1989. *A Sourcebook in Indian Philosophy*. Princeton: Princeton University Press.

Śaṃkara Miśra. 1923. "*The Vaiśeṣika Sūtras of Kaṇāda, with Commentary of Śaṃkara Miśra, Extracts from the Gloss of Jayanārāyṇa and the Bhaṣya of Candrakānta*." Translated by Nandalal Sinha. In *A Sourcebook in Indian Philosophy*. Edited by Sarvepalli Radhakrishnan and Charles A. Moore. Princeton: Princeton University Press.

Sharma, Ramesh K. 2018. *Yuktidipika: The Most Important Commentary on the Samkhyakarika of Isvarakrsna*. Delhi: Motilal Banarsidass Publishers.

Shastri, Dharmendra Nath. 1997. *The Philosophy of Nyāya-Vaiśeṣika and Its Conflict with the Buddhist Dignāga School: Critique of Indian Realism*. Delhi: Bharatiya Vidya Prakashan.

Tatia, Nathmal. 1951. *Studies in Jaina Philosophy*. Varanasi: P. V. Research Institute.

Welden, Ellwood Austin. 1913. "The Samkhya Karikas of Iśvara Krishna with the Commentary of Gaudapada." PhD diss. University of Pennsylvania.

Index

About the Author

Sonam Thakchoe received his PhD from and is a Senior Philosophy Lecturer at University of Tasmania, where he teaches Asian philosophy, coordinates the Asian Philosophy Program, and directs the Tasmanian Buddhist Studies in India Exchange Program. His research focuses on Indo-Tibetan Madhyamaka philosophy with a particular emphasis on ontology, epistemology, ethics, and Buddhist philosophy of mind. His publications include two dozen referred articles and six scholarly books: *Knowing Illusion: Bringing a Tibetan Debate into Contemporary Discourse, Vol. 1: A Philosophical History of the Debate* and *Vol. 2: Translations* (Oxford University Press, 2021, coauthored with the Yakherds); *Dignāga's Investigation of the Percept* (Oxford University Press, 2016, coauthored with the Yakherds); *Moonpaths: Ethics and Emptiness* (Oxford University Press, 2015, coauthored with the Cowherds); *Moonshadows: Conventional Truth in Buddhist Philosophy* (Oxford University Press, 2011); and his monograph *The Two Truths Debate: Tsongkhapa and Gorampa on the Middle Way* (Wisdom Publications, 2007).

What to Read Next from Wisdom Publications

Science and Philosophy in Indian Buddhist Classics
Volume 3, Philosophical Schools
His Holiness the Dalai Lama

"*Philosophical Schools* presents the seminal works of ancient Indian philosophy, bringing together the thoughts and views of both non-Buddhist and Buddhist schools. These ancient philosophical views can still enrich our understanding of how we humans engage with the world around us, particularly in our search for inner peace and in our understanding of the nature of experience, the origin of the world, and our role within it."—Khen Rinpoché Geshé Tashi Tsering, abbot of Sera Mé Monastery and author of the *Foundations of Buddhist Thought* series

Beautiful Adornment of Mount Meru
A Presentation of Classical Indian Philosophy
Translated by Donald S. Lopez Jr.

"This is a masterful translation of an extraordinary work by the great Tibetan polymath Changkya Rölpai Dorjé, a Geluk master of the eighteenth century. By providing a deep and systematic overview of the various schools of Indian Buddhism, it provides unique insights into some of the central tenets of Buddhist philosophy such as no-self and emptiness. This is the kind of work that one can return to again and again."—Georges Dreyfus, Jackson Professor of Religion, Williams College

About Wisdom Publications

Wisdom Publications is the leading publisher of classic and contemporary Buddhist books and practical works on mindfulness. To learn more about us or to explore our other books, please visit our website at wisdomexperience.org or contact us at the address below.

Wisdom Publications
199 Elm Street
Somerville, MA 02144 USA

We are a 501(c)(3) organization, and donations in support of our mission are tax deductible.

Wisdom Publications is affiliated with the Foundation for the Preservation of the Mahayana Tradition (FPMT).